Jesus of Africa

FAITH AND CULTURES SERIES
An Orbis Series on Contextualizing Gospel and Church
General Editor: Robert J. Schreiter, C.PP.S.

The *Faith and Cultures Series* deals with questions that arise as Christian faith attempts to respond to its new global reality. For centuries Christianity and the church were identified with European cultures. Although the roots of Christian tradition lie deep in Semitic cultures and Africa, and although Asian influences on it are well documented, that original diversity was widely forgotten as the church took shape in the West.

Today, as the churches of the Americas, Asia, and Africa take their place alongside older churches of Mediterranean and North Atlantic cultures, they claim the right to express Christian faith in their own idioms, thought patterns, and cultures. To provide a forum for better understanding this process, the Orbis *Faith and Cultures Series* publishes books that illuminate the range of questions that arise from this global challenge.

Orbis and the *Faith and Cultures Series* General Editor invite the submission of manuscripts on relevant topics.

FAITH AND CULTURES SERIES

Jesus of Africa

Voices of Contemporary African Christology

Diane B. Stinton

Maryknoll, New York 10545

Founded in 1970, Orbis Books endeavors to publish works that enlighten the mind, nourish the spirit, and challenge the conscience. The publishing arm of the Maryknoll Fathers and Brothers, Orbis seeks to explore the global dimensions of the Christian faith and mission, to invite dialogue with diverse cultures and religious traditions, and to serve the cause of reconciliation and peace. The books published reflect the opinions of their authors and are not meant to represent the official position of the Maryknoll Society. To obtain more information about Maryknoll and Orbis Books, please visit our website at www.maryknoll.org.

Manufactured in the United States of America.

Manuscript editing and typesetting by Joan Weber Laflamme.

Library of Congress Cataloging-in-Publication Data

Stinton, Diane B.
  Jesus of Africa : voices of contemporary African christology / Diane B. Stinton.
        p. cm. — (Faith and cultures series)
Includes bibliographical references.
  ISBN 1-57075-537-X (pbk.)
  1. Jesus Christ—Person and offices. 2. Theology, Doctrinal—Africa, Sub-Saharan. I. Title. II. Series.
  BT205 .S858 2004
  232'.096—dc22

                                        2003019856

To the African Christians

Theologians, church leaders and laity,
with gratitude
for willingly and joyfully relating to me
their understanding and experience
of Jesus Christ

Contents

Figures

Tables

Foreword

Robert J. Schreiter

Christology in Africa has been moving steadily ahead. How to name Jesus, by Africans and for Africans, was placed on the agenda early in attempts to create a genuinely African theology. For the first period of the development of African theology, after countries received their political independence from colonial powers, a great deal of effort had to be expended simply to legitimate the use of African concepts and images. That these could be a point of departure, and not merely decorative, took extended work. This task had to be undertaken over against the overweening power of North Atlantic academic theology. It also had to be in tandem with the nation-building dreams and aspirations of the people of the different countries.

As Diane Stinton points out in Part I, this groundwork has now been largely laid. A second generation can now build further. But African theology, and its presentation of Jesus within that theology, faces new challenges. Dealing with the colonial heritage still remains. Economic dependence, being excluded by fast-moving globalization, and the enduring legacy of the colonization of the mind (the most insidious aspect of colonialism) raise high hurdles. The social and political crisis in so many African countries, the devastating epidemic of HIV/AIDS, and the persistence of malaria are enervating two generations of Africans, depleting the possibility of their moving forward as they would wish. If Christ is to be relevant for Africa today, this hydra-headed challenge will have to be met.

In recent years a very thorough academic study of Christology in Africa has been published by a Danish theologian, Jørn Henrik Olsen (*Kristus i tropisk Afrika: i spaendlingsfeltet mellem identitet og relevans* [Uppsala: Svenska Institutet för Missionsforskning, 2001]). In his book both the progress and the limits of Christology in Africa are sketched out. It surveys nearly all the published materials on Jesus in Africa. This can provide a kind of baseline for the future. But African Christianity is much larger than its written texts. With more than three hundred million Christians, a considerable percentage of whom are not literate, to study only written texts is not enough. Theologians such as John Waliggo, Efoé Penoukou and others have been calling attention to this. We need to know more about what ordinary Christians believe and confess about Jesus Christ. Second, that which does appear in print is largely in English and French, colonial languages that many people do not use on a day-to-day basis. One of the few exceptions to this was a little booklet published both in Twi and in English that contained the ecstatic sayings about Jesus by a Ghanaian woman Afua Kuma (*Jesus of the Deep Forest: Prayers and Praises of Afua Kuma*, trans. Jon Kirby [Accra: Asempa Publishers, 1980]). As all these studies make clear, a different approach needed to be taken to get a fuller picture of what is going on in African reflection on the meaning of Jesus.

More recently, however, qualitative research has been undertaken to find out what people at the grassroots believe about Jesus and what sorts of images they have of him. In this regard I commend Carl Sundberg's *Conversion and Contextual Conceptions of Christ: A Missiological Study among Young Converts in Brazzaville, Republic of Congo* (Uppsala: Swedish Institute of Missionary Research, 2000).

The book you are about to read by Diane Stinton represents the most comprehensive of such studies to appear to date. While it only covers three countries in English-speaking Africa (Ghana, Uganda, and Kenya), it has the special merit of weaving together not only published material on Jesus in Africa but also interviews with people at different theological levels: the grassroots; informal, ongoing discussion groups; theologians; and theologians working together (such as the Circle of Concerned Women Theologians). By so doing, she gives us a much richer picture of how Christ is confessed in Africa today. Stinton's analysis of what she has found is rooted solidly both in the wider, ecumenical theological context and the issues, mentioned above, that challenge Christian faith in Africa today.

Needless to say, this is a first—but very important—step. The continent is vast, and the number of new Christians continues to burgeon. The rise of Pentecostal churches alongside more established historic mission churches and African-instituted churches (known by their acronym, AICs) presents a range that no single researcher could hope to encompass—and probably not a whole team of researchers, either. But Diane Stinton has given us an exemplary study in both senses of the word: it is exemplary in showing how to do such study, and exemplary in the results produced. To do effective planning in Africa's churches today, to take the pulse of how efforts to meet Africa's challenges are succeeding, we must know more about what people are thinking and how theologians are bringing that knowledge to bear on the articulation of Christology. This book will help move us along the road today.

Acknowledgments

Initial impetus for this book stems from conversations with Professor Kwame Bediako in Nairobi, Kenya, in 1994. Since then, my desire for a deeper understanding of contemporary African Christianity has been realized through Ph.D. research at the Centre for the Study of Christianity in the Non-Western World, New College, Edinburgh. I am deeply grateful to Professor Kwame Bediako, Dr. T. Jack Thompson, and Professor David Kerr, Director of the Centre, for their incisive oversight of this research project. I am also indebted to Professors Andrew F. Walls and John S. Pobee for their valuable critique and personal encouragement. Additional thanks go to Dr. William Burrows, Managing Editor of Orbis Books, for his key support in publication, and to Joan Laflamme and Catherine Costello for their able assistance in the editing and production of the book.

Certainly the highlight of the research experience was interacting with African Christians in Kenya, Uganda, and Ghana. Daystar University, where I lecture in biblical studies and theology, provided the home base for the fieldwork in Nairobi. The Akrofi-Christaller Memorial Centre for Mission Research and Applied Theology, founded and directed by Kwame Bediako, made possible the research in Ghana. I am thankful for the warm hospitality and practical assistance from both institutions. In addition, certain communities of African Christians extended themselves to me in unexpected ways. The Little Sisters of St. Francis adopted me for the week spent with them in Uganda, providing Christlike hospitality. I was also privileged to interact with the Circle of Concerned African Women Theologians and the Pan-African Christian Women's Alliance in both Kenya and Ghana. These experiences have served to deepen the esteem I have for the many African Christian women who have touched my life.

Friends have stood with me throughout this venture—in Edinburgh, in Canada, in Africa, and across the seas—and I thank God for the gift of each one. I must single out Eugene and Jan Peterson for their steadfast, prayerful support and for generously donating 150 copies of *The Message—New Testament*. These were given as gifts of appreciation to those who participated in the interviews with me.

Deepest gratitude goes to my family for its unfailing love and unending encouragement. I especially honor my mother, Margaret Stinton, and my late father, Dr. Arthur Stinton. Without their deep vision of God's kingdom worldwide and their devotion to nurturing me in my vocation, this research project would not have come to life.

For the profound privilege of witnessing Christ's presence in Africa, I thank God.

Abbreviations

AACC	All Africa Conference of Churches
AEAM	Association of Evangelicals of Africa and Madagascar
AFER	*African Ecclesiastical Review*
AJET	*African Journal of Evangelical Theology*
The Circle	The Circle of Concerned African Women Theologians
EAAT	Ecumenical Association of African Theologians
EATWOT	Ecumenical Association of Third World Theologians
NCCK	National Council of the Churches of Kenya
PACWA	Pan-African Christian Women's Alliance
WCC	World Council of Churches

Part I

Introduction
to Contemporary African
Christologies

1

Exploring African Christologies Today

At the heart of the Christian faith is the person of Jesus Christ. Consequently, the very core of Christian theology is Christology. John Mbiti, one of the pioneers of modern African theology, acknowledges that "Christian Theology ought properly to be Christology, for Theology falls or stands on how it understands, translates and interprets Jesus Christ, at a given Time, Place and human situation."[1] Other contemporary African theologians also stress Jesus' central place within African Christianity and the critical need to articulate the reality and significance of Christ in relation to the lives of African Christians. For example, J. N. K. Mugambi and Laurenti Magesa write:

> Christology is, in the final analysis, the most basic and central issue of *Christian* theology. The faith, the hope and the praxis of love that Christian theology attempts to explicate, and which Christians endeavour to witness to by their life, must have Christ as their foundation and goal. . . . In fact, to be precise, theology is not Christian at all when it does not offer Jesus Christ of Nazareth as the answer to the human quest.[2]

In the ongoing development of Christian theology African accounts of Christology warrant careful consideration in view of Africa's prominent place in Christian history at the turn of the millennium. According to Andrew Walls, leading scholar of world Christianity, one of the most important events in the whole of Christian history occurred in the twentieth century:

> It is nothing less than a complete change in the centre of gravity of Christianity, so that the heartlands of the Church are no longer in Europe, decreasingly in North America, but in Latin America, in certain parts of Asia, and, most important for our present purposes, in Africa.[3]

As a result of this remarkable shift in world Christianity, plus the observation that theology which endures is that which affects the minds and lives of a significant

3

number of people, Walls asserts that the theologies presently arising in Africa will have a determinative effect in shaping church history for centuries to come. Thus it is imperative to examine current christological trends in Africa in their own right and in order to further understand Christian tradition as it unfolds worldwide.

CONTEMPORARY AFRICAN CHRISTOLOGIES: CRISIS OR CONFIDENCE?

Recent reflections on African Christianity often identify a "christological crisis,"[4] with various explanations for why African believers struggle to appropriate Jesus Christ authentically. African Christians allegedly need to perceive and respond to Jesus in ways that are meaningful and relevant to their own mentality and experience. For example, in 1963 missionary John V. Taylor spoke passionately of "a sense of urgency in the search for the true meeting-place where Christ is conversing with the soul of Africa."[5] Elaborating on the significance of Christianity being perceived in Africa as a "white man's religion," Taylor pinpointed the heart of the problem in a most penetrating way:

> Christ has been presented as the answer to the questions a white man would ask, the solution to the needs that Western man would feel, the Saviour of the world of the European world-view, the object of adoration and prayer of historic Christendom. But if Christ were to appear as the answer to the questions that Africans are asking, what would he look like? If he came into the world of African cosmology to redeem Man as Africans understand him, would he be recognizable to the rest of the Church Universal? And if Africa offered him the praises and petitions of her total, uninhibited humanity, would they be acceptable?[6]

More recently Anselme Sanon, citing Ernest Sambou, emphasizes that "in most African countries, the prime theological urgency consists in discovering the true face of Jesus Christ, that Christians may have the living experience of that face, in depth and according to their own genius."[7]

On the other hand, christological confidence abounds in the perceptions of Jesus Christ "through African eyes," as operative among indigenous believers ever since Christianity arrived on the continent. The concept of looking at Jesus through African eyes can be seen, quite literally, in the iconography of the Coptic Orthodox Church in Ethiopia, where the "Ethiopianism" of the figures is established through the use of very prominent eyes. In the early twentieth century a non-literate South African prophet, Isaiah Shembe, gained renown as the founder of an independent church, the Ibandla lamaNazaretha. Among the many hymns Shembe composed, the following verse illustrates longstanding indigenous expressions of Christology:

Umuhle wanangwe yethu	Beautiful are you [our] leopard . . .
Umuhle wena Krestu wethu,	Beautiful are you our Christ,
Sukuma wena Nkosi yethu	Stand up you [our] iNkosi . . .
Uchoboze izitha zethu.	That you may crush our enemies.[9]
Amen, Amen, Amen.[8]	

Even more recently, Afua Kuma, a non-literate Ghanaian woman who worked her fields and served as village midwife, voiced striking images of Jesus in the vivid language and poetry of the Akan people. Examples include the following:

Obirempon Yesu a woye kramo kese,	O great and powerful Jesus,
owia ne osram na eye wo batakari,	incomparable Diviner,
eho rehyeren se anopa nsoromma.	the sun and moon are your *batakari*
Sekyere Buruku a	[robe].
woye bepow tenten;	It sparkles like the morning star.
amansan nyinaa hu w'anuonyam.	Sekyere Buruku,
	the tall mountain,
	all the nations see Your glory.

—ɯ—

Yerusalem mmepow	The mountains of Jerusalem surround
atwa yen ho ahyia;	us;
Sion mmepow ntam na yehye.	we are in the midst
Obonsam, wo tuo renka yen.	of the mountains of Zion.
Se obonsam se oresore yen so a,	Satan, your bullets can't touch us.
yeye Yesu nkurofo.	If Satan says he will rise up against us
	we are still the people of Jesus!

Yesu Kristo, wo na woye saremusee;	If Satan troubles us,
wo na wo bowerew ye nnam;	Jesus Christ,
yi obonsam nsono gu fam	you who are the Lion of the
ma nwansanapobi ne no nni.	grasslands,
	you whose claws are sharp,
	will tear out his entrails
	and leave them on the ground
	for the flies to eat.

—ɯ—

Yesu a wagye ahiafo	Jesus, Saviour of the poor,
ama yen anim aba nyam.	who brightens up our faces!
Damfo-Adu,	Damfo-Adu: the clever one,
wo na yeredan wo	we rely on you as the tongue relies
se tekrema redan abogye.[10]	on the mouth.[11]

The recent recording and publishing of her prayers illustrate an important point, that African Christians have naturally understood and responded to Jesus in light of received biblical teaching *and* their own cultural heritage.

In spite of the long history of these indigenous, oral Christologies, it is only in the past few decades that Christology has risen to a prominent position in the writings of African theologians south of the Sahara. In this regard, the "christological crisis" refers to a lack of critical and systematic reflection on Jesus Christ by Africans in light of their own cultural inheritance and identity. For example, in 1968 John Mbiti claimed that "African concepts of Christology do not exist."[12] Although he proceeded to delineate those aspects of Jesus that do indeed correspond to an African conceptualization of the world, Mbiti is quoted as an early spokesperson for the crisis in textual Christologies.[13] In 1982 Aylward Shorter affirmed that "folk Christianity in Africa is alive and well," while academic theology "is dying of theological neglect," specifying its "failure to provide a convincing African or Black Christology."[14] Likewise, a 1987 publication recorded Kofi Appiah-Kubi's verdict that "whereas there are volumes written on African ideas of God, surprisingly, there is a very thin literature on African Christology."[15]

In contrast to these assessments, other writers from the late 1980s express striking confidence in the subject. In 1989 theologian Charles Nyamiti identified Christology as the most developed subject in African theology to date. He reiterated this assessment in a 1994 publication, adding that writings had progressed beyond simply voicing the need or suggesting methods for what should be done to actually formulating Christologies.[16] Nyamiti noted that aside from certain academic dissertations, many of the writings remained on a rudimentary level. Nonetheless, his assessment signaled a shift in perspective on the status of contemporary African Christologies. Moreover, in 1994 historian John Baur highlighted Christology as the central theme in African theology.[17] Although he mentioned having only found four elaborate treatises on the subject, he drew attention to the proliferation of christological titles being explored in essay form.

The rapid flowering of African Christologies is evident in key anthologies, journal articles, and monographs published over the past few decades, and it accounts for a recent assessment of African Christologies as the "centre-piece" of African Christian theology.[18] Thus the current field appears strikingly different from a few decades ago.

HISTORICAL AND THEOLOGICAL CONTEXT

How is this shift from crisis to confidence to be understood? Why do African Christologies proliferate at this particular point in the history of African Christianity? While various scholars trace the rise of recent African theologies and Christologies, it is worth focusing on the historical and theological significance of this creative outburst of christological reflection across the continent from the 1980s onward.[19] For, as Kwame Bediako observes, these emergent Christologies are especially significant since they are conspicuously absent or minimal during the first phase of modern African theology (1950s–1980s).[20] So how is their apparently late arrival to be interpreted?

Phase One (1950s–1980s): Latent Christologies

Christology was certainly inherent in African theology from the outset, as Mbiti indicates in his quote above concerning the centrality of Christology to theology. Furthermore, the All Africa Conference of Churches (AACC), constituted in Kampala in 1963 in hopes of achieving selfhood for the African church and inspiring African theology, held an assembly in Abijan in 1969. Exploring indigenous liturgies and African expressions of Christian doctrine, the assembly firmly declared that "Christ must be the centre of this theology."[21] Hence christological concern was definitely present, yet not prominent during the early stages of African theology in the twentieth century.

Several factors contributed to this state of affairs. On the sociopolitical scene, African theology as an intellectual discipline arose during the 1950s, when the struggle against colonialism led to several newly independent states. For example in 1955, shortly before Ghana became the first African nation to attain independence in 1957, the Christian Council of the Gold Coast sponsored a conference in Accra, "Christianity and African Culture," which proved to be instrumental in forging new theological directions. Due to the widely perceived collusion between Christianity and colonialism, with African intellectuals consequently critiquing Christianity, African theologians were challenged to establish their credentials as "truly African and Christian."[22] Thus a first priority lay in formulating an apologetic for African theology in the face of nationalist critique and missionary domination of the church in Africa.

Along with the political wind of change came the cultural revolution that swept across the continent.[23] To counter the disdain with which local cultures had generally been held during colonial times, Africans made intensive efforts to reaffirm their identity and integrity in many spheres of life, including names, dress, music, dance forms, architecture, and other indigenous expressions affecting church life and practice. On the intellectual level, prior to the 1950s, literary writers induced the African Renaissance, particularly the Francophone movement known as *la négritude*, initiated by Léopold Senghor, Frantz Fanon, and Aimé Césaire, plus Anglophone writers including Nigerians Wole Soyinka and Chinua Achebe and Kenyan Ngugi wa Thiong'o. Writers on African philosophy further reinforced cultural revival, whether foreigners like Belgian Franciscan missionary Placide Tempels or Africans like Rwandan Alexis Kagame. Given the ferment of revitalizing local cultures, efforts to indigenize mission churches took place and took priority within this wider context of African reformation in literature, philosophy, and history. Apparently, immediate attention did not go to Christology.

Parallel to the African Renaissance a more widespread theological renaissance developed from the mid-twentieth century. On the international scene the Second Vatican Council (1962–65), with its theology of *aggiornamento*, sanctioned a radical reappraisal of Christian liturgy, catechesis, pastoral practices, theology, and ecclesiology, plus more positive reevaluations of non-Christian religions and cultures. Justin Ukpong summarizes the significance of Vatican II as follows: "In these documents, therefore, we find the first steps towards the realization of a 'world church' in which the universal is present in the particular, and in which there might be room for the development of autochthonous forms of Christian expression."[24] Pope Paul VI's visit to Kampala in 1969 gave further impetus to cultivating local African expressions of the Christian faith, when he urged the bishops, "You may, and you must, have an African Christianity."[25] New initiatives in Catholic and Protestant theologies coalesced and fostered growth through African participation in the wider context of third-world theology. In particular, Africa hosted the first Ecumenical Dialogue of Third World Theologians in Dar es Salaam in 1976, resulting in the foundation of the Ecumenical Association of Third World Theologians (EATWOT). In 1977 the corresponding foundation of the Ecumenical Association of African Theologians (EAAT) followed in Accra. Finally, on the continental scene, the remarkable rise in African initiated churches further stimulated theological fermentation. Fears of the exodus of African Christians from mission denominations to these indigenous churches encouraged theologians and church leaders to reformulate their faith so as to be more meaningful to their members.

Thus the academic discipline of African theology was born amid crosswinds of sociopolitical, cultural, and theological change. Fairly early in its development, Desmond Tutu affirmed African theology in its attempt to "rehabilitate Africa's rich cultural heritage and religious consciousness." He viewed it as "the theological counterpart of what has happened in, say, the study of African history. It has helped to give the lie to the supercilious but tacit assumption that religion and history in Africa date from the advent in that continent of the white man."[26] In spite of Tutu's strong validation of African theology, Bediako rightfully notes, "It still remains important to appreciate why this effort has been made as a self-consciously *theological* endeavour, and in a specifically *Christian* interest."[27] It could be added, to return to the issue at hand, within this specifically Christian agenda, why the seeming neglect of Christology initially?

Clues appear in various writings. For example, Kwesi Dickson, a pioneer in the scholarly examination of the Bible in relation to African life and thought, notes that several expatriate and African writers highlight the cultural continuity between Israel and Africa. On this basis, he explores "the African predilection for the Old Testament" in order to discern possible theological developments from this source.[28] While such investigation does not preclude christological inquiry, the evidence that African Christians often favor the Old Testament might provide some explanation for why Christology does not feature more prominently before the 1980s. Alternatively, John Parratt suggests that one reason for the initial neglect lies in the discontinuity between views of history inherent in Christianity and African religions. Since African religions are not "historical" in the sense of originating from a historical founder or having a tradition of "sacred history," the historical founder of Christianity arguably exacts less regard from African believers.[29] It is a moot point, but one that registers the inattention to Christology during the first phase of modern African theology.

As early as 1976 Adrian Hastings, a leading interpreter of African Christianity, drew attention to what he found perplexing. Assessing the initial developments in African theology, he noted that African traditional religions had assumed "the very centre of the academic stage" for first-generation theologians, whose chief task became "something of a dialogue between the African scholar and the perennial religions and spiritualities of Africa."[30] Hastings then identified the central concern of this "first flowering of 'African Theology'"[31] in the late 1960s: "The religious authenticity which is being sought by current African theology is beyond all else an authenticity of continuity, first and foremost the continuity of God." As a result, he voiced "a danger that areas of traditional Christian doctrine which are not reflected in the African past disappear or are marginalized, and this includes almost anything specifically christological."[32] Hence for Hastings, the preoccupation with the African past, apparently at the expense of Christology, was cause for concern.

In contrast, Bediako asserts that the inevitable theological concentration on Africa's primal religions actually lay at the heart of the achievements of first-generation theologians.[33] Far from being a diversion from interpreting the gospel in Africa, the very process of reassessing primal religions—previously declared by the 1910 World Missionary Conference in Edinburgh to contain virtually no preparation for Christianity—together with the profession of Christian faith enabled these theologians to demonstrate "the true character of African *Christian* identity."[34] In other words, the need John Pobee identified above, that is, to be truly African and Christian, has been met through the profound discovery of conversion to Christianity coupled with cultural continuity. According to Bediako, it was precisely "the missionary presumption of the European value-setting for the Christian faith"[35] that excluded Africa's religious past from serious theological reflection, which, in turn, produced the *problematik* Mbiti voiced concerning the lack of theology in the post-missionary African church. Thus the first generation of African theologians concentrated primarily on the pre-Christian religious heritage in an attempt to clarify the nature and meaning of African Christian identity, and their achievements have been duly noted.[36]

Phase Two (1980s–Present): Emergent Christologies

If the initial phase of theological endeavor focused on the gospel in relation to the African heritage, thereby delaying intensive christological inquiry, strong evidence suggests that the groundwork laid by the first generation has proved foundational for progress since then. The 1980s marked an important shift in theological development. A new generation of scholars explored additional themes in theology by employing genuinely African categories, legitimated by the first generation, to articulate new insights. Christology was foremost in this transition, now formulated in categories derived directly from the worldviews of African primal religions, such as Christ as healer, as ancestor, as master of initiation.[37] Other expressions, such as liberation and women's Christologies, addressed contemporary realities in African life. Without undertaking an extensive survey, brief introductions to four early christological explorations illustrate the creative outburst that spanned geographical and confessional lines.

With the year 1980 forming an approximate watershed between the first and second phases of modern African theology, the shift from crisis to confidence becomes apparent in christological reflections. In the preface to his 1979 *Toward an African Theology*, John Pobee made the stark statement that it was time to stop criticizing the work of early missionaries and to adopt a more positive and constructive approach to African theology. Shortly after Pobee's volume noticeable progress occurred in the proliferation of christological writings throughout the 1980s. One historical moment, 1983–84, saw the publication of a succession of monographs marking the emergence of African Christologies.

Enyi Ben Udoh

One early work was Enyi Ben Udoh's doctoral dissertation presented to Princeton Theological Seminary in 1983 and later published as *Guest Christology: An Interpretative View of the Christological Problem in Africa*. A Nigerian Presbyterian minister, Udoh recounts that his experience as a refugee in the Biafran war triggered the question of "the image, status and role of Christ in Africa."[38] The notion of crisis looms large in Udoh's thought. He initially states that "the traditional way in which Christ was introduced in Africa, was largely responsible for the prevailing faith schizophrenia among African Christians." He further defines the problem as a *"religious double-mindedness,"* or a "dilemma of combining the Christian principles with African traditional religion without being fully African or completely Christian."[39] The first third of Udoh's work develops the hypothesis that this African "faith pathology" is fundamentally christological, the origins of the problem lying in the nature of nineteenth-century European mission. Analyzing the Church of Scotland's mission to Calabar, Udoh concludes that "Christ entered the African scene as a forceful, impatient and unfriendly tyrant. He was presented as invalidating the history and institutions of a people in order to impose his rule upon them."[40] Udoh therefore deduces that many Nigerians view Christ as "merely a stranger," "an illegal alien," "a refugee, a dissident or a fugitive who in desperation has come to Africa for sanctuary," or as "the most visible and publicized symbol of foreign domination ever."[41]

Against this backdrop of crisis Udoh explores three proposals for African Christologies: *Bongaka* (doctor), liberator, and *Christus*-Victor. He argues that these promise genuine theological alternatives to any received Christology. He then expresses further confidence in his own proposal of a guest christological paradigm. In order to overcome Africans' sense of Jesus as stranger, Udoh urges that Jesus be welcomed first as a guest, according to indigenous concepts and norms of honor. Only after he resides intimately among them on this basis will the "faith schizophrenia" of African Christians be resolved by "recognizing Jesus' presence in our midst, no longer as a guest but as our kin."[42]

Kwame Bediako

Contemporaneously, another Presbyterian minister, Ghanaian Kwame Bediako, identified the christological problem and offered new insights in response to it. Although his doctoral thesis, submitted to the University of Aberdeen in 1983, provides in-depth treatment of the first generation of African theologians, his christological reflections were also published that year in essay form and subsequently reprinted as *Jesus in African Culture: A Ghanaian Perspective*.[43] Like Udoh, Bediako attends to the historical and theological dimensions of missionary engagement in Africa, underlining that the quality of contact between Christian proclamation and traditional religious life had a profound impact on present understandings of Jesus Christ. Bediako's analysis of that encounter outlines factors that contributed to the generally negative attitudes missionaries adopted toward African religious life. He further exposes "the missionary misapprehension of the Gospel" in the failure to appreciate adequately the "fundamental and primary universality of the Gospel, of Christ, and hence of his intimate relevance to all our *human* contexts."[44] As a result, according to Bediako, the Western missionary enterprise did not achieve a genuine encounter between the Christian faith and, for example, the worldview of his own people, the Akan. One "ominous implication" of the missionary shortcomings was that Africans' reception and articulation of the Christian faith was often restricted to models from the Christian traditions of Europe. On this basis, "Christ could not inhabit the spiritual universe of the African consciousness except, in essence, as a stranger."[45] Here Bediako concurs with Udoh's identification of the christological crisis. Thus the concomitant problem of African Christian identity—summed up in the question Must we become other than African in order to be truly Christian?—becomes fundamental to Bediako's theological project.[46]

In contrast to Udoh's approach, however, Bediako emphasizes that "the negative side of missionary history in Africa must not be exaggerated."[47] Despite his incisive analysis of shortcomings in the modern missionary enterprise, Bediako establishes confidence in African Christologies on the basis of the theological and cultural continuity inherent in African Christian conversion, indicated above. He also highlights the far-reaching implications of the Bible being translated into vernacular languages. Furthermore, he adopts a markedly different stance from Udoh in stating, "I also make the Biblical assumption that Jesus Christ is not a stranger to our heritage."[48] His fundamental premise is that Jesus is "the *Universal* Saviour and thus the Saviour of the African world."[49] Without downplaying the particularity of Jesus' Jewishness, Bediako emphasizes his incarnation for all of humanity and for all times. Consequently, he distinguishes "our natural past" from "our adoptive past," in which through faith in Christ African believers now share in all the promises made to the patriarchs and Israel, and the good news becomes "*our* story." So while Bediako's christological point of departure is located more in confidence than in crisis, like Udoh he acknowledges that "accepting Jesus as 'our Saviour' always involves making him at home in our spiritual universe and in terms of our religious needs and longings."[50] For this reason Bediako interprets the gospel in light of Akan traditional religion.

Since the spirit fathers or ancestors are central to the Akan heritage, Bediako develops the image of Jesus as ancestor, concluding that "Jesus Christ is the only real and true Ancestor and Source of life for all mankind, fulfilling and transcending the benefits believed to be bestowed by lineage ancestors."[51]

Charles Nyamiti

The proposal of Jesus as ancestor also appears in a 1984 publication by Charles Nyamiti, a notable Tanzanian Catholic theologian. While paying less attention to any sense of crisis stemming from the missionary transmission of the gospel to Africa, Nyamiti shares with Udoh and Bediako a deep confidence in the African religious heritage as fertile ground for theological construction. In his elaborate treatment of the christological image, *Christ as Our Ancestor: Christology from an African Perspective*, Nyamiti begins straight from the African religious heritage, calling for deeper analysis of the ancestral beliefs and practices in order to employ these more profitably for theological purposes. Consequently, he seeks to explicate the entire Christian message using the African category of ancestor as a point of departure for dogmatic theology, Christian morality and spirituality, liturgy, canon law, and catechesis. Within this overall scheme the concept of Christ as ancestor is pivotal. Specifically, he delineates Jesus as "brother-ancestor," based on "the type of ancestorship which exists between a dead individual and his fellow brothers and sisters in a nuclear family."[52] He concedes that this is a rarer ancestral relationship than parent-ancestors yet contends that it provides the closest analogy for Christ, though not the only one. He then develops the analogy both in relation to the Trinity and in relation to humanity. Adopting a comparative approach, he first juxtaposes Jesus and the African brother-ancestor figure and then compares this ancestral paradigm with both traditional and contemporary Christologies.

Certainly Nyamiti articulates new insights regarding the identity and significance of Christ from an African perspective. However, his attempt to develop an African scientific or systematic theology, favoring metaphysics and philosophical speculation over sociocultural analysis, diminishes the impact of his ancestral Christology in the contemporary context.[53] Although Nyamiti provides some reflections on pastoral implications, he draws criticism for writing abstract reflections without adequately addressing the contemporary situation in keeping with current priorities for contextual theologies in Africa.[54]

Takatso Mofokeng

A fourth christological work that emerged at this time is Takatso Mofokeng's *The Crucified among the Crossbearers: Towards a Black Christology,* soon acknowledged by John Mbiti as "the first major study of Christology by an African theologian of our time."[55] Mofokeng begins with a poignant expression of the conditions in his first parish ministry in South Africa, which prompted his central christological question: "How can faith in Jesus Christ empower black people who are involved in the struggle for their liberation?"[56] An introduction to the sociopolitical and economic factors that gave birth to black consciousness and its "twin sister," black theology, elucidates the deep existential crisis inherent in his approach of christological praxis. In Mofokeng's words, "This praxis starts with a crisis at the level of consciousness as well as that of the politico-economic." The crisis is "contained in questions like: 'Who am I?; How long shall the black Christian wait before he realizes true humanity which the gospel has promised him?' 'How can I be liberated to become my authentic self?'"[57]

In opposition to "the oppressiveness of the situation" and "the oppressiveness of the traditional language of faith as spoken in South Africa," Mofokeng advocates an epistemological break in a new praxis of liberation and a new theological language.[58] Christology is central to this project, and hence he seeks "fraternal assistance" from Jon Sobrino's Christology, particularly his dialectical interpretation of Jesus' life, and further insights from Karl Barth's "high" Christology, especially its trinitarian grounding and its emphasis on the resurrection. Assessing the relative strengths and weaknesses in the christological reflections of these two theologians paves the way for his own expression of black Christology. *Black* goes beyond color to signify the commitment of the poor and marginalized who seek to realize their humanity through humble dependence on Jesus Christ and obedience to his radical demands for establishing true humanity. Praxis is based on the birth, life, death, and resurrection of Jesus, for, as the lord of history, Jesus continues to live in community and in solidarity with them, suffering in every way with them but also inspiring the victory of resurrection as oppressed peoples are empowered to become agents of their own history.

Conclusion

This brief glimpse at four works published in the early 1980s illustrates the rapid rise of Christologies across the sub-Saharan continent and across confessional lines. It also introduces various approaches taken by African theologians, with points of departure and conclusions ranging across a spectrum of expressions representing crisis to confidence. Furthermore, the christological issues that surface provide directives for later analysis, namely, in the key questions posed, sources and methods employed, and central themes proposed. Whatever the precise contribution of each of the above authors, their combined witness confirms what Pobee asserted in 1979 and what Bediako reinforces as follows:

The era of African theological literature as reaction to Western misrepresentation is past. What lies ahead is a critical theological construction which will relate more fully the widespread African confidence in the Christian faith to the actual and ongoing Christian responses to the life-experiences of Africans.[59]

THE ANALYSIS OF CONTEMPORARY AFRICAN CHRISTOLOGIES

In view of the relatively recent entrance of these Christologies onto the stage of African textual theology, it is not surprising that there has been relatively little in-depth theological analysis of them. Hence, the present purpose is to analyze selected African Christologies according to certain presuppositions and procedures.

PRESUPPOSITIONS

Of the few requisite definitions, the term *African* can be problematic in examining African Christology. Scholars rightfully point out the danger of generalizations about Africa that lack sufficient regard for the vastness of the continent and the diversity of its peoples, languages, cultures, and histories. Nonetheless, as Mugambi cautions, the recognition of diversity in Africa must not overlook "the reality of and aspiration for a commonality and homogeneity in the African experience."[60] Overall, contemporary African theologians reveal awareness of the hazard of overgeneralization and guard against it by specifying the particular people group to which they refer.

While African theology is now established as a legitimate discipline, it is nevertheless appropriate to clarify its precise meaning as employed here. Certainly other theologies, traditional and Islamic, exist on the continent. Yet in the field of African Christianity, it is widely presupposed that the phrase *African theology* refers to African Christian theology. Within this sphere "critical African theology" is stated succinctly to be "the organized faith-reflection of an authentically African Christianity."[61] African theologians tend to expand the bounds of definition, however, as indicated, for example, in Mugambi's statement:

> I do not associate theology with literacy and high academic learning, even though such skills may greatly enhance theological expression. Rather, I associate it with systematic reflection and systematic articulation. . . . In Africa, there are numerous excellent theologians who cannot read or write.[62]

Both approaches are reflected in Charles Nyamiti's definition of African theology in its broad sense as "the understanding and expression of the Christian faith in accordance with African needs and mentality," and in its narrow sense as "the systematic and scientific presentation or elaboration of the Christian faith according to the needs and mentality of the African peoples." Corresponding to his definitions of African theology, Nyamiti defines African Christology more broadly as "*discourse on Christ in accordance with the mentality and needs of the people in the black continent,*" and more narrowly as the systematic and scientific elaboration of reflections on Christ in keeping with African concerns and thought forms.[63] While a preliminary definition provides orientation to the field of study, the meaning of African Christology requires extensive elaboration. As Bénézet Bujo points out,

> You cannot define Christology as such in Africa unless you *describe* it. You cannot *define* it as in classical philosophy, because I think African Christology is not yet shaped like that in Europe. We are trying to open many ways for African Christology or African understandings of Christ.[64]

Bujo's statement introduces the next clarification, concerning the plural form, *Christologies*. Rationale for a plurality of African Christologies is grounded in biblical and theological precedence. First, Christians understand Jesus' critical question, "Who do you say I am?" (Mk 8:29), to be addressed to every individual and generation in every context. As John Pobee explains, Christology pertains to

> people's attempt to articulate and portray the Christ who confronts them or whom they have experienced or met on a Damascus Road. And they do that articulation from their being and as they are. So one . . . can expect different and varying emphases in that articulation, differences determined by one's experiences, by one's heritage, by one's gender, by one's race. The encounter on the Emmaus road is not identical with the encounter on the Damascus road.[65]

Just as the gospel writers provide different portraits of Jesus, along with the interpretative statements of other New Testament writers, so too diverse Christologies arise in Africa today. In addition to the factors noted by Pobee, the pluriformity of Christologies stems from differences in academic, denominational, political, cultural, and linguistic backgrounds, and in the variety of theological approaches utilized.

Second, rationale for a plurality of Christologies is found in a major shift in the theology of mission that occurred in the mid-twentieth century. David Bosch explains a clear contrast between the "era of noncontextualization" in Protestant and Catholic missions and the new approach. The former method, lasting until approximately 1950, entailed theology (in the singular) being defined once and for all and then "indigenized" into third-world cultures without losing any of its essence. Hence Western theology, as the dominant theology, was regarded to have universal validity and was exported in its "unaltered—and unalterable—forms" to the younger churches overseas. In contrast, "contextualization" assumes "the experimental and contingent nature of all theology."[66] Instead of writing "systematic theologies" that attempt to construct comprehensive and eternally valid systems, contextual theologians seek an ongoing dialogue between "text and context" that necessarily remains provisional.

Given the diversity of contexts in Africa, it is natural to expect African Christologies because "each cultural context has come up with its own understanding of who Jesus Christ is for them in their given cultural, religious and political reality."[67] Pobee thus concludes, "No one Christology may encompass all the aspects of the subject. So many, if not all, of Christologies emerging from Africa need to be assembled and engaged in dialogue among themselves as well as with the church universal."[68] Moreover, Pobee is representative of many African theologians who call for the dialogue to take place in "an ecumenical arena for mutual challenge, correction, affirmation."[69]

The new era of contextual theologies not only acknowledges a plurality of Christologies but also signifies new ways of doing Christology in accordance with priorities emerging in the wider field of African theology. A landmark document in this regard is the "Final Communiqué" of the 1977 Pan-African Conference of Third World Theologians, held in Accra, Ghana. The concluding section, entitled "Perspectives for the Future," sounds a clear call for how theology is to be done: "The African situation requires a new theological methodology that is different from the approaches of the dominant theologies of the West. . . . Our task as theologians is to create a theology that arises from and is accountable to African people."[70] This new way is termed "contextual" theology, or "accountable to the context people live in."[71] The priority of contextuality resounds throughout the works of African theologians, including Bujo, who warned in 1986 that African theology to date had been too academic and therefore largely irrelevant to contemporary African society.[72] Instead, a widespread methodological presupposition is that "genuine Christological reflection cannot be separated from Africa's socio-political, religio-cultural and economic contexts—this is the real and concrete everyday experience within which we Christologise."[73]

Contextual theology also highlights the concept of community, or the whole people of God, as integral to christological formulation. Pobee and Amirtham put it succinctly: "People need theology and, more particularly, theology needs people. Theology needs the reflection of people committed to Christian practice to preserve its vitality and wholeness."[74] This means "everyone has a duty to theologise," including those "outside the elitist group of professional theologians." Yet the phrase "theology by the people" does not exclude the professional theologian; rather, it underlines that "what the theologian does is *in the context of* and *with* the people, not *for* the people gathered as a community of faith."[75]

While women form the strong majority of many communities of faith within African Christianity, women's perspectives have not featured prominently in African theology until recent times. Two leading African women theologians, Mercy Oduyoye and Musimbi Kanyoro, express the dilemma:

African women theologians have come to realize that as long as men and foreign researchers remain the authorities on culture, rituals, and religion, African women will continue to be spoken of as if they were dead. . . . Until women's views are listened to and their participation allowed and ensured, the truth will remain hidden, and the call to live the values of the Reign of God will be unheeded.[76]

Likewise Anne Nasimiyu Wasike, another notable African woman theologian, laments that very few women's Christologies have been written. Speaking from her own experience of theologizing in community, she states, "In order for a thorough investigation on Christology and the African woman's experience to be carried out, some oral interviews have to be part of the study."[77]

Nasimiyu's observation points toward another directive for the analysis of African Christologies. It is common knowledge that Christians in Africa have always theologized, if not formally, at least informally, for example, in singing, praying, and preaching. As Kwesi Dickson emphasizes,

> This is a point which cannot be made forcefully enough, for with the blossoming of theological exposition in recent years, particularly in the so-called Third World, there is the possibility—yea, a real danger—that Christians in Africa, and elsewhere, might come to associate theology solely with a systematic articulation of Christian belief.[78]

Pobee verifies that while the term *Christology* conjures up ideas of formal theses and discourses, the propositional style of expression is only one cultural mode of christological formulation. He emphasizes that "it does not always have to take the form of articulation by word, whether written or oral."[79] Rather, on the basis of his in-depth study of martyrdom in the New Testament as one form of christological confession, Pobee concludes that "Christology may sometimes have to be gleaned and articulated from the being and doing of people."[80] For example, what Henry Okullu states about African theology applies equally to African Christology:

> When we are looking for African theology we should go first to the fields, to the village church, to Christian homes to listen to those spontaneously uttered prayers before people go to bed. . . . We must listen to the throbbing drumbeats and the clapping of hands accompanying the impromptu singing in the independent churches. We must look at the way in which Christianity is being planted in Africa through music, drama, songs, dances, art, paintings. We must listen to the preaching of a sophisticated pastor as well as to that of the simple village vicar. . . . Can it be that all this is an empty show? It is impossible. This then is African theology.[81]

The search for African Christologies thus extends beyond formal written expressions to include informal expressions, for example, in worship, prayer, preaching, artwork, drama, gestures, and symbols.[82]

In view of these two dimensions of African Christology, namely, the formal and the informal, or the written and the oral, Kwame Bediako calls for African Christianity itself to be distinguished from the scholarly literature on it. He proceeds on Mbiti's distinction between the oral theology, which already exists in "the living experiences of Christians," and the academic theology, which can only arise afterward in attempt to "examine the features retrospectively in order to understand them."[83] Looking to the origins of theology in the New Testament, Bediako argues that "an authentic tradition of literary Christian scholarship" cannot exist apart from the "spontaneous or implicit theology" located in "a *substratum* of vital Christian experience and consciousness."[84] While the two elements of theology are not to be confused, Bediako underlines, the informal theology must be granted due significance. Consequently, in order to seek interpretative depth in the scholarly penetration of African Christianity, serious attention must be given to "the observation and study of the actual life of African Christian communities."[85] Bediako explains that the intention is not to set the study of the "lived" theology off against the written theology, since both are obviously important. Rather, it is because the informal expressions of theology cannot be fully circumscribed within the formal expressions that the former warrant particular attention. He thus asserts the following crucial directive for African Christian scholarship:

> If it retains and maintains a vital link with the Christian presence in Africa, and with the spontaneous and often *oral* articulation of Christian faith and experience that goes on, it will be in a position to contribute significantly to understanding, as well as shaping Christian thought generally for the coming century.[86]

Thus key considerations in the analysis of contemporary African Christologies include the plurality of African Christologies emerging in ecumenical dialogue, their contextual nature, the importance of the community of faith in their formulation with particular reference to the need for women's perspectives, and their dual dimensions of formal and informal expressions.

PROCEDURES

In response to the priorities outlined above, the present research integrates the analysis of written or textual Christologies with that of oral Christologies gained through qualitative field research. A qualitative approach serves theological analysis especially well, since it focuses on "*participant perspectives*" and seeks to discover "what *they* are experiencing, how *they* interpret their experiences.[87] Given the long history of interpretation and misinterpretation of Africans by non-Africans, the procedure adopted here is to capture and express African voices as authentically as possible, relating their words, discerning their meanings, and conveying these through extensive illustration. (All citations are from the oral interviews outlined below unless specified as published sources.[88])

The methodological approach combines data selected from three major sources: (1) African christological texts, (2) the authors of those texts, and (3) African Christians from various church traditions.

African Christological Texts

With the recent surge of creative Christologies across sub-Saharan Africa, many theologians warrant consideration for their christological reflections.

However, given the extensive theology arising from the historical context of southern Africa, theologians from this region lie beyond the present scope. The following six theologians are selected as a cross-section of leading men and women from various contexts across tropical Africa and from Catholic and Protestant traditions:[89]

- Bénézet Bujo: Congolese; francophone, Roman Catholic
- Jean-Marc Ela: Cameroonian, francophone, Roman Catholic
- J. N. K. Mugambi: Kenyan, Anglican
- Anne Nasimiyu Wasike: Kenyan, Roman Catholic
- Mercy Oduyoye: Ghanaian, Methodist
- John Pobee: Ghanaian, Anglican

African Authors of the Christological Texts

In-depth personal interviews with each of the six theologians enhance the discussion. The intention was to probe aspects of the authors' own theological formation, to clarify the contexts from which and for which they have written their theology, and to allow for further elucidation of their Christologies, including any current concerns not yet published and any anticipated priorities for the future.[90]

African Christians in Kenya, Uganda, and Ghana

The main sites selected for field research include Kenya and Ghana, with one extension into Uganda.[91] As important as it is to articulate the Christologies of particular homogenous Christian communities in Africa, it is just as vital to explore the burgeoning urban centers, where a mélange of cultures and languages exist and which equally compose the reality of contemporary Africa. Therefore, the interview respondents selected here consist of urban, educated African Christians, both clergy and laity. All interviewees are fluent in English, and many of them evidently function spiritually (that is, read the Bible, pray, and worship) as much or more in English than in their own vernacular.

While women are included in the confessional categories (except Catholic clergy), they are justifiably granted their own forum for discussion in light of their particular christological concerns. Consequently, two groups of women are considered, representing transcontinental organizations already established: the Circle of Concerned African Women Theologians ("the Circle"), who identify themselves as being ecumenical and interfaith in composition, and the Pan-African Christian Women's Alliance (PACWA), who are under the umbrella of the Association of Evangelicals of Africa and Madagascar (AEAM). In sum, both individual interviews and focus groups were conducted according to the following categories:[92]

- Catholic clergy
- Catholic laity

• Protestant clergy
• Protestant laity
• The Circle of Concerned African Women Theologians
• Pan-African Christian Women's Alliance

An additional category emerged during the course of fieldwork in Ghana:

• Local traditional leaders

Aside from pilot interviews in Kenya, I conducted thirty individual interviews in Kenya and thirty-five in Ghana. In addition, I conducted one focus group in each of the six main categories in Kenya and in Ghana, making a total of twelve focus groups.[93]

Finally, participant observation in a variety of natural settings for christological expression further informs the investigation. For example, I attended a broad spectrum of Christian worship services, taking note of liturgy, hymns and songs, preaching, prayers, iconography, and dance and other physical expressions in worship.

Thus I have utilized a variety of approaches in exploring contemporary African Christologies. Figure 1-1 summarizes the research procedures, with the triangular design intended to confirm findings and to increase the breadth and depth of information.[94]

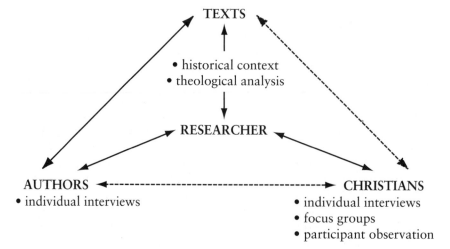

TEXTS

• historical context
• theological analysis

RESEARCHER

AUTHORS
• individual interviews

CHRISTIANS
• individual interviews
• focus groups
• participant observation

FIGURE 1–1. SOURCES AND METHODS FOR EXPLORING AFRICAN CHRISTOLOGIES

CONCLUSION

Contemporary African theologians identify a crucial issue: "From the African Church, a clear and convincing answer is demanded to this question: Who is Jesus Christ for you, Africa? Who do you say that He is?"[95] Consequently, the present purpose is essentially to explore how African Christians today respond to the fundamental question of Jesus Christ, "Who do you say I am?" (Mk 8:29). Critical analysis focuses on central themes that emerge in textual and oral Christologies, their sources and shaping influences, and their significance to African and world Christianity. The underlying argument is that the African Christians selected for consideration do indeed reveal confident, contextual engagement with the key christological question highlighted above. That is to say, responses to this question are articulated not only in light of biblical revelation and Christian tradition but also in terms of African realities both past and present. In so doing, these contemporary African Christologies represent a significant landmark in the development of African theology.

This is not to suggest that the current Christologies are either static or faits accomplis. Rather, the following analysis seeks to discern the present shape of Christologies in their ongoing development. They are therefore configured here in four broad categories intrinsically related to one another. Each category represents a cluster of christological images: (1) Jesus as life-giver, with special reference to the images of healer and traditional healer, (2) Jesus as mediator, developing the image of Jesus as ancestor, (3) Jesus as loved one, concentrating on images of family and friendship, and (4) Jesus as leader, focusing on the images of king/chief and liberator. Critical engagement with the expressed Christologies proceeds on the basis of criteria specified by African Christians for their own theological agenda. Assessment acknowledges strengths or conscious appropriations of Jesus in keeping with their stated priorities. It also recognizes areas of controversy that are as yet unresolved. Increased awareness of contested issues then invites further investigation to discern what prompts and what constrains the more controversial christological reflections. The outcome, then, does not reveal a tidy, systematic progression but rather a continued process of forging Christologies in the furnace of contemporary African realities. Strikingly, it is in confronting these contextual realities that the African Christologies take on particular urgency and potency. The very conditions that spawn the current christological reflections are also redressed by the creative images of Jesus as these are appropriated in Christian praxis. Significance thus emerges in their shaping of African Christianity and their importance for world Christianity.

2

Understanding Origins
of African Christologies

As long as one people is in the image and likeness of another, we do not reach
the real purpose of being Christian, namely to be human in the image of
Christ.

—JOHN POBEE, GHANAIAN THEOLOGIAN

Chapter 1 explored the historical and theological contexts of contemporary African Christologies, and established procedures for their analysis. This chapter examines the origins of these Christologies by identifying critical issues that prompt their present expression. Key factors include the sources and methods of christological formulation, as well as various issues regarding contextual relevance. The expressed priorities of African Christians, summarized in the conclusion, provide the criteria for engaging critically with the current Christologies.

ISSUES REGARDING SOURCES AND METHODS

From the outset of modern African theology theologians clearly delineated the sources for christological discourse. Mbiti, in a 1968 essay lamenting the lack of African concepts of Christ, likewise stated that the African church was "without a theology, without theologians, and without theological concern."[1] He therefore urged his fellow Africans to develop theological reflection on the basis of four rich sources of material. The first of these four "pillars" is the Bible, which he asserted must be the final authority on religious matters. The second was the theology of the older Churches, referring especially to the scholarship and tradition of the church in Europe. The third pillar is the traditional African world, which he insisted must be taken seriously since "it is within the traditional thought-forms and religious concerns that our peoples live and try to assimilate Christian teaching. These traditional thought-forms strongly colour much of their understanding of the Christian message."[2] Finally, the living experience of the church is an important source of theological reflection. In this regard Mbiti showed openness to further investigation of the African Independent Churches as an authentic expression of African Christianity.

Looking back over the development of African theology since Mbiti's appeal, these four pillars have evidently supported the theological endeavors of Africans thus far. While the relative weight given to each source differs among theologians, they certainly tap the potential for drawing upon all categories. The "Final Communiqué" of the 1977 Pan-African Conference of Third World Theologians, held in Accra, Ghana, provides clear indication of wider assent regarding these sources. Like Mbiti before them, these theologians point to the Bible and Christian heritage as the first source, insisting that "the Bible is the basic source of African theology, because it is the primary witness of God's revelation in Jesus Christ. No theology can retain its Christian identity apart from Scripture."[3] Second, they point to African anthropology and cosmology, stressing that the salvation of the human person is inextricably bound to that of the cosmos. Third, African traditional religions are central to their fundamental premise:

> The God of history speaks to all peoples in particular ways. In Africa the traditional religions are a major source for the study of the African experience of God. The beliefs and practices of the traditional religions in Africa can enrich Christian theology and spirituality.[4]

The African Independent Churches form the fourth source. These theologians then add another source: other African realities, a broad category covering everything from cultural forms of life and arts, to family and communal life, to the struggles against racism, sexism, and any other form of economic, political, social, and cultural oppression.

Given the rich variety of sources potentially drawn upon in formulating African Christologies, a corresponding array of methods is detectable in emergent African Christologies. Preliminary observations are confined here to identifying possible approaches, which are then illustrated in the Christologies examined throughout Part II. Within his typology of inculturation and liberation Christologies, Charles Nyamiti summarizes two main methods in the inculturation approach: (1) "from the Bible to African reality," or starting from the biblical material about Christ and moving to the African cultural context to discern relevant christological themes, and (2) "from African reality to Christology," or drawing upon the African cultural background as the point of departure for christological elaboration. Regarding the second category, Nyamiti explains, "In this approach the author examines the mystery of Christ from either the perspective of the African worldview, or from the angle of some particular theme taken from the African worldview or culture."[5] This latter "thematic" approach is said to be used most frequently and to represent the area in which African Christologies have especially flourished. Liberation Christologies likewise find points of departure in (1) the Bible, particularly reflecting a "Christology . . . from below,"[6] beginning with the man Jesus of Nazareth and highlighting the liberating dimensions of his ministry, and (2) the contemporary context as the locus for christological formulation. For example, Magesa summarizes these methodological considerations in outlining the need for Christians to commit themselves to following "Jesus Christ the Liberator" in this historical experience:

> Drawing on the experience of the general mass of the African peoples, and also on the work of the various social sciences which have analyzed the codified experience, a theological examination of the socio-economic and political situation prevalent in Africa brings to the fore numerous ethical and moral questions. . . . All of these are questions of suffering, issues of lack of freedom in its various aspects. Further problems to be seen all over the continent—problems of ignorance and preventable disease, of famine and ethnic wars, of class antagonisms and racial persecutions—are the direct consequence of ignoring this basic question of "unfreedom." They are a result of not confronting it in time with the active, liberating word of God.[7]

In addition, Nyamiti makes passing reference to "African feminist theology (centred on the emancipation of women)"[8] within this category of liberation, and John Parratt likewise refers to feminist theology as a second-generation liberation theology.[9] While Nyamiti's typology is by no means exhaustive, it is perhaps the simplest and most lucid overview of the complex subject of christological methodology.[10]

Following this skeletal outline of potential sources and methods, it remains to examine how they are fleshed out in the selected Christologies under consideration. Instead of analyzing these factors in isolation, they are treated within the context of investigating the central themes in Chapters 3 through 6. Nonetheless, this brief introduction raises criteria for consideration in engaging critically with the African Christologies. For the sake of cohesiveness with additional criteria, plus ease of reference, the criteria regarding sources and methods are set forth in the conclusion to this chapter along with those of contextual relevance.

ISSUES REGARDING CONTEXTUAL RELEVANCE

Recent trends in contextual theologies highlight the need to discern the questions arising in a particular context of the gospel and to develop theological formulations in response to those questions. Certainly the African theologians under consideration are cognizant of this methodological priority. For example, Mercy Oduyoye introduces the liberation of Christian theology by summarizing the shift in perspective:

> Theologians throughout the world who felt a call to speak more relevantly to their age and generation freed themselves from traditional dogmatic and systematic theology and focused on life issues. Instead of telling people what

questions to ask and then furnishing them with the answers, theologians began to listen to the questions people were asking and then seek the answers.[11]

Moreover, Jean-Marc Ela demonstrates his commitment to such a contextual approach in his practical ministry and his theological reflection. He insists, "Our response to the God who has spoken through his Son has to be formulated from the struggles of our people, from their joys, from their pains, from their hopes and from their frustrations today."[12] He further commented in the oral interview:

> Personally I would not want to do Christology simply for its own sake. We must see how Christology is written in reflecting together on Christian ministries actually experienced in Africa, taking account of the questions that the people ask themselves.

What, then, are the central questions being asked across the selected contexts in Africa today? The purpose of this section is to introduce key christological issues regarding contextual relevance, as identified by the selected African Christians in the textual and oral Christologies.

One succinct expression that captures the multifaceted complexity of theological issues is John Pobee's description of African Christianity in terms of "the North Atlantic Captivity of the Church." Representing widespread conviction, he explains the predicament in relation to Christology:

> Christianity in Africa starts with an assumed definition of the Christian faith which is definitely North Atlantic—intellectually, spiritually, liturgically, organisationally. Missionary preaching in Africa has been so shaped by the North Atlantic cultures and contexts, that the African is unable to see beyond that picture of Christ of the biblical faiths.[13]

He also laments that "some have misused the Christian faith to oppress Africans. In the name of bringing 'Christian civilization' to the so-called benighted Africans, they have oppressed Africans intellectually, physically, spiritually, economically, and culturally."[14]

Pobee's summary statements reflect the fact that most of the christological issues are intrinsically related to one another. Nonetheless, for the present purpose of analysis, the major critical issues are distinguished under the following headings: (1) historical and missiological issues, (2) theological issues, (3) issues of African Christian identity, (4) gender issues, (5) issues of contemporary Christian witness, and (6) issues regarding language. Many of the points raised echo matters outlined in Chapter 1 concerning the initial emergence of African Christologies this century. However, the present discussion traces the continued development of christological reflection by highlighting the specific concerns voiced by these current representatives. In view of their experience of "the North Atlantic Captivity of the Church," it is especially important that African Christians articulate their own perceptions of the christological issues. Therefore this chapter, in particular, employs extensive direct quotes, as well as autobiographical reminiscences of the selected theologians. Finally, the present discussion identifies the most vital problems but neither develops them at length nor engages with them critically. Rather, these christological concerns form the backdrop against which to interpret and assess the models of contemporary African Christologies in later chapters.

HISTORICAL AND MISSIOLOGICAL ISSUES

The ills Africans have suffered through contact with Europeans are well known. Yet, according to Ugandan Catholic priest J. M. Waliggo, for anyone seeking to truly grasp contemporary African Christologies, it is fundamentally necessary

> to understand the African experience, if you can, before and during the one hundred years of Christianity or even five hundred years of Christianity. The episode of slave trade is very important. The episode of colonization is very important. The episode of neo-colonization and the betrayal of the real Christian people who did take on power at independence. The *suffering* we have passed through is very important.

Granting the veracity of Pobee's remark that "all theology is biography," it is not surprising that those with firsthand experience of Christianity during the era of colonialism and Western missions voiced the historical and missiological issues most poignantly. Thus Mugambi gave forceful expression to a central christological issue of ongoing struggle:

> I am wrestling with a contradiction: The gospel proclaims good news in specific cultural and historical terms (Lk 4:16–22). Yet missionary Christianity has reached Africa as terribly *bad news*, in which people have been taught in church to despise their culture, their ancestry, their history and their knowledge. How can Jesus the Son of God, Who created Africans in His own Image, condone such dehumanization? Either this negative teaching is theologically erroneous (heretical); or it is imperialist ideology rather than theology; or the God this teaching proclaims is an idol created in the image of its proclaimers. The implications of this concern are far reaching and it is too early to predict the outcome.

The intensity of Mugambi's assertion is best appreciated in light of his autobiographical reflections on influences that shaped his theology. Recalling how part of his childhood was spent at a mission station, he recounted:

> This was during Kenya's war of independence from British colonial dominion. The conduct of missionaries in that war was, in my view, inconsistent with the Gospel. The Gospel proclaims liberty to the captives, but we were taught to acquiesce in our oppression and aspire for "freedom in Christ."

This was hypocritical, because they were free, and we were captive. They seemed not to mind about the loss of African lives, including devout Christians, during that war. There was a great deal of emphasis on "new life in Jesus-Christ." But there was hardly any willingness to talk publicly about the necessity to end colonial rule. In their public profile they portrayed hardly any difference between themselves and the colonial oppressors. This conduct had a lasting impact on me, and helped me to distinguish between the Gospel, and missionary appropriations (or misappropriations) of it.

Therefore the close association between Christianity and colonialism as well as missionary attitudes and actions have had a decisive influence upon emergent African theologies. Theologians question missionary practices like uprooting converts from their home environment and denigrating African culture. Hence, in Mugambi's estimation, "the Christian missionary enterprise has had the greatest impact in the disintegration of African cultural and religious heritage."[15]

As a result of these historical and missiological factors, some Africans in recent times, especially intellectuals, have rejected Jesus as a foreign "white" god and Christianity as a European religion.[16] While acknowledging the reality of such twentieth-century intellectual criticisms, it must also be noted that these views are contested by African Christians today.[17] However, for the present purpose of identifying christological issues, it remains indisputable that colonialism and the modern missionary enterprise have had a deleterious effect on some Africans' perceptions of Christ. Both church leaders and lay people attest to this. For example John Gatu, the former moderator of the Presbyterian Church of East Africa, spoke candidly to the issue:

That was my experience before my conversion. That indeed was the one reason why I did not want to belong to the church. Because for me, the introduction of Jesus, which more or less came at the time to destroy everything else that was African, and that all that mattered was what the *mzungu* [white or European] would say was a concept that I could not perceive.[18]

Likewise Kenyan Catholic layman Gerald Wanjohi, a retired philosophy professor from the University of Nairobi, voiced the common complaint that Christianity was brought to Africa "in the garb of the white man." He then related his own conviction, plus a well-known story:

But the main problem is the way Christianity was introduced, especially coming in and banning so many of our cultural practices and values. The most serious of these complaints is how the missionary and colonialist worked together to deprive the African of his heritage, especially of his land. The story goes like this, that the missionary would come and preach to the people and then tell them, "Now, we close our eyes to pray." And they closed their eyes and started praying, all right. But at the same time, another *mzungu*, the colonialist, was busy taking away the African land!

In view of this strongly perceived historical collusion between missionaries and colonialists, plus the association between Christianity and Western culture, African Christians are compelled to question their own appropriation of the gospel of Jesus Christ. A Ugandan religious sister, Mary Savio, put it this way:

> But the problem was that when we got the gospel, it had changed so much that it had a different culture. We were absorbing it through many cultures that had touched it. But now it is for us Africans to think, which is the real Christ? And which is the other culture? Where do I fit in? Should we be going for everything that came with this gospel? How can we make it our own? Or how can we really belong to Christ? And not to the Canadians! And not to the French! And not to the British! That is not easy—it needs a lot of discernment and faith.

Hannah Kinoti, professor of religious studies at the University of Nairobi and Kenyan representative of the Circle of Concerned African Women Theologians, explained further:

> We have been struggling to see Jesus with an African face, and that is a struggle that we have to continue. The kind of face that Jesus has been given, to me, is a white face. A white face, Jesus or God, even the images we see of Jesus—and it becomes a struggle.

Salome Okeyo expressed similar sentiments in the focus group of Kenyan Catholic laity: "At first there was something which I kept on wondering when I was a child. Why is it that whenever I see the picture of Jesus, it is in a European form? So at first I used to think, did he come for only these Europeans and not the Africans?" Finally, among the many respondents who lamented the proliferation of white images of Jesus in Africa, Kenyan pastor J. B. Masinde stated the problem in this way:

> Concerning the Christ that we have to present now, we have to peel off some clothes that he's been packaged in. I don't mean it in a bad way, but those who presented Christ to Africa, say in my area, they presented him packaged in the Western kind of model, in the sense that the perception many people got was not even that Christ was a Jew! The drawings they had in their churches, the pictures they had in their homes did not even look like Jewish men! 'Cause most of them were drawn in the Italian fashion. So the perception was, "Oh, he must have been a white man! Ah, like the white missionary! He must have been closer to God than we are!"

A whole complex of issues thus arises from the missionary transmission of the gospel to Africa during colonial times. While the theological texts and oral interviews reveal many other related concerns, attention has been restricted to the main historical factors prompting contemporary christological questions, namely, (1) the close association of Christianity with colonialism, and (2) missionary attitudes and practices, particularly the denigration of African cultures. Like chisel and hammer, these two aspects of recent African history have together helped to carve the "disfigured" face of Jesus in Africa today: as white, as European, as consequently alien, as marred with suffering yet submissive to those upholding the status quo. Catholic layman George Hagan, director of the Institute of African Studies at the University of Ghana, Legon, observed:

> The early missionaries were not preaching Christ to heal our bodies, preaching Christ to liberate us. They were preaching Christ who made us able to accept our position in life. Not Christ as the agitator. Theirs was a Christ of submission, that would enable the African to accept leadership from the Church, leadership from the colonial masters.

Finally, Nasimiyu Wasike's conclusion provides an apt summary of the historical and missiological issues:

> Therefore, the Jesus that the Africans received from the western European missionaries was a Jesus who had been clothed in many layers of cultural realities. He was imagined as an imperialist, racist, cultural and . . . religious colonialist, and as hierarchical and patriarchal in his relationships with people.[19]

THEOLOGICAL ISSUES

"The North Atlantic Captivity of the Church" has also created a cluster of overlapping issues that are theological in nature. For Africans have endured not only political, economic and cultural imperialism, but also the domination of Western theology and church polity. Despite much effort and progress in cultivating African Christianity, according to Kwesi Dickson, the current president of the AACC, "colonial theology is very much in place still. There's no question, even though people have gone to seminary and all that. The colonial theology is alive and well."

The defect here is not merely ecclesiastical hegemony or Western ethnocentrism and paternalism, however much these symptoms violate the gospel of Jesus Christ. Rather, the root problem is much more pernicious, for it raises the very theological question of missionary misapprehension of the gospel itself. Mugambi's explanation is worth quoting at length for its clarity:

> Christian missionaries came as agents of western civilization which, they believed, was the "Christian civilization." They went out to Africa and Asia in the name of "Christendom" rather than in the name of Christ. The modern missionary enterprise in Africa was founded upon an erroneous theological presupposition. By identifying the Christian faith with western "Christendom" the missionaries ignored or overlooked one of the most important theological affirmations of the Christian faith since the time of Jesus—that *conversion* to Christianity did not necessarily demand *acculturation* into the culture

of the missionary. Interestingly, this issue of demanding converts to denounce their cultural heritage and accept that of the missionary precipitated the first great controversy in the history of Christianity. It led to the significant theological conflict between Peter and Paul.

One of the most disturbing ironies of the modern missionary enterprise, was that the missionaries were biblical literalists, yet they did not take cognizance of the resolution of the first ecumenical council of Jerusalem which declared that it was not necessary for a Gentile to become an "honorary" Jew in order to become a Christian. Most missionaries insisted that an African must become an "honorary white," as a precondition for becoming a Christian. This was a gross theological error.[20]

Thus the missionary association of Christianity and European civilization went beyond a mere cultural blunder to evidence a theological misconception.[21] As a direct legacy of the missionary enterprise, African Christians face the fundamental problem of appropriating Christ as Africans despite the "judaizing" tendencies of Western missionaries to fashion Christian faith according to their own image. This challenge surfaces in the autobiographical reflections of the selected African theologians and contributes significantly to the agenda voiced regarding African Christologies. Reminiscing about his own theological formation, Bujo commented:

> It is difficult to say, but maybe what has influenced me is that I grew up in the colonial period, and I saw how the African culture was not taken seriously into account. We didn't understand many things in our prayers, or in our life in the school. What we were taught was not according to our African life—it was strange to us. So that has been the starting point. Then, when I was studying theology at seminary, what we learned was all Western philosophy. Especially in the ethical problems, all the problems were concentrated on the Western life. But nobody took into account our own problems in Africa.

In contrast to the estrangement from African life he experienced at school, Bujo explained: "Then at home, my parents taught me the African way of life. So, I wanted to know Christ, to understand Christianity in my culture—to find the roots of my culture also in the Christian faith. That has been the starting point." Consequently, assessing how his background in Africa and his experiences in the West shaped his present understanding of Jesus, Bujo concluded: "Jesus Christ, the Risen Christ, no longer belongs to one culture. So Europe cannot impose on us a model from Europe. Everybody has to understand Christ in his own culture, so we have the right to understand Christ in our culture." All these experiences and convictions therefore elicit the key christological question that stands at the heart of Bujo's agenda for African theology: "*In which way can Jesus Christ be an African among the Africans according to their own religious experience?*"[22]

Discussing this agenda for African theology, Bujo underlined an important observation:

Christian theology in the African context entails not only the problem of culture as ethnology, but also the new problems that came to Africa with colonialism and with the new civilization—the technology and all that makes up the African context today. We have to understand the gospel in this context today, and not be one-sided, considering only the old culture. We have to take into account this new culture in Africa, and build a new dynamism—maybe go out from the old culture, because there are some elements from the old culture still surviving today.

Elsewhere he concludes that indeed "the future of Christianity in Africa depends on getting the right balance between the old and the new."[23] In keeping with this stated priority, the theological issues confronting African Christologies can be set forth as follows: first, Jesus in relation to the African heritage; second, Jesus in relation to contemporary realities in Africa; and third, fundamental christological questions arising from the biblical witness concerning Jesus' life, death, and resurrection.

The paramount priority of relating Jesus to the African heritage rings clear across the continent from Catholics and Protestants, theologians, church leaders, and lay people alike. Beginning with the latter, Catherine Mwango, from the focus group of Kenyan Catholic laity, pointed out the particular problem of relating Jesus to the traditional understanding of God:

The problem is that when you talk about God and Jesus, I think God is more pronounced in the African setting, in the form of mountains, in the particular names in different languages, like *Nyasai* in Luo and Luhya, and *Ngai* in Kikuyu. So, it looks like God the Creator was more pronounced, and for a long time Jesus remained like somebody from *out*.

In neighboring Uganda, Catholic priest J. M. Waliggo explained further:

I think the figure of Jesus Christ was not brought out clearly from our cultural milieu. God the Father we knew, everybody knew who God was. But the Son was something new. And they tried to present the gospel as new, and as such, it has really had very little impact. Jesus Christ just somehow appears, and he's the one more repeated by preachers. But the interaction does not really carry as much weight as when you talk about God, because God is the center of African religion and African culture. But now, to bring in a new person, through whom salvation is made, you had to very much know the culture, and then see, how do I present it, which is the question most theologians and preachers have never solved.

Waliggo stressed that when Jesus is introduced in this way, as a "new person" unrelated to the God previously known in Africa, "the notion of Christology can only come in when you unite them in such a manner as they did in the Trinity. But there is a big question there, a problem." Peter Bisem, Deputy Secretary General of the National Council of Churches of Kenya, concurs in establishing that if in our teaching, our emphasis of Jesus is as if he is distinct from the Father, as if he's not one in action as the Godhead, that has created something of a problem. But when we understand God in Christ, then that is not a crisis at all. In fact, when you speak to people, surprisingly they don't find it as something new! They say, "Yes, what we're hearing from the gospel message is what our people have always believed."

Across the continent, in Ghana, Protestant leader Kwesi Dickson attested to the same dilemma and set it in historical perspective:

The way that Christianity was presented, and still is in some cases, Christ didn't seem to fit in too well. Because we had God, we talked about *Nyame* the whole time, God, everybody understood that. But Christ didn't seem to fit in so well. It was in the eighteenth century, around 1751, that one missionary, Thomas Thompson of the SPG,[24] wrote that whenever he preached about God, the people were very happy. When he turned to Christ, they lost interest and started to wander off, because Christ didn't seem familiar. Didn't fit, and this was apparently the result of the way the church, the missionary preaching, went. But Christ matters, because he makes clear to us who God truly is. Without that knowledge, we get a very attenuated understanding of God. And that's why I take Christ so seriously. He makes God clearer to me, than otherwise he would be, without Christ. So, we've had this problem from the very beginning, of Christ not fitting in. The evidence is quite clear from the eighteenth century. And I'm afraid that we have not always done the right sort of preaching or teaching on the matter. So I feel strongly about Christ being understood better so that we would understand God better.

As these voices indicate, one of the most critical theological issues in the transmission of the gospel to Africa concerns the very nature of the Christian God and God's self-revelation in Christ to African peoples. In other words, what concept of God was imparted through missionary preaching and received by African Christians? How faithful was this concept of God to that of the biblical witness? Peter Kiarie, former director of education at the Catholic Secretariat in Nairobi, asserted:

Jesus Christ came as part of the Bible. In terms of where Christ fits into the African heritage, Christ does not come to replace the African God because— I am a Kikuyu, and the people here have a very strong faith in God the Creator. And they did not worship images or any idols.

Kiarie continued by explaining how the missionaries "presented Jesus as the Son of God who created heaven and earth," and taught the creed referring to "*one* God, Creator of heaven and earth, God the Father Almighty." Therefore, in addressing the relationship between Jesus and the Father and how best to communicate this understanding of God to the African context, Kiarie insists upon beginning from Genesis and the creation story. He explained:

So Jesus is seen in context. There is no Jesus, just a Jesus—you bring him in. No! You have to go back even to the preexistence, the Jesus even before Christmas. You come first of all from the Old Testament about God, because you don't tell the Africans about Jesus before you tell them about God. If Jesus is not rooted to God, then he's nowhere. So, it must be about God, and Jesus must be seen active and related to this God—there must be evidence. So that's why Jesus, his name and his very presence, then becomes meaningful.

Locating the presence of Jesus in their pre-Christian past thus becomes a central concern for many African Christians. Gatu has been a leading proponent of this endeavor within Kenyan Christianity, yet he related the opposition he still encounters when doing so. For example, referring to the East African Revival movement, he described that

one time, when I was trying to talk about the images of God in the African setting, and what God has done and how God has revealed himself through all nations, I found it very difficult to put it to the Revival brethren, particularly when I was trying to use traditional tunes to convey Christian messages. They were challenging me and in fact accusing me of taking the church back to heathenism. And I said, "Brethren, now look! If the God that I believe in, who is the Father of Jesus Christ, did not reveal himself in any way to my people of Kikuyu-land, I will have nothing to do with that kind of God! Because I believe if he is that kind of God, he must have revealed himself in a certain way to my Kikuyu people, in preparation for the coming of his Son, Jesus Christ." And I said, "This is why, for me, he's such an important person in my life. And this is why this God is so important, because he never left my people without any witness, even before the coming of missionary Christianity, as it were."

Gatu went on to cite examples of traditional Kikuyu religious rites, such as selecting a goat or sheep with "no blemish at all" and cutting the animal vertically and horizontally in "a sign of the cross" when sacrificing it, which he interprets as follows:

Those for me are signs that God gave to my people of the coming of the Lord Jesus Christ. And for that reason, I believe all the more, that while the Kikuyu people may not have seen Jesus, the cross, as it were, they already had enough to prepare them for the coming of the Lord Jesus Christ. And my criticism of missionaries is that they sort of degraded all that, or even rubbed away all that, and more or less said, "Let us start on a clean slate."

In contrast to this tabula-rasa approach commonly taken by early missionaries, the selected African theologians locate the crux of their christological questioning in the interface between the biblical revelation of Christ and the African context. Hence Ghanaian Protestant Pobee asks the crucial questions: "Who is Jesus Christ? What manner of man is he? How does he affect my life? Why should an Akan relate to Jesus of Nazareth, who does not belong to his clan, family, tribe, and nation?"[25] Kenyan Catholic Nasimiyu Wasike agrees, for when asked to identify the key christological issue for Africans today, she replied:

> It stems out of the whole theological formation that we have received. It was the way the Western theology interpreted who Christ is, and that's what we received. But now we have to look at Christ as he is in the scriptures. Who is he for us? And I think, that is the crucial, crucial point.

Another aspect of missionary preaching that did not adequately consider the traditional African worldview it encountered concerns the nature of Christian salvation. While a vast topic in itself, the specific focus here is the present and future dimensions of Christ's saving work. It is now widely acknowledged that African ontology is essentially anthropocentric and the focus of life is decidedly "this-worldly."[26] Yet mission Christianity tended to present the gospel of Christ as primarily otherworldly. Speaking of the legacy of Western missions, Amoah and Oduyoye explain:

> The eschatology that accompanies this Christology has, however, focused almost entirely on "the end of the age" and often on a supramundane realm where all is well. African Christians have had to support this Christ with spiritualities from their own traditions, which assure them of immediate well-being in the now and in the near future.[27]

Likewise Africans are known for their holistic view of life, yet the missionary transmission of the gospel, marked as it was by the effects of the European Enlightenment, often separated the material from the spiritual. These authors conclude:

> This mission Christology, we suggest, is not up to the task of empowering Christians for life in Africa today, with its material and spiritual demands. It masks the relevance of Christ in the business of living today and in the immediate future. Africans require a holistic view of life. This demands a Christ who affects the whole of life and demonstrates that there is nothing that is not the business of God.[28]

Thus a number of significant theological issues arise in the attempt to relate Jesus to the African heritage, from the very nature of God and his self-revelation in Christ to the eschatological dimensions of salvation and the relevance of Christ to life today.

The second dimension of theological issues concerns the relation of Jesus to contemporary realities in Africa. While the subject is broad, two aspects are introduced here: (1) the socioeconomic and political context, and (2) the religious context. Regarding the current socioeconomic and political context, Ghanaian Protestant clergy member Margaret Asabea echoed the preliminary comment above by Waliggo concerning the need to understand Africa's present situation in light of her former suffering under the impact of Europe:

> This African-European struggle—economic disorder, slave trade and things like that, they are a problem, real problem which happened, historic. And we can't change the history. The atrocities that came about through this trade, they are there. They are landmarks there.

Bujo concurred, emphasizing the following:

> In fact, the catastrophic economic situation that prevails in Africa today cannot easily be isolated from the long-lasting oppression which foreign powers once imposed on it. Besides the loss of human potential and without considering the physical and moral sufferings of slavery, the colonial period initiated and ruthlessly carried out a large scale exploitation of Africa's natural resources. The transfer of capital towards the North is just one aspect of this unpleasant reality.[29]

However, it is Ela who comes to the fore in denouncing contemporary economic and political injustices from a theological perspective. He places his fundamental christological issues squarely in the current contexts of neocolonialism and globalism:

> How can we believe in Jesus Christ in a context in which the rich countries refuse to grant to the black peoples the status of historic subject? It is in today's world that we have to respond to the question Jesus of Nazareth asks us: "Africans, for you, who am I?" . . . How can we express our belonging to God in a continent that does not belong to itself? Should we allow ourselves to be enclosed in a three-dimensional religious universe of sin, sacraments, and grace at a time when, under cover of cooperation, economic and financial groups freely dispute over land, beaches, bauxite, copper, and diamond mines, commerce and tourism, and of course uranium and oil, and, certainly, the very conscience of the African people. For the economic penetration is always coupled with cultural domination. It will be more and more difficult to separate the questions of faith in the African environment from the questions asked everywhere about the process of recolonization currently under way in the countries of Africa, which appear to be a sort of fiscal paradise of multinationals that demand a climate of stability and security essential to the pillage of national resources.[30]

Further examination of these economic and political challenges awaits the exploration of christological responses to them. However, the point underscored here is the crucial need for contemporary Christologies to address life's current realities in addition to the African heritage.

Another aspect of the contemporary context that arises in discussions about Christ is that of denominationalism and religious pluralism. These concerns are voiced less frequently than other issues, and in general are raised by those who are theologically trained. For example, Mugambi warns that "the plague of Christianity in Africa is its internal division and rivalry, not external threat."[31] Likewise, Oduyoye calls for African theologians "to face the scandal of the divisions and competition within the church, as 'original tribalism' is being replaced by the Christian 'tribes'—Anglicans, Methodists, Roman Catholics, Baptists."[32]

Pobee questions, "Are we preaching the same Christ—Anglicans, Methodists, Roman Catholics? If so, why are we at each other's throats?" He also illustrates such interdenominational tensions from his own experience of marrying a Catholic woman and facing criticism for not having married an Anglican. Stressing yet again that "all theology is biography," he ponders, "So what does it mean now, in this Roman Catholic/Anglican family, to affirm one and the same Christ?"

Addressing the christological concern in the wider context of religious pluralism in Africa, Pobee observed:

> When I go to West Africa, it becomes, as in the case of Nigeria, "Who is Christ in this pluralistic society?" Because you have your Muslim tackling you, your traditionalist. So you have to define your Christology in a pluralistic context—unlike in the North, in the early church, when it was the Christian ideology, as if the others didn't exist.

Therefore, a critical issue to emerge is that of the uniqueness of Christ amid religious pluralism. Oduyoye emphasized:

> It is important for us that we are able to state who Jesus is. Because we are living in a multi-religious context, we recognize the multi-religious context, and there's a big challenge that comes to us out of the Johannine exclusivist Christology about Jesus alone as the way, the truth. You take that, and you take your multi-religious community, and you have a task on your hands. Now how do you work out the Christ in that context? It's one of the challenges that I hope more people will work on.

Besides these challenges of relating Jesus to the African heritage and to the contemporary realities, there are certain christological questions deemed quintessential to the Christian faith. Main concerns can only be identified at present, and these include understanding Jesus as human and divine, his relation to God the Father and the Holy Spirit, and the meaning and significance of his death and resurrection. A vital question from Ela not only reflects this latter issue, but also serves to sum up the previous sections regarding historical and theological issues concerning Christology. In pointing out the problem of theological ethnocentrism that has dominated Christianity for centuries, Ela explains:

> For the "irruption of the Third World" is shaking up theology. It is necessary to underline here the extent of the "shift" that is taking place in a turnaround of history where theology elaborated in the West is less assured of remaining the official theology of the entire church. The rupture with North Atlantic

theology is henceforth imperative if we want to rediscover God from the "periphery." . . . In short, a critical and responsible reappropriation of the scandal of Jesus obliges us to remain faithful to the places where the irruption of the poor in history questions our understanding of the faith.[33]

In this process of reappropriation that Ela advocates, the meaning of Christ's death and resurrection in relation to the African experience of suffering is absolutely central:

If Christianity wishes to avoid the temptation of the priest and the Levite in the parable of the Good Samaritan (Luke 20:31–32), it must assume the tragedy in Africa of those whom Frantz Fanon has called "the wretched of the earth." In this situation, the return to Jesus makes it absolutely necessary that our Christian reflection becomes incessantly suspicious toward any God-talk that attempts to "pass on the other side" of the actual situation in Africa. How can we rediscover God from the perspective of "a crucified messiah" (1 Cor. 1:23) while at the same time covering up the other scandal that is at the center of the human adventure of our era? Here is this scandal: for five hundred years, the West has chosen the Christ without the cross, while the people of Africa live the cross without the Christ. It is this passion without redemption in which Africa continues to live that must question our understanding of Jesus Christ. Taking into consideration such a basic situation, how can we articulate the crucifixion of Jesus and the historical suffering of our people? In other words, how can we reread in our own way the narratives of the Passion of our Lord Jesus Christ taking into account the stations of our memory? Such is the question that comes out of the black continent where—if one really dares to admit it—God speaks to the world and to the church.[34]

ISSUES OF AFRICAN CHRISTIAN IDENTITY

For many African theologians, the problem of African Christian identity lies at the epicenter of African theology.[35] At the confluence of the historical, missiological, and theological issues delineated above, issues of identity run deeply and personally in the lives of African believers. Reflecting upon it historically, Bujo affirms: "In offering us fullness of life, Jesus offers to the people of Africa true development. After the traumas of the slave-trade and colonialism, and now the horrors of the refugee situation, the African people are searching for a new identity."[36] This quest for a new identity, according to Pobee, concerns what it means to be human "as nuanced by African identity and Christ."[37]

Examining the issue missiologically, Bisem explained:

But it is now plainly understood that the style of mission and approach, that is, the missionary practice of uprooting converts from their traditional environment, sometimes tended to create, you could say, an identity crisis in the hearer of the message. Because the presentation was as if God speaks to this person, and now, cuts him off or cuts her off from his initial identity—up-roots, if you like.

Various expressions emerge to describe this duality often experienced by African Christians. For example, Ela speaks of "the split personality that one observes in the Churches in which the cultural and symbolic universe of indigenous Christians has never been taken seriously in the manner in which the Gospel has been presented to them," or "the dichotomy in the life of certain Christians," or "their spiritual schizophrenia."[38]

Considering the issue theologically, Protestant lay woman Irene Odotei, a history professor at the University of Ghana, Legon, put it succinctly:

> Christianity came to us wrapped in a cultural garb. And the Bible is within a certain cultural context, that's the Jewish context. So now, how do we bring it within the Ghanaian context? Does it mean by being a Christian, you have to stop being Ghanaian? Or, is it by being Ghanaian, you cannot be a Christian? So how to be very Ghanaian and very Christian is the problem.

Her questioning resonates with that of Anne Nasimiyu Wasike, who articulated from her own experience this fundamental issue of African Christian identity. Recalling her sense of utter bewilderment in discovering "ethnic affiliation churches" in America, she recounted:

> I began to think, then, we ought to be African Christians. There has to be something like that! Otherwise, who am I? I'm not Polish, I'm not Irish, I'm not English, I'm not German. And so, how do I affiliate myself with this church, then? Because I saw it there, and all of a sudden I was convinced, I have to go back to my roots! What were they? Because for my whole traditional upbringing, my father and mother actually had nothing to do with the traditional rituals and worship, and they would never allow any of us to participate. So I was totally brought up in a culture I believed was Christian. But then the Christianity which I received from my formation was not bringing me to where I want to be or who I want to be. I suddenly had to think, who am I? Who am I really? What kind of Christian am I? That question became very powerful and strong, and that is the moment I said, I have to think like an African. I have to believe like an African. And how do I begin?

Nasimiyu Wasike went on to explain how, despite misunderstanding and opposition from her parents, she went to her grandmother, a diviner, to begin researching her own traditional culture. She concluded: "So from that moment, I decided I am really going to get into inculturation now. I want to really see myself as an African Christian believer." This priority influences the shape of contemporary Christology for Nasimiyu Wasike and Odotei, and for many other African believers like them.

GENDER ISSUES

While the issues outlined thus far indicate further developments in the matters explored in Chapter 1, the subject of gender in relation to emergent African Christologies is relatively recent. To illustrate, Oduyoye traces the "irruption within the irruption" of EATWOT, when the 1981 Fifth International Conference in New Delhi confronted the challenge that "the irruption of women in church and society is an integral part of the voice of the earth's voiceless majority" in need of attention. From this challenge stems the fundamental methodological stance: "The concerns and experiences of women as women are yet another *locus* for liberation theology."[39] Therefore, EATWOT was called to expand its borders from doing theology based on experiences of classism and racism in the socioeconomic and political realms, to include sexism anchored in religio-cultural perceptions. Some third-world representatives maintain that issues of sexism are not indigenous to their contexts, arising instead from "a minority of disgruntled, leisure-saturated, middle-class women of the capitalist West." Yet Oduyoye retorts, "The fact is that sexism is part of the intricate web of oppression in which most of us live, and that having attuned ourselves to it does not make it any less a factor of oppression."[40] The feminist claim that women are oppressed in male-dominated structures of church and society is thus said to challenge not only "the dominant theology of the capitalist West," but also "the maleness of Christian theology worldwide, together with the patriarchal presuppositions that govern all our relationships."[41] The goal of feminism, according to Oduyoye, is for women and men from the Northern and Southern hemispheres to join in the common search for what it means to be fully human. "The way forward is a 'new community of men and women,' not reversal; participation, not takeover or handover. Feminism in theology springs from a conviction that a theology of relationships might contribute to bring us closer to human life as God desires it."[42]

Toward this aim, African feminist theologians seek to discover the sources of their oppression. Three main sources come to light, which in turn evoke christological questions. First, aspects of Christian tradition are deemed to conceal Jesus' "revolutionary" approach to women in granting them equal status to men and thus restoring the original relationship God established between the sexes at creation. Nasimiyu Wasike traces the origin of the problem to the early church era, when christological formulations were being forged in the context of Jewish and Hellenistic categories of thought. As a result of the patriarchal realities of the time, the term *Logos* applied to Christ as creator also became associated with the rational principle of the human soul, presumed to be male. Therefore theological references to Christ became heavily androcentric, reinforcing the assumption that God was male. Only male metaphors were considered appropriate to speak of God; moreover, "Christ had to be male in order to reveal a male God, and this was taken literally."[43] While man was understood to be made in the image of God, woman was only seen as the image of man and only saved through man. Such concepts about God and Christ in relation to man and woman colored the development of theology in Europe for centuries and consequently tainted perceptions of Christ brought by modern European missionaries to Africa. Nasimiyu Wasike summarizes the problem as follows:

> The African church has inherited the misinterpretation of woman and her relation to God and Jesus from the European church. Therefore, the African woman, in addition to being under her cultural bondage and oppression, also experiences the socio-economic oppression of neo-colonialists in the church.[44]

Feminist theologians further lament the fact that until recent decades, most critical reflection on Christology was written by men and from a male perspective. Not only was the female perspective left unarticulated, but also "the theology on the person of Jesus tended to be much more philosophical and abstract than that of the existential Jesus of the Gospels who calls people as individuals and as a community to authentic human existence."[45] As a result of this historical neglect, African women now pose basic questions such as those of Amoah and Oduyoye: "What have women to do with the concept of Christology? What do women say about Christology? Is there such a thing as a women's Christology? Do the traditional statements of Christology take into account women's experience of life?"[46]

The concern for reflection upon women's experience leads to a consideration of additional causes of oppression. The second source identified is sexist cultural orientations, such as the appeal to blood taboos from African traditional religion in protest against women's ordination to the priesthood. Theology is said to arise from women's painful experiences of the structural and domestic violence enshrined in religio-cultural traditions. A third related source that compounds women's oppression is the contemporary sociopolitical context. Women are noted to be the easiest targets and the most frequent victims of suffering across Africa today. As Oduyoye describes it, "This politico-economic machinery of death, with its militarism, arbitrary arrests and so-called popular democracy, also promotes the abuse of women. This is the situation out of which third world women do their theology." [47]

As women reflect on Christ from these contexts of oppression, *Jesus* is considered to be "no swear word but a cry. It says, 'save me, save us, save them.'" Oduyoye stresses further that the answer to who Jesus is, is neither a historical quest nor a probe into his being. In contrast to traditional Christology's presentation of Jesus' two natures and consubstantiality with God, she states that women seek "the immediate quest—what does all this mean to our ailing world with its ailing people?"[48] It is questions like these, elicited by situations of suffering, that fuel the efforts and inspire innovative methods and fresh insights in contemporary women's Christologies.

Finally, the need to address gender issues in contemporary African Christologies is increasingly recognized to extend beyond the domain of women's concerns alone. Thus Ela affirmed:

> I think that the question of gender challenges our christologies. It is not only the concern of women. Every theologian must be able to show regard for

Jesus Christ in taking account of the fact that humanity is at the same time masculine and feminine.

Pobee concurs, for when asked about critical issues regarding African Christologies in future, he responded:

> In the next century, I think, how women articulate their experience of Christ will become very important. They are more than one half of the world. More than one half of the population of the church. I have heard loud and clear, women have been smarting under all kinds of oppression in society and in the home. So, what they say about Christ as the hope and fears of all the years, as we sing at Christmas, will be one of the crucial things.

It is interesting to note the extent to which both of these male theologians attribute important aspects of their theological formation to significant women in their lives, particularly their mothers. However, further exploration of gender issues in relation to theology awaits the elaboration of the christological models in Part II.

ISSUES OF CONTEMPORARY CHRISTIAN WITNESS

If christological concerns arise out of past experience, as indicated by the issues discussed thus far, they also originate in present witness to Jesus Christ. For as Mugambi and Magesa stress:

> No Christological discussion in Africa today can avoid the question of the credibility of Christ. . . . It is the question not only of effective evangelization but also of the praxis of faith of the followers of Christ. It is the question of how we can present Christ to the African world as truly its Lord and Saviour in a convincing manner. Even more important, it is the question of how this conviction can be lived out.[49]

What threatens the "credibility of Christ" in contemporary Christianity in Africa? Numerous challenges surface in this respect, only two of which will be summarized briefly.

Oduyoye introduces the first factor succinctly in highlighting "the gap between 'Christianity preached' and 'Christianity lived.'"[50] The cry echoes across the continent. For example, Kenyan Circle member Hannah Kinoti lamented: "Well, I must admit there is a lot of disillusionment for any thinking African. There are some who are very disillusioned because of the many discrepancies of the message and the reality of life." What are these discrepancies? B. Y. Quarshie, lecturer in the Department for the Study of Religions at the University of Ghana, Legon, and former chairman of a Presbytery, observed:

> The way I look at the Christian scene, vis-à-vis all the difficulties we face, as a nation—the fact that when you go into government circles you encounter

people who say they are Christians. You go into businesses they are there! Private enterprise and so on, you will find people who claim to be Christians, who therefore claim to know Christ. And yet by what they do day in and day out six days of the week, apart from Sunday going to service, there is no indication that they have met this Christ or that he means anything to them. And *that* is what I find rather disturbing. In other words, I don't think Christians are making a difference. And you have to ask whether they actually know this Jesus Christ at all.

Similar regret is expressed about the contemporary scene in Kenya; in the Circle focus group Emily Choge remarked:

> To analyze the life of Christ in our situation here in Africa, and leading that life in which he will be seen as relevant, I think is the issue here. There is a lot of superficiality, a lot of lack of understanding of what it really means to be a follower of Jesus Christ. It has been estimated that Kenya is supposed to be 80 percent Christian, and yet it is also third in the corruption hierarchy in the world. So how do the two go together? How can we be Christian and yet have this corruption?

As a result of such discrepancies, African Christians ask themselves serious questions. For example, Marie Gacambi, lecturer at the Catholic University of East Africa in Nairobi, queried, "Does our belief really touch our concrete life situation? Or is the Christian belief something put on, which we can discard at any moment?" She presented the problem as follows:

> I do believe that somehow, we may not have been able to help the believer to grasp the message completely—who Jesus is, the kerygma and not the Jesus that is given out there as an ideal. Otherwise, if we really have grasped who Jesus is, and the values that Jesus lives, then somehow once we embrace the Christian life, a complete transformation, a conversion, a change of heart and mind and attitude should take place. This is one of the questions.

Protestant lay man Alex Glover-Quartey concluded with a common criticism that "Christianity in Ghana is skin-deep. You know, once you scratch the skin, what you see is not actually what ought to be Christianity."

A second issue related to the credibility of Christ is the appropriateness of certain expressions of Christian witness as currently found in these African contexts. For example, concern is expressed about witness to Christ being marred by undue stress on the "health and wealth" gospel. As Quarshie remarked, "The trend is now you go to church to become prosperous. So the pursuit of materialism, with the church as a front, is just what is going on." Or, as Protestant lay man John Muriithi, a fruit-hawker on the streets of Nairobi, observed frankly, "Well, my colleagues, some of them don't go to church. They believe church people cheat, they just want money. Church is a kind of business, something like that."

Oduyoye called attention to another challenge regarding appropriate witness to Christ, in a new generation of "cultured despisers" who impede the cultivation of African Christologies:

> We are using cultural symbolisms that are being deliberately eroded by some Western charismatics and neo-Pentecostal Christianity. So, for how much longer will this language communicate? In the theology that we are doing in Africa, we're using concepts of ancestors, we're using the carrier, we're using what we know. But there's a generation that's going to some of these newer churches, and they are being told, "Forget it. You can't even do a naming ceremony, let alone pour libation. When you're getting married, it doesn't matter if you don't do the traditional marriage, just come to church." There's a whole generation that is being deliberately alienated from the African culture. So I'm asking myself, What kind of theology will communicate with this generation? And where are we going to find that theology? Or are we going back to the colonial Western situation where you just imbibe the theology that was brought to you from somebody else's context. That, for me, is a challenge.

These few examples, intimating hypocrisy, nominalism, superficiality, prosperity preaching, and deliberate alienation from African culture, illustrate the range of issues that contemporary African Christians must address in order to render credible and appropriate witness to Christ.

ISSUES REGARDING LANGUAGE

The impact of language in shaping various expressions of the Christian faith has long been recognized. As Pobee emphasizes, language is symbolic, going beyond syntax and morphology to being "the vehicle for assuming a culture, a civilization. It is the vehicle for possessing the world-view."[51] He points out, however, that African languages were considered barbarous in the nineteenth and into the twentieth century. Hence, Africans were taught colonial languages to "redeem" them from their barbarism, and these colonial languages have continued to dominate in the African context, including African theology, to the present. Given this reality, Pobee presents the following challenge:

> Convenient and useful as these established foreign languages may be, their symbolism is different from the one an African naturally appreciates through his vernacular. The result is that often there is no harmony of his intellectual perception with his emotional needs. This cannot lead to wholeness, to total salvation. So I see much soundness in the Reformation principle that all must hear the word of God in their mother-tongue or vernacular. There is need to use the vernacular to communicate the scriptures and for the administration of the sacraments, for prayers, music, etc.[52]

Other theologians and interview respondents corroborate this view. Ela in particular stressed the centrality of language in doing theology in Africa today.

He emphasized, with slight laughter, how the language of Western creeds means nothing to rural Africans, and then stated his own methodological priority:

> See, when we take these formulas, Jesus Christ, a single person united in two natures in a hypostatic manner, that is the formulation of Westerners. For me, an African, that means nothing. If I say that to the people of my village! If I take these formulas to the Kirdis, of the mountain, they say, "What? What?" And I believe that if I ask the same question of Jesus himself, he will say to me, "What? What are you saying to me?!" He does not understand, Jesus himself, what one says about him in the West. If I bring that back from the West and I want to speak in Africa, that will be an obstacle. This is why I want to be obliged, myself, to return to the New Testament to try to understand its message and to find what is most meaningful for the people when I speak about Jesus Christ. Indeed, that is the question. All the problem of theology is there: to discover what is the most meaningful for them.

Ela illustrated this priority with respect to the use of vernacular in his ministry among the Kirdi of northern Cameroon. He recounted that, in preparing for Christmas celebrations, people asked how they might present Jesus. Ela held meetings with his catechists:

> I said to them, "Listen, you know your language better than I do." (I learned the language, but they spoke it better.) "We want to find the right language to speak of what the gospels say. What expressions can we find in order to speak to the people who come from the mountain?" And that is the work we did, every Sunday for fourteen years, working from the gospel, then seeking the words and images of the people to present these things.

Consequently, the villagers were urged to draw upon their local language and thought forms and were thus able to connect their own context meaningfully with that of Jesus' birth, saying, "For us, Jesus' birth is like the children of the mountain. He was born like the children in our homes." In a later conversation Ela returned to this central conviction regarding language and its use in the formulation of African Christologies. He concluded with this challenge:

> I have wanted the African christologies to take into account the language that the people speak Jesus, themselves. Because they speak of Jesus! And I have seen an actual situation, where the women sing Jesus. They start to sing "Emmanuel," like we rock an infant. They sing lullabies about Jesus, the child of Mary. Therefore I say, these women are captured by something in Jesus Christ. So these songs of women are a language that is spoken about Jesus Christ. What is the significance of this language, what is its depth, what is its richness? And therefore how do we articulate a coherent theological discourse on Jesus Christ in listening in to the women who sing the gospel?

Issues related to language as expressing worldview, therefore, warrant careful consideration in constructing African Christologies.

CONCLUSION: CRITERIA FOR CRITICAL ENGAGEMENT
WITH AFRICAN CHRISTOLOGIES

An initial investigation into the origins of African Christologies brings to light a number of interrelated concerns. Whether stemming from Africa's past history or present realities, the questions raised are fundamental to the perceptions of Christ articulated by African believers today. Consequently, the issues introduced in this chapter do not recede in the following chapters. On the contrary, they remain foundational to the interpretation and assessment of the Christologies articulated. For, in identifying the matters of utmost concern to them, the African Christians accordingly voice the priorities they seek in forging their own experience and expression of faith in Christ. These stated priorities therefore form the basis for critical engagement with the contemporary African Christologies.

On the basis of their own assertions, then, the following indicators have emerged that can function as criteria for assessing the current Christologies.

APPROPRIATENESS OF SOURCES

Do the African Christologies draw upon the recommended sources outlined in the first part of the chapter, which can be conflated as (a) the Bible and Christian heritage, (b) the African heritage, including history, religion and culture, (c) the living experience of the Church, and (d) contemporary realities in Africa? Are some sources evidently favored above others? If so, what impact might this have upon the current configuration of contemporary African Christologies?

APPROPRIATENESS OF METHODS

While attention is paid to the ways in which all the selected African Christians reason in arriving at their perceptions of Christ, two main methodological questions are addressed primarily to the African theologians under consideration. The first query stems from the call made by African theologians, recorded in the "Final Communiqué," for "a new theological methodology" that would serve to produce the kind of contextual theology being advocated for Africa.[53] The question, therefore, is what contributions have been made toward this end by those who have articulated more formal expressions of African Christology? Or, more precisely, are the christological methods effective in pursuing the priorities expressed regarding contextual relevance?

The second main question is related to the first, and it arises from Mugambi's assertion that "African Christian theology is in a methodological crisis, owing to the lack of methodological consciousness."[54] Contending that "the African Church will only come of age when it becomes self-critical," Mugambi calls for a thorough critique of theological method as part of the overall theological introspection recommended.[55] In view of this assessment, the question arises as to whether the selected African theologians evidence the methodological "introspection and self-criticism" that Mugambi urges.

FACTORS OF CONTEXTUAL RELEVANCE

The second part of the chapter has examined critical issues regarding contextual relevance attested in the theological literature and the oral interviews. A number of factors have been distinguished in this regard:

- *Historical relevance*: Is Jesus understood meaningfully in relation to Africa's history, particularly in relation to the suffering of Africa?
- *Theological relevance*: How is Jesus understood in relation to (1) Africa's pre-Christian heritage; (2) the contemporary context of religious pluralism; and (3) fundamental biblical affirmations regarding Jesus' identity, life, death, and resurrection?
- *Cultural relevance*: Is Jesus presently perceived as a "foreigner" (e.g., "white," "European") by African Christians, or, in the memorable phrase of Welbourn and Ogot, has he found "a place to feel at home" in Africa?[56]
- *Contemporary relevance*: Do African Christians view Jesus as being significant to the contemporary realities of life in their own context, for example, politically, economically, and socially? In particular, do the emergent Christologies bear witness to the liberating dimensions of the gospel? The "Final Communiqué" from the Pan-African Conference of Third World Theologians stresses that "African theology must also be *liberation* theology."[57] Therefore, do the contemporary African Christologies meet this expressed directive?
- *Gender appropriateness*: Are the contemporary African Christologies adequately addressing the concerns outlined in this regard?
- *Credibility of witness*: Do the African Christologies lend credible and appropriate witness to Jesus today?
- *Linguistic and conceptual relevance*: Do the current Christologies capture and incarnate the existential realities of life and African self-understanding? How far is the concern for language actually translating into the whole worldview? In other words, do the Christologies reflect indigenous perceptions that indeed "the gospel has become *our* story," not simply a foreign story transliterated into local languages?

The criteria regarding sources and methods and the seven factors of contextual relevance serve to guide the critical examination of contemporary African Christologies presented in Part II.

Part II

Models
of Contemporary African
Christologies

THE PREVAILING PARADIGM: INCULTURATION AND LIBERATION

African theology is commonly introduced according to two main trends that emerged from the late 1950s to the late 1980s: African or inculturation theology, and black or liberation theology. The former category entails theological exploration of African indigenous cultures in an attempt to integrate the African pre-Christian religious heritage with the Christian faith so as to "ensure the integrity of African Christian identity and selfhood."[1] The latter category has been further subdivided into South African black theology, arising out of the particular context of apartheid in that country, and African liberation theology, found throughout independent sub-Saharan Africa and broader in scope. Its intention is to integrate the theme of liberation in the rest of the African cultural background. Liberation is not confined to modern socioeconomic and political levels but includes emancipation from other forms of oppression such as disease, poverty, hunger, ignorance, and the subjugation of women.[2]

African Christologies are naturally presented in keeping with the twofold classification of inculturation and liberation, as in the case of Charles Nyamiti's simple typology. Defining Christologies of inculturation as an effort "to incarnate the Gospel message in the African cultures on the theological level," Nyamiti maintains that these Christologies are "on the whole, more numerous and in many cases relatively more profound" than those of liberation Christologies.[3] However, Mugambi criticizes Nyamiti's categorization for being too sharp, contending that commitment to one approach does not necessitate inattention or opposition toward the other approach.[4]

While in-depth analysis of the relationship between inculturation and liberation theologies lies beyond the scope of the present discussion, the contrasting views above reflect an extended debate within the field of African Christianity. Certainly the broad twofold classification has served an important purpose in distinguishing the various contexts eliciting African theologies, plus the sources favored and the methods employed in their construction. It thus retains instructive value for an overview of theological development in Africa.

Nonetheless, despite qualifications made that inculturation and liberation theologies are not mutually exclusive and that they are best viewed in terms of concentric circles,[5] the tendency remains to perpetuate a false dichotomy between the two trends. As a result, African theologians have increasingly objected to sustaining such a dubious division. For example, Ela decries "the traps of Africanization," in the proliferation of research on the confrontation between the gospel and African authenticity, and "the dead-end of ethnotheology."[6] Against any such one-sided approach, Ela protests with his central thesis that "*liberation of the oppressed must be the primary condition for any authentic inculturation of the Christian message*."[7] Bujo strongly concurs, and these two theologians express mutual acknowledgment in this regard. Building upon his initial premise that true African liberation is impossible "without rediscovering deeply rooted traditional cultural values,"[8] Bujo denounces any theology of inculturation focusing on "anthropological poverty"[9] without adequately addressing the ills of the post-colonial context that inculturation alone cannot remedy. He accuses this theology of being too academic and "a pompous irrelevance, truly an ideological superstructure at the service of the bourgeoisie."[10] Further charge is leveled against theologians promoting such "bourgeois religion" when Bujo questions how a theology done in and for Africa can so persistently close its eyes to the immense wretchedness and misery which is all around us. He asks if a nation can develop culturally while being politically oppressed and economically exploited to such a horrifying degree, and while its people, faced with starvation and many other catastrophes, are struggling for survival.[11]

Bujo then concludes, "We cannot take pride in the fact that our theology has *such a onesided interest in culture* that it is little concerned with the liberation of the People of God from their misery."[12] Instead, a synthesis of the two approaches is required. Or, as Nyamiti declares, "In fact, all true and integral inculturation christology must also be one of liberation, and vice versa."[13]

Once it is established that inculturation and liberation are intrinsically related, the theological dilemma of one approach versus the other is acknowledged to be a false dilemma.[14] Both sides of the debate are limited by a deficient understanding of what constitutes culture in the African context, as Emmanuel Martey ably demonstrates. In opposition to those assuming that culture is past oriented and static, Martey stresses that Africa is currently marked by "*both cultural continuity and change.*"[15] As a basis for further penetrating African theological realities, he advocates a reexamination of African culture:

> A thorough study of African culture cannot take place unless the power structures in African societies and the forces that offer resistance to these powerful structures are well understood. Analysis of contemporary African culture cannot therefore be limited to "traditionalism." It must include the whole totality of African existence—politics, economics, religion, pre-colonial worldview and thought forms, philosophy, language, ethnicity, music, arts, sexuality, and changes brought about by modern science and technology that have had an impact on African people. These are not separate parts of the whole African existence, but, rather, they are *intersecting dimensions* of the African experience and African existence.[16]

He sums up that, "in point of fact, culture to the African is *life*; therefore our perspective on culture must be holistic."[17] Finally, he explores the implications of this understanding of culture for theology in Africa and concludes with the necessity of a unified interpretation of the two foci of inculturation and liberation:

> A relevant, contextual and authentic theology for Africa must have a unitary perception of inculturation and liberation. Such a dynamic definition

of inclusive theology would lack *neither* an appreciation for traditional religious culture—the context from which the overwhelming majority of Christians in Africa come, and in which many of them still continue to live—*nor* refuse engagement in dialogue with the crucial issues raised by contemporary political and economic factors—factors that are the main reasons for Africa's crisis and backwardness in world affairs. . . . It is when both the liberationist and inculturationist analyses of African reality are integrated that we arrive at a new perspective in the creation of a unified theology of cultural and political liberation.[18]

Thus most African theologians clearly call for an integrative approach to constructing contextual theologies. Accordingly, an attempt is made here to utilize a synthesizing approach in the analysis of contextual Christologies.

A CURRENT CONFIGURATION OF AFRICAN CHRISTOLOGIES

In seeking to attain the "unitary perception of inculturation and liberation" highlighted above, an alternative configuration is proposed here in order to portray the research findings. Since the model approach is now familiar not only in the physical and social sciences but also in theology, it is adopted here for the purpose of interpreting contemporary African Christologies.[19] In *Models of the Church* Avery Dulles notes that theology depends heavily on images in order to faithfully communicate the Christian experience of God. He then provides the following definition: "When an image is employed reflectively and critically to deepen one's theoretical understanding of a reality it becomes what is today called a 'model.'"[20] It is in this sense that the present models are offered as one way of interpreting the highly complex realities evidenced in the textual and qualitative research, without precluding other possible interpretations of the data. Since some theoretical framework is required for representing the christological data, the configuration set forth in Figure II–1 serves as an abstraction of the concrete evidence collected, and it is therefore derived directly from the data. Its main strength thus lies in that it is firmly grounded in the context of christological investigation in Africa.

This configuration seeks an appropriate balance of simplicity and complexity in displaying the most significant aspects of the research findings. Hence a "meta-model" portrays the overall investigation, setting forth its major components: sources and methods, critical issues, central themes, and the significance of the contemporary African Christologies to African Christianity. Within that overarching structure, distinct models corresponding to the central christological themes are depicted as interlocking circles. While the thematic titles are placed in the outer spheres for clarifying distinctions, the circles show significant overlap that occurs among christological images. Part II elaborates on these christological models. The arrows indicate that the current Christologies both emerge from the critical issues identified in Part I, and are also significant in redressing those very issues, discussed in Part III. Rationale for this particular

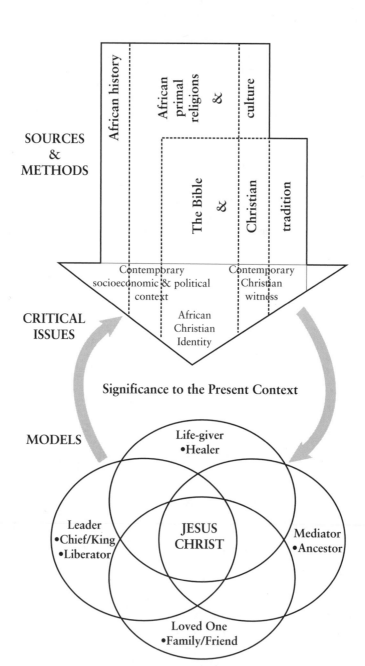

SOURCES
&
METHODS

African history

African primal religions & culture

The Bible & Christian tradition

CRITICAL
ISSUES

Contemporary socioeconomic & political context

Contemporary Christian witness

African Christian Identity

Significance to the Present Context

MODELS

Life-giver
•Healer

Leader
•Chief/King
•Liberator

JESUS CHRIST

Mediator
•Ancestor

Loved One
•Family/Friend

FIGURE II–1. MODELS OF CONTEMPORARY AFRICAN CHRISTOLOGIES

design lies in the convergence of two goals: (1) the integrative approach to theological realities as advocated by the African authors, and (2) the need for complementary models that allow various aspects of the christological perceptions to be teased out without losing sight of the overall view of the material. Both priorities are in accordance with the holistic nature of African ontology and epistemology.

One final point concerns the problem of verification in theology. Dulles notes that "religious imagery is both functional and cognitive," so "religious experience, then, provides a vital key for the evaluation and interpretation of symbols."[21] Consequently, verification of the christological models ultimately depends upon corporate discernment by those whose perceptions they portray. The extent to which the models resonate with the understanding and experience of the selected African Christians will determine their value as a contribution to the study of African Christianity.

3

Jesus as Life-giver

What do you think is the main or the most significant contribution that African Christology has to offer world Christianity?
  "I would think that one of the main things would be Christ, the giver of life. I feel that the idea of Christ as the source of real life, the giver of life, is extremely vital to us."
                                      —KWESI DICKSON, PRESIDENT OF THE AACC

"The concept of Jesus as a life-giver, a life-promoter, I would say, comes out very, very significantly."
                   —MARY GETUI, THE CIRCLE OF CONCERNED AFRICAN WOMEN THEOLOGIANS

INTRODUCTION

The first christological model to be explored is that of Jesus as life-giver. Arising from the data of textual and oral Christologies, this central theme is fundamental to all other themes and therefore provides the appropriate starting point. So essential is the African estimation of life that Bénézet Bujo selects it as the basic conceptual framework for his theological and ethical investigations. When inquiring into the compatibility of the Christian message and the black ethos, he notes that Christianity encountered many values in Africa, the chief of which he identifies as follows:

> Among those values we have to underline life, which was the cardinal point for all the rest. Life is, of course, that to which all humanity aspires, but the way in which the African systematically centres community and ethos around life deserves particular attention. The Christian message cannot ignore this fact without exposing itself to failure.[1]

54

How Jesus is perceived in relation to life, with respect to traditional thought and contemporary realities in Africa, features prominently in African Christianity and thus forms the focal point of this chapter.[2]

This chapter is divided into four main sections. The introduction considers concepts of life in traditional African thought as interpreted by selected African Christians, and their conviction of Jesus as life-giver or the one who fulfills African aspirations for life. Textual and field research unearths various images of Jesus in relation to life, images such as creator, preserver, protector, provider, and architect or planner. The central image in this respect is undoubtedly that of Jesus as healer, or one who restores life; therefore, the second main section explores this image. The related image of Jesus as traditional healer warrants close scrutiny, undertaken in the third section. The conclusion offers critical engagement with the African Christologies, and more extensive treatment in this chapter allows briefer conclusions in Chapters 4 through 6. The overall aim of the chapter is to examine the rationale for this christological model in terms of African thought and biblical witness, to interpret its meaning in contemporary Christian reflection and practice, and to assess its significance to African Christianity.

CONCEPTS OF LIFE IN TRADITIONAL AFRICA

"Life is so central that it must be characterized as sacred."[3] Thus Bujo introduces the life concepts of African clan society as the starting point for his theology. He delineates several characteristics of life, some of which require further elaboration in later chapters. The first point Bujo underlines is that pre-Christian black Africa, assumed to be largely monotheistic, recognized God as the source of all life and the one who alone possesses fullness of life. Citing previous studies by Vincent Mulago, Bolaji Idowu, and John Mbiti, Bujo explains that African tradition views God as the creator and sustainer of all life, culminating in human life.[4] He then notes that a crucial point concerning life is its hierarchical ordering, defined as follows: "Life is a participation in God, but it is always mediated by one standing above the recipient in the hierarchy of being. This hierarchy belongs both to the invisible and to the visible world."[5] In tracing the hierarchy of invisible and visible powers, from God through deceased clan and family members, through royalty, chiefs, and elders, to heads of households and family members, Bujo acknowledges Mulago's influence. Mulago had previously studied three Bantu peoples and established his main thesis that participation in a common life is absolutely foundational to their family, social, political, and religious customs. Mulago spells out this concept in terms of "unity of life" or "vital union," which he defines as "a relationship of being and life between each individual and his descendants, his family, his brothers and sisters in the clan, his antecedents, and also with God, the ultimate source of life." After specifying that it also extends to inanimate life resources, Mulago concludes, "What is this life? It is a whole life, individual inasmuch as it is received by each being which exists, and communal or collective inasmuch as each being draws from a common source of life."[6]

Mulago's statement reflects two additional characteristics of life in traditional African thought: holistic and communal. Again, Mulago's thought is echoed in Bujo, who stresses that life goes beyond the biological to embrace "the whole of human existence, life understood as the totality of the dimensions which constitute the human as a person."[7] Elsewhere Bujo specifies that "to an African there is no dichotomy between private, social, political and religious life."[8] Likewise John Pobee affirms this fundamental perception of life in the ontology and epistemology of many traditional African societies: "Being and existence are seen very comprehensively—they are as physical as they are spiritual, as external as internal. They have a wholistic view of life."[9] Finally, Mulago points out the significance of life being communal in Africa:

> The Bantu believe firmly in a vital communion or life-bond which creates solidarity between members of the same family or clan. . . . The family, clan or tribe is a whole, of which each member is only a part. The same blood, the same life which is shared by all, which all receive from the first ancestor, the founder of the clan, runs through the veins of all. Every effort must be directed to the preservation, maintenance, growth and perpetuation of this common treasure. The pitiless elimination of everything which hinders this end, and the encouragement at all costs of everything which further it: this is the last word in Bantu customs and institutions, wisdom and philosophy.[10]

Several aspects of traditional African concepts of life thus emerge in the writings of these theologians: its centrality as the focus of many African religions and worldviews, its origin and fullness in God, its hierarchical ordering and demand for participation, and its comprehensive character in encompassing all realms of existence and incorporating the individual and communal dimensions. According to the data from textual and oral Christologies set forth in the next section, these facets of life influence African Christians' perceptions of Jesus and the life he brings.

JESUS AS LIFE-GIVER

Akin to Mulago's concept of "vital union" as the unifying principle of Bantu thought is Placide Tempels's notion of "life-force," proposed in his work *Bantu Philosophy*.[11] Bujo refers to both writers in explaining black African concepts of life. In particular, he states that one of Tempels's most important findings is this vital force reckoned to be at the heart of African worldviews and religions. He notes that Tempels went to the extent of claiming that "for the African, 'to be' was the same as 'to have life-force.'"[12] He further points out Tempels's conviction that the African quest for life in its most comprehensive sense was not restricted to Africa but rather signified a fundamental human instinct. So this was one area, according to Tempels, that an understanding of the African view of life could make a contribution beyond the continent of Africa. Tempels linked the African search for life to Jesus' claim in John 10:10 that he had come to bring life and to bring it more abundantly. Bujo relates this insight as follows:

"If Jesus is truly the Way, the Truth and the Life, then he is the final answer to the aspirations of the whole human race and not only of Africans. All human cultures manifest the human longing for fullness of life."[13]

Bujo clearly concurs with Tempels's approach in this regard, for in another publication Bujo reiterates that "what is most sacred in the negro-African tradition is life which must be encouraged in all its dimensions."[14] He then makes the following affirmation concerning Jesus Christ: "He is the unique manifestation of the life of God, he is source and proto-model of all life. It is he who teaches us what . . . is the true life, what is to live. He has come that we might have life and have it in abundance *(Jn 10:10)*."[15] Elsewhere, the convergence of the traditional African concept of life with the biblical witness concerning Jesus as life-giver is explicit. Having again quoted John 10:10 and summarized additional Johannine texts on Jesus and life, Bujo declares Jesus to be "the true vital force and energy *par excellence* which flows into all his descendants."[16] The import of this observation is further elucidated with respect to Jesus as ancestor in the following chapter. The stress at present is upon the significance of "Jesus as new source of life,"[17] understood and conveyed through African and biblical concepts.

Pobee takes a similar tack in reflecting as an Akan Christian upon life and peace. Like Bujo, he begins by examining these two concepts in traditional African thought, emphasizing their holistic and communal character. However, he clearly asserts the priority of the biblical revelation in stating his methodological approach:

> The traditional African concept of well-being can only be the *starting point*. In any case, as a Christian I believe Christ adds a new dimension, challenging the traditional culture. The task before us then is to attempt to construct a view which has for its elements the Gospel of Jesus Christ, the traditional African insights with regard to a wholistic view of life, at once vertical and horizontal, and the realities of today's world.[18]

Pobee then looks to the Fourth Gospel for relevant metaphors of life, including bread of life, water of life, and light of life, all of which he states Africans are seeking. Dwelling particularly on the bread image, he undertakes exegesis of Jesus' miraculous feeding of the multitude in John 6. He concludes, "Of that life Jesus of Nazareth, now Lord, was and is the example *par excellence*. Jesus is the bread of life in the sense that what he represents is absolutely necessary for a genuine life and peace, in short for well-being."[19]

In another example Pobee explores the meaning and significance of Jesus as the life of the world, drawing upon biblical evidence and aspects of traditional Akan culture. Again, he stresses that "the Bible is of crucial importance for the statement of the African's vision of Christ; the Bible remains the charter document of the church."[20] Working from the Fourth Gospel, he first defines the two Greek words translated as "life": *zoe*, referring to biological or physical life; and *psyche*, used metaphorically for religious or spiritual life, especially in relation to Christ. Pobee then draws parallels between the biblical and Akan concepts of life and death. For instance, he outlines the Akan view of life as going beyond biological life to represent all the material prosperity and spiritual values that constitute well-being, summed up in the "seven graces." Pobee explains:

> The Akan prays for the seven graces: life and good health *(nkwa)*, God's grace *(adom)*, peace of society and mankind *(asomdwee)*, potency and fertility of sex *(abawotum)*, powerful eyesight *(anihutum)*, good hearing power *(asotatum)*, and rainfall and general prosperity of the clan and tribe *(amandoree)*.[21]

Having juxtaposed the biblical and Akan materials, Pobee concludes:

> The Akan concept of life outlined in the seven graces is a welcome starting point for evangelism. For all the coalescence Christianity goes further to make the unique claim that life is found in its fullness in Christ, e.g. John 1:4: 'In him (i.e. Christ the Logos) was life.' . . . Thus the biblical faith affirms the centrality of Christ to and for the life of human beings; the basic necessities of life are to be sought and found in Christ. In our context we can assert that the seven graces for which the Akan prays are met in Christ.[22]

African concepts of life as met in Christ are also evidenced in the oral Christologies. The central preoccupation with life is manifest in the extent to which African Christians speak of Jesus in relation to the life he brings. In the individual interviews, thirty of the sixty-five respondents in Kenya, Uganda, and Ghana initiated perceptions of Jesus specifically related to the image of life-giver as expounded above. That is to say, no set question was asked in this regard, yet respondents volunteered comments to this effect, and these comments were aside from those concerning Jesus' relevance to life or even Jesus giving his own life to accomplish salvation. For example, representative expressions included the following: "Jesus is life to me"; "Jesus is life, life itself"; "Jesus, the source of our life"; "he's your life-giver"; "he is the giver of life—not only now, physical life, but even eternal life"; he restores "the wholeness of life" or "the fullness of life." Equivalent findings occur in the focus groups, for seven of the twelve groups convened in Kenya and Ghana reveal similar perceptions.

Biblical influences in shaping such perceptions are certainly evident. For example, five of the sixty-five individual respondents either quoted John 10:10 directly or alluded to the "abundant life" Christ brings, making this one of the verses referred to most often in the interviews. Other respondents quoted Jesus' claims, "I am the bread of life" (Jn 6:35), or "I am the way, the truth and the life" (Jn 14:6). For instance Florence Y. B. Yeboah, national director of the Ghana Congress on Evangelization Women's Ministry and a PACWA representative, responded as follows when asked who Jesus is to her:

> Jesus, for me, is the one who is the creator of the universe. He holds the universe together. In fact, the whole scripture revolves around him. He is life,

and the Bible says, "The life," his life, "is the light of men." He has said in John 14:6 that he is the way, the truth, and the life.

So the Bible is definitely highlighted as a key source for understanding Jesus as life-giver. Yet the biblical witness concerning Jesus has clearly taken root in local idiom. To illustrate, during the same interview Yeboah spontaneously sang the following Twi hymn:

So Yesu mu yie	Hold fast to Jesus.
Na mma wanfi wo nsa	Do not lose your hold on him.
Se wonya no a, woanya nkwa	If you choose him, you have life.
Se wopa no a woafa owuo	If you avoid him, you meet death.
Nti so Yesu mu yie,	So hold on fast to Jesus,
Na mma wamfi wo nsa	and do not lose your hold on him.[23]

In another example Joseph Lamptey, from the focus group of Ghanaian Protestant clergy, offered this image of Jesus derived from the Bible yet expressed in vernacular hymns, in this case in Ga:

Jesus is perceived as the fountain of life, an idea taken from when Jesus talks with the woman at the well. This idea of fountain of life can be seen in some hymns and songs that we sing. That Jesus *wela bubu* is the fountain of life. He provides our needs, both physical and spiritual. We see him as a well of life, a fountain that is always there.

Not only are biblical images of Jesus translated into local idiom, but also African vernacular terms related to life are ascribed to Jesus. For example, Ghanaian Robert Aboagye-Mensah, superintendent minister for the Methodist Church—Dansoman Circuit, explained how a Twi term traditionally referring to God is now extended to Jesus:

One of them is the *Oye, Oyeadeeyie*. That is, "he does things well," "he makes things well," or "he brings life into things." When you use it in the context of human well-being, it means "he makes them whole," "he brings the whole"— like the shalom—he brings wholeness. So sometimes you hear people, in their prayers, refer to Jesus as *Oyeadeeyie*.

Grace Sackey introduced the same Twi term in the focus group of Ghanaian Protestant laity, defining it as "restoration, someone who restores life or health, everything that is lacking in your life, Jesus is able to do it. To renew your life, your faith, your sickness, deliverance—anything." Strikingly, this traditional concept seemed to resonate in the perceptions of Jesus voiced by some Ghanaian Christians. Although no vernacular term was used, when asked who Jesus is to her, Protestant clergywoman Margaret Asabea immediately replied:

He is the one who, as it were, brought me from nothingness to life. What do I mean? It's like, something which has been disintegrated, shattered, and then he brought the wholeness of life back to me. And the process is not completed. He still goes on and on and on and on with me.

According to these African Christians, then, a coalescence evidently forms between African and biblical traditions concerning life. The centrality of life is certainly manifest, and the source of life traditionally acknowledged in God is now extended to Jesus. Ghanaian clergyman Quarshie provided a clear summary statement regarding this convergence of African and biblical thought, for in response to the question of who Jesus is to him personally, he replied that no single symbol can capture all of it. Yet in attempting to synthesize central truths concerning Jesus' identity, he focused on the single concept of life, saying, "Probably to put it very simply, I would say he is *life*." He continued by explaining that to elaborate on specific aspects, he would speak of Jesus as savior, as Lord, and as king, yet these biblical categories are all placed within the overarching framework of the concern for life. He concluded: "I say I have life. Without him, there is no life. That's how simply I would put it, if you ask me, in a nutshell."

The implications of African and biblical life concepts merging in Christ are manifold, yet many surround the central notions of life being holistic and communal. For example, in a later conversation, Quarshie returned to the fundamental view of Jesus as life-giver and related it to the critical issue of African Christian identity as identified in Chapter 2:

It's precisely what I referred to earlier on as the personal or the identity crisis. And I think that is something that we need to address, in terms of Christ making us whole, in terms of eliminating this identity crisis that we have. And in so doing, once again, affirming the life that he offers to us. I think that probably for me, for us so-called theologians, that should be the greatest challenge. Because I don't think we are really doing it. At least for the average Ghanaian Christian or African Christian, that crisis is still there.

Apparently, then, the contemporary African Christologies not only emerge from the critical issues in the current context but also provide a response to those very issues. In this case the issue of African Christian identity arises from the historical and theological context outlined in Part I, yet, according to Quarshie, the discovery and affirmation of Jesus as life-giver potentially overcomes that identity crisis.

The Circle women emphasized the same aspect of holistic life in Christ especially, though not exclusively, with the implications for gender issues in Africa. Ghanaian representative Elizabeth Amoah described the importance of the traditional religious heritage to the women in Ghana and what influence this background exerts when these women convert to Christianity. She explained: "So they will take Jesus! Because they see him as a powerful, miraculous healer—everything. They will even say, 'Jesus is my everything,' emphasizing the holistic, the totality of life that you get in Jesus." Furthermore, Kenyan representative Mary Getui quotes John 10:10 in both her individual interview and in the focus group of Circle women, and underlines its significance for African Christians today. Just as Jesus gives life physically and spiritually, so women give life physically, through conception, pregnancy, birth, and breast-feeding, and spiritually, through their many "mothering" roles in the community regardless of biological motherhood. Therefore the image of Jesus as life-giver potentially enhances the position of women in the community. For as Getui concludes, "Life needs both male and female. So if we are going to look at Jesus as life or as life-promoter, then we need to bring in this contribution of the place of men and women."

The founding director of the Circle, Mercy Oduyoye, also expressed deep concern for holistic and communal life in Christ. In her address to the World Council of Churches' Sixth Assembly in 1983, Oduyoye began by stressing that Africans have ways of viewing life that differ from the prevailing perspectives in Western societies. She lamented that Christianity in Africa has not adequately absorbed, or even considered, the primal worldviews it has encountered. Instead, the Euro-American expressions of the faith have dominated. Oduyoye maintained that "African Christians, however, whether Anglican, Protestant or Roman Catholic, see life basically as Africans," and hence their sympathy and appreciation for the life exhibited in the African Independent Churches.[24] Oduyoye then offered a poem, "Reflections on Wholeness." This poem reflects the integration of African and biblical concepts of life discussed above, as well as the contemporary realities and the call for liberationist theology. It also demonstrates the conviction of African theologians that theological reflection need not be expressed in the same format as the systematic exposition associated with Western theology. For Oduyoye unequivocally brings a theological as well as an African perspective to what she introduces as "the challenge of Christ to an Africa that thinks whole, preaches wholeness and yet is riddled with divisiveness and brokenness."[25]

Finally, Oduyoye made the important point, echoing Bujo in the introduction to this chapter, that the yearning for wholeness and the problems that hinder its realization are not exclusively African. Yet, she asserted, the African worldview is nevertheless an asset in developing a holistic approach to life. In response to the gap between the ideal and the actual, as outlined in Chapter 2 on critical issues concerning contemporary Christian witness, Oduyoye stressed that this very gap is the crucial point where the cross of Christ is placed. She concluded:

To heal this sinful human condition, Christianity claims, "Christ is the Answer." Jesus Christ is presented to the world as its very Life. In Africa where religion is still taken seriously and is accepted as filling the whole of life, the claim "Jesus Christ, the Life of the World" is of crucial consequence.[26]

Once again, the very issues arising in context are addressed and potentially redressed by the appropriation of Jesus as life-giver.

JESUS AS HEALER

INTRODUCTION

Oduyoye is not alone in expressing the yearning for wholeness of life in Africa and lamenting the "litany of brokenness."[27] Bujo also queries, "In Africa the importance of life has always been underlined for the family, the clan, and the community of the ancestors. But what has happened to this life today? Is there still the same respect for life in this post-colonial world?"[28] Apparently not, according to his reflections on how life is "scoffed at in Africa." He levels sharp castigation against the political leaders in many countries across Africa whose dictatorial regimes radically contradict widespread ancestral traditions regarding chieftaincy. These leaders thereby violate the sacredness of life entrusted to their oversight. Yet culpability does not rest with such leaders alone. Bujo continues:

> But not only the political chiefs, much more in a general way, we are all colonized by the new mights: money, power. . . . That leads us to pooh-pooh life: this only has value for us in the measure that it concerns our person alone. Today there is killing in Africa like killing snakes, like removing weeds.[29]

He therefore contends that while "the whole of Africa is pregnant with the life of God," it must be defended in combating injustice, ethnocentrism, regionalism, and racism, and in establishing human rights and solidarity with the marginalized.[30]

By expressing such concerns, Bujo confirms the predicament Appiah-Kubi voices:

> Jesus Christ is thus conceived by many African Christians as the great physician, healer and victor over worldly powers *par excellence*. To many, Jesus came that we might have life and have it more abundantly. But the perturbing question is, where is this abundant life, when all around us we see suffering, poverty, oppression, strife, envy, war and destruction?[31]

In view of this dilemma, Cécé Kolié raises a legitimate challenge: "To proclaim Jesus as the Great Healer calls for a great deal of explaining to the millions who starve in the Sahel, to victims of injustice and corruption, and to the polyparasitic afflicted of the tropical and equatorial forests!"[32]

Another crucial dimension concerns the relation between the image of Jesus as healer and traditional concepts of health and illness. As Jean-Marc Ela emphasizes, a primary task of Christian reflection in black Africa is to reformulate the faith so as to allow the gospel to speak to Africans through their primordial symbolism. To illustrate, Ela addresses sickness and notes that in black Africa it is generally "not experienced as an objective fact," but rather as "a scandal that

belongs in the anthropological realm of evil and misfortune."[33] Illness is viewed
as a calamity that not only strikes the particular individual, but also indicates a
disruption of social relationships, thereby making it a family and communal
concern. Where health is viewed as being more than biological, encompassing
physical, mental, spiritual, social, and environmental well-being, illness signifies an unfortunate disruption of harmony in these factors. Organic causes may
well be recognized, yet the overriding belief attributes sickness to spiritual or
supernatural causes such as offending God or ancestral spirits, possession by
evil spirits, witchcraft, breaking taboos, or curses from offended family or community members.[34] Illness is therefore inextricably linked to human relationships with one another and with the universe. Since "the African universe of
sickness is inseparable from the universe of spirits," Ela underlines that "the
techniques of healing cannot be separated from the symbolic universe from which
they emerge."[35] He thus challenges the church with the vital importance of providing answers to the questions of life and death for which Africans still seek
out marabouts, diviners, and healers.

The problem here, as Pobee points out, is that the early missionaries tended
to deny the reality of malevolent powers at work in the community and to dismiss belief in witchcraft as superstition and heathenism.[36] Instead of attending
to the needs within the African worldview of spirits and sickness, missionaries
often reproached or ignored African approaches to illness and denounced African medicine and medical practitioners as devilish. Moreover, while some Western medical missionaries adopted a holistic approach in preaching Christ as a
healer-savior who redeems humanity from sickness, sin, and all forms of dehu-
manization, in general the proclamation of the gospel was skewed toward a
"spiritual salvation" of the soul. As Philomena Mwaura explains, "The healing
and evangelical missions directed to the Africans did not have a holistic impact
but were seen as directed to different parts of the same person, the body and the
soul, whereas in Africa this dualistic view of the person is not existent."[37]

As a result of the dissonance between aspects of mission Christianity and
traditional views regarding health, ambiguities and contradictions often arise in
the African experience of Christian faith. Hence the notorious characterization
of African Christians adopting forms of piety from the missionary enterprise
while still maintaining their traditional beliefs and practices, especially during
sickness or critical life stages.[38] Ela expresses the dilemma as follows:

"Christians, you unfortunate people! In the morning at mass, in the evening
at the diviner's! Amulet in your pocket, scapular around your neck!" This
Zaïroise song reveals the tragedy of the majority of black African Christians.
. . . For a great number of baptised people, conversion to the Gospel is a
veritable "ambiguous Adventure."[39]

The extent of this problem leads Kolié to pose a grave question: "The bipolarity
of the religious loyalties of our baptized who carry a rosary in their hand and a
'fetish' under their clothing leads us . . . to ask whether Jesus can honestly be
present in Africa as a healer."[40] This quandary is intensified by Kolié's recounting

how, over the previous year, he had asked various catechists and community leaders of villages and quarters to list their own personal names for Jesus. Pointing out that Christ had come to his region sixty years earlier, and that customarily within a year black African communities grant newcomers a nickname expressing the type of relationship held with them, Kolié relates his findings as follows:

> They all gave titles taken from the Bible or missals. Not one of them came out with a term that translated his or her personal relationship to Christ. . . . They all told me that Christ is the Saviour, the Son of God, the man of peace, and so on. Certainly none of them told me that Jesus is a healer. And they would certainly not have been able to tell me why.[41]

Following this report, Kolié raises the critical question as to whether this is not what the majority of African theologians do:

> Since their communities cannot name Christ personally without going to the Bible or catechisms, they do just the opposite, and attribute to Christ the traditional titles of initiator, chief, great ancestor, and so on, that they would *like* to see him given in the communities. Once more we impose on our fellow Africans the way of seeing that we have learned from our Western masters. Shall we be followed by our communities, when we have finally gotten the prayers of the missal translated into these titles for Jesus whose real effectiveness has not really been tested in Africa?[42]

Thus contemporary realities and traditional worldviews pose serious challenges regarding Christ as healer in Africa. In a continent of massive suffering, is Jesus truly known as healer? Or, as Kolié suggests, is this concept yet another foreign imposition on Africa? The question warrants careful consideration, particularly in light of Kolié's observation that these titles have not been adequately tested in Africa. Toward that end, then, the image of Jesus as healer forms an important component of the present research design.[43] The findings, however preliminary in the overall field of contemporary African Christologies, enable further consideration of Kolié's question whether Jesus can honestly be perceived in Africa as a healer. First, the qualitative data are set forth, followed by analysis of the rationale for the image, its meaning, and problems with it.

THE DATA REGARDING JESUS AS HEALER

The image of Jesus as healer is indeed operative among the selected African Christians, as demonstrated conclusively in the oral interviews conducted in Kenya, Uganda, and Ghana. The overwhelming majority of individual interview respondents attested to this image being meaningful to them, with fifty-seven of the sixty with whom it was discussed responding positively.[44] Not a single person denied or rejected the image, although three voiced certain reservations related to how it is understood or practiced in contemporary Christianity.

In contrast to Kolié's informants, none of whom identified Jesus as healer, it is significant that four of the twenty-seven Kenyan and Ugandan respondents with whom it was discussed and ten of the thirty-three Ghanaians volunteered the image themselves in various contexts of conversation. For example, several raised it when asked for images of Jesus that resonate especially with African Christians. Often in this context it was the first idea offered. Religious sister Marie Gacambi, lecturer at the Catholic University of East Africa, immediately replied:

> Obviously for any African, the image of healing is important. Healing is a ministry within the African tradition, because our understanding is that a person is whole and we try to alleviate anything that interferes with the wholeness of life. So, when we speak of Jesus as a healer, that is an image that touches an African very much. You will see this even with these ministries where people come in big numbers. So Jesus as a healer is an image that is powerful.

Likewise, Catholic Mary Kizito, lecturer at Daystar University in Nairobi, straightaway spoke of Jesus as healer and explained why it is a meaningful category:

> You read it in the Bible, but [it is] because Africa is so much plagued with disease—AIDS, malaria, and all these other diseases which kill people. So, I look at him as a healer, and I think many Africans do. The most powerful image of Jesus is Jesus the healer. He can take away our diseases.

Noteworthy here is not only that the image of Jesus as healer is the first to be expressed, but also that the reasons given reflect the issues discussed above. That is to say, Jesus is perceived both in relation to traditional concepts of life and health, as Gacambi indicated, and in relation to contemporary realities, as Kizito attested.

The same pattern held true in the focus groups; all eleven of the groups with whom it was discussed agreed that the image of Jesus as healer is appropriate and meaningful. Even more significantly, the concept was volunteered by various members within six of the eleven groups. Interestingly, in the focus group of Kenyan Protestant clergy, John Gichinga challenged the question about the image of Jesus as healer, insisting that it is not an "image" but a "reality" in Nairobi Baptist Church, where he is senior pastor: "It's beyond a perception, it's beyond an image. It is really recognizing that some of the things that were happening in Jesus' time are possible in our day through his name."

Thus the data generated from the individual interviews and focus groups unequivocally show that these African Christians identify Jesus as healer. Likewise, the textual Christologies lend strong support for the image (discussed below). Additionally, widespread contextual evidence corroborates that Jesus is viewed as healer. For example, confirmation came through participant observation in various church services across a range of mainline denominations, conferences, Bible studies, prayer meetings, and informal conversations. Numerous instances of liturgy, preaching, prayers, hymns and choruses, and testimonies reflect belief in Jesus as healer. From the extensive materials gleaned through this informal research, only one textual illustration is offered from each of the main contexts of field research. First, the following chorus, sung in Nairobi Chapel on April 26, 1998, reflects the intrinsically related images of Jesus as life-giver and healer:

> *Jabulani Africa*
> Jesus, life and hope to heal our land
> Savior, reaching out with your mighty hand
> > Sing for joy, O Africa
> > The Lord your God is risen upon you
> > Sing for joy, O Africa
> > The Lord your God is risen upon you now
> > *Jabulani, jabulani Africa* (4x)
> Jesus, river of life to our thirsty land
> Saviour, meeting our needs with Your mighty hand.

The following Twi hymn is found in *Legon Praise*, a collection of hymns published for use in the Legon Interdenominational Church in Legon, Accra, Ghana:

Din Bi Wo Ho	*There Is a Name*
Din bi wo ho, din no fi soro	There's a name, the name is from heaven
Din no reye anwanwa adwuma	The name does perform miracles
Din no ne Jesus (2x)	Jesus! is the name (2x)
Din no ma anifraefo hu ade	The name makes the blind see
Din no ma akwatafo ho san	The name heals the lepers too
Din no ma abubuafo nante	The name makes the cripple walk
Din no ne Jesus	Jesus! is the name
Din no obonsam suro	The name is feared by the devil
Din no abeyifo suro	It is feared by witches
Din no abosom suro	It is feared by other gods
Din no ne Jesus	Jesus! is the name.[45]

Finally, the photograph in Figure 3–1 provides a visual indicator that further substantiates the widespread perception of Jesus as healer.

THE RATIONALE FOR JESUS AS HEALER

It is not enough to establish that the image of Jesus as healer is indeed pervasive in the contexts specified for field research. It is also necessary to determine the substance of this image, including its rationale, meaning, and significance. Unlike the informants of whom Kolié writes, the African Christians considered here not only name Jesus as healer but also indicate why they perceive him so.

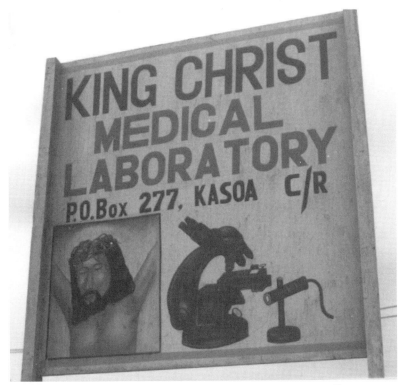

FIGURE 3–1. SIGNBOARD FOR MEDICAL CLINIC, KASOA, GHANA

The main reasons given may be summarized as, first, biblical and theological rationale, and second, contemporary experience, although often these two aspects of the rationale were combined in the interviewees' responses.

Biblical and Theological Rationale

Biblical precedent featured significantly in the reasons stated for understanding Jesus as healer. Often respondents cited the gospel evidence of Jesus' healing ministry first, with its application to the contemporary context either stated explicitly or assumed. For example, Ndingi Mwana a'Nzeki, archbishop of the Roman Catholic Church in Kenya, replied firmly to the question of Jesus as healer: "I am convinced myself. Absolutely." He argued first from the Bible, pointing out that there is not a single instance of Jesus turning away anyone in need of healing, except for the Canaanite woman whose faith he tested by delaying the healing. After recounting that story, he continued: "And even now, today, he heals! The problem with the people is we don't pray for healing. We are embarrassed to pray for somebody who is sick to be healed. Personally I have no problem with that." He then spoke from personal experience of having prayed for people who were subsequently healed. Ghanaian Catholic lay man George Hagan shared this confidence:

Jesus as healer is not an extraordinary thing. The image is a biblical one. Jesus heals our souls, and he heals our bodies too. And in fact, during his sojourn on earth, he used the healing of the physical body to point to the healing of the soul. So, that is not surprising.

Beyond the gospel record of Jesus' healing ministry, respondents reasoned on the basis of wider biblical evidence. Kenyan Protestant J. B. Masinde, pastor of the Deliverance Church in Umoja, Nairobi, elaborated on the rationale for understanding Jesus as healer in this way:

> He *is* a healer. Because he is God, and God says, "I am Jehovah Rapha, I am the Lord your God that heals you." And lots of times in the gospels we see Jesus as a healer. The summary that Peter gives of him in Acts 10:38 says that "God anointed Jesus of Nazareth with the Holy Spirit and power, and because of that he went about doing good and healing." Matthew 8:17: "He himself bore our sin, in his own body, bore our infirmities." The prophecy of Isaiah 53: "He himself, in his own body, was wounded for our transgressions, bruised for our iniquity." And so by his stripes we are healed. So you cannot separate God from that. And you can't separate Jesus from that.

Hence interviewees appealed primarily to the gospel accounts of Jesus' healing ministry but also to the wider context of Old Testament and New Testament materials to justify their belief in Jesus as healer.

Masinde's quotation above reveals more general theological grounds also found elsewhere in respondents' reasoning. Kenyan fruit-hawker John Muriithi reckons that because Jesus is God, he can do anything however big or small. Therefore, "Jesus is a *real* healer. He can heal!" Across the continent, a traditional Akan leader and third-generation Christian combines biblical and theological justification in reaching the same conclusion. Nana Addo Birikorang, *apesamakahene* (official spokesman) of the traditional Council of Akropong-Akuapem, reasoned as follows:

> Well, the Bible provides examples of Christ healing. But I think that whatever Christ has done is an extension of the power of God. In *our* concept of God, God is omnipotent. Now, the spiritual attributes of God can be quite safely accredited to Christ. So I do not see any problem with accepting Christ as a healer. He was both a physical and spiritual healer.

Another example holds special interest due to the background of the respondent. Kenyan lay man Morompi Ole Ronkei, associate director of Communications for Compassion International—Africa, is a Maasai who had had virtually no encounter with Christianity until he attended Starehe Boys' Secondary School in Nairobi. His particular clan of Maasai are set apart as the spiritual leaders of the community, a role that encompasses political, prophetic, and medicinal functions. Now a self-confessed Christian, Ole Ronkei responded to the question of

Jesus as healer by stating, "Yeah, absolutely." He interpreted the image in terms of physical healing, affirming, "I see him healing all the time, whether it's just from a headache to physical deformities of one sort or another. I think that is quite applicable." He then connected this conviction to the traditional healing practice of the Maasai, explaining, "Does God heal? Yes, God does. The Maasai herbalist, the spiritual leader, will give you medicine, and he says, 'Well, my friend, I want you to know you're in the hands of *God*. You're *not* in my hands.' Oh, yes, and he says that all the time!" Thus it becomes apparent that Ole Ronkei's firm conviction of Jesus as healer is partially informed or at least colored by his background in traditional Maasai culture. Stating explicitly elsewhere that the God of the Bible is "*really* identical" with the God of the Maasai, *Enkai*, and that there is "virtually no difference" between them, Ole Ronkei has no hesitation in ascribing the healing powers of that God to the person of Jesus.[46] Thus there are clear theological grounds for perceiving Jesus as healer according to the witness of these African Christians. Biblical teaching is certainly central to the justification given by the respondents. Yet in some cases, like Ole Ronkei's, the healing power assumed in relation to the traditional concept of God converges with the biblical affirmation of God as healer and is then extended to Jesus.

Contemporary Experience

If the biblical/theological rationale was fundamental to the interviewees, contemporary experience of Jesus as healer was even more prominent in the perceptions articulated. A number of the respondents, at least sixteen of the sixty individuals with whom the issue was discussed, plus additional focus group members, bore witness to Jesus having healed them personally. Nana Dokua I, *okuapehemmaa* (queenmother) of the Akuapem traditional area since 1966, offered striking testimony when volunteering the image of Jesus as healer. Seventy-six years old at the time of the interview, Nana Dokua recounted how one time she had become so sick she could no longer walk. She then related with considerable animation, "He's my healer, my doctor. Formerly, I couldn't walk properly. Now I can run! *Yes!*" She further narrated how she had suffered gall stones requiring an operation abroad, which eventually took place unexpectedly and for free in a top hospital in the United States, one which normally costs a thousand dollars per night. After narrating her experience enthusiastically, she exclaimed, "Thank you, Jesus! He is Lord. He's Lord. So when I call him 'my healer, my daddy, my husband'—my [deceased] husband used to do that [care for her], but he hasn't got enough money to pay one thousand dollars a night! Only Jesus can do it!" Then, even more poignantly, Nana Dokua speaks candidly of her own experience of childlessness and the intense suffering this situation creates for women in the traditional culture. Yet she identified Jesus as the one who has enabled her to transcend this grief.[47] She concluded by speaking joyfully, with laughter, of Jesus' impact "in everything! In all my ways. Jesus has been a good friend. A doctor, a healer! My protector! My fortress! My shield! Everything."

Ghanaian Protestant lay woman Irene Odotei also initiated her conviction of Jesus as healer: "I reached a point where I was breaking. And it was when I committed my life to Christ, I saw healing in my own life: physical healing, and even my mind, you know, emotional and all that. So I see Jesus a lot as a healer, as a repairer." Sister Marie Gacambi voiced the most dramatic witness to personal healing. In response to the central question of who Jesus is to her personally, she spontaneously spoke of Jesus as a friend and the impact this has had upon her life. To explain, she recounted having been in a serious car accident in 1973, in which the driver was killed and she was hospitalized for almost a year. She described how, unexpectedly to her, Archbishop Milingo, the Catholic bishop from Zambia renowned for his gifts of healing, came to pray for her. Her experience is well worth citing, despite its length, for the extraordinary outcome and for her conclusion regarding Jesus as healer:

> And he prayed over me. I had a broken pelvis. The bottom part and the top were separated, and so even staying in the hospital, I would never be able to walk. I could never stand—if I stood, my leg would swell like a balloon. And I had a big lump here, on my back. I used to go every month for physiotherapy with a machine, so that the liquid could be removed. So I had all those disabilities. When he came, and after we had spoken, he said, "Can I pray? Let us pray." So I just sat on a chair like this, and he stood next to me. And he put his hand on my face and said, "Mama, go to sleep." And I literally went to sleep! That type of sleep where you can hear what is happening, but you are not able to open your eyes! But I could hear him saying, "In the name of Jesus, pelvis go back to your place." And literally, I felt the bones moving, moving! Then he would order the blood: "Heart, pump the blood to all parts of the body, in the name of Jesus." And I literally felt a current! So, at the end of it, he said, "Mama, wake up. The Lord has healed you." When he said those words, "The Lord has healed you," I came to realize something had happened! So, for me, the whole question of Jesus being a friend to me is not only intellectual; I have *experienced* it. I've experienced his healing power, not only physically but also psychologically. I'm able to cope with things that previously I could not. So that's why it is not only physical but also psychological and spiritual—a wholeness of healing.

These accounts typify the witness of many African Christians in the oral interviews concerning their own experience of Jesus healing.

An even greater number of individuals attested to their experience of seeing others healed by Jesus. Examples are akin to those previously cited, reflecting healing in various dimensions of life. Still others, though far fewer in number, spoke of their own personal involvement in healing ministries, as did Nzeki above. For example, Ghanaian S. S. Quarcoopome, senior research fellow in modern history and politics at the Institute of African Studies, Legon, and also resident pastor of a charismatic church, gave a succinct summary of the components of rationale discussed thus far: "Yes, Jesus is a healer. He healed when he was on earth, and he's still healing now. I can testify to this, because I have used

his name, 'In the name of Jesus be healed,' and things have taken place. Simple—
just on faith. He *is* a healer." Masinde concurred on the basis of his ministry
experience. Yet he also stressed that God does not heal everyone:

> See, you've got to realize, physical healing is not our aim. Our aim is to serve
> God with our lives and glorify him in our death. And if God's going to take
> someone home through the way of sickness and disease, I won't question
> him. That doesn't stop him from being a healer. I still preach him as a healer.

Contemporary experience therefore plays a crucial role in determining Christians' perceptions of Jesus as healer, whether the healing is experienced personally, witnessed in others, or sought on behalf of others. Additional evidence
arising from the current context includes the proliferation of healing ministries
depicting Jesus in this role. Respondents refer to healing masses and church
services, as well as large evangelistic crusades or rallies that incorporate prayer
for healing, such as those held in Nairobi's Uhuru Park or Kasarani Stadium.
Kenyan Circle member Mary Getui pointed out further indications of widespread interest in Jesus as healer, including crowds flocking to evangelists from
Kenya, the West, and from the Far East who advertise for people to "Come for a
Miracle," or to the powerful healing ministry of Kenyan Mary Akatsa. She also
noted the centrality of healing among African Independent Churches, plus the
close connection between healing and evangelism in hospital and prison ministries. While problems related to these manifestations have yet to be addressed,
all these factors confirm the extent to which contemporary experience fortifies
African Christians' identification of Jesus as healer.

THE MEANING OF JESUS AS HEALER

Four main affirmations serve to summarize the interpretations of African
Christians in this regard. First, the image of Jesus as healer corresponds to that
of Jesus as life-giver, for it asserts that Jesus restores life where it has been
diminished, that he repairs life where it has been broken. Bujo draws a fundamental connection between healing and life as follows: "And even the healings
that Jesus performed must not only be seen as the revelation of his divinity, but
also Christ wants to stress that in his role as the Messiah, he comes to give
fullness of life at all levels."[48] Ghanaian Protestant clergyman Aboagye-Mensah
claimed that this christological image "is one of the major ones." He described
"Jesus as the healer, one who heals not only our sicknesses but our deeply
wounded souls. One who puts us together, as it were." Similarly Kenyan Protestant lay woman Marcy Muhia offered her understanding of Jesus as healer in
terms of "one who is able to restore the inner man, to create wholeness in the
inner man." She explained:

> When Christ comes into your life, something fundamental happens within
> you, and he begins a process of restoration. Your body disintegrates—that's
> fine—and I think, as life has gone on, I'm more and more accepting that,

because we live in a fallen world, disease is a must. Loss is a must. But, more and more, I think I'm understanding what it means for Christ to really heal, that there's a restoration of the inner man that is taking place as well. We're broken: we're broken in our sinfulness, broken in our relationships because of that sinfulness, broken in our emotions because of unhealthy patterns of life. Those things have brought about a brokenness in us. And I think Christ is able to heal that, to heal very completely.

The second major affirmation is closely related to the first, in that the African theologians, church leaders and lay people alike emphasize Jesus' healing as the re-creation of wholeness in all aspects of life. Pobee encapsulates the notion, stating, "Healing is at base a quest after wholeness of being and person, body, soul and mind."[49] Attention has already been drawn to the holistic approach to healing generally characteristic of African peoples, and certainly the textual and oral Christologies depict Jesus as healer in this light. Approximately one-quarter of the sixty individuals and one-third of the focus groups with whom this image was discussed stressed that Jesus' healing goes beyond the physical to encompass, in combined responses, the spiritual, emotional, moral, psychological, and relational dimensions. Kenyan Protestant lay woman Mabel Correa added further facets in stating that Jesus heals not only diseases but also "situations of finances, because Jesus is an *all-round healer*. He's opened up doors for jobs, for marriage, for a husband and wife to get together, things like that."

Furthermore, the holistic interpretation of healing extends beyond the individual to incorporate the communal dimensions of life. For example, Anne Nasimiyu Wasike underlines that Jesus' healing in the gospels was both physical and spiritual, and she concludes, "Jesus inaugurated the restoration of individuals and societies to wholeness and he invited the disciples to participate in this re-establishment."[50] Elsewhere she outlines the significance of this interpretation of healing for the African context, in referring to an editorial from the *Daily Nation* in Kenya that lamented that Kenyan society was becoming increasingly immoral, sick, corrupt, and in a state of total decay. In response, she voices the call of liberation theologians for "a spirituality of justice" to permeate all the activities of Jesus' disciples both as individuals and as communities.[51] Bujo underlined the same point. While full explication of the ancestral paradigm for Jesus awaits the following chapter, the integral relationship between the images appeared when Bujo remarked:

Jesus Christ as a healer, for example, is very actual here in our society. This healer is not only for sickness, but he has to heal all the misery in society, if we believe he is a new Proto-Ancestor, because the Proto-Ancestor is the one who is giving life in all the areas—not only the biological life.

Thus the portrayal of Jesus as healer signifies the restoration of life in its various dimensions, both for individuals and for communities.

Within this comprehensive view of life one area requires particular attention in outlining a third affirmation concerning Jesus as healer in Africa. Ela insists

that the African universe of sickness is inseparable from the spirit world and
that consequently healing must be addressed within this symbolic universe, and
thus he acknowledges that the ongoing propensity for Christians to seek out
traditional priests is a serious challenge to the Church of Africa. He therefore
urges Christians to consider carefully the role such traditional healers play in
the life of local populations, and he questions, "In the African environment,
shouldn't the church take Jesus at his word in the gospels in making use of the
power granted to it to lay hands on and heal the sick? (Mk 16:18)."[52] Ela emphasizes the importance of such healing ministries, and again calls for the Bible to
be reread in such a way as to relate the African person to the invisible world,
thereby assuming the symbolic universe of sickness and healing in order to
effect the salvation power inherent in the gospel. He then concludes,

> In a context where the African is confronted with invisible forces at work in
> the universe, the church has to find an adequate manner of proclaiming the
> primacy of Christ (Col 1:15–20), remembering that Saint Paul did not con-
> demn the powers and the principalities to which the new converts from the
> Greek world still accorded great importance. For he applied himself above
> all to specifying the paramount position of Christ from whom comes all sal-
> vation. In Black Africa, the world of the Night or of the Invisible is perhaps
> the privileged place in which we must understand the good news of the de-
> scent of Jesus into hell (1 Pt 3:19–20) in order to announce liberation to the
> African menaced by occult power.[53]

Oduyoye also points out what is at stake:

> It is therefore not strange that if relief from evil influences, from the spiritual
> oppressors, is not felt by members of Christian churches, they move from
> church to church as well as to-and-fro between the church and the *Odunsini*,
> the traditional healer of body and soul. Nevertheless, Jesus, "the Great Phy-
> sician," is the anchor of their faith, for he is preached as the healer par excel-
> lence.[54]

The image of Jesus as healer prevailing over evil powers features very prominently among the African Initiated Churches. Hence reference must be made to
them, despite the fact that they lie beyond the present scope, for the challenge
they bring to the historic churches. Amoah and Oduyoye observe the remarkable growth of these churches and note that "Christ, the great Healer, is seen as
the center of the Christology of these charismatic churches."[55] Pobee, among
others, adds that healing is the most important reason for people joining these
churches, often in reaction to the attitudes of the mission churches. Following
his own examination of the biblical evidence concerning Jesus as healer, Pobee
concludes:

> Evidently, the gospel's healing and exorcism by the Spirit of God were a
> significant part of the ministry of Jesus and his followers, even if he did not

overplay it. It accords well with the contemporary worldview in which ailments were not just matters of cause and effect but also have spiritual ramifications, if not origins. That whole world now accords well with the African story even today. On the other hand, the churches founded by missionary bodies in Europe and America have been reluctant, if not unwilling, to accept this healing and exorcism by the power of the Spirit, especially if it is through Africans.[56]

While acknowledging the positive role of medical missions and granting the growing awareness of the importance of healing within the historic churches, Pobee nonetheless calls for rehabilitation of the healing ministry as a significant part of mission in Africa today.

The combined proclamations of these theologians, together with the witness of the African Initiated Churches, indicate the third main point regarding the meaning of Jesus as healer. That is, the image conveys Jesus' supremacy over every form of evil operating in the universe, whether it is manifested in the physical, mental, emotional, spiritual, social, or any other sphere of life. In this sense Jesus as healer overlaps with closely related images like victor, conqueror, and warrior, or the one who defeats all that is life-negating instead of life-affirming. That Jesus is indeed perceived in this role emerged in the oral interviews, in which twelve of the total sixty-five individual respondents initiated comments to this effect, such as Jesus having conquered all enemies including disease, evil spirits, and death itself.

Strong evidence for this perception emerges particularly in the Ghanaian context. For example, Ghanaian Protestant clergyman Aboagye-Mensah highlights the image of Jesus as healer, and continues:

> Related to this is Jesus as the victor, one who is victorious over the spiritual forces, whether it's in the powers of darkness, principalities and powers and so on. These are some of the areas that most people, when they come to you, want solace and prayer for, because they believe that Jesus has overcome these powers of darkness and therefore can set them free from those.

Additionally, Ghanaian clergyman Dan Antwi, principal of Trinity Theological College, stressed the importance of the vernacular in expressing this image far more vividly than English translations convey. He responded enthusiastically to the image of Jesus as healer, underlining its importance to the Ghanaian context and citing three vernacular titles as corroboration:

> Ah! That one? It's an amazing and powerful one, especially because we are in a society where we are exposed to ailments and so on. "Savior," the expression "savior," in the vernacular *ogyefo*, "one who really rescues you," and he may rescue you not only from danger but from disease. *Osa osahene*, you can have *osahene*, who is "the conquering king," the one who leads in battle and so on. You can also have *Osofo Yesu*, "the one who heals." We have those categories, and sometimes you hear people praying in those categories:

"Jesus, a healer who heals and who doesn't accept down payment for healing. But he heals and heals completely."

Thus, despite the general reluctance of the modern missionary movement to portray Jesus as healer in the light of African concepts of healing and sickness, many African Christians today nonetheless view him in this traditional role as triumphing over the powers of darkness, disease, and death.

Jesus as healer means that he restores life, and life in all its dimensions, encompassing individual and communal aspects. The image further signifies that Jesus is perceived as supreme over every life-diminishing force. The vernacular titles introduced above lead to a fourth and final affirmation regarding the meaning of Jesus as healer; namely, the image is intrinsically related to other significant roles such as savior, liberator, and redeemer. For example, Oduyoye makes the fundamental assertion that "the cry for salvation/liberation in Africa is primarily a cry for health and wholeness."[57] Likewise Nasimiyu Wasike sets forth the premise that "healing is part and parcel of liberation and inculturation,"[58] which she argues on the basis of Jesus' healing ministry and its significance to Africa today. The interrelatedness of the concepts of saving, healing, conquering, and protecting came through in discussions of vernacular terms employed for Jesus. For example, in speaking of Ghanaian Christians, Protestant lay woman Irene Odotei explained: "They see him as a protector, like a savior. *Agyenkwa*, he's given you life, the savior. And they see him as a warrior, *Osa, Osa-berima Yehowa*. And protector, the big rock, the big fortress."

Ghanaian Catholic lay man George Hagan spelled out how Jesus is understood as healer not only in line with biblical teaching, but also in accordance with cultural expectation. With respect to the latter he explained:

> Now in the African cultures too, healing is a holistic thing. It is always seen as having a spiritual dimension, so you would expect a charismatic figure, a spiritual figure—in fact our healers were all spiritual figures. Our herbalists were supposed to know things physical and things spiritual. Our fetish priests and priestesses were operating in the realm of the spiritual; they were supposed to have powers of healing. So the association between spirituality and healing is already there in the minds of our people. And if you have come to say that Christ is a redeemer, and yet a redeemer who did not have the power to heal, it would have sounded very odd in the ears of an African. So the healing image of Christ is a very vivid one, something that is very, very important, that strikes a chord in the mind of an African.

PROBLEMS WITH THE IMAGE OF JESUS AS HEALER

While the image of Jesus as healer is evidently important to many African Christians, some express alternative views. For example, Ghanaian Protestant clergyman B. Y. Quarshie certainly affirmed Jesus as healer, yet he ruled against seeing this as anything specifically African: "When I think about healer, what comes to mind is not strictly speaking a typical African healer or anything of the sort." Instead, he stated that "it's really a matter of trying to see that yes, Christ is the answer to every situation, every matter pertaining to any given context. So if in that given context, the issue is one of disease, then Christ can be presented in that context indeed as a healer." Yet his overall contention relates back to the central concept of Jesus as life-giver, for he concluded: "If we talk, for example, about Christ being life, and therefore everything that life is, we would do away with things that negate life. I would see Christ's affirmation as meaning that indeed he can heal. But that would only be one aspect of it."

The contrasting perspectives are not necessarily contradictory, but they do reflect certain tensions inherent in depicting Jesus according to traditional African categories. On the one hand, African concepts of healing and healers inevitably influence the interpretations of African Christians regarding Jesus as healer. Often this background serves to enhance the understanding of Jesus in this role, as clearly manifest in the textual and oral data presented thus far. On the other hand, however, such cultural constructs can potentially diminish one's apprehension of Jesus, as Quarshie, among others, intimated. Again, the issue is not so much diametrically opposed views, but more a matter of balance and proportion as certain voices seek to guard against the reduction of Jesus to any role defined too narrowly. Hence Protestant clergyman Abraham Akrong, research fellow in African religions and philosophy at the University of Ghana, Legon, voiced both a ready acceptance and a certain extension of the concept of Jesus as healer:

> Yeah, Jesus as healer. You see, in the traditional society, the healer is not just a herbalist. The healer combines prophecy or divination. He will combine wisdom, insight—they are very good counselors—so that when Christ also becomes a healer, he combines all these things. He does not only heal, he counsels you, he brings fullness into your life. So in that sense, Christ as a healer is also part of the wider scope within which we want to understand the nature of Christ.

Further challenges regarding the image of Jesus as healer emerged in the oral interviews. In line with these cautions about narrowly skewing perceptions of Christ, Ghanaian Catholic priest Joseph Aggrey voiced the danger of simply fashioning ideas about Jesus according to one's own understanding and current needs. Although Aggrey volunteered the image of healer for Jesus, he warned:

> So sometimes what Jesus is to somebody can be seen by what the person is going through. There are some people who see Jesus only as a healer, because they are sick. There are some people who, because they are poor, want Jesus to change stones into bread for them. So if you don't take care, you will be kind of parochial in your thinking about Jesus Christ. But Jesus Christ embodies *everything*. So there is that danger, of losing sight of who Jesus is. You're only thinking of who Jesus is in reference to your problem, the situation in which you find yourself.

Additional problems can be summarized briefly. Ghanaian Catholic Bishop Palmer-Buckle related his experience of parishioners who come to him expecting instantaneous, miraculous cures, some of whom are "shattered" when he not only prays with them but also advises them to go to the hospital. As indicated at the outset of this section on Jesus as healer, certain respondents found problems not with the image per se, but with how it is portrayed in contemporary healing ministries. In this case Palmer-Buckle regretted that "most of our preachers present slambang miraculous healing as the only form of healing Jesus presented, but that's not true from the scriptures." Likewise, Kenyan Peter Gichure, lecturer at St. Thomas Aquinas Seminary and at the Catholic University of East Africa, lamented that "the emphasis on Jesus the healer can be another euphoria," with evangelists openly exploiting Africans "in very desperate situations," unable to afford drugs or medical care. He objects to the widespread healing ministries which in his mind distort the true meaning of Jesus' healing as related to "the kingdom, or the reign of God." Furthermore, Ghanaian Bishop Peter Sarpong was among those who decry any undue stress on Jesus' physical healing. As Juliana Senavoe, Ghanaian Protestant clergywoman and principal of Christian Service College, Kumasi, explained:

> He heals, because he's involved in the totality of life. But his primary intention is not to heal the body, because I believe that healing this body is just a postponement of death, for a while. Then it will have to succumb to death, and therefore healing is not the primary thing. So yes, he does heal. He heals me, I definitely saw that with my cancer, earlier on. But that's not his primary task.

Finally, Kwesi Dickson was among those who criticized unwarranted focus on the human minister of healing, remarking that "in many instances, Christ plays second fiddle to these human leaders, I suspect." He further pointed out the problem of inadequate teaching regarding Jesus as "the one who overcomes all," citing his experience with particular church leaders who feared that a certain sick person would be "finished off" by his enemies through witchcraft. Thus various challenges definitely arise with respect to the image of Jesus as healer in Africa, primarily stemming from its portrayal in the practice of certain healing ministries.

Yet the most incisive critique of the image came from Ela. While in no way denying that Jesus is healer, Ela criticized the way in which African theologians commonly depict the image through the approach of christological titles, the results of which are not sufficiently serious and rigorous. In his opinion African Christology has only begun; he explained his own approach as follows:

> It is to recapture all the richness of meanings of the New Testament, the core essence of the New Testament—to understand Jesus Christ, God in Jesus Christ—from what I call the people at the bottom of the heap. I know well enough that it is important to present Jesus as ancestor, as the master

of initiation, as the healer, that's all fine. But in the context in which I myself have tried to elaborate on Jesus Christ, I start with the people at the bottom.

Ela's point of departure clearly lies in the contemporary context, for he begins with the presupposition that faith must intersect with "the totality of existence and all of its problems," and that in Africa, "it must begin with the people's struggle to escape from the hellish circle in which they risk being permanently imprisoned."[59] Hence, he focuses on the structures of daily life and examines the social problems, citing recent research that indicates that "health is their priority (75%)—even before family (48%) or job security (33%)."[60] His central question therefore challenges the churches to consider their response to this general concern and whether an alternative health care system ought to be developed.

In examining health issues in the contemporary context Ela traces their roots first through the medical systems established under colonialism, in which health facilities and treatment became integrated into an overall system of domination and exploitation. Since independence, the situation has only worsened with the increasing disparity between the rich and poor and the perpetuation of a socioeconomic system in which health care is the privilege of the wealthy minority. In brief, Ela sums it up as "'class' medicine" and again calls for the churches to respond to this form of social injustice. He then inquires into the relationship between Christian missions and health programs in Africa, pointing out certain ambiguities in that missionaries provide solid medical care, yet sometimes "the connivance of evangelization with medical work arouses the mistrust of various African sectors," particularly among Muslims.[61] In light of the historical collusion between Christianity and colonialism, Ela highlights the ensuing problem as follows: "Thus the salvation of the soul and efforts to heal are both interpreted as consolation within a system of oppression and domination."[62] From this contemporary context, then, with the complex health issues arising from colonialism, neocolonialism, and Christian mission, crucial questions arise concerning health care in relation to salvation and the kingdom of God.

Having set forth the critical issues regarding health in Africa today, Ela tackles the emergent questions in light of biblical teaching. He explores Jesus' healing ministry within the wider context of sickness and sin in the Bible. On this basis Ela draws out the theological significance of Jesus' healings in terms of salvation and liberation. That is to say, the healings are not merely proofs of Jesus' divinity, but rather they reveal the inauguration of a new age, the fulfillment of messianic hope in the presence of God's kingdom in the world. So Jesus is not simply a miracleworker, but "one who roots salvation in the web of history. . . . Whenever a person is reborn to life by the force of the gospel operating through the words and actions of Jesus, salvation is available in 'bodily' form."[63] Salvation is presented in its communal, cosmic and eschatological dimensions, the latter summarized from Romans 8:20–24 as follows:

In this context, human health appears as one dimension of the salvation whose fullness we await in a glorious future. Strictly speaking, to be healed—that is, to be delivered from evil—is in itself to be saved. Humanity is invited to enter into that state of creation marked by the saving power of the Resurrection.[64]

However, Ela's acknowledgment of the eschatological dimension of healing is not prey to the tendency of some forms of mission Christianity that have condoned present suffering in hopes of future bliss in heaven. On the contrary, Ela takes a strongly liberationist approach, first depicting Jesus' healing ministry as indication that he is the "new Moses (Acts 3:22; 7:37; Deut. 18:15), the Messiah announced by the prophets and awaited by the poor and oppressed."[65] Ela thus concludes:

> The many forms of deliverance signified by healing in the gospels define the liberation of humanity through Jesus Christ. They allow us to hear and see the liberating activity of the Messiah on behalf of the poor and oppressed. The incarnation is the time when God decisively announces the gospel and frees the captives (Luke 4:18–19). How can this time of God be actualised in contemporary African society, apart from reference to questions of health? What's the use of a "medicine" coopted for the benefit of wealthy minorities, when the "*lives*" of those neglected by its progress are stuck in structures of inequity and injustice?[66]

The theological interpretation of Jesus as healer therefore informs the agenda Ela advocates: first, exposing the structures that contradict God's will for humanity and the world; then analyzing the socioeconomic factors that imprison humans in sickness and misery; and finally, participating in active resistance to current socioeconomic structures that are incompatible with the gospel as an essential feature of Christian practice. Ela thus challenges Christians to examine the roots of sickness in the unjust organization of African societies, and to live the gospel by totally restructuring the living conditions within those societies.

Ela's contribution to the discussion underlines the fact that although the image of Jesus as healer may be widely held among the selected African Christians, it is not necessarily a foregone conclusion that Jesus fulfills this role in the contemporary context. Critical issues regarding the image were raised in the introduction to this second section, including the challenges inherent in relating Jesus to contemporary suffering across the continent and to traditional concepts of illness and healing. These complexities led to serious and legitimate questions concerning whether Jesus can truly be interpreted as healer in Africa today. In response, the data have shown conclusively that the image is indeed operative in the understanding and experience of the vast majority of African Christians considered here. However, acknowledging manifestation of the image does not approve any sense of triumphalism. For analysis of the substance of the image has brought to light not only positive affirmations concerning its meaning, but also problems hindering its realization more adequately in the lives of Africans today. Affirmatively, respondents interpreted Jesus as healer to mean that he restores life wherever it has been diminished; that his healing extends to all aspects of life and encompasses the individual, communal, and cosmic spheres; that it signifies Jesus' supremacy over all powers, however evil; and that its content overlaps with other images such as savior, liberator, and redeemer. Yet contrasting views also emerged, calling for caution against any undue restriction of Jesus by fashioning him according to human cultural constructs or personal needs. Further reservations stem from certain healing ministries considered detrimental to a sound portrayal of Jesus as healer. Ultimately, though, the most acute criticism came from Ela who, in opposition to the common approach of developing christological titles, champions a much broader methodology of interpreting Jesus as healer in terms of his liberating activity on behalf of the poor and oppressed and his ongoing establishment of the kingdom of God among those who suffer today.

JESUS AS TRADITIONAL HEALER

INTRODUCTION

The centrality of life and healing in African thought underpins the portraits of Jesus as life-giver and healer. As Cécé Kolié asserts, "For the black African person, the aspiration to *life*, to eternity, is so primary that the persons called to administer it hold a place of eminence. Soothsayers and healers, medicine persons of all kinds, are the pillars of social life."[67] Kolié further points out that while other traditional leaders such as chiefs and masters of initiation are on the wane, traditional healers are not. The consequent question is whether the traditional healer provides a salutary image for African Christians to apprehend Jesus.

The suggestion of interpreting Jesus in relation to the traditional healer finds early attestation within African theology. Buana Kibongi's 1969 essay "Priesthood" outlines four main roles of the *nganga* or "priest" in the Congolese cultural context: (1) mediator against evil forces, (2) healer, (3) magician, and (4) prophet or visionary.[68] Kibongi goes on to compare this notion of priesthood with that found in the Old Testament and with Jesus as the high priest of the new covenant. Despite drawing a significant contrast between Jesus and *nganga*, Kibongi nonetheless states:

> However the activities of *nganga* throw into relief the idea of salvation or deliverance. *Nganga* is certainly the saviour or the liberator of *Muntu* ["human, person"]. *Nganga* has undoubtedly contributed to the maintenance of the idea of salvation or deliverance. The desire for salvation or deliverance is fully satisfied by the Son of God, the Saviour and Lord of the World.[69]

Kibongi thus distinguishes their roles in concluding that "*Nganga* willed to save man, but did not succeed in doing so; Christ did so fully once for all. Christ has therefore accomplished the work of *Nganga*."[70] Kibongi nevertheless highlights the significance of the traditional healer by elucidating how African Christians interpret both Jesus and Christian priests, including missionaries and Africans, in light of their prior experience of *nganga*.

Ten years later, Gabriel Setiloane proposed the image of Jesus as traditional healer. Yet he recounts:

Some German theologians were scandalized when I suggested that I would look for the Messiah-*Christos* idea in African thinking somewhere in the area of the African *Bongaka* [traditional doctor—often derogatorily called witchdoctor or jujuman] and in the possession of individual persons by Divinity. I still believe that an authentic African Christology lies in that direction, and the future of African theology lies in digging it out and presenting it to the world.[71]

Most African theologians, however, have been conspicuously reticent about recommending the image of Jesus as traditional healer. Matthew Schoffeleers questions why it has not been acknowledged and utilized by African theologians, with the exception of a few like Kibongi and Setiloane, whom he states have not been treated seriously with respect to this point. He offers two reasons by way of explanation: First, the *nganga* paradigm is viewed as an intrinsic part of indigenous African religion and therefore "tainted too much with syncretistic connotations," according to the official church; and second, both missionary and African Christian ministers tend to view the *nganga* as a rival with whom they must compete for the same clientele.[72] Hence, Schoffeleers concludes that most Christian leaders evidently consider it improper to construct a Christology on the basis of the *nganga* paradigm.

Certainly the observation of relative silence on the topic is borne out by the textual evidence considered here. Of the six theologians selected, I found no explicit reference to Jesus portrayed as a traditional healer. In contrast, Schoffeleers maintains that "at the level of folk theology—at least one christological paradigm exists that is used over large areas of sub-Saharan Africa. That paradigm is the medicine person, known in many Bantu languages by the noun *nganga* or one of its cognates."[73] In view of the dichotomy Schoffeleers posits between professional theology and folk theology, certain questions call for attention. First, to what extent does the image of Jesus as traditional healer function, either explicitly or implicitly, among the selected African Christian respondents? What meaning do they ascribe to it? And what rationale do they express either for supporting or for rejecting the image? Findings from the field research, first from Kenya and Uganda, then from Ghana, form the basis for conclusions drawn from all the materials considered together. Since no distinct pattern emerged from the field data to suggest that individual respondents' views may be correlated to variables such as nationality, age, gender, church affiliation, favored language for Bible reading and prayer, or theological education, analysis concentrates on the expressed meanings and rationale.

JESUS AS *MGANGA* OR TRADITIONAL HEALER IN KENYA AND UGANDA

The Data

Responses from individual interviewees to the question of Jesus as *mganga* or traditional healer ranged from an enthusiastic, "Yes! I would have no problem with Jesus as mganga. He is *mganga*," to a firm, "No, no, no. Jesus has no comparison with *mganga*. I would say that's an insult to Jesus Christ."[74] Most responses fell in between these extremes. While some respondents voiced only positive or only negative responses, others weighed the pros and cons in presenting Jesus this way. Therefore, if the weight of the evidence or the overall verdict expressed by each person is considered, fourteen of the twenty-two respondents with whom the question was discussed agreed that *mganga* is a meaningful way to depict Jesus.[75] Of the remainder, seven disagreed that the image is suitable for Jesus, and one concluded neither positively nor negatively but stressed that it depends on the geographical context (that is, acceptable in Tanzania, not so in Kenya). Thus approximately two-thirds of the available responses were favorable towards Jesus as *mganga*, while approximately one-third were not (see Table 3–1).

A similar pattern holds true for the focus groups in Kenya with whom the image was discussed (see Table 3–2).[76]

The Meaning of Mganga

One of the major problems with presenting Jesus in the image of the traditional healer was the confusion surrounding this figure in terms of definitions and roles.[77] Perceptions have become clouded through colonial and mission history in East Africa, as respondents verified. For example, Peter Kiarie, former director of education at the Catholic Secretariat in Nairobi, who has done extensive research among his own Kikuyu people, pointed out the anachronism of African medicine men being referred to as witchdoctors, a term that "is actually a contradiction because 'witches' are 'witches,'" that is, distinct from "doctors." Before further clarifying the distinction between various terms employed, it is noteworthy that some respondents attributed the negative connotations associated with the traditional healer to false assumptions and teaching on the part of Christians. Catholic religious sister Gacambi explained concerning the term *mganga:* "So it's that Christian dimension that really put everything that is done by the African as bad. It gave that negative connotation, because that's the way we were taught in our catechism." Consequently, rather than seeking to clarify definitions from anthropological or religious studies literature, the present aim is to discern how the term *mganga* functions in the thinking of these selected African Christians. For it is in this arena of religious understanding and imagination that the image of Jesus as *mganga* rises or falls.

In defining the terms as traditionally understood, many respondents made a clear distinction between two kinds of figures. The first is *mganga*, referring to the healer, the one who heals, the best doctor, *daktari*,[78] medicine man, a spiritual *mganga* or herbalist who mixes herbs to administer to the sick, or a *seer* who can convey good messages to you. Masinde pointed out that the root meaning of the Swahili verb *kuganga* is "to treat," so that the *mganga* is essentially a doctor who treats people. Returning to the observation above concerning the anachronistic term *witchdoctor,* Kiarie explained that Africans distinguish "the witch, the sorcerer," from "the healer, or the medicine man, or the diviner, a herbalist who uses herbs." He stressed that in the traditional African context, there was no single individual who could diagnose and deal with all the social

Individual Responses	Statistic	Percentage
Positive responses only	8/22	36%
Negative responses only	5/22	23%
Positive and negative responses	9/22	41%
Overall verdict positive: 6/9		
Overall verdict negative: 2/9		
Overall verdict neutral: 1/9		
Total responses overall positive	14/22	64%
Total responses overall negative	7/22	32%
Total responses overall neutral	1/22	4%

TABLE 3–1. INDIVIDUAL RESPONSES IN KENYA AND UGANDA TO THE IMAGE OF JESUS AS *MGANGA*

Focus Group Responses	Statistic	Percentage
Positive responses only	1/5	20%
Negative responses only	0/5	0%
Positive and negative responses	4/5	80%
Overall verdict positive: 1/4		
Overall verdict negative: 1/4		
Overall verdict neutral: 2/4		
Total responses overall positive	2/5	40%
Total responses overall negative	1/5	20%
Total responses overall neutral	2/5	40%

TABLE 3–2. FOCUS GROUP RESPONSES IN KENYA TO THE IMAGE OF JESUS AS *MGANGA*

problems; hence there were "*mganga* or *waganga*—medicine men—of different kinds." He further identified two main roles of the medicine man: (1) divination, to discern why someone is sick, for example, if a taboo has been broken or a demand by the ancestors is unfulfilled, and (2) prescription, to remedy the situation through actual medicine, sacrifice, or "praying for healing directly from the spiritual powers, from the divine powers."

Kiarie then distinguished these "experts" who have learned some trade, such as the herbalists, from the second kind of figure "who would be very suspicious." He continued, "Some *waganga* claim to have other superior powers—they are not divine powers." In this category he placed people dealing with *majini*, or power from "the evil spirits or the demons," and also "astrologers, the people who are reading your palms and claiming to have magical powers."

He summarized: "There are people who are out there to control, and even make a lot of money. And they survive on people's enmities." Again, in contrast, he stressed that "in the positive African context, people respected very much the medicine man." Likewise in the focus group of Kenyan Catholic clergy, Njorogi Mwangi distinguished the positive role of the *mganga* or medicine man from its negative counterpart: *mchawi* in Swahili, defined as "a sorcerer," "a witch," "a wizard," or "somebody who can bring bad things."

Additional respondents further confirmed the negative connotations that they or others associate with the term *mganga*. Kenyan Catholic Archbishop Nzeki spoke of how it has become blurred in Kenya with "the *mganga* witchcraft" or the "one who puts fear into you." The former chairman of the department of philosophy at the University of Nairobi, Gerald Wanjohi, explained that *mganga* is also understood as "a wizard, who is actually a sorcerer, who finds ways to eliminate people; one who practices black magic, so to speak." Additional descriptions included "a person who practices superstition," who "is associated with evil," and "a kind of seer, in a negative way," or someone who uses spiritual power in a malicious way. The term *witchdoctor* continues to be used, as evidenced in the oral interviews. For example, Masinde employed it referring to one who "doubles in the spiritual underworld, the dark world, devil worship. And his powers are not from God, or from herbs—it's actually demonic." Various members of the focus group of Catholic laity also spoke of the witchdoctor as, for example, "one who kills."

Given these contrasting interpretations of the same term, *mganga*, it is not surprising that the application of the term to Jesus is controversial. To illustrate the extent of the confusion regarding terminology, it is notable that Catholic priest David Kamau volunteered the image of Jesus as "the greatest African medicine man." He explained why this image is so significant to African Christians in light of the context of widespread African belief, and his summary is worth citing in full for its recapitulation of the meanings delineated above:

> Yeah! Yeah, it is there, in the sense that Africans believe in witchcraft, sorcerers, wizards, and these affect our lives even today. According to African cosmology, worldview, it starts with God, then the spiritual beings. Below the spiritual beings, you have man. And below man, you have the living and non-living beings. Within this hierarchy penetrates a mystical power, and this mystical power gives life according to this worldview. Now, there are people who have the knowledge of this mystical power, and they use this mystical power to harm the people. These are the sorcerers and wizards. But again, there are also other people who use this power to do good to the people. These are African medicine men. So they confront the other group that want to harm the people. Now, Jesus is the greatest African medicine man. He can use that power to heal, to help the people. So as an African, I would say Jesus is the greatest medicine man who fights the witchcraft and sorcerers. And therefore we should not be afraid of these people.

While advocating that Jesus be understood in these terms, Kamau nevertheless rejected the image of Jesus as *mganga* because of its negative connotations. He concluded that Jesus is a medicine man but not a *mganga*, despite the fact that his interpretation of the "medicine man" correlates closely with what others attribute to *mganga*. Hermeneutical complexities of this nature account for the ambivalence African Christians expressed in relation to the image of Jesus as *mganga*, as delineated in the following sections.

Rationale for the Image of Jesus as Mganga

The data findings presented above show that approximately two-thirds of the individual interviewees and almost half of the focus groups with whom the image of Jesus as *mganga* was discussed were by and large favorable in response. Three main reasons were given in support. First, it was argued that the term *mganga* has been condemned or has gained negative connotations without adequate investigation. Hence there is need to recover traditional terms and concepts that may enhance African Christians' understanding of Jesus and their practice of healing ministries. As Catholic lecturer Gacambi put it, "I feel it would be good to start reclaiming those titles and showing the positive element. Yes, because as long as we keep away from them, then we lose this element that we are trying to enhance." The basis for recovering traditional terms is the conviction that Jesus fulfills the role that the traditional healer plays in many African societies. For example, Bonifes Adoyo in the focus group of Protestant clergy took a somewhat pragmatic approach:

> Healing is healing! If somebody is sick, as long as he knows there is a place for healing, that's where he goes. And that is the context in which we are saying, if people would go to a *mganga* for healing—maybe they have a need that medical science has not been able to resolve—they will come to Jesus to heal! In that sense, that is why we are saying that he is perceived in that role, that if you are sick, he will cure you!

The main reason developed in support of the image, however, concerns the parallels between the ministries of Jesus and those of the traditional healer. These parallels are believed to provide grounds for interpreting Jesus in this light and to allow African Christians to appropriate Jesus in a more meaningful way. One clear correspondence is the power to heal and to confront and conquer evil powers. In addition to Catholic priest Kamau's statement above to this effect, Protestant lay woman Sarah Nabwire spoke of the human *mganga* as merely a "photocopy" of "the big *mganga*, Jesus." A second parallel concerns special powers of knowledge attributed to traditional healers and to Jesus. Kiarie drew the comparison, yet intimated that Jesus supersedes the traditional healer:

> So in that context, you can see Jesus comes out very powerfully as the healer, because he demonstrates he knows people. He doesn't have to have a gourd, and do things to diagnose what is wrong. He looks at Nathaniel, and says, "Here is an Israelite without guile." And he says, "I saw you while you were there under the tree." This kind of approach, that Jesus had that knowledge of

persons—he *knew*, you don't have to tell him. So this is something that Africans admire—they liked the medicine men.

A third parallel is that, like the traditional healer, Jesus uses many different ways to heal. Again Kiarie provided lucid explanation:

And when it comes to healing, he uses so many ways. He can touch you, he can put mud or saliva on your eyes, he can command these spirits. He has all manner of ways: by his word, he can even heal at a distance, like this Roman soldier, "You just go, your son is healed." He can even speak to forces, so he is a real miracleworker.

It is noteworthy, in this regard, that Kiarie is among three of the twenty-two individual respondents and one of the five focus groups who find justification for interpreting Jesus as *mganga* in recalling the particular example of Jesus healing the blind man by mixing mud and saliva and placing it on his eyes, an action considered akin to certain practices of traditional healers. So in light of these parallels, some African Christians contend that Jesus may be understood through the image of the traditional healer for he, and the healing ministry extended through his followers, provides the healing which was formerly sought through the human *mganga*. Kiarie concluded:

Jesus is actually the supreme *mganga*. You see, with Jesus you don't have to go to the *mganga*. And this is where the church, when it now offers healing services, either through prayers or through the sacrament or through medical, hospital services, is an extension of the same healing.

Finally, limited contextual evidence further supports the view of Jesus as *mganga* or traditional healer. First, Getui observed that the existence of "Christian herbalists," or Christians who practice healing ministries that blend the Christian faith with traditional African healing practices, supports the notion of understanding Jesus in this same light. She also spoke of a pastor she knows who "simply got this gift of using herbs." Following a brief description of his ministry of healing, she concluded: "Jesus can actually be seen as a *mganga* if you look at it from that perspective." In a focus group discussion, Kenyan Catholic priests confirmed this perception based on their own experience as priests. They discussed parishioners coming to them with various requests for healing, including those "seeing snakes" sent by others to harm them. The priests interpreted such "symptoms" as indicators of personal problems like jealousy and rivalry, and described the "Christian rites" they perform in praying for each person with oil and holy water. Njoroge Mwangi then concluded, "So, if you can try to bring those qualities, try to cultivate that attitude, like Jesus Christ as a healer, it's going to bring a lot of impact."

A second aspect of contextual evidence is Swahili songs about Jesus as healer. While the songs may not portray Jesus specifically in the role of traditional healer, two individual respondents introduced songs in the context of discussing

Jesus in this role. For example, Kiarie cited and interpreted one Swahili song that he reports is frequently played on the radio: "'Nataka uguzo—uguzo wa Yesu,' 'I want to be touched, to be touched by Jesus.' You see, if Jesus touches me, I'm okay. I am healed, you know, 'I want to be touched, to be healed.'" Also, fruit-hawker Muriithi mentioned and sang, "Daktari, Yesu daktari," which is one verse of a Swahili chorus commonly sung in Kenya. When probed as to whether *daktari* means the same as *mganga*, he replied, "It's almost the same. It's just a similar word, but there's a slight difference, because nowadays people go to doctors, they don't go to *mganga*." Thus African Christians bore witness to some current perceptions of Jesus as traditional healer in the contemporary context from their experience of the confluence of biblical and African traditions plus the process of modernization.

Problems with the Image of Jesus as Mganga

Not surprisingly, the most common reason given for rejecting or cautioning against the image of Jesus as *mganga* was the negative connotations associated with the term, as outlined above. John Gatu responded favorably to the image himself, in keeping with his leading role in interpreting Christianity from African perspectives. However, he noted the main problem with this particular image:

> The only problem is that in our own concepts today, *mganga* is seen as a person who practices superstition. We don't see him as the healer in the sense that you're talking about Jesus now. And so, if you say to somebody, "Kristo Yesu ni mganga," the immediate concept—because of the distortion that has been made in some of our concepts—you're talking about that fellow who plays juju.

Furthermore, Catholic lecturer Peter Gichure voiced strong objection on the theological grounds that it places Jesus on par with evil, or the devil, rather than adequately acknowledging his omnipotence over all forces of evil. While conceding some instructive value to Jesus as the *mganga* or traditional healer who works good for the community, he nonetheless warned, "But it's the mentality, it's what you instruct the people, that is very dangerous." He elaborated with an example: If you tell an African that Jesus is *mganga*, the African will conceptualize it as a competition between two *waganga*, like the story of Moses confronting the wise men of Pharaoh in the contest of powers. In contrast to this approach, Gichure insisted, "But the evil has *no power*. The devil's power is so limited that it's incomparable! The mere presence of Jesus—without telling people he's a *mganga*—the mere presence of Jesus should be able to say no to the evil. So, the emphasis should not be on the *mganga*, but should always be on Jesus' presence" and his ultimate power over all evil, for "Jesus Christ stands against all evil."

Finally, the image was rejected on additional theological grounds as compromising the divinity of Jesus. Given Titus Kivunzi's role as bishop of the Africa

Inland Church, a large denomination planted by the Africa Inland Mission, which was generally negative toward African traditional religions, it is not surprising that he vehemently opposed Jesus as *mganga* and its equivalent term in his vernacular, Kikamba. Kivunzi explained, "I'm looking at Jesus as God himself, the creator of the world, so to look at him as *mganga* is really minimizing his divinity." Interestingly, Ole Ronkei, the Maasai Christian from a clan of spiritual and medicinal leaders, argued along similar lines that the image reduces Jesus to being lower than God and thereby creates confusion for traditional Maasai. He advised:

> If you introduce Christ as God, you're going to put Christ in exactly the same position, same capacity as God—no difference. And then you have to start being careful how you're going to refer to that, that you're not lowering God to the level of the healer that God uses.

With respect to the traditional Maasai context, Ole Ronkei emphasized that God is understood to be the healer, and that he can heal either directly through prayer or through people such as a medicine man or herbalist. Like Gichure above, he grants that there may be room to understand Christ in this capacity. However, he cautioned against it, stating, "He could be presented as a healer, but overall as a healer who heals, but not reducing him down to the person who has to go to the bush and cut a branch and show you that it's a branch from that tree and a leaf from this one that will heal you." So whether from contexts of conservative Christianity or traditional Maasai culture, respondents voiced theological grounds for objecting to Jesus as *mganga*.

Conclusion: Jesus as Mganga

Approximately two-thirds of the individual respondents with whom the image of Jesus as *mganga* or traditional healer was discussed in Kenya and Uganda concluded that they would support its usage, provided the term is adequately qualified to mean a healer and not a witch or sorcerer. However, primarily in view of the negative connotations already associated with the *mganga* or traditional healer, the remaining one-third either discourage the image or reject it outright. Focus group findings corroborate that the image is controversial, with 40 percent concluding positively in support of it, 20 percent concluding negatively in rejecting it, and 40 percent expressing pros and cons without reaching a consensus. Summarizing perceptions from the individual and focus groups combined, some interviewees voiced strong opposition on the theological grounds of compromising the divinity of Christ. Yet others displayed openness to portraying him in this way, arguing for the need to recover and purify traditional terms that may enhance Africans' understanding of Jesus. One major aspect pointed out in this regard, in accord with the previous discussion of Jesus as healer, was that both Jesus and the *mganga* reveal a holistic approach to healing. For example, when asked if he would recommend the image of Jesus as *mganga* for Kenyan Christians, Gatu made this striking assertion, "Oh, yes! And I would say, like, this word that I was using now, *murigiti, murigiti*—it has a very deep Kikuyu meaning, that 'he comes to doctor.' He comes to not only cleanse, in the sense of cleansing, but in terms of total healing."

One last witness warrants full citation, for she both summarized key aspects of the preceding discussion and provided a compelling example of African Christians reappropriating aspects of traditional culture in light of Jesus' ministry and that of the Bible. Her comments are especially striking, coming from one who was raised in the East African Revival and therefore considerably cut off from her roots in traditional culture. Yet after intensive study of the African heritage, Hannah Kinoti, former chairperson of the Department of Religious Studies at the University of Nairobi, responded to the question of Jesus as *mganga* as follows:

It would be meaningful, yes. In this country, both *waganga* and the witchdoctor are traditional healers. You have herbalists, you have diviners, you have bone-setters, you have even just seers who give advice. With the coming of mission Christianity, they all went underground because there was a lot of hostility against them. So my own ideas of who a *mganga* is, from my own studies, show me yes, Jesus is a *mganga!* Because a *mganga,* traditionally, is not one who will run to give you some concoction or do some magic. Okay, they have their paraphernalia, as modern doctors have their stethoscopes and white coats and all that. It's a question of which situation you are in—they behave in the same way. But a *mganga* would really question you, to try and place your problem. And often the problem was not just here, where you're hurting, but the relationships in your own social setting, family setting. And the *mganga* took your mind back to your social setting. How are your relationships? And I see Jesus doing the same because when you have a problem, through the Bible, reading the words of Jesus, it will pinpoint some things that you should put right. And in that sense I see Jesus as a *mganga,* yes.

JESUS AS *ODUNSINI* OR TRADITIONAL HEALER IN GHANA

The Data

Like the data presented from Kenya and Uganda, individual responses to the question of Jesus as *odunsini* or traditional healer in Ghana are best conveyed on a continuum ranging from a positive acceptance, "Yes, Jesus is *odunsini,* that's a healer. Yes," to a vehement rejection, "Christ could *never* have been an *odunsini.*"[79] Most responses fall between these two poles, with many interviewees weighing the positive and negative factors in depicting Jesus this way. A summary of the views expressed indicates how controversial the image is to these Ghanaian Christians. Table 3–3 displays the responses of the twenty-eight individuals with whom the question was discussed.

Once again, data from the focus groups with whom it was discussed further confirm that the image is disputable, as evidenced in Table 3–4.

Individual Responses	Statistic	Percentage
Positive responses only	6/28	21%
Negative responses only	12/28	43%
Positive and negative responses	10/28	36%
Overall verdict positive: 6/10		
Overall verdict negative: 4/10		
Total responses overall positive	12/28	43%
Total responses overall negative	16/28	57%

TABLE 3–3. INDIVIDUAL RESPONSES IN GHANA TO THE IMAGE
OF JESUS AS *ODUNSINI*

Focus Group Responses	Statistic	Percentage
Positive responses only	3/5	60%
Negative responses only	1/5	20%
Positive and negative responses	1/5	20%
Overall verdict positive: 0/1		
Overall verdict negative: 1/1		
Total responses overall positive	3/5	60%
Total responses overall negative	2/5	40%

TABLE 3–4. FOCUS GROUP RESPONSES IN GHANA TO THE IMAGE
OF JESUS AS *ODUNSINI*

The Meaning of Odunsini

The image of Jesus as *odunsini* is contentious in Ghana primarily due to the different interpretations of the term, particularly in light of modern mission history in Ghana. As in Kenya and Uganda, respondents express various denotations and connotations of *odunsini*. The first range of meanings clusters around the perception that *odunsini* is a healer. Samuel Aboa, former principal of the Presbyterian Teachers' College in Akropong-Akuapem and a resident expert in the Twi language, pointed out that the root word refers to cutting the bark of a tree and on this basis concluded, "I understand *odunsini* as someone who uses plants to heal." Others, including Catholic lay man Samuel Asubonteng, voiced corroboration of this interpretation of the "herbalist":

> My understanding of *odunsini* has nothing to do with fetish, with the worship of lesser gods. My understanding of *odunsini* is a herbalist, somebody who has been trained or been gifted to heal or cure, with the admixture of herbs and the earth. Maybe we can relate him to an alchemist, that's *odunsini*.

The term *medicine man* is also used synonymously, with a few respondents describing their own experience of treatment by this kind of traditional healer. For example, despite being raised in a Christian home, Kwesi Dickson has no hesitation in relating how he grew up being treated by "the local medicine person, who would apply herbs and things to cure us." Asked if these healers were understood to draw upon other spiritual powers, he replied, "No, no, no. They're those who have the expertise to cure." Moreover, members of the focus group of Ghanaian Protestant laity interpreted *odunsini* in relation to Jesus as "the great physician." Finally, Catholic priest Matthew Edusei added the further dimension that "*odunsini* provides protection against witches and other evil forces."

A second range of meanings, however, conveys more negative connotations surrounding the term *odunsini*. Dickson clearly contrasted his understanding of the *odunsini* as herbalist, delineated above, to "the charlatans who would ask you to go and bring the left ear of a crow and that kind of thing." Others interpreted *odunsini* as "the fetish priest," "people who will consult oracles, consult their *deities*," or "*odunsini* might have reference to other things apart from God. And intermediaries that can be described as idols." Another respondent spoke of "a typical Akan *odunsini*—we used to use the word *obosomfo*—the fetish priest who worshiped an idol is regarded as *odunsini*." Further descriptions included "a spiritualist," a "witchdoctor," a "medicine man" who incurs spirits in healing, or "a juju man." According to Florence Y. B. Yeboah, "*Odunsini* is one who heals with evil powers," a perception confirmed by Protestant clergyman Thomas Oduro, who summed up:

> Well, the plural for *odunsini* is *adensiufoo*. The *adensiufoo* work through some spirits. They consult spirits to heal. It's something like an occultic practice, depending on the spirits to know what herbs to use, and also to know the cause of the disease and the prescription for the disease.

Thus the selected Ghanaian Christians clearly expressed contrasting interpretations of the term *odunsini*, and this accounts significantly for the ambivalence regarding the image of Jesus as *odunsini*. Before exploring further reasons for the mixed reactions, it is worth noting alternative suggestions for vernacular expressions considered more constructive for portraying Jesus. For example, Nana Dokua I countered the idea of *odunsini* with another Twi term, saying, "*Oyaresafo*, that's how we call him, *Oyaresafo*." She stated that this term means "a healer," and admitted that she associates *odunsini* with "fetish." Probed further for the difference between the two terms, she explained that Jesus as *oyaresafo* "doesn't do with the roots and the leaves and so on. He just speaks one word and you are healed." Another vernacular term recommended for Jesus was *oduyefoo*. Catholic lay man George Hagan explained it as "someone who treats us. Someone who makes us whole, heals us." Likewise, Catholic Bishop Palmer-Buckle suggested the same term meaning "somebody who makes healing or medicines," and he differentiated it slightly from *odunsini* as "somebody who deals with herbs, roots, and the rest of it." Finally, Catholic Bishop Peter Sarpong suggests the same term and outlines its significance in relation to Jesus:

> Jesus as *Oduyefoo*, the doctor or the medicine man. Jesus is the answer to all ailments—ailments of the body, ailments of the soul, ailments of the mind. He is the only one who has the power to unite human beings so that there is no friction between one individual and another, one group and another. Jesus does not only heal, he enables the healed to heal. After making you whole and sound, Jesus is able to empower you to be the transmitter of this wholistic healing to others.[80]

Rationale for the Image of Jesus as Odunsini

The three main reasons put forward in support of Jesus as traditional healer in Kenya and Uganda are similarly expressed in Ghana. Hence, where perceptions overlap, the discussion of the Ghanaian material is minimized. First, a few Ghanaians asserted that Jesus fulfills the role that the traditional healer plays in their African society. Therefore, it is meaningful to portray Jesus in this way in order to inculturate the gospel. For example, Catholic priest Aggrey equated *odunsini* with "healer" and fully agreed with its application to Jesus. Probed further as to whether he personally thinks of Jesus as *odunsini*, he responded, "Oh, yes. Because he heals, he cures sickness." More significantly, Catholic priest Edusei initiated the following perspective on Jesus' relevance to life in Ghana, that is, before any question of Jesus as *odunsini* arose in discussion:

> And because people have a sense of fear, given by the cultural milieu, Jesus now becomes, if you want, almost the role that the traditional witchdoctor was playing. Because the traditional witchdoctor was protecting those who came under him from the influence of the devil, or witches. Now, Jesus provides that. So some commentators are saying, they are performing the same role as the traditional witchdoctors, and the methods can be the same. So, for a lot of these people, that is what is happening.

Later in the conversation he responded to the question posed regarding Jesus as *odunsini*:

> *Oh*, yes! *Odunsini*, that's what I was saying about the role of Christ in our traditional context—how the tradition is shaping our understanding of Christ, and the emphasis. *Odunsini* provides protection against witches and other evil forces. They believe that Jesus can do that. There are two ways that is done: one is prayer, with nothing involved, just prayer. The other one is using all kinds of things, it can be blessed water, or a candle, or something. But people do have faith in these things!

It must be noted that Edusei voiced serious reservations about the image of Jesus as *odunsini*, aspects of which are incorporated in the next section. However, the observations underlined here include, first, his recognition of how the image meets people's perceived needs through concepts they understand, thereby inculturating Christianity in a meaningful way. Second, he explicitly acknowledged that the traditional context "is *shaping* our understanding of Christ." And finally, despite admitting "a lot of reservations," he called for dialogue, "because through dialogue we can *purify* the concepts, we can educate ourselves, we can learn from others." It is this openness to inculturation, then, which fuels the motivation for some Ghanaian Christians to consider depicting Jesus as *odunsini*.

The main reason expressed for accepting the image of Jesus as traditional healer, akin to the situation in Kenya and Uganda, is the correspondence found between the ministries of the traditional healer and of Jesus. Parallels include their respective powers to heal and to confront and conquer evil forces. Raphael Avornyo, in the focus group of Ghanaian Catholic laity, drew the correspondence explicitly:

> What the *odunsini* does is to try to help that particular person, to draw him out of sickness. And he uses all his strength, all his power, all his faculties to try to help that person. And that is just exactly what Jesus Christ does. He is there to help us out of the situations which we have, and so they are the same, it's the same thing.

Ghanaian Christians also draw attention to seemingly parallel methods employed for healing. It is again striking that four of the twenty-seven individual respondents with whom it was discussed single out the story of Jesus mixing saliva with mud in healing the blind man as biblical rationale for viewing Jesus as *odunsini*. One example of this reasoning comes from Protestant lay man Lawrence Darmani, who wrestles with the image partly on account of a negative personal experience with a traditional healer. In his words,

> If I call Jesus *odunsini*, I have to sieve a few things out of that name in my mind, and I'm capable of doing that. I would see the end result of it. I will see him as a person who is *odunsini* who eventually does the healing. Fortunately I have concepts like Jesus spits onto the ground and makes some mud, and then heals somebody by putting it on the eyes, and the person is healed. Now, that's very helpful for me to see him as *odunsini* because he used something. He used some object, and then smeared it on the eyes of this blind person, and then says, "Go and wash," and then the person is healed. *Odunsini* is somebody like that! So yes, I can see Jesus as *odunsini*, in that respect.

Finally, a few respondents bore witness to contextual evidence for Jesus being perceived as *odunsini* or traditional healer. Catholic priest Aggrey in Mampong-Akuapem not only attested to the image being operative for him personally, but also responded with some degree of surprise in his voice when asked if he speaks of Jesus as *odunsini* to his parishioners: "Yes, I do! Yes! Because *odunsini* cures sicknesses, and Jesus also cures sicknesses. So, Jesus can be compared to the *odunsini*." Moreover, members of the focus group of Ghanaian Protestant laity confirmed, when probed, that the image of Jesus as *odunsini* is already part of their own Christian experience and that it is used in public ministry, although they do not apparently differentiate *odunsini* from healer.

Furthermore, a few respondents referred to vernacular songs that employ terms for Jesus as the traditional healer. Catholic Bishop Palmer-Buckle cited a vernacular song referring to Jesus as *oduyefoo*, the term suggested as an alternative to *odunsini*. Anthony Kornu of the focus group of Catholic clergy explained that the Twi term *odunsini* is equivalent to *doyola* in his vernacular, Ewe. He cited a song employing the term, which he paraphrased as "Cure me. Cure me of my illness. When I am well, I will follow you." Lastly, Johnson Asare of the focus group of Ghanaian Protestant clergy added, "And I think in our songs, we sing something like "*odunsini*—he is a healer who doesn't use herbs." So I think we got it right—he's *odunsini*, but one who doesn't use herbs or stones." Hence the contextual evidence for Jesus being perceived as *odunsini* or traditional healer was not widespread in the research findings, yet there were some indications that the image is operative among Ghanaian Christians.

Problems with the Image of Jesus as Odunsini

As in Kenya and Uganda, the most common reason given by the selected Ghanaian Christians for rejecting the image of Jesus as traditional healer is the negative connotations associated with *odunsini* or its equivalent in other vernaculars. For example, Protestant clergyman Dan Antwi stressed the importance of Jesus as healer and offered vernacular titles to that effect. However, when asked about *odunsini*, he replied, "*Odunsini*? That one would be getting to the pagan expression. People wouldn't take that one." Similarly, Hagan concluded, "There *must* be a Twi word which is useful, but *odunsini* can *only* refer to Christ metaphorically, and in a very weak way, most inadequate way."

Next, if some of the Ghanaian interviewees found support for Jesus as *odunsini* in light of parallels drawn between the healing ministries of the two figures, other respondents pointed out contrasts in this regard. After defining the term through its root derivation, traditional leader Nana Addo Birikorang objected, "There is no example of Christ ever having used herbal medicine or anything for anything, in the Bible. And therefore Christ, to me, could never have been an *odunsini*." Likewise Oduro, who was quoted above regarding the traditional healers consulting with spirits to effect cures, pointed out:

> But that is different from Jesus as a healer. He does not depend on any spirit to tell him, "This is the cause of the sickness," and also, "Use this and use that." No. The moment you approach him he knows what is wrong with you, and he tells you. He does not wait to be possessed by any spirit for the prescription or for the cause. So that is the basic difference between Jesus as a healer and then *odunsini*.

Thus juxtaposing the healing ministries of Jesus and the *odunsini* can potentially work positively or negatively in assessing this image for Jesus, according to the witness of these Ghanaian Christians.

Other dangers evidently emerge in drawing close correspondences between Jesus and the traditional healer. Despite the openness to inculturating Christianity that Edusei expressed, he added, "I also see a lot of dangers with that, of people not making a complete distinction between the two. Because as you know, *odunsini* might have reference to other things apart from God, and intermediaries that can be described as idols." He further noted people's propensity for "personalizing the power" and locating it in the Christian minister rather than in Christ himself. He warned, with slight laughter:

> "A powerful minister," they would say, you know? You're not a powerful minister! You're an instrument. And the tendency is that it stops them from going to Christ themselves; they run to the minister. They might not have the basic confidence to sit down and pray themselves. But the minister just leads you to Christ; he is not Christ, he cannot be.

Related to this factor of human engagement in healing ministries, Dickson expressed caution on the basis of personal experience encountering "bizarre practices" employed in healing by certain church members. On this basis he concluded, "So one has to be careful how one uses *odunsini* and things. You have got to qualify them very carefully, in order not to give very strange misunderstanding."

Finally, a few Ghanaian respondents expressed the equivalent concern voiced by Kenyans and Ugandans regarding the image of the traditional healer reducing Jesus in such a way as to jeopardize his rightful status. For example, Protestant lay woman Virginia Dankwa, a medical doctor, interprets *odunsini* as "medicine man." When probed for her understanding of the term, she replied, "*Odunsini*? Well, medicine men usually incur some spirits in their practices and so on. I think the name, as far as I'm concerned, is a bit *below* the status of Jesus. I wouldn't describe Jesus as *odunsini*." Another Protestant lay woman, Grace Nartey, responded in similar fashion. She explained from her vernacular, Dangme, the equivalent term for traditional healer:

> Unfortunately, for me, *tsofatse* refers to the traditional healer. And I see the traditional healer in a very small light. And therefore for me, Jesus is much, much, much, much bigger than that. But he *is* a healer, I mean he is the ultimate healer and the all-embracing healer.

Conclusion: Jesus as Odunsini

The controversial nature of portraying Jesus as *odunsini* is clearly evident in the almost equal split between those who favor its usage and those who do not. Most of those who accept the image stressed that their support is conditional upon the image being communicated with appropriate qualifications. For example, Darmani was cited above with respect to the biblical rationale he finds for employing the image and the "sieving" process required in doing so. He stressed:

> But it's very, very important for those of us who have grown out of our traditional set-up, that when we are assigning certain traditional names or ascribing certain traditional titles to Jesus Christ, that we are careful to explain the details—especially to even understand the concept behind the use of certain names, and then apply it to the Lord Jesus Christ.

He elaborated further on how he has the scriptures to guide him in discerning what correspondences may be drawn between Jesus and the *odunsini*, while a person from traditional background "hearing about Jesus for the first time, as an *odunsini*" would need "a lot of explanation." For that reason he emphasized the need for Christian teaching, and reflecting his role as the founding editor of *Step Magazine—Ghana,* he concluded:

> For those of us who write about these things, it is very, very crucial that we go back and try to explain the reason for certain names given to certain people within the society. And how, when we are going to later on use that name, we understand that we are not picking all the moss together with the good thing, you see.

Related to this observation, a few respondents noted that the image might be meaningful within academic contexts, but perhaps not elsewhere. For instance, when probed for her overall verdict on Jesus as *odunsini*, Protestant clergywoman Asabea replied, "Yes, yes. To the academia, yes. But I wonder how the typical traditional Christian would take it? Because there might be some confusion." This point was also made by Stephen Antwi, a member of the focus group of Ghanaian Protestant clergy which was conducted during an extended seminar on gospel and culture at the Akrofi-Christaller Memorial Centre for Mission Research and Applied Theology. While the views expressed within this group about Jesus as *odunsini* were largely negative, Antwi admitted, "Actually, a seminar like this will make me accept it, you know, but if I want to go by the way the traditional *odunsini* does his method of healing, then you have to be careful."

A further complication emerged with respect to language(s) employed in ministry, a point that illustrates the critical issue outlined in Chapter 2 concerning the continued domination of colonial languages and their impact upon African Christianity. In this case Kwesi Dickson had agreed that the image of *odunsini* fits with Jesus conceptually. Yet when queried about the term experientially, whether he had spoken of Jesus this way in his own ministry, he responded:

> I *have* spoken, not used the word, I must say. See, part of the problem is that usually as I travel around, I have to use English. But occasionally I will use the word—*odunsini* is the Twi; Mfantse is *nensini*, but it's close. We've used

it but unfortunately the word tends to be understood also in the sense of the mystical, you know, using concoctions or strange things and that kind of charlatan I've been talking about. It tends to be understood also in that sense. So one has to be careful how one uses it.

Thus linguistic factors can seriously impede the use of *odunsini* or its vernacular equivalents, either conducting ministry in colonial languages or, once again, the negative connotations surrounding the term(s). The result is that several respondents confirmed that they have not or would not employ the image in their own ministry, even when they have affirmed that the image fits conceptually. For example, although Darmani is most positive about the potential for understanding Jesus as *odunsini* and acknowledged the stress on Jesus as healer in the ministry of *Step Magazine—Ghana,* he admitted they have never used the term *odunsini* in *Step.* He summed up, with slight laughter:

> As healer, yes. Not as *odunsini* the way we have seen him in our traditional set-up: the old man who sits there, who people go to and he concocts things and then he heals them. But it's a term that can be used. We have not used that term in *Step,* nor even the concept of it, because of the other side of the *odunsini.* We are careful especially because in Ghana we have a lot of traditional practitioners.

Thus a number of factors contribute to the ambivalence with which these Ghanaian Christians respond to the image of Jesus as *odunsini* or traditional healer, yet the expressed reservations evidently cluster around the nucleus of negative connotations surrounding the term.

CONCLUSION: JESUS AS TRADITIONAL HEALER

The central question addressed here is whether or not Jesus as traditional healer is a constructive image for contemporary African Christians. Despite the fact that a few African theologians, such as Kibongi and Setiloane, have proposed the image, most African theologians to date have been reluctant to promote it. Observing this hesitation, Schoffeleers poses a dichotomy between the views of professional theologians and those representing folk theology, or the population at large in sub-Saharan Africa where the *nganga* christological paradigm is said to be widespread. Consequently, the aim of the present discussion has been to discern to what extent the image functions either explicitly or implicitly among the selected African Christians in Kenya, Uganda, and Ghana; how the image is interpreted; and the rationale expressed for supporting or rejecting it.

On the basis of the findings set forth above, all four of Schoffeleers's conclusions are corroborated, yet with some nuancing. First, Schoffeleers's main conclusion is that "in large parts of Black Africa the medicine person [*nganga*] provides a framework within which to conceptualise the person of Christ and the role of the Christian minister."[81] Data from the present qualitative research certainly confirm that the image of Jesus as traditional healer is functioning at least implicitly and to a considerable degree explicitly for significant numbers of the selected African Christians, that is to say, a minimum of almost half of those interviewed. Given that this particular sample represented Christians from mission churches, presumed to be subject to "the Christ of the established churches" or "a Westernized image of the Savior," in Schoffeleers's terminology, the extent to which the image is operative is all the more striking.[82]

Notwithstanding this evidence, it remains questionable whether the image functions as widely as Schoffeleers intimates. Further research, particularly integrating quantitative methods, would be necessary to ascertain the degree of usage more precisely. However, concern stems from the premise upon which Schoffeleers constructs his case for the *nganga* paradigm. Introducing his research by way of the "christological crisis" said to exist in African theology to date, he states:

> Although several christological studies have appeared since, a feeling of crisis persists because those involved in christological research have been unable to reach even a modicum of consensus about a suitable African paradigm for Christ. Some prefer to cast him as Victor, others as Chief, yet others as Ancestor, without any party being able to establish a convincing claim.[83]

From this basis, then, the *nganga* paradigm is purported to be an image already widespread throughout sub-Saharan Africa and therefore, presumably, to warrant such a convincing claim. The question arises, however, as to the rationale for insisting upon a consensus regarding a suitable African paradigm for Christ, when this contravenes the current call for cultivating a plurality of christological images.[84] Therefore, insofar as the *nganga* paradigm is advocated as one image for Jesus currently operative among African Christians, the data from this research definitely provide substantiation. However, in view of the serious reservations voiced by respondents with respect to the image, the present findings do not support any suggestion, whether explicit or implicit, that the image of traditional healer is in any way primary or the most prevalent christological paradigm.

Schoffeleer's second conclusion is that "the *nganga* is a folk paradigm, not a paradigm consciously constructed by professional theologians for the purpose of 'indigenizing' the person of Christ."[85] He further suggests a possible contrast on this account between the *nganga* paradigm and other christological images, such as victor, chief, and ancestor, which are likely not rooted in folk theology. In so doing, he apparently concurs with Kolié's contention, which he notes elsewhere, that African theologians are attempting to introduce christological paradigms that are unknown to the people at large.[86] Once again, the present data clearly confirm Schoffeleer's second conclusion. For, in this case, a definite divergence emerges between the absence of the image in the textual Christologies of the professional theologians under consideration and the presence of the image in the oral Christologies articulated in Kenya, Uganda, and Ghana. Thus there would be no grounds for any claim that this image is created by African theologians and imposed on African Christians, as Kolié suggests with respect to other traditional titles.

However, according to the present research findings, the clear-cut distinction Schoffeleers posits between "elite theologians" and "folk theology" cannot be sustained. Analysis of the oral Christologies reveals that there are respondents who would rightfully be classified as the intellectual elite, that is, highly educated experts who have published in the field of African Christianity, who do express considerable support for the image of Jesus as traditional healer.[87] Conversely, there are significant numbers of those representing the population at large, at least of the urban, educated Christians specified in the research sample, who voice strong opposition to the image. The simple dichotomy proposed, then, is not borne out by the evidence.

Perhaps Kwame Bediako offers a more helpful avenue for interpretation in his insistence upon the need to distinguish African Christianity from the literature on it. Examining the birth of theology in the New Testament and its implications for African theology today, Bediako concludes, "An authentic tradition of literary Christian scholarship can exist only where a living reality of Christian experience is, and is felt to be, relevant to daily life."[88] If the image of Jesus as *mganga* or *odunsini* is considered in light of this process of theological development, the oral Christologies demonstrate that Jesus undoubtedly functions in a way that corresponds to the traditional healer in the living experience of many African Christians. As to why the image is not often found in written or academic theology, two possibilities may be suggested. Perhaps it is a matter of time, for, as Mbiti points out, "African Christianity cannot wait for written theology to keep pace with it."[89] In other words, if the image truly functions meaningfully for Africans in the "substratum of vital Christian experience and consciousness,"[90] it may yet emerge more significantly in academic theology. On the other hand, and especially in view of the three decades since Kibongi suggested the image in writing, if it has not progressed in academic theology, perhaps there are significant reasons to account for this state of affairs. Hence the concerted effort made here to ascertain those factors that prompt and those factors that constrain the image. Before further consideration of these factors, it must be stressed that the complex issue concerning the presence or absence of Jesus as traditional healer within various expressions of African Christianity cannot be adequately explained on the basis of a simple dichotomy between "professional" and "folk" theology. Instead, any divergence between manifestations of "living" and "academic" theology calls attention to the precise nature of the image and to the very process of theological development itself.

Schoffeleers's third conclusion may again be confirmed, yet slightly nuanced on the basis of this research. He underlines that precisely because the *nganga* paradigm is inherently part of folk theology, it allows privileged access to African conceptions of Christ, of sin, and of redemption. Since Schoffeleers's research is largely informed by anthropological literature on the role of *nganga*, his christological interpretation of the traditional healer is shaped accordingly. So, while details of his interpretation may vary somewhat from the views expressed here by the selected African Christians, the present findings concur with

Schoffeleers's observation: "Christ is often referred to as the one true *nganga* because this is an image that the audience intuitively understands and at the same time is seen as rooted in scripture."[91] Thus, in the juxtaposition of these two figures, Jesus and the traditional healer, new horizons of understanding are potentially opened for interpreting Christ and his relation to the existential realities of Africans today. Accordingly, the witness of many of the selected African Christians affirmed that the image does indeed enhance their apprehension of Jesus and his significance to their lives.

In his final conclusion Schoffeleers returns to the initial question, "Why has this *nganga* paradigm, which is so tangibly and extensively present in folk theology, not been exploited by the professional theologians?"[92] The first reason he offers by way of explanation is that there may be "a conscious or unconscious fear of introducing syncretistic notions and practices."[93] Close inspection of the present research data reveals that only two respondents actually used the term *syncretism,* one Catholic priest and one Protestant lay man, and only one employed it in the context of discussing the image of traditional healer. Catholic priest Edusei is quoted above with respect to his call for dialogue in order to purify traditional concepts and to promote further learning. Yet despite his openness to inculturation, he voiced his own reservations about the *odunsini* image and concluded, "I fear it is easy to fall into syncretism, or just merging two things that need to be carefully brought together." Even where the explicit term is not used, the implicit concern undergirds considerable opposition to the image. In the preceding discussion attention was drawn to the enduring negative connotations, the warnings about possible confusion, and the consequent need for care in employing the image, the emphasis on the contrasts between Jesus and the traditional healer, and the genuine concern about reducing Jesus to a level below his rightful status. Moreover, even when the image is accepted, very often support is only granted on the condition that adequate instruction accompany its usage in order to differentiate Jesus from the traditional figure. Thus, for example, Samson Obwa in the focus group of Kenyan Protestant clergy concluded from his own ethnic society, "The Luos argue that he is a *mganga waganga*—they differentiate Jesus, that one they know. He is more than just a *mganga*. He is a *mganga waganga*, so with that one they can refer to Jesus." Thus Schoffeleers is accurate in identifying the fear of syncretism as a major cause for neglecting the image of Jesus as traditional healer in written theology, for such apprehensions evidently account for many of the reservations expressed by the selected African Christians.

What, then, can be concluded about this controversial image for Jesus? The relatively equal weighting of acceptance and rejection is abundantly clear from the numbers represented and the reasons cited. The range of possible responses was well summed up by Jane Mathu in the focus group of Kenyan PACWA women, and her explanation serves to recapitulate central points of the preceding discussion:

I think it would depend on the community that you have come from. Like, in my community there are no *wagangas*, or not many. But there are some

communities where actually almost everybody depends on the *waganga*, especially those who have not come across Christianity. And if you told them
Jesus is a *mganga* they would be really excited. But for those people who
have learned about the love of Jesus, it will be almost a heresy, I mean an
insult to Christianity, because a *mganga* is not somebody you would be proud
to be identified with. It's somebody I would associate with a lot of Satanism
or demons. The kind of things I have heard of or read about *waganga*—I
don't think I would associate Jesus with the *mganga*. But as I have said, it
depends on the people you are talking to, the community where they have
come from, and how much they have heard about Jesus or Christianity.

Given this spectrum of potential perceptions regarding Jesus as traditional healer,
strict conclusions are inadvisable. However, a brief consideration of the critical
issues prompting African Christologies and the criteria set forth for engaging
critically with them sheds light on current complexities concerning the image.

On the one hand, negative factors constraining this depiction of Jesus are
clarified in light of certain critical issues concerning the Christologies. For example, historical and missiological factors, specifically colonial and missionary
practices, account significantly for the hostility toward the African traditional
healers, for the distortions in terminology describing these figures, and for the
consequent alienation of African Christians from traditional healing practices. As
a result, linguistic factors feature prominently in restricting the use of the image,
primarily due to the negative connotations but also the continued domination of
colonial languages. In addition, concern has been expressed about contemporary
Christian witness where certain questionable practices encountered in some healing ministries hinder further promotion of Jesus as traditional healer.

On the other hand, positive factors supporting the image are more understandable when considered against the criteria African Christians have set for
their own christological agenda. Certainly the aspects of theological and linguistic relevance form crucial factors, as the evidence has shown that this portrait of Jesus may potentially deepen African Christians' understanding of him
in relation to concepts from the African heritage. The findings have definitely
confirmed Kibongi's suggestion in 1969 that Jesus is perceived to accomplish
the work of *nganga* in terms of healing, protecting from evil powers, and restoring community relations where disruption has occurred in the social fabric.
Not only may Jesus' role be understood to fulfill that of the African traditional
healer, but also the role of this healer may serve to enhance Africans' understanding of the biblical affirmations regarding Jesus' life, death, and resurrection. That is to say, the holistic approach to healing in African tradition may
foster insight into biblical affirmations regarding Jesus' healing ministry as
signifying the inauguration of the kingdom of God in all its individual, corporate, and cosmic dimensions. Aylward Shorter builds a strong case for this
observation in his in-depth analysis of Jesus in relation to the "witchdoctor."
After a close comparison of their respective healing ministries, he forms the following conclusion concerning how the African traditional healer may point to
larger tenets concerning Jesus:

Jesus, therefore, used the techniques of popular healers and exorcists of his time, and to that extent, at least, he was like a traditional diviner-healer or witchdoctor. Scientific medicine was not a possible option in his lifetime, or for many centuries afterwards. Nevertheless, in antedating medical science, Jesus also escaped its limitations, notably its comparative lack of interest in the environmental, social and moral aspects of healing. Jesus shared the integrated approach to healing which characterizes the so-called witchdoctor, but he carried it infinitely further in every dimension. In his own life he offered a comprehensive redemption for the world's sickness, and in his own person he offered a release for the sick, the sinful, the sad, the aliens, the outcasts, the poor and the ritually unclean. In Jesus' message there was no condition of diminished humankind, no sickness, disability or guilt which was impervious to the liberating and restorative power of God's love encountered in his own life and person.[94]

Therefore the image bears potential theological relevance for Christians today, not only in Africa, but for those from different medical traditions as well.

Further consideration of the criteria for assessing the African Christologies awaits the conclusion to the chapter. For the present, it is tentatively suggested that the positive factors that might ensue from portraying Jesus as traditional healer allow room for the cautious promotion and the judicious employment of this image for Jesus, provided it is accompanied with adequate instruction. Part of that educational process will require an honest reassessment of "the despised witchdoctor," as Shorter emphasizes:

For the image of the traditional doctor to become respectable enough to be applied to Christ, we must not only renounce the exaggeration which turned him into an agent of Satan, but we must purify and transform the concepts of healing and divining with which he is factually associated.[95]

At the same time, however, negative connotations surrounding the traditional healer may be accounted for significantly, but not entirely, by colonial and missionary influence. Whatever the source and the legitimacy of such reservations about this traditional figure, as long as negative associations endure, African Christians will rightfully resist making facile comparisons between this healer and Jesus, especially if to do so would create confusion.

Presenting the negative and positive factors together does not entail contradiction; rather, the two must be held simultaneously in creative tension. Issues of gospel and culture inevitably require honest and careful assessment of the potential for creating understanding or misunderstanding, for opening or obscuring horizons for understanding Jesus. Nor is such a dialectical approach without precedent. A return to the witness of Kibongi indicates that, following his explication of Jesus as *nganga*, he nonetheless concludes, "Our attitude towards *nganga* in particular, and negro-African culture in general, or any other value, is both negative and positive. This double attitude seems to be dictated by revelation itself."[96] Citing examples from Abraham, Israel, and Paul, he underscores how any point of contact between human culture and biblical revelation necessitates the dual process of being "continually called both to leave our world behind, and to take it with us, so that Christ may become more and more our Saviour and Lord."[97] Or, as one of the African voices above graphically put it, to ensure that "we are not picking all the moss together with the good thing."

CONCLUSION: JESUS AS LIFE-GIVER

This first christological model emerges from the centrality of life in black African thought. Traditional concepts of life, as interpreted by selected African Christians, form the intellectual constructs that converge with biblical affirmations to formulate the image of Jesus as life-giver, or the one who fulfills the aspirations for life in black Africa. The corresponding image of Jesus as healer adds further signification that Jesus restores life wherever it has been diminished, and that he upholds life against any powers that threaten it. Both of these associated images are well attested in the oral and textual Christologies under consideration. Attention has also been extended to the related but controversial image of Jesus as traditional healer.

The focal point of interpreting Jesus in relation to life is certainly not original here. On the contrary, the concern is fundamental to the birth and growth of African theology in recent times. It is especially noteworthy that the closing words of the "Final Communiqué" encapsulate the stated aim in forming EAAT as follows: "We undertake this journey of service through theology so that all the women, men, and children of our lands may be able 'to have life and live abundantly.'"[98] In attempting to pursue this aim, these theologians specify their task as addressing the needs of post-independent Africa from the standpoint of their belief in Jesus Christ. To do so, they call for "an interdisciplinary methodology of social analysis, biblical reflection, and active commitment to be with the peoples in their endeavors to build a better society."[99] In view of this overall aim, then, the present question is what progress has been made toward this end with the particular images of Jesus as life-giver, healer, and traditional healer. The interrelated images are considered together in light of the criteria set forth in Chapter 2, namely, the appropriateness of sources and methods, and the seven factors of contextual relevance.

Analysis of the sources underlying these images of Jesus reveals that the African Christians draw upon all four of the recommended sources, but to different degrees. First, the Bible and Christian heritage find strong attestation in the textual and oral Christologies, primarily in the gospel accounts of Jesus' life-giving and healing ministry, but also in wider biblical sources and theological affirmations. The primary place of the Bible has been highlighted through quotes from Pobee that are representative of the expressed views of other respondents. Second, the African heritage also features prominently in the African concepts of life and healing that shape contemporary views of Jesus, and especially the image of Jesus as traditional healer. Third, respondents appealed to the living experience of the church as grounds for both promoting and for curbing the portrayal of Jesus as healer. That is, they claimed strong justification for this image on account of contemporary experiences of healing. Furthermore, they underscored the import of widespread healing ministries, including how the historic churches have been influenced by the African Initiated Churches and by the Pentecostal movement. However, they also voiced certain cautions arising from some healing ministries in order to restrain distorted images of Jesus as healer.

The fourth source recommended for constructing African theology is contemporary realities in Africa. Here, respondents acknowledged the extensive suffering in Africa as reason for approaching Jesus as life-giver and healer, and certainly this contributes to the effectiveness of the image as a lived reality for many African Christians. However, the predominant perspective voiced in the oral Christologies concerned Jesus healing through prayer, or through medicine, or sometimes a combination of the two. While in no way disparaging these perspectives, it must be stressed that relatively few of the selected African Christians articulated the need for sociopolitical analysis of the contemporary realities related to health as a starting point for understanding Jesus as healer. Nor did they generally address the structures that significantly account for people's suffering ill health, nor advocate theological commitment to challenge such unjust structures. Ela is the obvious exception in this regard, followed by Bujo, Nasimiyu, and Pobee, who move in the same direction. More of the interview respondents' views along these lines will be brought to light in Chapter 6, "Jesus as Leader." Nonetheless, further theological reflection upon current issues related to health across black Africa would enhance the understanding and experience of Jesus as healer and help to guard against undue emphasis upon "faith healing." For example, given the scale of devastation wrought by AIDS in Africa today, it is surprising that relatively few respondents referred to this crisis in relation to Jesus as healer or in relation to his significance to life in their context.[100] Clearly the ongoing scourge of AIDS calls for much greater attention by way of orthopraxis than the present research data reveal. Thus the main point here is the present imbalance among the first three sources as grist to the mill of christological formulation, and the relative neglect of the fourth source.

A variety of methods have been exemplified in employing the sources delineated above. Drawing upon Nyamiti's typology of inculturation and liberation Christologies, there is evidence for each of the main approaches he outlines. With respect to inculturation methodologies, clear substantiation is found for movement from the Bible to "African reality," or applying biblical teachings about Jesus to the contemporary African situation. Conversely, there is ample demonstration of movement from "African reality" to Christology in traditional concepts of life and healing being used to open new avenues for understanding Jesus. Moreover, the data show that personal experience of Jesus as healer featured prominently in shaping these African Christians' views about Jesus. Their combined witness thus attests to the vitality of Christian experience that marks African Christianity. Then, with regard to liberation methodologies, the discussion above indicated the limited evidence of methodological departure in the contemporary context as the locus for christological reflection. Again, more concentrated efforts in these directions will deepen the efficacy of African Christologies.

Further considerations regarding christological methodology stem from the two questions raised in Chapter 2 and addressed specifically to the African theologians under consideration. The first question concerns what contributions have been made toward a new theological methodology that will produce the kind of contextual theology being advocated for Africa. Here the combined efforts of various theologians drawing upon their respective fields of expertise indeed signaled new gains in creative methodologies. For example, from his background of New Testament scholarship, Pobee models in-depth biblical exegesis integrated with intensive analysis of aspects of Akan culture, resulting in fresh christological insights for Christians in Ghana and beyond. Similarly, Oduyoye's extensive knowledge of African cultures and religions provides a firm foundation for elucidating the significance of Jesus in relation to the African heritage. She further exemplifies new modes for expressing theology, as illustrated by reference to her poem on the wholeness of life. In addition, Ela's expertise in sociology fosters acute analysis of the contemporary health-related issues that, together with incisive biblical investigation, enhances his approach to understanding Jesus as healer. There is no doubt that these theologians pave new directions for christological inquiry and expression in Africa today. They further reveal varying degrees of self-assessment, as concerns the second question derived from Mugambi's call for "introspection and self-criticism." For the present, Ela can be singled out for his achievement in this regard, as he clearly distinguishes his theological approach from the common trend of developing christological titles and stresses his priority of beginning with the people "at the bottom." Thus distinct methodological advances are detected in the textual Christologies of these selected theologians.

Finally, a brief summary of the seven aspects of contextual relevance underlines various points made in preceding discussions. Perhaps the greatest strength of these particular images lies in their theological relevance. The evidence has shown that Jesus is understood effectively in relation to the African heritage in terms of his fulfilling the aspirations for life in traditional black Africa and providing the healing previously sought from traditional concepts of God and through traditional healers. This strongly confirms Mbiti's assertion decades ago that the portrait of Jesus as *Christus Victor* is of utmost significance to African Christians:

> The Christian message brings Jesus as the one who fought victoriously against the forces of the devil, spirits, sickness, hatred, fear, and death itself. In each of these areas he won a victory and lives now above the assault of these forces. He is the victor, the one hope, the one example, the one conqueror: and this makes sense to African peoples, it draws their attention, and it is pregnant with meaning. It gives to their myths an absolutely new dimension. The greatest need among African peoples, is to see, to know, and to experience Jesus Christ as the victor over the powers and forces from which Africa knows no means of deliverance.[101]

Not only is Jesus understood in light of African traditions, but these traditions concerning life and health evidently enhance African Christians' grasp of biblical affirmations regarding Jesus' life, death, and resurrection. For example, the holistic, communal, and cosmic dimensions of life and healing according to African and biblical traditions are illuminated. Furthermore, the African Christians establish grounds for interpreting Jesus' healing in light of his comprehensive ministry encompassing healing, salvation, and liberation, an observation to be further elucidated in later chapters. Once again, this corroborates Mbiti's earlier insight concerning the integral relationship between healing and salvation in African Christianity. With healing said to be the highest ministerial office in many African contexts, Mbiti observes: "Consequently this is the peak of the Christian experience of God and Jesus as 'our Saviour.' Divine healing is an extension of the 'saving' benefits of God and Jesus." He concludes:

> Healing brings or increases life. . . . This is a major, if not central, outcome of coming into a faith relationship with "our Saviour." The question is not so much one of "salvation from what," as it is "salvation into what." The answer is clearly that Christians are rescued or saved into a life, a life whose source and sustainer is God or Jesus "our Saviour."[102]

Herein lies the rationale for the first christological model being that of Jesus as life-giver and healer, for certainly these concepts are fundamental to salvation from the perspective of African Christians.

The degree of cultural relevance flows from the theological relevance combined with the vernacular or conceptual relevance of the images. These christological portraits clearly capture the existential realities of life for the overwhelming majority of the selected African Christians, thereby reflecting indigenous perceptions of Jesus operating at the level of religious experience. Thus, to the extent that Jesus is comprehended in light of African concepts of life and healing, to that extent is the sense of his foreignness diminished. Even where African traditions may be waning, Jesus is nonetheless hailed as the one who can revive the former ideals, like wholeness of life. As Oduyoye concludes:

> Much of what we pride ourselves in has become a mirage, hence the relevance of the Christ-event for Africa. In him we see the pattern of life that is capable of resuscitating these ideals and empowering us to gain the wholeness of life that comes out of being taken into his sphere of influence in which we shall live under the rule of God. In Jesus we see the life of one for whom the spirit world is a reality and the reign of God over all, the operative dynamic of life. Jesus becomes for the African, the Finisher of our Wholeness.[103]

Oduyoye and the Circle, among others, also articulate the life-giving and healing images of Jesus in relation to gender issues. For example, they develop the significance of Jesus as life-giver in association with women as life-givers. Also, implications for gender relations stem from the recognition of life being communal and of humanity being made up of male and female.

Certain aspects of the contemporary relevance of these christological images may be added to the strengths outlined above. Research findings certainly manifest the importance of Jesus as life-giver and healer to African Christians today. However, weaknesses emerge with respect to both historical and contemporary relevance. In general, insufficient attention is paid to the history of health-related suffering in Africa and to the church's role in alleviating the current misery ensuing from that history of suffering. Again, Ela has paved the way in this direction, and other theologians follow suit, thereby strengthening the case for African Christianity.[104] For, as Kolié accurately points out, Christians "have, and will continue to have, credit with the African only to the extent that they share, side by side with the African person, *the struggle for life.*"[105] So further christological reflection and action concerning the liberating dimension of the gospel in relation to health issues, such as corrupt health systems, the AIDS pandemic, the lack of potable water, the scandalous proliferation of preventable diseases, and politically induced famine, would fortify African Christianity on the continent. Hence Bujo's call for the church of Africa to become a community of healing, for "Jesus Christ has healed us. He heals all the members of the community, giving life to everybody. And this is a very important aspect of Christology."

Finally, the criterion regarding credibility of witness reinforces key strengths and enduring challenges within African Christianity. Again, the research findings patently demonstrate the vitality of Christian witness to Jesus as life-giver and healer. However, certain reservations regarding the efficacy of the christological images stem from some contemporary healing ministries and from current realities in Africa. Thus, by way of conclusion, there is need to highlight Pobee's exhortation that the healing ministry is a significant part of the mission of God's people and his proposals for Christian involvement in enhancing health education and medical work.[106] No African Christian would likely disagree with Pobee on this account, yet it appears that Christian witness through the ministry of healing needs to be understood and actualized far more comprehensively.

In view of the serious issues that make the images of Jesus as life-giver and healer contestable today, it is crucial that African Christians address the enduring challenges that threaten to distort perceptions of Jesus. As Kolié rightfully insists, "It can only be from the experiential advent of Christ in the vital problems of our communities that a coherent theological discourse will arise and not remain superficial."[107] He further emphasizes, after raising the question of whether Jesus can truly be present in Africa as a healer, that "to give Christ the face of the healer in Africa (even though this was his principal activity in Israel) will not be feasible until the manifold gifts of healing possessed by all of our Christian communities have begun to manifest themselves."[108] Thus Kolié makes the vital point that it is not simply a matter of naming Jesus or ascribing African titles to him, but rather of witnessing that Jesus actually fulfills these important roles in the lives of African Christians today. So in spite of the strong evidence in this chapter for the significant presence of Jesus as life-giver and healer in Africa, there is need to attend to the legitimate challenge Kolié voices as follows:

We must bring it about that Jesus be named precisely by those who will have received and welcomed him. This Jesus will be Healer, Grand Master of Initiation, Ancestor par excellence, or Chief of Chiefs, not because I shall have declared him to be such, but because he will have wrought cures, presided over initiations, and given birth to a free person. His hosts will believe in him no longer on my word, but because they will have seen and heard them themselves, because they will have experienced the liberation he brings, the exodus he works.[109]

With this sober challenge in mind, further facets of Jesus' identity and significance are investigated in the next model of Jesus as mediator.

4

Jesus as Mediator

Jesus Christ is the ultimate embodiment of all the virtues of the ancestors, the realization of the salvation for which they yearned. Further still, Jesus Christ is the Proto-Ancestor, the proto-life-force, bearer in a transcendent form of the primitive "vital union" and "vital force."

—BÉNÉZET BUJO, CONGOLESE THEOLOGIAN

An African ecclesiology can no longer dispense with a christology based on Jesus Christ as Proto-Ancestor and as the source of proto-ancestral vital force. . . . An ecclesiology incarnated into this African world of thought will produce unheard of prophetic consequences in society and community life in modern Africa.

—BÉNÉZET BUJO, CONGOLESE THEOLOGIAN

I think the strongest profile of Jesus that comes through, which I find helpful for my own life, is that of a living companion on your life's journey. The closeness of Jesus, for me, is like the way we appropriate the presence of our ancestors. Jesus functions for me as an ancestor functions for any Akan—an invisible companion, a person whose presence you can sense very keenly, mentors you in your life and he's just there, he's around. So it's this lively presence that I think is most useful for me.

—MERCY ODUYOYE, GHANAIAN THEOLOGIAN

INTRODUCTION

In the interface between biblical and African traditions, concepts of mediation are central. The second christological model investigates how Jesus is understood and experienced as mediator in selected contemporary African contexts where these traditions meet. The chapter is divided into three main sections.

First is a brief introduction to intermediaries in the African heritage, according to selected African Christians, and how these believers view Jesus as mediator. Textual and field research reveals numerous images of Jesus in relation to mediation; the images overlap with one another and with those from other christological models. Some of these images include Jesus as mediator, prophet, priest, lamb, sacrifice, reconciler, advocate, and peacemaker. One of the more significant images to emerge in this category is that of Jesus as ancestor. Attention focuses on this image in the second section of the chapter, before conclusions are drawn in the final section. In keeping with the previous chapter, the aim of this chapter is to outline the rationale for the second christological pattern in the convergence of African and biblical traditions, to interpret its meaning in contemporary African usage, and to consider its significance for contemporary African Christianity.

INTERMEDIARIES IN AFRICAN RELIGIONS

The first christological model began with concepts of life in Africa, since the very foundation and purpose of African religions, as Laurenti Magesa notes, "is life, life in its fullness." Magesa explains:

> The logic of the moral/ethical orientation of African Religion is unmistakable: wherever and whenever there is a diminishment or a destruction of the force of life, something must be done to restore it; whenever there is a breach of order in the universe as established by God through the ancestors, humanity must see to it that harmony is restored. Failing this, humanity will suffer.[1]

When afflictions occur within a community, such as wrongdoing, illness, or witchcraft, African religions recognize various means to discover the reasons for the disharmony in the universe and to prescribe measures for rectifying the problem, thereby restoring the force of life. Intermediaries are those beings who function in these roles of discernment and mediating reconciliation.

Mbiti claims that intermediaries in Africa are found "almost everywhere" and derived from common social and political custom in which people of higher status are approached indirectly through a third party. "It is a widespread feeling among many African peoples that man should not, or cannot, approach God alone or directly, but that he must do so through the mediation of special persons or other beings."[2] Mbiti identifies two types of intermediaries. Some are human beings, including "priests, kings, medicine men, seers, oracles, diviners, rain-makers and ritual elders."[3] The main functions of these human mediums are (1) helping humanity to maintain liturgical contact with God and the spiritual world and (2) attending to the needs of the community. That is, when people relate their needs to the appropriate religious specialist, it is the medium's duty to approach God or the spirit world through prayers, sacrifice, offerings, divination, or dream interpretation according to the need presented.

The second type of intermediary, according to Mbiti, includes spiritual beings believed to assist people in approaching God. He distinguishes between divinities, or "spiritual beings of a relatively high status" such as "nature spirits" or the spirits of deified heroes, clan founders, kings, and chiefs, and the "common populace" of spiritual beings.[4] While human relationships with the spirits certainly vary among different African societies, Mbiti emphasizes the powerful place that many societies grant to the "living dead," the spirits of those who have died recently. These are considered to be the closest links that humans have with the spirit world. They are also regarded as the best intermediaries because they know the needs of humans, from whom they have only recently departed, and they are "bilingual" in speaking the language of humans and the language of the spirits and God. Consequently, they are approached more often than God for minor needs in life. While people are definitely free to approach God directly and do so often, according to Mbiti, they nonetheless feel the need for a bridge between themselves and God. Hence the spiritual intermediaries are seen as "windows and channels through which people may come closer to God."

The idea of intermediaries fits well with the African view of the universe, which holds that the invisible world is in some ways higher than that of man, but God is higher still. In order to reach God effectively it may be useful to approach him by first approaching those who are lower than he is but higher than the ordinary person.[5]

JESUS AS MEDIATOR

With concepts of mediators so important in the African heritage, African Christians have naturally interpreted Jesus in relation to such notions. Kofi Appiah-Kubi observes that the idea of a mediator or intermediary is common among most African societies and asserts that Christ plays the role of the traditional intermediary, approaching God on behalf of the people.[6] François Kabasélé notes contextual evidence in that "most of the movements of spiritual awakening in black Africa are marked by an acute sense of the concept of the intermediary."[7] For example, certain catecheses arose during the era of "adaptation," which sought to relate the worship of Christ to the ancestral concepts widespread throughout Bantu-speaking Africa. In view of this association of Jesus with traditional intermediaries, and in particular the ancestors, this question arises: Can the category of African ancestors function meaningfully as a hermeneutical key for interpreting Jesus Christ in Africa? The remainder of the chapter addresses this central question by introducing ancestors in traditional African thought, raising critical issues surrounding the image of Jesus as ancestor, exploring the image as expressed in the textual and oral Christologies, and arriving at conclusions regarding its significance for African Christianity.

JESUS AS ANCESTOR

INTRODUCTION

Concepts of Ancestor in Africa

The vital role of the ancestors in traditional African thought lies beyond dispute, with clear attestation in the literature on African religions and on African Christianity.[8] Among the primary sources in this study, Bénézet Bujo asserts that the notion of communion with the dead is central to the worldview of African peoples, citing evidence from funeral rites, initiation rites, hunting ceremonies, and other rituals among the Bahema of Congo.[9] Likewise, although Jean-Marc Ela notes that veneration of the ancestors takes different forms in different societies, he concludes:

> In many traditional societies, the cult of the dead is perhaps that aspect of culture to which the African is most attached—the heritage clung to above all else. Indeed, the cult of the ancestors is so widespread throughout Africa that it is impossible to avoid the questions this practice raises for Christian life and reflection.[10]

Offering examples from various contexts across Africa, from the formal recognition of the ancestral cult by some governments, such as the Congolese, to African art including statues and masks, Ela reserves his explanation of the ancestral cult for the Kirdi peoples of Cameroon, among whom he ministered. He acknowledges the threat that increasing urbanization poses to belief in the ancestors, pointing to research conducted in Abidjan that revealed that young people distance themselves from traditional customs or are even unaware of them. In response, Ela questions how the traditional cultural inheritance can be maintained in Christian practice as society changes. He underlines that what is at stake is "an African vision of humanity" enshrined in honoring the ancestors and even urges the church to consider how Christianity in the West could benefit from studying black Africans' communion with their ancestors.[11] Hence he undoubtedly concurs with Bujo's observation that ancestral veneration is one of the fundamental pillars of religion for many ethnic groups in black Africa, and Bujo's consequent conviction expressed as follows:

> In reality, anyone who would propose e.g. an ecclesiology, a christology or a sacramental theology from the point of view of African ancestral veneration, would have to pay particular attention to those living dead, whose commemoration is regarded by their descendants as indispensable and beneficial or even salvific for their earthly existence.[12]

If this is the case, then what is the place and role of the living dead in black Africa? Tanzanian theologian Charles Nyamiti observes that "there is no uniform system of beliefs on ancestors in black Africa."[13] Divergences may be found even within the same social or tribal group, and not all African peoples practice ancestor veneration. Despite such differences, Nyamiti contends that there are enough beliefs shared by most societies to affirm certain common ancestral beliefs in black Africa. He outlines five common elements:

1. *Natural relationship* between the ancestor and his or her earthly relatives, usually based on parenthood, but sometimes on brotherhood or on membership in a secret society.
2. *Supernatural or sacred status* acquired through death and understood in terms of super-human powers and nearness to God. Ancestors are often presented as ambivalent in character, for they can be benevolent to their earthly kin but can also intervene in human affairs to bring harm, particularly punishment for relatives who have neglected them or committed some offense within the community. Consequently the ancestors are sometimes feared, although the living normally expect care and protection from them as well as various benefits like long life, children, and wealth. Angry ancestors are generally appeased through prayers and various rituals involving food or drinks.
3. *Mediation* between God and humanity because of their supernatural status and proximity to God.
4. *Title to regular sacred communication* with earthly relatives, with whom the ancestors long to maintain contact.
5. *Exemplarity*, as models of good behavior.[14]

Ghanaian theologian Peter Sarpong adds the central conviction that not everyone becomes an ancestor, but only those who fulfill specific conditions. The first condition is to pass through the critical stages of life to attain adulthood, which is generally determined by marriage rather than age and which assumes procreation. An unmarried person, however old, is disqualified from ancestorhood because of not having transmitted life to another person and is therefore considered "a useless person whose name should be blotted out of memory."[15] A second requirement is to die a natural death, excluding tragic deaths such as those by accident, suicide, unclean diseases, or in childbirth. A third qualification is an exemplary life by tribal standards, demonstrating good character and behavior according to traditional morality.

Finally, in summarizing the role of ancestors in Africa, several main points emerge from the literature. Aylward Shorter draws attention to one approach in which ancestors are very often understood as no more than liturgical companions of the living. He explains that the spirits of the dead are not always invoked as those to whom veneration is addressed. Rather,

the worshipper prays in solidarity with them to the Creator, using prayer-formulas or sacred places which they have bequeathed to him. These are regarded as pledges of divine favour, since the dead are held to stand in a close relationship to God, even if they are not invoked themselves.[16]

According to Shorter, this approach is found among numerous African peoples, including a cluster of those in central Kenya. A second key role, identified above, is that of mediators between God and humanity, whether the ancestors are interpreted as intercessors or plenipotentiaries. A third function of the living dead Mbiti summarizes as "guardians of family affairs, traditions, ethics and activities."[17] They are said to be the makers and custodians of tribal law, and the conviction that the ancestors are watching over the human community to regulate daily life and behavior serves as a potent sanction to morality.

Much more than spiritual law-enforcers, however, the fundamental role of the ancestors is as invisible participants in the ongoing life of the human community. One vital component here is that they continue the ties of kinship beyond death, linking together family and clan members in the visible and invisible worlds. Thus kinship lies at the very heart of ancestral concepts. As Magesa explains, "Kinship is what in large measure constitutes life itself and its mystique. And kinship is most intensely and most meaningfully realized and expressed in and by the ancestor relationship."[18] Ancestral communion therefore entails acts of remembrance that actualize the presence of the departed for the living with whom they are in continuity. Moreover, ancestral communion is marked by a reciprocal relationship of mutual action that enhances life for the community in human and cosmic solidarity. Magesa notes further: "The ancestors and their descendants are in a constant state of exchanging gifts and favors. This is what communion requires; it is what remembrance means. This dialectic strengthens the life force of the world for the sake of living humanity."[19] Thus the ultimate goal of ancestral veneration in Africa, encompassing ancestral communion as well as rituals of preventing and redressing harm in the community, is to seek balance and harmony among all aspects of the created order, that is, between the living and the dead, among the living, and with creation. It is this harmony that constitutes the abundant life the ancestors received from the founders of the clan, lineage, or ethnic group, which they observed themselves, thereby becoming ancestors, and which is to be transmitted from generation to generation.

Critical Issues regarding Jesus in Relation to African Ancestors

Before considering how this brief overview of ancestral concepts bears upon the image of Jesus as ancestor, certain critical issues must be raised regarding Jesus in relation to African ancestors. Methodological concerns begin with the problem of terminology, for the word *ancestor* is one of many attempts to translate various African vernacular terms. For example, Mbiti objects to the terms *ancestors* and *ancestral spirits* being used generally for the departed because not all spirits are ancestors; instead, he advocates simply "spirits" or "the living dead," whichever is applicable.[20] Shorter concurs, yet calls for further clarification to justify the apparent paradox of the living dead. After weighing other

English translations, such as *ghost, shade,* and *those who are dead,* he suggests the phrase "spirits of the dead."[21] The concern extends beyond the lack of terminological agreement, however, for as Shorter observes, "It is very instructive to note the difficulty African Christians have in translating the English term 'ancestor' back into an African language."[22] Citing an example of Swahili words under consideration for use in the All-Africa Eucharistic Prayer, he underlines how certain vernacular terms carry associations deemed incompatible with a Christian attitude to the departed. Therefore, akin to the situation with the image of Jesus as traditional healer, the connotations surrounding vernacular terms and their English translations will necessarily influence the interpretation of Jesus as ancestor.

Related to the linguistic concern of translating vernacular terms is the deeper issue regarding the theological interpretation of African ancestral spirits. One's view of these spirits will patently affect one's receptivity toward the use of this category for depicting Jesus Christ. For example, in contrast to the delineation of ancestors summarized above, Richard Gehman, an evangelical missionary in Kenya, builds on the premise that "traditional African belief in the ancestral spirits is one of those items in ATR [African Traditional Religion] which is totally incompatible with the Christian faith."[23] Given this starting point, he draws radically different conclusions concerning these spirits:

> In biblical perspective these are none other than the unclean spirits, the fallen angels who serve their master, even Satan. Nothing could be plainer in the Bible than the divine abhorrence and active opposition to any contact, communication or relationship with the ancestral spirits, divinities or other spirits.[24]

In addition to divergent interpretations of African ancestral spirits, theological problems concerning the image of Jesus as ancestor are multiplied by three critical questions intrinsically related to one another. The first is the longstanding question of whether the African ancestors are actually worshiped or merely venerated. In discussions of African theology in the twentieth century, Harry Sawyerr pointed out the difficulties manifested by the opposing views of those who consider ancestral cults as "abominable idolatry" and those who deny that real worship takes place.[25] These contrasting interpretations likewise emerge in the present research and undoubtedly color perceptions of Jesus as ancestor, as evidenced in the analysis to come.

A second, closely connected question is the place of the African ancestors in the Christian faith. Ela forms a key witness here, for in accordance with his criticism of a titular christological approach referred to in the discussion of Jesus as healer, he dissents from those enthusiastically endorsing Jesus as ancestor. In conversation he acknowledged the image as a prominent theme at present and commended Bujo's contribution in this regard. Nevertheless, he argued that the Christology of the ancestor Christ is not new, being essentially Pauline Christology, and that it has not yet been examined at a sufficiently systematic and critical manner in Africa. Instead, he asserted: "For me the central question that has to be reconsidered is that of the place of the ancestors in an African christology. We have not elucidated this problem." Elsewhere he has indeed tackled the issue, identifying it as of crucial importance to any discussion of the Christian faith that takes into account an existing culture in order for the gospel to purify and liberate it. After highlighting the pervasiveness of honoring ancestors in Africa and explicating one example of it in Cameroon, he pinpoints the real issue for Christians: "Is there any place in our life in Jesus Christ for maintaining a relationship between the living and the dead? Or must Africans break their relationship with their ancestors if they are to be converted to the gospel?"[26] Varying responses to these questions surface in written and oral discussions of African Christology, particularly in relation to the veneration of saints in Catholic tradition, and again influence receptivity to the image of Jesus as ancestor.

A third question stems directly from the second, as clearly indicated in the conversation with Ela. Immediately following the statement above regarding the place of the ancestors in African Christology, he raised the fundamental question of ancestral mediation in light of New Testament claims for Jesus as the only mediator between God and man. If Jesus is the universal savior, then what is the role of the ancestors in the history of salvation? Certainly questions regarding the uniqueness and normativeness of Jesus amid contemporary religious pluralism are pivotal in the field of global Christologies today.[27]

Thus important questions arise regarding the African ancestors in connection with Christology: the theological interpretation of their identity; their place within African religions, including whether they are worshiped or venerated; and their place within the Christian faith, especially in light of Christian saints, and their role as mediators in relation to Christian claims of the sole mediation of Jesus Christ. While in-depth inquiry into these issues lies beyond the present scope, they are introduced here as aspects of the theological matrix in which the image of Jesus as ancestor has developed.

JESUS AS ANCESTOR IN SELECTED TEXTUAL CHRISTOLOGIES

With the exception of Ela all six of the selected African theologians lend varying degrees of assent and priority to the image of Jesus as ancestor. Present elaboration centers upon the two leading proponents in this regard, namely, John Pobee and Bénézet Bujo. The fact that these two are, respectively, a West African Protestant Anglophone and a Central African Catholic Francophone reflects the widespread appeal of the image throughout the continent.

John Pobee

Pobee was among the earliest advocates of the ancestral image for Jesus in modern African theology, as expressed in his 1979 work *Toward an African Theology.* The stated aim of this volume is to translate the Christian faith into genuine African categories and thought forms. Among the main aspects of the

Akan worldview on which he focuses, Pobee explains, "perhaps the most potent aspect of Akan religion is the cult of the ancestors. They, like the Supreme Being, are always held in deep reverence or even worshipped."[28] He then delineates the beliefs about their identity as departed clan members, their qualifications for ancestry, and their ongoing participation in the community in terms similar to those outlined above. He later returns to this traditional category of the ancestors in his concentrated reflections on Christology. In light of the fundamental role of ancestral veneration within Akan thought and society, Pobee poses his critical christological questions as follows: "Who is Jesus Christ? What manner of man is he? How does he affect my life? Why should an Akan relate to Jesus of Nazareth, who does not belong to his clan, family, tribe, and nation?"[29] The answers to these questions, in his view, will largely determine the rooting of Christianity in Africa.

Before tackling the questions directly, Pobee highlights the problem raised because the Nicene Creed, ratified and expanded by the Council of Constantinople, became the plumb-line of orthodoxy for Western Christianity. That creed was forged in a predominantly Hellenistic society and articulated in the language and concepts of the time, such as "substance" and "hypostasis," which are now alien to the language and thought forms of both Europe and Africa. Yet, due to the enduring impact of Greco-Roman culture, the tendency remains to discuss Christology in metaphysical terms. Emphasizing that the creed was itself an attempt to "translate" biblical faith into contemporary idiom, Pobee asserts his methodological priority of getting behind the creed to the biblical faith that constitutes the plumb-line for assessing any subsequent Christology. Consequently, the question for him is "What has the biblical tradition to say on Christology?"[30] In contrast to metaphysical speculation, Pobee argues that biblical faith presents Christology in very functional terms, depicting Jesus in terms of his activity, and that this approach fits well with Akan thought. He therefore advocates and models the use of proverbs, used for serious discussions in Akan society, as a more apt approach for an Akan Christology than the process of philosophical abstraction from biblical texts that has governed Western theology.

Having established his methodological rationale, Pobee attends first to the biblical presentation of Christology. He notes the diversity of christological formulations within the New Testament, based on different writers' experiences and cultures, yet arrives at his central thesis, expressed as follows:

> The diverse Christologies converge and agree on two points: "Jesus is truly man and at the same time truly divine." It is these two ideas that any Christology, whether African or European, American or Chinese, Russian or Australian, Akan or Ga, Ewe or Dagbani, Yoruba or Igbo, is concerned to capture, even if the imageries or terminologies may change. All the christological titles come back to these same two ideas. The humanity and the divinity of Jesus are the two nonnegotiables of any authentic Christology.[31]

These two components, the humanity and divinity of Jesus, form the twin foci of Pobee's christological reflections as condensed in this particular work on African theology.

It is within this context that Pobee formulates the image of Jesus as ancestor. As he seeks to relate aspects of biblical teaching about Jesus to the Akan worldview, Pobee returns to the concept of ancestors to interpret Jesus' divinity in terms of his authority and power as judge of people's deeds:

> In Akan society the Supreme Being and the ancestors provide the sanctions for the good life and punish evil. And the ancestors hold that authority as ministers of the Supreme Being. Our approach would be to look on Jesus as the Great and Greatest Ancestor—in Akan language *Nana*.[32]

He immediately stresses that "even if Jesus is *Nana* like the other illustrious ancestors, . . . he is superior to the other ancestors by virtue of being closest to God and as God."[33] He also points out that as *Nana*, Jesus has authority not only over the human realm but also over all spirit beings including the ancestors. Additionally, Pobee recounts how reflecting on the term *Nana* as used for Jesus, the ancestors, and the Supreme Being triggered the intrinsically related idea of Jesus as chief.[34] The two images thus dovetail in his conclusions regarding the implications of *Nana Yesu* for Christian life:

> To say Jesus is *Nana* is to let his standards reign supreme in personal orientation, in the structures of society, in the economic processes, and in political forces. It means in practical terms personal and social justice and re-creation. An African who affirms that Jesus is *Nana* also should relate that message to the issues of human and social justices in African countries as in the rest of the world.[35]

Pobee addresses his initial christological questions through the image of Jesus as ancestor as only one possible christological portrait intended to speak to the hearts of Africans. In its formulation to date it remains regrettably limited, as Pobee himself lamented in conversation. For example, inadequate attention is given to the thorny issue of how Jesus can be linked with African lineage ancestors, a concern inherent in Pobee's own christological query. Doubtless further consideration of Jesus' role as ancestor, beyond functions of power and authority to judge, would enhance his presentation of the image. Nonetheless, by drawing upon his personal experience of the ancestral motif, Pobee portrayed Jesus as ancestor "because it's the language the Akan of Ghana would use. It's a way of saying, What is the living connection between me and this Jesus Christ?"

Bénézet Bujo

This living connection between the African believer and Jesus Christ also lies at the heart of Bujo's theological agenda, as may be recalled from his central question introduced in Chapter 2: "*In which way can Jesus Christ be an African among the Africans according to their own religious experience?*"[36] To address this challenge Bujo begins, like Pobee, with the historical precedent of early Christians bestowing upon Jesus titles from contemporary culture. These have remained throughout Christian tradition despite their meanings becoming obscured and the consequent need for reinterpreting Christology in today's changing cultural contexts. Given the centrality of ancestral beliefs throughout black Africa as outlined above, Bujo develops an entire ancestral theology on the presupposition of "ancestor-preoccupation as a typical, anthropocentric, African 'mode of thought.'"[37] Present elaboration is confined to the most salient features of his christological formulation, including his interpretation of ancestral veneration, its connection with Jesus, and the significance of the ensuing image of Jesus as ancestor.

If the first christological model presents life as fundamental to African worldviews, the second model reflects how life is inextricably bound up with the ancestors according to widespread African belief. Ultimately life comes from God, as indicated in Bujo's thought conveyed in the previous chapter, yet the ancestors play a vital role in mediating that life force to the living. For this reason Bujo asserts both eschatological and salvific dimensions inherent in ancestral communion:

> Here we begin to understand the supreme importance of the past for the African: for the secret of life is to be found above all in the hallowed attitudes and practices of the ancestors. In their wisdom is to be found the key to a better and fuller life, and it is therefore crucial that the rites, actions, words and laws which the ancestors have bequeathed to their descendants be scrupulously observed: they are the indispensable instruments of salvation. The way a person treats this inheritance is decisive, for life or for death. The ancestral traditions are gifts of God, they have a truly sacramental character. The life-giving traditions of the past must determine the present and the future since in them alone is salvation to be found.[38]

The African heritage is thus interpreted as having sacramental meaning and efficacy, for only in honoring and appropriating the traditions of the past can the human community secure life for the present and the future. Through the acts of ancestral remembrance, states Bujo, Africans are seeking not just earthly prosperity but "salvation in all its fullness."[39]

In order to relate the African heritage to biblical sources, Bujo draws a striking parallel between ancestral beliefs and "narrative theology" rooted in the Bible. In other words, he likens African traditions of remembering and reenacting the deeds of the ancestors as a "memorial-narrative act of salvation" to "Exodus Theology."[40] Thus the ancestors are models for the living, not simply to be imitated, but the recalling of ancestral traditions is thought actually to bring into effect the fullness of life they signify. So the African traditions do not function in a deterministic way, but rather as a potency that the individual decides whether or not to actuate. By recalling the life-giving words and actions of the ancestors, one chooses life; by neglecting them, one chooses death. Personal responsibility lies with each individual to follow the path of the ancestors, which is known to bring life.

It is on this basis that Bujo proposes the image of Jesus as the ancestor par excellence or the proto-ancestor. Due to the anthropocentric nature of African thought, Bujo stresses the importance of "ascending Christology" or "Christology from below" for the African context. He therefore employs Jesus' earthly ministry as a point of departure and interprets it in terms of those virtues and actions that Africans attribute to their ancestors:

> If we look back on the historical Jesus of Nazareth, we can see in him, not only one who lived the African ancestor-ideal in the highest degree, but one who brought that ideal to an altogether new fulfilment. Jesus worked miracles, healing the sick, opening the eyes of the blind, raising the dead to life. In short, he brought life, and *life-force*, in its fullness.[41]

As Bujo's words indicate, the analogy drawn between Jesus and ancestor by no means suggests that Jesus is merely one founding ancestor among many. On the contrary, he specifies the title proto-ancestor to signify that Jesus "infinitely transcended" the "authentic ideal of the God-fearing African ancestors."[42] He further clarified in conversation that the term *proto-ancestor* does not only mean "first," as some African and European critics have construed it, but also "model." It is akin to the biblical imagery of Jesus as the "new Adam," for just as Adam revealed sin and brought death, so Jesus reveals sinlessness and brings life. Hence, as Bujo explained, "*Proto* can mean 'model.' So we have somebody from whom we can learn how to be a human being, how to be perfect, and so on. That is a proto-ancestor." Elsewhere he provides the following succinct summary statement: "In this sense, Jesus Christ is the Proto-Ancestor for the Africans. The law for living as good and wise Africans came to us by the intermediary of the ancestors, the divine grace and wisdom to clothe us with the new man have come to us by Jesus Christ."[43]

Complementing a Christology from below Bujo also emphasizes "the supraterrestrial Christ, who by his death and resurrection was established by the Father as our Proto-Ancestor."[44] This, he underlines, is a thoroughly biblical thought that is at the center of Paul's Christology and soteriology. For example, the parallel between the "first Adam" and "last Adam" (1 Cor 15:45; Rom 5:12–13) is interpreted along these lines. Further rationale for the proto-ancestral image is found in Christ being portrayed as the head of the body in Pauline ecclesiology and cosmology (Col 1:18; Eph 1:23), the firstborn in all creation (Col 1:15), the beginning and firstborn from among the dead (Col 1:18), the firstfruits of all who have fallen asleep (1 Cor 15:20), and the one in whom the fullness of divinity is to be found and through whom reconciliation is accomplished (Col 1:19–20; cf. 2:9). Bujo thus concludes that Jesus as proto-ancestor in no way contradicts New Testament thought. Rather, the image reflects the belief that he is the "firstborn among all the ancestors," not on a biological level but on "a soteriological level of re-birth to a mystical and supernatural life and mode of existence."[45]

It is important to note that Bujo's explanation of the proto-ancestral image forms a key context for his reflections on Jesus as life-giver (presented in the previous chapter). His rationale for employing the African category of "a great founding ancestor" to portray Jesus is summarized in this way:

> If the vital force emanating from God actually passes through our ancestors, and, in particular, through the proto-ancestor of a clan, the Christian believer is convinced that God is similarly communicating His own divine life to us by means of His Messiah and Son, whom He thereby constituted as our Proto-Ancestor.[46]

Again, he stresses that "this is not just a question of imitating prior examples, but as Proto-Ancestor, He is the one who invites men to take part in his life-giving, creative activity. Jesus Christ is thus the life-giving, proto-force of the whole black ethos."[47] So the image has vital significance for a number of areas within African Christianity to which Bujo attends, besides theology and Christology, including pneumatology, ecclesiology, and especially ethics. While the subject is vast, attention is confined here to certain christological issues already raised, which may be profitably addressed through considering the image of Jesus as ancestor.

First, Bujo's response to his own christological query highlighted above is to set forth an African interpretation of the incarnation that takes cognizance of the role of the African ancestors in God's saving activity. He asserts that Christ as proto-ancestor has to do "with the very essence of the Word's becoming man,"[48] for in revealing both God and true humanity, Jesus identifies fully with humankind and thereby encompasses all of the ancestors' striving after righteousness. Bujo then voices an important conclusion:

> Above all, Jesus Christ himself becomes the privileged locus for a full understanding of the ancestors. The African now has something to say about the mystery of the Incarnation, for after God had spoken to us at various times and in various places, including our ancestors, in these last days he speaks to us through his Son, whom he has established as unique Ancestor, as Proto-Ancestor, from whom all life flows for His descendants (cf. Heb 1, 1–2). From him derive all those longed-for prerogatives which constitute Him as Ancestor. The African ancestors are in this way forerunners, or images, of the Proto-Ancestor, Jesus Christ.[49]

Thus Jesus becomes the savior whose passion, death, and resurrection must be remembered and retold down the generations, for he is the one who opens up the future that the ancestors had sought to secure. By exegeting Jesus in relation to the African ancestors reinterpreted in this fashion, Bujo not only reverses the negative estimation of the ancestors characteristic of much of the modern missionary enterprise, but also demonstrates an openness to acknowledging them within the mystical body of Christ and including them in Christian liturgy. So Bujo, along with Ela and others, offers a positive contribution to the question of the place of African ancestors within Christianity.

Furthermore, Bujo insists that the christological title proto-ancestor, when translated into a corresponding theology and catechesis, will be far more meaningful to Africans than titles such as *logos* ("Word") and *Kyrios* ("Lord"). He explicitly denies any wish to suppress these latter titles. He simply underlines that they are derived from a particular culture far removed from the African's experience and therefore may not effectively touch African sensibilities. Consequently, he argues for the legitimacy of granting titles to Jesus that are more deeply rooted in the culture of those to whom the gospel message is being addressed. The significance of this approach is then stated clearly in terms of the critical issue of African Christian identity:

> It is important that Christianity show the Africans that being truly Christian and being truly African are not opposed to each other, because to be a true Christian means to be a true human being, since it was Jesus himself who was truly human and who humanised the world. Once however we have established that the legitimate yearnings of the African ancestors are not only taken up in Jesus Christ, but are also transcended in him, can we not use the concept of Proto-Ancestor as the starting-point of a Christology for which the enthusiasm of the African will be more than a passing fashion?[50]

It becomes apparent once again, then, that the critical issues that prompt contemporary African Christologies are addressed and potentially redressed by those very Christologies. In this case Bujo's voice was presented in Chapter 2 regarding Africans' search for a new identity after the traumas of the slave trade, colonialism, and the present plight of refugees across the continent. In response, he proposes the proto-ancestral image as a means for communicating to Africans that the identity, the true humanity they seek, and the fullness of life that their ancestors sought, are ultimately found in the person of Christ:

> Jesus Christ the Proto-Ancestor wants nothing more than full life and the total and comprehensive development of the new People of God in Africa who, setting out from a remote past, and the drama of the masses of refugees in so many places, continues on its way to eternity, searching for greater autonomy and true identity. To present Jesus Christ in this tragic situation as Proto-Ancestor is of the greatest significance. It amounts to saying that he is the new Moses who, through so many obstacles, sufferings, tears and oppression of all kinds, is steadily leading his African people to the waters of life.[51]

This statement leads to the final point regarding the significance of Bujo's proto-ancestral image to African Christianity. For whatever contribution Bujo makes to inculturating the gospel through employing the indigenous category of ancestors, by juxtaposing the images of Jesus as proto-ancestor and the "new Moses" he paves the way for developing further liberative dimensions of the gospel in the contemporary context. Indeed, Bujo writes primarily on Christian ethics, yet the foregoing discussion introduces his proto-ancestral Christology as the nucleus for what he terms a "Christocentric-black-African morality."[52] While his application of Christology to ethics lies beyond present exploration, suffice it to stress his fundamental assertion that "to understand Jesus as Proto-Ancestor means accompanying him on the way of the Cross."[53] This means, among other things, to enter into solidarity with the poor, the feeble, and all those marginalized in society, and "to declare a merciless struggle against the many ills which rob modern Africa of its vital force and lead its nations, slowly but surely, to a premature death."[54] So the strength of Bujo's christological contribution lies not only in the content of his proto-ancestral model, but also in the method advocated therein. As he points out, "It is in the line of orthopraxy that our considerations of Jesus Christ as Proto-Ancestor and source of life could become a veritable ferment for the transformation of a post-ancestral and post-colonial Africa."[55] Here, then, is an African theologian who supersedes the inculturation-liberation divide. For, in contrast to any such artificial dichotomy, Bujo concludes his christological reflections as follows: "I believe that a truly dynamic Christianity will only be possible in Africa when the foundation of the African's whole life is built on Jesus Christ, conceived in specifically African categories."[56]

JESUS AS ANCESTOR IN THE ORAL CHRISTOLOGIES

After introducing the image of Jesus as ancestor through a consideration of its derivation in African traditions, various critical issues it elicits, and its emergence among selected African theologians, the question remains as to how this image fares among African Christians today. Is it operative in the lives of individuals and Christian communities? How is it understood? What factors either encourage or restrain its usage? And what significance is it perceived to have for contemporary African Christianity? These questions are investigated by outlining data findings from the interviews, the rationale expressed for the image, problems with it, and aspects of its significance as articulated by the selected African Christians. The results of field research in Kenya, Uganda, and Ghana are juxtaposed, with convergences and divergences between nationality or other variables pointed out as appropriate.

The Data

That Jesus as ancestor is a controversial image immediately comes to light in the statistical findings from the qualitative interviews. In Kenya and Uganda, of the twenty-seven individual respondents with whom it was discussed, 48 percent were positive in their overall verdict compared with 44 percent who were negative (see Table 4–1). Contrasting responses also occurred in Ghana, although in this case, of the thirty-two respondents with whom the image was discussed, 63 percent were overall negative as opposed to 31 percent positive (see Table 4–2, percentages rounded up).

Individual Responses	Statistic	Percentage
Positive responses only	10/27	37%
Negative responses only	11/27	41%
Positive and negative responses	6/27	22%
Overall verdict positive: 3/6		
Overall verdict negative: 1/6		
Overall verdict neutral: 2/6		
Total responses overall positive	13/27	48%
Total responses overall negative	12/27	44%
Total responses overall neutral	2/27	8%

TABLE 4–1. INDIVIDUAL RESPONSES IN KENYA AND UGANDA
TO THE IMAGE OF JESUS AS ANCESTOR

Individual Responses	Statistic	Percentage
Positive responses only	5/32	16%
Negative responses only	13/32	41%
Neutral responses only	1/32	3%
Positive and negative responses	13/32	41%
Overall verdict positive: 5/13		
Overall verdict negative: 7/13		
Overall verdict neutral: 1/13		
Total responses overall positive	10/32	31%
Total responses overall negative	20/32	63%
Total responses overall neutral	2/32	6%

TABLE 4–2. INDIVIDUAL RESPONSES IN GHANA TO THE IMAGE
OF JESUS AS ANCESTOR

On the basis of matrix tables exploring variables that might reflect patterns of differentiation in the individual responses, a few observations are apposite. The most obvious divergence occurs between Catholic and Protestant respondents, with Catholics being more favorably inclined toward the image than Protestants.[57] This factor probably accounts for the majority of negative responses in Ghana, since more Protestants than Catholics were interviewed in this context. Further differentiation might be detected on the basis of the language favored for personal Bible reading. While those reading in the vernacular are divided roughly equally in their views, those reading in English are more readily opposed to the image. Additionally, there may also be some divergence in responses because of theological education, for those who are theologically educated are divided approximately equally in their views, while those who are not theologically educated are more negative in response. This might suggest that theological education encourages at least consideration of the image, that is, acknowledging positive and negative factors about it even if the overall verdict is negative. It must be stressed that these findings from qualitative research indicate certain clusters of responses within this particular sample. However, further quantitative research would need to be conducted to establish more definite conclusions regarding possible variables at play in respondents' views.

The pattern of conflicting responses indicated in the individual responses is also found in the focus groups. Combining all the groups together for the present purpose, the following findings emerge: Of the ten groups with whom the image was discussed, the consensus from four groups was positive while that from six groups was negative (see Table 4–3).

Focus Group Responses	*Statistic*	*Percentage*
Positive responses only	3/10	30%
Negative responses only	2/10	20%
Positive and negative responses	5/10	50%
Overall verdict positive: 1/5		
Overall verdict negative: 4/5		
Total responses overall positive	4/10	40%
Total responses overall negative	6/10	60%

TABLE 4–3. FOCUS GROUP RESPONSES IN KENYA AND GHANA
TO THE IMAGE OF JESUS AS ANCESTOR

Finally, a few observations are noted concerning the prevalence of the image of Jesus as ancestor in the selected contexts for field research, as well as its sources and shaping influences. The first consideration is the extent to which respondents volunteered the image themselves, as opposed to the interviewer raising the idea and requesting their response to it. In Kenya and Uganda only two individuals initiated discussion of Jesus as ancestor, and both did so in the context of question three regarding images of Jesus especially meaningful to African Christians. While one of these interviewees admitted that he wrestles with it, voicing pros and cons, the other raised it as a negative example, arguing strongly against African theologians assigning such christological titles. In Ghana, four respondents volunteered the image, with three voicing fairly strong support and one acknowledging awareness without personal assent. Thus six of the total of sixty-five respondents volunteered the image of Jesus as ancestor.

It is noteworthy that all six who raised the image are theologically educated. While not all of these support the ancestral model for Jesus, as mentioned above, it does indicate that the image is under discussion in theological circles across Africa. Further evidence is found in respondents volunteering the names of specific theologians who articulate the image. For example, Kenyan and Ugandan respondents referred to Nyamiti and Bujo, and Ghanaian respondents mentioned Bediako, Bujo, and Pobee. Once again, all the respondents who did so are theologically educated and are not necessarily supportive of the image. However, these findings reveal that the fairly recent christological discourse derived from ancestral concepts is being disseminated to some degree through theological education. Also, a few interviewees explicitly stated that their theological studies have had some impact upon their view of Jesus as ancestor. What is more, two respondents argued that the image is advocated by academic theologians but is not in use by "ordinary people."

This view was countered by the witness of Catholic parish priest Joseph Aggrey, who confirmed that the image is operative within his own life and church community in Ghana. Moreover, Catholic Bishop Charles Palmer-Buckle and Protestant Dan Antwi, principal of Trinity Theological College, Legon, admitted that it is not meaningful to them personally yet affirmed that it is functioning for some local parishioners. In the focus group of Ghanaian Protestant clergy, Joseph Asare voiced an interesting corroboration when he stated, "There is a song which says 'Yesu oye made nyinaa. Oye magya. Oye mene.' So we pray to our ancestors." The Twi song is translated literally as "Jesus is everything to me. He is my father. He is my mother," and it signifies that a song which traditionalists would normally sing to their ancestors, specifying the relations, is now addressed to Jesus as the father, mother, and hence the ancestor. Also in Uganda certain members of the Little Sisters of St. Francis, including Nasimiyu Wasike, related how their experience of celebrating Mass, during which an expatriate priest incorporates prayers of invocation for the African ancestors to join in worship, has enhanced their understanding and appropriation of Jesus as ancestor.

So no clear-cut picture appeared regarding the prevalence of the ancestral image for Jesus in the selected African contexts, yet a few contour lines emerge through the present research. First, the image is decidedly controversial, as demonstrated in the statistical findings. Second, Catholic Christians show greater proclivity to adopt the ancestral image than Protestants. Third, theologically educated respondents show greater awareness of theologians' proposals for Jesus as ancestor than those without theological education. While this point seems obvious, it was also noted that increased awareness does not necessarily mean increased affirmation, and that there is some contextual evidence to indicate that the image is operative beyond the realm of academic theology. Thus it is necessary to turn to the respondents' expressed views to clarify further the emerging picture of Jesus as ancestor in Africa. Rationale for the image is examined first, followed by problems with the image. Finally, conclusions are offered regarding its significance to African Christianity.

Rationale for the Image of Jesus as Ancestor

Several reasons are advanced to explain why Jesus as ancestor is a viable and meaningful image for African Christians. The reasons reflect the interplay between biblical and African concepts and elucidate how Jesus fulfills the role that was traditionally played by the ancestors in Africa. Four main ancestral functions are evidenced, all of which reflect aspects of the summary introduction to the ancestors above: mediation, founder of a community, ongoing participation in the life of the human community, and provider of life.

The first major role in which respondents perceive Jesus is that of mediator between God and humanity, analogous to the ancestors. Ghanaian Protestant clergyman Samuel Aboa summarized clearly:

> Well I can think of Christ as an ancestor, because we believe that our ancestors are also mediators. Those who have died before us continue at least in spirit, and they can mediate between us and the gods or other ancestral spirits, or other powers. And it becomes more meaningful to me when it's said that Christ has died for us and he mediates for us. In this way, I equate him with our understanding of the ancestors.[58]

Later, Aboa reiterated how the notion of Jesus as ancestor helps him to understand the vicarious death and the resurrection of Jesus, asserting that "our traditional worldview gives us an idea" of how to comprehend these biblical affirmations. Kenyan Catholic sister Marie Gacambi also interprets Jesus as ancestor in this way and relates the image to his role as the firstborn of all creation. She argued:

> After all, in the scripture we say he's the firstborn of all creation. And so, someone that has an interest in us. Our ancestors have an interest in the well-being of the family. They are the mediators between us and God. So really, Jesus is *the* ancestor, from that perspective, because he's the one that has this whole human link with the transcendent.

Gacambi's insight introduces the second key parallel between Jesus and the ancestors in that he is the founder of a new community and, as such, establishes its identity. Kenyan Catholic lay man Peter Kiarie explained, "If you look at it that way, you will see that Jesus fits exactly as the supreme ancestor, because he comes and he founds a new community." From Johannine teaching Kiarie outlined the nature of spiritual rebirth into the new humanity, and from Pauline teaching he added the concepts of the mystical body of Christ with Jesus as the head. He then spelled out the significance:

> His ancestry is so physical, in the sense that not only was he there, at that time, but he continues. So you can see Jesus presents himself as an ever-present ancestor—he's actually there all the time, and he was there before, and now he continues. So this makes the people feel very much at home.

Similarly, Kenyan Protestant clergyman Peter Bisem volunteered the image of Jesus as "the great ancestor," and despite its shortcomings, contended that "it is very appealing, and quite exciting in the sense that it re-creates, if you like, the identity of a people, or of a community. Because it is from the ancestor that you have your name. It is from the ancestor that you have your identity." Ghanaian

Protestant clergyman Emmanuel Martey concurred, drawing a parallel between naming as fundamental to identity in African tradition and the first Christians being called after Christ in Syria: "So, from him, from the head, from the ancestor, we got our name, in African understanding." With respect to Jesus as "the founder of the Christian family," he concluded, "So with that concept, it explains Christianity better to the African, especially Christ to the African."

Concerning the critical question of how Jesus becomes the lineage head for Africans today, only one respondent, Ghanaian traditional leader Birikorang, claimed a common ancestry with Jesus in Jewish origins.[59] Others responded by stressing Jesus' incarnation for all humanity and believers' adoption by faith into the family of God. For example, in the focus group of Kenyan Catholic laity, Charles Otieno pointed out that Jesus belongs to the tribe of Israel and that "Abraham is actually our father in faith. So if Jesus came from Abraham, then he is our ancestor." He further stated that, despite the fact that Jesus had no children, he belongs to the race of Abraham as "we all" do: "black, white, red, and different colors." Hence Jesus "is part of our ancestry." Also, in the focus group of Kenyan Protestant laity, Purity Nguhiu noted that the gospel genealogies record Jesus' ancestry "up to the birth of Jesus Christ. And that is it, full stop. But from there, the next introduction is that we are heirs with Christ Jesus." She further pointed out that he was of the lineage of David and by faith we have entered that family. So, for many of the respondents, questions of biological ancestry are not considered problematic in comprehending Jesus as ancestor on account of New Testament teaching regarding the spiritual adoption of believers into Jesus' family.

A third major role of African ancestors understood to be fulfilled in Jesus is that of ongoing participation in the life of the human community, specifically as family guardian. Concepts clearly overlapped in this regard, for, as already noted, Jesus is believed to have founded a new family and to continue making his presence known to that family. Joseph Aggrey cited one of the more common reasons for viewing Jesus as ancestor: "He also came to live here on earth, and has died and gone. But we still remember Jesus Christ, because we know he is still in our midst, spiritually." Regarding Jesus' ongoing participation, Kwesi Dickson explained:

> The question is, who is ancestor? It is not everybody who dies who becomes ancestor. The person who is to become an ancestor must have lived an exemplary kind of life, and because of that, that person never dies—he's always present, and he's involved in the life of the people, even though he is across the borders, as it were. And we have this idea of communing with ancestors.

The analogy of ancestral communion was discussed further in the focus group of Kenyan Catholic clergy, with Elijah Chege disclosing the corresponding image of Christ as brother. While this latter image features in the next chapter on Jesus as loved one, Chege's comment reveals the overlap between ancestor and brother, and hence between the two christological models:

An ancestor is someone who is close to the people from which he came. And he is considered like a brother, because if people ask him to pray for them, then he will do that. Jesus himself said that if we ask anything through his name, we will get it. Also we know that our ancestors—we never worshiped them; instead, they used to pray for us—are there to intercede for us, they are like today's saints. But, although we call Jesus an ancestor, he is an ancestor but somehow slightly different because he is God.

Besides intercession, Jesus continues to participate in the human community by way of protection. Kenyan Catholic priest Kamau drew attention to this facet of ancestral communion and its significance:

The one who protects people now, is Christ! Then Christ becomes an African ancestor because he takes care of the people, like ancestors. And you know the comparison—he's the true ancestor, because he is playing the role of ancestors. This is how we have Christ as ancestor, African ancestor.

Closely related to protection is the traditional belief that "power emanates from the ancestors and from the spirit world." So commented Oscar Muriu in the focus group of Kenyan Protestant clergy, when he cautiously considered Jesus as ancestor and conceded that "if you were to look at ancestors in *that* sense, as a source of power, maybe." Thus several dimensions of Jesus' ongoing involvement in the human community come to the fore, including his presence, prayer, protection, and power. In these respects he is understood in an analogous way to the African ancestors, and especially to the corresponding role of brother.

The final point is essentially a culmination of the three aspects of ancestral communion outlined above; namely, Jesus, as firstborn of all creation, mediates between God and humanity, he establishes a new human family, and he continues to participate in that community. That is to say, just as the goal of ancestral veneration in Africa is to foster abundant life, so Jesus is believed to provide the fullness of life that the ancestors sought themselves and continue to transmit to their descendants. Ghanaian Protestant clergyman Abraham Akrong expressed this notion clearly in discussing Jesus as ancestor, explaining:

It's a meaningful category to me, in a way, because the ancestors stand for what we call fullness of life. You know, it's the ideal life. If you want to ask the African, "What is your ideal?": it's to grow up, go through the rites of passage, and die and become an ancestor! That's an ideal. So the ideal nature of the ancestors for me would be a way in which we could also articulate the ideal nature that Jesus Christ came to teach us about what we really ought to be.

Echoing Pobee and Bujo's fundamental assertion that Jesus as ancestor exegetes both God and humanity, respondents affirmed that Jesus reveals the humanity, in terms of the qualities, that the African ancestors exemplify. For instance,

Kiarie remarked, "It's very clear that Jesus presents himself as the man. You know, he even calls himself the son of man, that human image that we are actually growing like. So, I think that calling Jesus the ancestor fits in very well." Furthermore, focusing on the qualities of Jesus in this manner is perceived to overcome the hurdle of physical ancestry in depicting Jesus as ancestor to Africans. Kenyan Circle member Mary Getui commented: "I would not want to look at it [the image] from the physical perspective, but I would like to look at it from the qualities that my ancestors wanted to promote." Likewise Ugandan Catholic priest J. M. Waliggo interpreted the image as linking Jesus to the traditional values in African religion, with the advantages of this approach spelled out in this way:

> People then may be able to begin linking with Jesus as ancestor without excluding their own ancestors. And the idea is to take away the duality between the ancestors who were not baptized and ancestors who were baptized, and use Jesus to be the link between the values in the African religion and the new values of understanding. For mediation to go on in that way, therefore, also leads to a spirituality which is drawing from the ancestorship of Jesus.

Thus the convergence of Jesus as life-giver and Jesus as ancestor comes to light in the textual and oral Christologies, with implications for spirituality and ethics in the African context. Before exploring the significance of Jesus as ancestor, however, it is necessary to examine various problems with the image.

Problems with the Image of Jesus as Ancestor

Like the controversial image of Jesus as traditional healer, objections to Jesus as ancestor stemmed primarily from historical and missiological issues, theological problems, and challenges of contemporary relevance. In Kenya, Protestant clergyman John Gatu was again a leading witness to the missiological issues. With respect to Jesus as ancestor, Gatu began with "the concept that was introduced by missionaries," and explained the problem in presenting the image as follows:

> I would have to first of all clarify this ancestor understanding, because the way it has been understood is very negative. It is very, very negative. The idea that has been given, because of the comparisons between the Western concepts and African concepts, is that ancestors are pagans who had no knowledge of God and so on. I would challenge that view.

Despite efforts by some African Christians to reinterpret the concept of ancestors more positively, Ghanaian Catholic priest Edusei summed up the present situation by remarking, "It's just the connotations associated with the term." For example, Ghanaian Protestant clergyman Aboagye-Mensah pointed out that "most people have associated ancestorship with forces that are anti-Christian, demonic forces and so on." Certainly the term *ancestor worship* arises in conversation, revealing commonly held perceptions. On this account, many respondents shared the verdict of Ghanaian Protestant clergyman S. S. Quarcoopome: "I would not use the word *ancestor* for Jesus."

As a result of missionary denigration of African ancestors, many contemporary Christians no longer identify with this aspect of their cultural heritage. Kenyan Protestant lay woman Marcy Muhia offered striking witness, when asked if she thinks about Jesus as ancestor:

> Not really, because for me there's been that severance, that separation. In that, my ancestors have come to mean not very many positive things, because it's associated with ancestor worship. And my grandparents, coming out of that, rejected it completely, completely. And so I don't know too much about my ancestors, which makes it difficult for me to associate Christ with ancestry. It's easier for me to think, I'm descended from Noah, I'm descended from Adam, but I don't think of Christ as my ancestor.

Combined with the missionary inheritance are other historical factors like modernization and urbanization, which have further alienated Africans from traditional culture. Ghanaian Catholic Bishop Palmer-Buckle attested to these forces:

> Because I grew up in a Christian environment, the role of the ancestors was overshadowed already at a very early age by the saints in the Catholic faith and by Jesus Christ. So I've never had a very big, call it reverence of ancestors as such. But I grew up in Accra. Maybe that's another negative aspect of it, that I grew up in the urban area, so something like pouring libation, calling on the ancestors, something like a stool, ancestral stools, never played much of a role in my life.

Given these historical and missiological factors, then, it is not surprising that many African Christians reject proposals of Jesus as ancestor.

The most serious objections to the image, however, are theological, grounded in concepts of the African ancestors deemed inapplicable or inappropriate for Jesus. Arguments are summarized here in terms of conflicting definitions, qualifications, and characteristics of ancestors, all of which are contrasted with Jesus. The foregoing discussion has amply shown that perceptions of the ancestors vary widely among the selected African Christians. While many defined the African ancestors positively, emphasizing the exemplary life required for becoming an ancestor, others defined them more generally as "those who have gone before us," including both the virtuous and the disreputable. For example, Kenyan Catholic priest Peter Gichure pointed out the shortcomings of the African ancestors and, on that basis, vehemently opposed the image for Jesus. Among other vices, such as authoritarianism and being "really treated as gods," Gichure pointed out:

> The history of Africa is also very, very terrible. For example, slavery—who really sold the Africans? They were the ancestors! Who really discriminated?

It was our ancestors. There's no way Christ will fit that—you could only use that as a way of explaining, but *never* as a model.

So different estimations of the ancestors obviously lead to different views regarding the suitability of the analogy for Jesus.

If the concept of Jesus as ancestor falls strangely upon African ears, the reasons most commonly expressed stem from the qualifications associated with the ancestors. First, the fundamental notion of lineage ancestors prevents some Christians from conceiving of Jesus in this way. Nearly ninety-year-old Ugandan Catholic sister Mary John stated that she has never heard of Jesus as ancestor before, and he would not fit into that role "because he is not of my tribe. The ancestors of Buganda must have been the Baganda—only." Likewise, Ghanaian Protestant clergywoman Margaret Asabea insisted that "an ancestor in the context of the African is your kith and kin, mother, father, grandfather, great grandfather," and that any attempts to construe Jesus as kindred to Africans are simply "academic gymnastics." Ghanaian Catholic Bishop Sarpong concurred, stressing that "ancestor is very restrictive" because it is an "ethnocentric concept." He explained:

You don't have the ancestors of the Asantes, you have the ancestors for the clans. My father is my ancestor, he's not your ancestor. And so before you adopt Jesus as an ancestor, you must be able first of all to convince the whole world that Christians are one family.

Although he admitted it could be done, using the African family as a model for the church, he also cautioned as follows:

It can be very good and it can be very dangerous, in the sense that the African family is characterized by love, sharing, sensitivity to one another, sharing problems, joint ownership of property, and so on. These are all excellent things. But, at the same time, the African family excludes other families. It's very ethnocentric. And what is happening in the African world, in Rwanda, in Burundi, is all an enlargement of the idea of the African family. The person who is outside my family is not as important as those in my family. I can band together with my own family members against another person from another family. When somebody from my family has done something, no matter how obnoxious, I support him or her, you see? So whereas the concept of the family can be used beautifully as for the church, in some respects it can be very dangerous.

In addition to physical lineage, objections were raised on the grounds that Jesus did not fulfill the traditional requirements of an ancestor in terms of age, marriage, and offspring. Kenyan Protestant lay man Ole Ronkei gave lively expression to these problems from the Maasai perspective:

Christ can't be an ancestor! No! How can he be? He was a young kid! Culturally speaking. An ancestor has this connotation of age, where I come from.

You need to reach a certain stage, you pass away, and we classify you as one of our ancestors. If a young person dies, he will just go into historical oblivion! An ancestor is somebody who is here, he's one of us, born, raised his own family until he passed away, and so we're looking at him as an ancestor, as a line that we've come through. Then Christ even becomes more problematic. He didn't have a wife! He didn't have children! Where are the offspring? Ancestor! Very problematic where I come from.

One last requirement traditionally held for African ancestors is a "good death." Asabea questioned whether Jesus' death would be considered so in African understanding, unless, she suggested, it was underscored as a sacrificial death. These examples therefore illustrate the kind of conundrum that the image of Jesus as ancestor poses to some African Christians who interpret the image more literally.

The third area of theological problems stems from characteristics of ancestors considered contrary to Jesus. Kenyan Protestant Bishop Kivunzi and Ghanaian Protestant clergyman Oduro both stressed that ancestors are creatures while Jesus is the creator of the ancestors; hence, he cannot even be called ancestor par excellence. Ghanaian PACWA member Florence Y. B. Yeboah added that although Jesus represents believers in heaven, he does so as creator and not as an ancestor from whom she comes. Therefore "even though he's condescended to come and dwell within us, he's still our Lord, our creator, our maker." Concomitantly, the ancestral image is deemed insufficient because while ancestors come to an end, once forgotten, Jesus is eternal. The ancestral paradigm is further limiting, according to Bisem, speaking from a Kalenjin perspective, in that "it would exclude women, because women have no identity in my community themselves. They get their identity in terms of their husband." He therefore concluded that the image "is not as all-embracing as we see in the Bible in terms of embracing the whole aspect of humanity, including male and female."[60]

Perhaps the most common objection regarding ancestral characteristics is that ancestors are "dead and buried" while Jesus is "alive," "contemporary," and "present." Kenyan Archbishop David Gitari acknowledged that "to the African, the living and the dead are very important. They are part of the family. But Jesus died and rose again, and he's living. Therefore he is *more* than an ancestor." Likewise, Ghanaian Oduro emphasized that "the fact of his resurrection makes him greater and more important than any ancestor I can think of." Implications for the Christian life were also identified. For example, Bishop Palmer-Buckle explained: "The tendency is that ancestors are a shade removed from that which is happening, unless they are invited to it. Whereas Jesus is always present, whether invited or not." Ghanaian Protestant lay man Lawrence Darmani concluded along the same lines:

I would picture him as rather much bigger than an ancestor. I see ancestors as, in the traditional concept, living in ghost land—vaguely alive, but hardly having bodies and not being able to interact with people. Jesus as ancestor would only mean to me that he's died and gone, but my difficulty with the use of that word *ancestor* for Jesus Christ has to do with my understanding of who Jesus is. You see, he died, but he rose again! And therefore I can't relate with ancestors, but I can relate with Christ.

Consequently, Kenyan Catholic lay man Wanjohi concluded that Jesus as ancestor does not make much impact on him personally because "we know Jesus much, much better than we know our ancestors."

These theological problems contribute to the conviction that Jesus is above the ancestors and must remain so to be on par with God. So, for some respondents, presenting him as ancestor, even distinguishing him as ancestor par excellence or proto-ancestor, risks compromising his divinity. Representative comments include the following: "He's higher than an ancestor [and] on that human basis, we could say he was an ancestor, but then coming back to his divine nature, that is where the difference lies"; "you are hitting a problem, because Jesus is worshiped, but the ancestors are not worshiped"; "I think I have reservations, maybe because I view him more in terms of his divinity than his humanity!"; "Jesus is the son of God—we don't see him as an ancestor"; and "he's the firstborn of God, so we don't see him as an ancestor." In Kenya a notable example came from Ole Ronkei, who stressed that he would not advocate the image for his Maasai people because it would be problematic according to their traditional piety. Referring to the Old Testament approach to prayer, addressing God as "the God of Abraham, the God of Isaac, the God of Jacob" to signify their ongoing covenant relationship with him, he explained:

We pray exactly the same way! "The God of our forefathers." Then we name them, according to the generations, not an individual person. I think you say, "The God of Isaac," and you're talking about this Isaac and his own entire generation. But, we talk about it in terms of those age groups. So, we say, "The God of that age group, and the God of the next age group," to show that we have not deviated, that we are still believing in exactly the same God that our ancestors believed in. Do you want to put Christ in that category when you talk about ancestors? See, if I put Christ there and he's God, he can't fall in that category! He has to be above!

In Ghana, Protestant lay woman Irene Odotei voiced a related concern. Although she responds positively to Jesus as ancestor, desiring to see some traditional concepts recovered to enhance African Christianity, she emphasized that Jesus is "unique" and there is danger of "mixing" him with hordes of other ancestors. While granting that it is possible to distinguish him as ancestor par excellence or proto-ancestor, she nonetheless cautioned:

There's no group with only one ancestor. There are so many of them. And even the gods, there are so many gods, and there are so many ancestors. And if you come to Accra and they're pouring libation, they will mention so many names, and then the gods, and then they will say, "From this place to that place, from the east to the west," then they call all of them and say, "I don't even know your number, so come, all of you, come, both great and small." Now, getting Jesus mixed up with "all of you," [then] "Come and drink," that will mean, would *take out* of the uniqueness of Christ.

So the crux of the matter stems from the two nonnegotiables pointed out previously by Pobee: the humanity and the divinity of Jesus. The spokespersons above clearly consider the ancestral image to compromise the divinity of Jesus, and on this basis reject it.

Finally, respondents voiced various problems related to the contemporary relevance of the image. Some pointed out that the image may be more meaningful among those ethnic groups whose ancestral beliefs have featured more prominently. For instance, Bisem affirmed that "it would be fascinating for a community like the Dogos of Ghana, who have a wonderful, mystical representation of the ancestor. Our communities didn't have that kind of thing." Similarly, the processes of modernization and urbanization, referred to with respect to historical factors, may diminish the relevance of the image, especially for young people in urban contexts. More significantly, Waliggo cautioned that "the model of ancestor may not change much in society. It may make us re-own our culture within Christianity, but may not touch very much the injustices that have been done to us and which we are doing to each other." The inculturation-liberation dichotomy reflected in this comment challenges the pertinence of the image and calls for further attention in the conclusions regarding christological method. Last, among those respondents who agreed that portraying Jesus as ancestor is appropriate conceptually, several admitted that it does not function for them experientially. Kenyan Circle member Hannah Kinoti concludes, "There is no problem about seeing Jesus as an ancestor, to me," yet she admitted that "it is not an image that I entertain a lot, or think too much about." Interestingly, Kenyan religious sister Gacambi spoke enthusiastically about the image, and when asked if it is meaningful to her personally, she replied, "It is starting to be meaningful to me, because before I did not study that aspect of Jesus as the ancestor." Gacambi's statement corroborates a few points made thus far: first, the challenge of contemporary relevance, since presumably the image was not meaningful to her previously; and second, the perception that it is being promoted by academic theologians, perhaps more than in the church context as a few suggested above. Yet it also illustrates the potential for the image to become personally significant to Christians when it is disseminated through theological education. So, despite the complex problems associated with depicting Jesus as ancestor, including historical and missiological issues, theological problems, and issues of contemporary relevance, it remains to attempt some assessment of the evidence in order to discern its current significance within African Christianity.

CONCLUSION: JESUS AS MEDIATOR

The second christological model reflects the importance of mediation in the African context. Among the mediatorial images that arise in the interface of

African and biblical traditions, Jesus as ancestor is a fairly recent and notable proposal. Francois Kabasélé sums up the perspective of many African Christians in stating that "Christ fits the category of Ancestor because, finally, he is the synthesis of all mediations (Heb. 8)." After exploring the analogy, he further concludes that "for Bantu Christians, Christ performs the role of Ancestor, by the mediation he provides. He is the exemplar, Ancestor, who fulfils in himself the words and deeds of the mediation of our Ancestors."[61]

Not all African Christians favor this portrait of Jesus, however, as the evidence above clearly demonstrates. Hence, the need remains to consider whether the category of African ancestors does indeed provide a hermeneutical key for interpreting Jesus meaningfully to African Christians today. A brief assessment of the image, in light of the criteria established in Chapter 2, attempts to recapitulate those factors that promote and those that restrain this particular christological image. In the process, observations are offered regarding its significance for contemporary African Christianity.

First, regarding the appropriateness of sources and methods, the image of Jesus as ancestor is clearly rooted in the African heritage. As Nyamiti explains, "Each author starts, in his own way, with the African ancestral beliefs and practices and tries to confront these with the Christian teaching on the Saviour."[62] Rationale is grounded in the pervasiveness of the ancestral paradigm and its enduring presence despite certain threats mentioned from the missionary inheritance, modernization, and urbanization. Granted, the relative strength of ancestral veneration varies among African societies, as repeatedly stressed. Consequently, depictions of Jesus as ancestor based on generalized summaries of ancestral concepts must be reexamined in particular contexts where the gospel encounters ancestral beliefs. According to Akrong, "Among the Akan, for example, it's very deep and strong." He explained that the average person may not be able to articulate fully ancestral beliefs, "yet ancestral symbol is the underlying paradigm of all social interactions." Probed further as to whether it is still operative among African Christians, Akrong maintained that it is, explaining that "it's so deep! The African culture controls us. Don't be deceived by anything. Don't be deceived by their cars, the external Westernization. I mean deep, deep, deep down, we're moving into the world from an African premise, deep, deep, deep down." For this reason he contended that the ancestral image

> could help us to reveal the mystery of Christ, because I believe that Christ is a mystery and you cannot exhaust him. It's a mere attempt to understand. We produce our ways by which we can build traditional bridges, where we don't tax them too much. They're contributing to, in a deep way, these traditional symbols are powerful in terms of capturing that mystery.

Therefore, among those peoples for whom the ancestral paradigm remains operative, the ancestral image potentially provides building materials for "traditional bridges" connecting the African heritage with the biblical witness of Christ.

If the "bridge" begins from the African heritage, it nonetheless joins with biblical affirmations about Jesus, according to proponents of Jesus as ancestor.

The matter is contested here, however, for the textual and oral sources reveal both acceptance and rejection of Jesus as ancestor on account of particular interpretations of biblical teaching. On the one hand, for example, a lay person interprets the image more literally in terms of Jesus' descent from African lineage and rejects it saying, "I just go for what the Bible tells me." On the other hand, among those who interpret the image more figuratively, Bujo insisted that "this proto-ancestor is biblical" and Ela remarked that the image is not original, since it is simply an "African recovery" of Pauline Christology and not specifically African. This conflicting evidence demonstrates the urgent need for closer analysis of contextual biblical hermeneutics. As Ernst Wendland points out, a serious problem with comparative analogy

> occurs when the analogy is not recognized at all, and people either interpret it literally or begin to identify the image and the topic. In either case, the result is confusion, whether it is recognized or not, and a serious breakdown in understanding and/or communication ensues.[63]

Such confusion definitely emerged in the mixed responses of interviewees to the proposal of Jesus as ancestor. Conclusions concerning the aptness of the image thus diverge. For example, Wendland notes in his article that the risk of conceptual misunderstanding did not prevent either Jesus or the apostolic writers from employing analogies and figurative language, and he acknowledges the need for theological analogizing in missiological contextualization. Yet he dismisses the ancestral image for Christ on the basis of a highly selective reading of African theologians, plus his own presuppositions regarding African ancestral cults and Christian doctrine.[64] In contrast, many African Christians selected for this study, even those whose overall verdict is decidedly negative, displayed openness to the image, provided it is qualified with adequate instruction. For example, Bishop Sarpong's response to the image is primarily negative, as indicated above, yet he acknowledged that you could "use the blanket term ancestor for Jesus Christ," but it "needs a lot of explanation." Above all else, that explanation must distinguish Jesus from the level of human ancestors so as not to jeopardize his divinity, the main theological problem voiced above. Representative remarks include insistence upon Jesus as a "superior ancestor" or as "a great ancestor, an ancestor with a difference!" Interpretation of the image therefore requires clear indication of the differences as well as the similarities between Jesus and the ancestors. The ancestral analogy must function to elucidate biblical affirmations about the identity and significance of Christ, rather than reading the African category back into scripture in such a way as to distort the biblical message, as Wendland, citing Tite Tiénou, cautions.[65] Furthermore, despite the hermeneutical complexities involved, both sides of the debate clearly follow Pobee's directive that the fundamental plumb-line for assessing these contemporary Christologies is their faithfulness to biblical teaching. In that sense, the Bible is again underlined as a central source for African Christologies.

If allowance is made for an appropriate convergence of biblical and African sources, there is certainly potential significance for African Christianity.

Ghanaian Protestant clergyman Emmanuel Martey spoke of the ancestral image as theologically appealing because "it fits—if you read scripture, and the African concept of ancestry." He further clarified how the analogy functions as follows:

> This is an image which can explain who Jesus is better, because Africans understand the concept of ancestry. Every analogy breaks down at a point. We are not saying that Jesus is an African ancestor, per se. What we are saying is that we're taking the concept, that image, the metaphor, to explain to the *African* who Jesus Christ is.

He then pointed to the christological questions that Jesus addressed to his disciples in Mark 8: Who others and then who they themselves thought he was. Martey stressed that the responses given to both questions—John the Baptist, Elijah, one of the prophets, as well as Messiah—were all derived from Judaism. He explained:

> His disciples use their previous religious understanding and experience to answer the reality of Jesus. So what African theologians are arguing is that in answering the christological question, one cannot ignore one's previous religious understanding and experience. That's why some of us go back into African traditional religion and African culture, to see what images, what symbols, are there, which will help us to understand who Jesus Christ is for the African.

Thus Martey concluded that the ancestral concept is especially significant for explaining Christ to Africans.

A few final observations are germane to examining sources and methods. First, Pobee and Bujo in particular, although others as well, emphasize the humanity and the divinity of Jesus, as well as the need for complementary approaches of "Christology from below" and "Christology from above." Second, while the ancestral image definitely draws more heavily upon the Bible and the African heritage as sources than the living experience of the church and contemporary realities in Africa, Bujo's firm stress on ecclesiology and orthopraxy in relation to the ancestral paradigm helps to counter any undue tendency toward a purely cultural Christianity. Furthermore, despite Waliggo's caution that Jesus as ancestor may not sufficiently address past and current injustices in Africa, he nevertheless validates the image. Moreover, it is in this context that he underlined the interrelatedness of various christological models:

> I always object to any theology which tries to be either merely liberation, because you cannot have inculturation without liberation, and you can't have liberation theology without inculturation. I would want to see all the different models interacting and being interplayed, rather than taking any title at the exclusion of another.

Within this interplay of christological models, where do the relative strengths and weaknesses of the ancestral image lie? Following from the preceding discussion and considering the seven criteria for contextual relevance, it becomes apparent that the portrait of Jesus as ancestor contributes less to the issues of historical relevance and gender appropriateness. Likewise, some have voiced caution concerning its contemporary relevance, and with that, the credibility of Christian witness. To the extent that the ancestral image truly inspires and elicits an orthopraxy grounded in Jesus as model or exemplar, it has potential relevance for the current context. As Oduyoye commented, "For me, the ancestor Jesus as the example, the person whose life you admire and therefore would like to live like that, is paramount." Otherwise, the image risks losing its contextual significance.

The ancestral image, however, contributes to the concerns of cultural relevance, as highlighted throughout the chapter. Martey stated that it explains Christ better to Africans; and Kiarie claimed that it "makes the people feel very much at home." Akrong summarized, "For me, once the ancestral symbol is used as understanding Christ, it makes Christ very, very close and near."

Jesus as ancestor also carries considerable theological relevance, as indicated in the reasons cited for and against the image on theological grounds. Strengths lie in relating Jesus to the African heritage and in employing aspects of this heritage to deepen African Christians' understanding of Jesus' life, death, and resurrection, to which Aboa and Gacambi, among others, attested. Yet controversy continues regarding the significance of the ancestral image to the contemporary context of religious pluralism. While many African Christians currently question claims of Jesus' sole mediation, the community of faith must examine the extent to which the ancestral image may be legitimately stretched in this regard, for certain christological expressions call for serious questioning.[66]

The discussion has also intimated that for some African Christians, particularly Catholics, the ancestral image for Jesus provides a link between the African ancestors and the Christian doctrine of the communion of the saints.[67] Yet, various Christian traditions hold different views concerning the role of human mediators, whether living or deceased, and these theological presuppositions inevitably influence perceptions of Jesus as ancestor.[68] In turn, there is potential ecclesiological relevance as various approaches are taken with respect to incorporating the African ancestors, and Jesus as ancestor, into the liturgy. For example, the Little Sisters of St. Francis relate how their personal and corporate worship has been enhanced through the African ancestors being invoked to join in worshiping God in the Eucharist. After consecrating the host, Father Peter Korse, missionary for thirty-five years in the Congo and Uganda and currently chaplain to the Little Sisters of St. Francis, Jinja, pours a little wine on the ground while informally invoking the African ancestors to join them in worshiping God.[69] (See Figure 4–1.) Likewise, regarding the Zaire Mass, Kabasélé explains,

FIGURE 4–1. INVOKING AFRICAN ANCESTORS TO JOIN IN CELEBRATING MASS, JINJA, UGANDA

Thus we have proposed to retain the offering of libations to the Ancestors. Instead of simply replacing them with the Mass, we have decided to integrate them into the Eucharistic celebration, so that they may express that Jesus Christ is the fullness of being, that he is the very essence of Ancestor—in brief, so that our libation may signify that, without the body and blood of the Son of God, our Ancestors do not attain the fullness of life, and thereby proclaim that Jesus Christ is Lord, to the Glory of God the Father.[70]

Clearly the ancestral portrait of Jesus has significant ramifications for the ongoing development of African theology and ecclesiology.

Finally, the criterion of linguistic and conceptual relevance, with its concern that current Christologies truly capture and incarnate the existential realities of life and African self-understanding, takes on heightened significance with respect to Jesus as ancestor. As Oduyoye explained, echoing Pobee, the image of Jesus as ancestor emerges as an attempt "to marry the two ideas, because that's what people will understand. You see, you're using a model which is already in their language." The problem that arises, however, as indicated in the introduction to this chapter, is that the English term *ancestor* is a translation of vernacular terms, but it is not identical with indigenous concepts. So, for example, when asked if he would speak of Christ as ancestor in his church setting, Akrong replied, "We would not, but you see, you can use the *title*—the ancestors are normally referred to by titles. *Nana,* and significantly the same title you give to an elder, you give to a chief, you give to an ancestor, you give to God." This statement corroborates Bediako's observation that even though *Nana* recalls the category of "ancestor," and so, in that sense translates the term, in actual fact it is not adequate to leave it at that. For whereas "ancestor" is a generic term in English, "Nana" is both a title and a personal name, in the same way that "Christos" (Christ) was both a title and a personal name in early Christian usage. This means that in point of fact, "Nana" is a more satisfactory term for speaking of the actuality of Christ than "Ancestor." It should therefore be clear from this that the real theological problem here has to do with the English word "ancestor" and not with *Nana*.[71]

Problems with the English word *ancestor* arise not only in translation, but also in cross-cultural interpretation. For example, Bujo related his experience of Europeans or Americans studying African Christology and responding with criticism based on Western philosophy. He recounted one instance in which a European priest teaching at the Gregorian University in Rome critiqued African ancestral Christology:

According to him it is not possible to do African christology with a concept of ancestor. Ancestorship means for him to be old, and to be old in today's world means you are not attractive anymore. So Christ will not be attractive for young people! And that means, for me, we are not understanding the same thing with the same concept. To say "ancestor" in Europe is something different from saying "ancestor" in Africa.

On this basis Bujo insists that "we should write our theology in African languages, because otherwise there are so many misunderstandings."

Bediako strongly concurs with the need for cultivating African theologies in the vernacular and goes a step further in stressing that mother tongues potentially carry new idioms that are crucial for discovering fresh insights into our common understanding of Christ. He thus concludes that "culture, and especially the new cultural entities that are becoming incorporated into the church worldwide, will continue to have a decisive impact on the shaping of Christian thought."[72] Herein lies a central aspect of the significance of African Christologies to world Christianity, also asserted by Fergus King. In examining possible correlations between angelic mediators in inter-testamental Judaism and ancestors in African religions, or shared features that might yield insights regarding the development of local theologies, King raises the theological question of how the person of Christ fits into existing theological categories. To this he responds by arguing that Christ transcends all categories, citing C. F. D. Moule:

Just as, in the New Testament period, Christ was recognised, indeed, in terms of various familiar categories and yet each time proved to be too big for that category and burst out of it in startling ways, so one might deduce, by extrapolation from this, that he would continue to confront each generation in the same way—familiar, yet startling, recognizable yet always transcending recognition, always ahead, as well as abreast: the ultimate from whom each generation is equidistant.[73]

If this is the case, King contends, then Christ may be recognized in the category of ancestor, but his confrontation with African traditions will transform those very concepts. The Christian theology of ancestors will be transformed, for example, in terms of liberation from fear of the ancestors or in terms of doctrine such as eschatology. Thus King concludes:

> The underlying feature of theological engagement with the Risen Lord is that theological categories and concepts are changed, whether that change occurs in the first century A.D. or the twentieth. It is a meeting that has happened in every place and time, that of Christ meeting his people in their own place and saying to them, "Come and see" (John 1:39).[74]

So, the controversy continues as some African Christians come to see Jesus as one who "fits" but also "transcends" the category of ancestors. Evidently, the image is already operative to some extent in the religious experience of African Christians, and it is being further disseminated through theological education. Abraham Akrong voiced openness to the ongoing process of christological formulation and its significance, noting that "if we have musicians and theologians who begin to use these things, so that once they get in language, their conceptual Jesus may be changed by the use of this kind of language." Other African Christians, however, remain reluctant for the reasons outlined. Despite the current inconclusiveness, what lies beyond dispute is that Christianity in Africa is posing questions and problems from its own context of faith in Christ for which it received no preparation from Christianity in the West. Nor is there any reason to expect that African theological endeavors should be any less arduous than they have been in other contexts of world Christianity. Yet this very process of forging creative contextual Christologies reveals that the new languages of Christian experience from non-Western cultures are assuredly making a decisive impact on the development of Christian thought.[75]

5

Jesus as Loved One

As a Ghanaian, one of the things we cherish is the family. And many people feel Jesus as a member of their family. People like to relate to Jesus as they relate to a member of the family.
—CHARLES PALMER-BUCKLE, CATHOLIC BISHOP OF KOFORIDUA, GHANA

Well, Jesus, he's my brother! He's the God-made-man who unites us all into one family of God, and who leads us to the Father. He is my brother, he's my friend, king, and spouse, as a religious sister.
—MARY SAVIO, LITTLE SISTERS OF ST. FRANCIS, UGANDA

I know Jesus Christ as a friend. In fact I know Jesus is Lord, and he's God— I've no doubt about the fact that Jesus is God. But I see him as a friend, very, very significantly.
—LAWRENCE DARMANI, FOUNDING EDITOR OF STEP MAGAZINE—GHANA

INTRODUCTION

This chapter continues to explore how African Christians perceive Jesus not only in light of biblical teaching and the Western missionary inheritance, but also in light of their own cultural heritage and existential realities. In this case family and communal experience, so central to traditional African cultures, clearly influence how Jesus is appropriated by the selected African Christians. The third christological model, Jesus as loved one, represents a cluster of relational images portraying Jesus as intimate family member and friend. For example, the research reveals conceptions of Jesus as brother, mother, father, parent, elder, and uncle. Further examples convey consciousness of the companionship and personal presence of Christ as friend, lover, guide, counselor, comforter, and visitor. From this wide array of christological portraits, key images are

143

analyzed in terms of their prevalence, their meaning, and their significance for African Christianity today.

CONCEPTS OF COMMUNITY IN TRADITIONAL AFRICA

Community life is a keystone upon which traditional African cultures are built. The first christological model, Jesus as life-giver, introduced Vincent Mulago's thesis that "unity of life" or "vital union" is fundamental to the family and social structures of many African peoples. Mulago asserts that "the key to an understanding of Bantu customs and institutions would thus appear to be the fact of community, unity of life. The handing-on of this life, the sharing in this one life, is the first link which unites members of the community."[1] He elaborates further that the individual's life is only meaningful as it is shared: "The member of the tribe, clan, the family, knows that he does not live to himself, but within the community." He concludes, "For the Bantu, living is existence in community."[2]

The second christological model, Jesus as mediator, highlights traditional views regarding the vital role of ancestors as ongoing participants in the life of the human community. Ancestors are often considered primary in the "mediating community," which Kabasélé explains as follows:

> The reason why the community is of the first importance for black Africans is the African awareness of the community as the principal mediator of the individual's initiation to life. Not only can the human individual not do without the community of human beings, but his or her existence would be devoid of all sense and meaning outside the community. In the Bantu world, one lives by and for the community.[3]

This conviction is symbolized in the widespread birth rituals that occur in two phases: biological birth into the family, followed by public reception into the wider community of extended family and friends. Moreover, these birth rituals and other rites of passage reflect African concepts of community as encompassing the living, the dead, and the not-yet-born. Indigenous concepts of community, mediation, and kinship are thus foundational to the ancestral paradigm for Christ.

The third christological model, Jesus as loved one, likewise builds upon core notions of communal life in Africa. Echoing the insights above, John Pobee contrasts Western ontology and epistemology with that of Africans, specifically the Akan:

> While Descartes philosophised *Cogito ergo sum* [I think, therefore I am], the Akan society would rather argue *Cognatus ergo sum*—i.e. I belong by blood relationship, therefore I am. In other words, in Akan society a man fully realizes himself as a man by belonging to a society. There is meaning and purpose to his life only because he belongs to a family, a clan, and a tribe.[4]

Elsewhere Pobee summarizes, "To be is to belong and live in a kinship group."[5] That is, personal individuality is only affirmed and fulfilled in relationship with other people. Therefore the crucial events of one's life, whether rites of passage or other crisis points, are experienced in relation to significant groups of people, the kinship group primarily, but also friends and neighbors.

While the emphasis on kinship is characteristically African, it is not peculiarly African, as Pobee points out. Rather, it is the form of kinship in Africa that is significant, in that the stress is on the so-called extended family rather than the nuclear family. J. N. K. Mugambi notes that the definition of family as a nuclear social unit is not strictly biblical, but rather a product of industrialization and urbanization.[6] Bénézet Bujo explains further, with respect to the church:

It is necessary to underline then the Church as *family*, not in the Euro-American sense of the nuclear family, but rather in the Negro-African sense of the large family which includes even cousins, distant cousins, and can go as far as to integrate friends and acquaintances; yes, even the dead are part of it.[7]

Certainly traditional family structures and communal life are under assault from urbanization, industrialization, and rising standards of living that adversely affect group solidarity. Nonetheless, Pobee notes that communalism remains a characteristic feature of many African societies, citing evidence in the continued preoccupation with religious rites of passage and the rise of new societal groupings in urban centers where kinship groups are less prevalent.

Finally, Anne Nasimiyu Wasike also underlines traditional African concepts of community. She draws upon John Mbiti's observations regarding African communalism, that "in traditional life, the individual does not and cannot exist alone except corporately," and cites Mbiti's well-known statement:

Whatever happens to the individual happens to the whole group, and whatever happens to the whole group happens to the individual. The individual can only say: "I am, because we are; and since we are, therefore I am."[8]

Once again, a cardinal point in African anthropology is that individual identity is established and fulfilled only in the context of community. To be is essentially to participate in family and community. Nasimiyu Wasike therefore concludes:

Community participation is a very prominent value among the African people. It permeates all life; it is the matrix upon which all the human and social values, attitudes, expectations and beliefs are based, and it is the foundation of an African theology, catechesis and liturgy.[9]

Jesus as Community Member

Given the fundamental place of community within African societies, traditional concepts of kinship and community inevitably color contemporary African Christologies. Pobee states that because an individual is identified as belonging to a kinship group, a construction of African Christology would emphasize the kinship of Jesus. Pobee explores Jesus' identity first in his relationship to his immediate family. From Mary he is said to have gained membership in a particular lineage and clan, and from Joseph as "a father of sorts," lineal descent from David (Lk 2:4; cf. Mt 1:16). References to Jesus' siblings (Mk 6:3), including his brother James the Just, further reinforce his identity in belonging to a kinship group. Rites of passage also give indication of Jesus' identity. For example, in outlining the significance of Jesus' circumcision Pobee integrates circumcision within Judaism, where it marks a child as belonging to the people of God, and within Akan society, where it incorporates a child into a kinship group:

> In the Akan context, the circumcision of Jesus would underline Jesus' belonging to a kinship group and therefore demonstrate his humanity. There will, however, be some difference in content between the biblical and the African traditional views: in our reinterpretation of African theology, the circumcision speaks not only of his belonging to a human kinship group, but also of his belonging to a religious human group which has entered into a covenant relationship with God.[10]

Likewise, interpreting Jesus' baptism in terms of his identification with the rest of humanity, Pobee speaks of it as "a rite of solidarity" that marks Jesus as a man in the African sense: "He was declared a man because by the rite he was declared a member of a group. *Cognatus ergo est*."[11]

Where Pobee questionably overlooks evidence of Jesus' alienation from his biological family (for example, Mk 3:21, 31–35; 6:1–6; and parallels), Mugambi provides a balancing viewpoint:

> In His public ministry Jesus affirms His ties with His immediate and extended family, and at the same time He distinguishes Himself from the rest of his kith and kin through His unique ministry to the Jewish community in general and the world at large. This double identity of Jesus as family member should be holistically maintained. Jesus is at the same time a member of His immediate family, the Jewish community and the universal community.[12]

The remainder of this chapter explores this "double identity" of Jesus, both as intimate family member and friend, and as member of wider human communities. In the specified contexts of this research, African Christians meaningfully appropriate Jesus as a close member of their community.

JESUS AS FAMILY MEMBER

Yesu e, Oye M'ade Nyinaa
Yesu e, oye m'ade nyinaa (2x)
Oye me na, m'agya, menua barima
Oye m'ade nyinaa

Jesus, He Is My All in All
Jesus, He is my all in all (2x)
He's my Mother, my Father, my strong Brother
He is my all in all.[13]

The Twi chorus above provides clear and appropriate evidence of indigenous African perceptions of Jesus as family member. The following discussion concentrates on three main family images among those that emerged in research: Jesus as brother, mother (also father/parent), and lover.

JESUS AS BROTHER

The importance of the image of Jesus as brother came to light in the interview with Nasimiyu Wasike. Asked to define African Christology, she immediately replied, "I think to define African Christology, you have to look at the various names that we give to Christ, to make him one of us. And I think that we look at him mainly as one of our brothers, the first of our brothers."

If the perception of Jesus as brother is prominent in Nasimiyu Wasike's present-day thinking, she stands in line with earlier African Christians who made the same claim. For example, Pobee cites a hymn from the early 1920s by disciples of Simon Kimbangu:

> Our God, Jesus, brother of us all
> Jesus, take us out of our sufferings
> Come and help us on earth, O Jesus![14]

In the mid-twentieth century Harry Sawyerr opposed the image of Jesus as chief and instead advocated Jesus as elder brother. Quoting Paul's statement that Jesus is the firstborn among many brethren (Rom 8:29), Sawyerr argued that just as the eldest of the elders is the lineage head, so Christ is the head of every family. According to Sawyerr:

> To represent Jesus Christ as the first-born among many brethren who with him together form the Church is in true keeping with African notions. For Christians an effort must be made to bring home the mystical relation between Christ and the Christian of which St. Paul speaks (Eph. 2:19ff.).[15]

Given these historical precedents, how does the image of Jesus as brother fare in contemporary Africa? Findings from the present research are set forth below in terms of the data, the rationale, the meaning, and the significance of the portrait of Jesus as brother.

The Data

In the oral interviews no set question was asked regarding Jesus as brother. It is therefore interesting to note the extent to which respondents volunteered this image. In Kenya and Uganda, eight of the thirty individual respondents voiced this perception of Jesus as being meaningful to them personally. In Ghana, seven of the thirty-five individual respondents did likewise, and an additional two referred to the concept without explicitly advocating it. Strikingly, the same image was initiated in eight of the twelve focus groups, thereby strengthening the observation that this particular christological portrait is significant to many African Christians.

No specific pattern of responses emerges from the data; Catholics and Protestants, men and women, clergy and laity articulated the image. Representative expressions included "my brother," "our elder brother," "Jesus Brother" or "Brother Jesus," "a big brother," "my bigger brother," "the senior brother," and "the universal brother." Moreover, respondents attested to contextual evidence of the image being presented in songs and prayers, as well as in their own interpretations of certain signboards. For example, Ghanaian queenmother Nana Dokua referred to a signboard publicizing "I'm redeemed by the blood of Jesus." Explaining what this means to her, she stated, "I've been redeemed. He died for us, so that now we can call God our Father. Jesus is our brother." Hence the oral and contextual data definitely indicate present perceptions of Jesus as brother.

Rationale for the Image of Jesus as Brother

African Christians cite various reasons for interpreting Jesus as brother. Biblical teaching, African concepts, and personal experience combine to provide grounds for the christological image. Sometimes respondents expressed biblical rationale more generally; for example, Ghanaian Protestant lay man Yeboah Amoa remarked, "Jesus Christ is my brother—the Bible says so." Other times they specified the biblical grounds more explicitly, particularly as it derives from Jesus' teaching. For instance, Ghanaian PACWA representative Felicia Opare-Saforo claimed: "Jesus called us his brothers, so I am a sister to Jesus. That one I know." Similarly, in the focus group of Kenyan Protestant clergy, Anne Wambugu explained, "I think most of us take Christ as a brother where he said 'my father and your father,' and where it says that 'we are co-heirs with him.'" Ghanaian Protestant lay woman Irene Odotei stated: "Jesus is my brother because that's what the Bible says—joint heirs with Christ, children of God and Jesus is the Son of God. If I believe in him and become a child of God, then of course I have a big brother!" Clearly, then, the Bible is a primary source for the conviction that Jesus is brother.

Traditional African concepts of brotherhood also shape perceptions of Jesus, according to the selected African Christians. Odotei continued her reflections, emphasizing that

> in the African context, having a brother means so much. So I suppose that's my Africanness—that's why I always want to think of Jesus as a brother, somebody close to me, a big brother who can take care of me, somebody I relate to. He's God, but he's also my brother.

Mary Koinange, in the focus group of PACWA women in Kenya, elaborated:

> He is actually my first love, in everything, because he has paid all my debts, and he has become my bigger brother. In the traditional way, the bigger brother becomes the father. He becomes responsible for what the father has been

doing. He is accepted as the head of that home after the father is gone. So Jesus Christ is accepted as the Son, the first Son of God, who is responsible for us. And we are becoming sons as he brings us home.

As with the christological images discussed in previous chapters, biblical and traditional African concepts are fused together through personal experience. Ghanaian queenmother Nana Dokua admitted candidly that Jesus acts

> like a brother, any time you call him. I used to have so many brothers, and they are all dead, left me alone. We were ten children—all dead!—and I'm the lastborn. At times, I say, "Oh, Jesus, everybody is gone. I need advice. I wish I had a brother." Then Jesus acts as a brother to me.

Ghanaian Charles Palmer-Buckle reinforced this perception from his experience as a Catholic bishop:

> Very often when you have a member of the family who is well off, who is more endowed, financially or intellectually or in other forms, there is a tendency that people lean on him, for his wisdom, for financial help. Many of the people I have come into contact with look at Jesus from that point of view, somebody they can go to and look for help. So, they often see Jesus as more or less a member of the family, a head of the family, to whom they can relate very personally.

Thus the selected African Christians perceive Jesus as brother on the basis of biblical teaching that is often understood and appropriated through their experience of brotherhood in the African context.

The Meaning of Jesus as Brother

What does the image of Jesus as brother mean to Christians in Africa today? One important facet is the humanity of Jesus it conveys. In this regard it overlaps with Jesus as ancestor, according to Catholic Archbishop Ndingi Mwana a'Nzeki, who summed up as follows: "Jesus is our elder brother in life, he is our ancestor. He was born of Mary, he was the Son of God, he was a man like ourselves." Irene Odotei first voiced her understanding of Jesus as brother, cited above, in relation to the incarnation. Asked who Jesus is to her personally, she immediately responded:

> Jesus Christ for me today is God-made-man, who became man because of me, to know how I feel, to know how I think, and to die for me and go back up there. So then because he has become like me, he knows where I'm hurting. He knows and he, being there, intercedes for me to the Father. So to me Jesus is a representative who understands, I mean a brother.

A similar statement from Kenyan Catholic clergyman Peter Gichure under-lines the intimacy associated with this human portrait of Jesus. Like Odotei, Gichure straightaway replied to the question of who Jesus is, as follows:

> I think Jesus Christ for me today is really my brother. I think that's why he came, as the Son, to make that link, that I am to him as a brother, that God, in a very special way, wants me to have that close relationship. As Hebrews says, God wants us to be sons and daughters of God and Jesus Christ brings that union. So, for me, Jesus is the one who will treat me like my brother, a brother who loves me, who wants anything good for me, who will stand for me even when I'm troubled and who will rejoice with me when I'm happy.

Not only the intimacy but also the human solidarity comes to light in interpret-ing Jesus as brother. Interestingly, Kenyan Protestant clergyman John Gatu raised this image in the context of discussing Jesus as liberator, explaining, "This is why even the word *brother* would mean so much. He's so *concerned*, he is *that* concerned, as a brother who suffers with me. And therefore he is certainly my liberator." So the humanity of Jesus, as the image of brother highlights, clearly connotes intimacy, attentiveness, solidarity, and support.

Another facet of this christological portrait is the emphasis on Jesus being present and contemporary, particularly in contrast to the ancestors. For example, David Gitari, archbishop of the Anglican Church of Kenya, objected to the im-age of Jesus as ancestor "because he is contemporary, whereas ancestors are dead." He continued, "In fact, in our prayer book, we call him 'Jesus Brother,' 'I am Brother Jesus.' He is contemporary, he is with us." Jesus' presence, con-veyed through this image, also speaks of his availability to Christians. For in-stance, Catholic Mary Kizito related what she learned of Jesus as a young girl: "My mother used to say, 'Jesus is, I mean, God, but Jesus is also like your brother. He's somebody you can run to when you have a problem.'" These early impressions of Jesus evidently marked Kizito's later understanding, for when asked who Jesus is to her today, she replied, "To me, Jesus is a friend, Jesus is a brother, and Jesus of course is God and he is the savior." She elaborated on how these convictions were reinforced through her experience as a nun and con-cluded with a statement of how she developed "a special relationship with Jesus as a friend, as a brother." Moreover, if Jesus as brother portrays his contempo-rary presence and his availability, it also suggests his protection. In the focus group of Ghanaian Protestant clergy, Stephen Antwi volunteered the image of Jesus as brother and explained it as follows:

> I see him as a big brother who protects me from witches and all the juju. When you say "juju," that is evil spirits in our system. So I see him as a big brother who has power to protect me when I am in trouble with those things which can harm our life.

Finally, African Christians stress the image of Jesus as universal brother in relation to serious tensions among ethnic groups within their life situations. In the focus group of Ghanaian Catholic clergy, Anthony Kornu described traditional acts of valor in eliminating people from other societies. While admitting that ethnicity and ethnocentrism are inescapable, Kornu asserted that a true understanding of "Jesus Christ the universal brother" militates against ethnic war and genocide. Bénézet Bujo has developed this christological image in accord with Jesus as life-giver and as ancestor who, by surpassing all other ancestors, alone unites all humanity into a single clan and ethnic group. He delineates the ramifications for appropriating Jesus in this way:

> He has come to bring peace and to bring back all men to brotherhood by suppressing every ethnic difference and also racial and others. He is the ancestor of all humanity, for he is the second Adam who creates a new man. From now on there is neither black nor white, neither yellow nor red; there is neither Jew nor Greek, neither Tutsi nor Hutu, neither Luba nor Munyamwezi nor Chagga nor Agikuyu; there is neither slave nor free man, neither man nor woman, neither cultivator nor minister of states, *"for all you are only one in Christ Jesus. But if you belong to Christ, you are therefore the descendants of Abraham, heirs according to the promise" (Gal 3:28–29).*[16]

Thus the image of Jesus as brother is said to communicate his humanity in a meaningful way, incorporating notions of intimacy and solidarity, contemporary presence and availability, protection from harm, and peace amid the hostilities of divided humanity.

Conclusion: Jesus as Brother

While the image of Jesus as brother was not specifically tested in the present research, the extent to which it emerged confirms its importance to many African Christians. On the basis of the rationale and meaning outlined above, several points of significance are noteworthy. First, akin to the image of Jesus as ancestor, this christological portrait serves as a hermeneutical bridge joining biblical and African concepts. In other words, it allows the clear affirmation of key biblical teachings about Christ in a way that truly resonates with many Africans' understanding and experience of brotherhood from their cultural heritage. For example, of the various perceptions discussed above regarding Jesus as brother from biblical and African perspectives, the intimacy of relationship clearly comes to light. Often personal testimony suggested the depth of closeness experienced, as when Kenyan Protestant lay woman Mabel Correa's eyes filled with tears in responding to the question of who Jesus is to her: "He's my *most* beloved, best, precious friend in the *whole* world! He's my elder brother— I'll start crying in a minute! He's the most, most—my treasure and my delight. Those are the ways that I describe him."

Second, according to these African Christians, the image of Jesus as brother clearly enhances one's understanding of the incarnation. Consequently, they claim to grasp the reality and significance of Jesus more deeply and personally, as Irene Odotei attested. Following her interpretation of the incarnation, out-lined above, she concluded:

> So to me Jesus is real, more real than the Jesus I learned about, who wasn't interested in my pair of shoes or in all the mundane things of life. He's inter-ested and he does everything well. So that's what Jesus is to me, a big brother and God made man.

Furthermore, the implications of the incarnation emerge in relation to human hostilities, particularly those based on ethnicity. Obviously, African Christian reflection on Jesus as universal brother does not automatically resolve the wide-spread ethnic tensions in many African contexts. Nonetheless, the fact that Afri-can Christians do reflect theologically on Jesus as brother, and relate personally the impact this has had upon their own prejudices, demonstrates the potential for this christological portrait to address crucial issues in Africa today.

Finally, expressions of Jesus as brother, among other family images, contrib-ute to the comprehensive character of many African Christologies. That is to say, when African Christians articulate the identity and significance of Jesus, they often convey an all-encompassing view of the person of Christ. A typical illustration came from Protestant lay man Yeboa Amoa, managing director of the Ghana Stock Exchange. Asked who Jesus is to him personally, he responded:

> Jesus Christ is everything. I mean, Jesus Christ is creator—he made every-thing, including me. Jesus Christ, at the same time, is my brother—the Bible says so. Jesus Christ is my friend. Jesus Christ is my father, because he and the Father are one. Jesus Christ is my provider, he's my healer, he's my sanc-tifier, he's my righteousness—all those things. He's my peace, he's my strength, and so on. There's plenty! Jesus Christ is all in all—the Bible says that everything consists in him, so, he's all. He's the Alpha and the Omega, the beginning and the end.

Within this sweeping description of Jesus, the relational images, including that of brother, are prominent. The significance of this observation is developed fur-ther in the following sections on Jesus as mother, lover, and friend.

JESUS AS MOTHER

African perceptions of Jesus as family member extend to parental images of Jesus as mother and father. The present discussion focuses primarily on Jesus as mother, since this portrait carries the weight of evidence, for reasons outlined below. In keeping with the preceding discussion of Jesus as brother, this section explores the data, rationale, meaning, and conclusions regarding the image of Jesus as mother.

The Data

As with the image of Jesus as brother, no set question was asked in the oral interviews regarding Jesus as mother. Nonetheless, certain theologians, church leaders, and laity voiced perceptions to this effect. Nasimiyu Wasike is noteworthy as a theologian consciously promoting the image of Jesus as mother in theological publications and in personal conversation. Yet if the concept arises as an academic construction "from above," it also emerges as an indigenous insight "from below." That is to say, church leaders attest to prayers, songs, and sermons expressing Jesus as mother, particularly in vernacular languages. For example, Catholic and Protestant church leaders in Ghana related how Christians sometimes refer to Christ as "Mother Jesus." Catholic Bishop Palmer-Buckle remarked, "Don't be surprised to hear them call Jesus *Obatanpa, Yesu Obatanpa. Obatanpanpa,* that means 'a good mother.' They do refer to him that way in their prayers and in their songs." Protestant minister Robert Aboagye-Mensah made the same observation, explaining that "*Obatan* is a very feminine expression, a motherly person who has a motherly care, which is very fascinating, actually."

Data consisting of vernacular expressions of motherhood applied to Jesus were evidenced more in the Ghanaian context than in Kenya or Uganda. This may reflect the more extensive use of vernacular languages in Ghanaian Christianity witnessed in the specified contexts of this research. Nevertheless, even though very few Kenyan and Ugandan respondents explicitly volunteered the image of Jesus as mother, they did articulate perceptions of Jesus that are closely associated with the concepts underlying this christological portrait. For example, Kenyan Catholic clergyman David Kamau volunteered notions of Jesus as father and as an African parent. In response to my subsequent question about the idea of Jesus as mother, he replied:

> First of all, who is a mother in our African context? A mother is one who is concerned about the children. Actually mother is the immediate person that the children will go to. They will never fear a mother. If they want to go to the father, they will go through the mother. So mother is a person who is very close to the children, who understands the children. When they cry, when they want food, mothers understand. So, I think Jesus is a mother, in that sense that he understands us, he is very close to us, and therefore you should not be afraid of going to him.

Probed further as to whether he had previously thought of Jesus as mother himself, he admitted that he had not consciously considered it. Interestingly, however, he affirmed that the idea has operated at some level in his understanding, and that when someone else names the image, it does indeed make sense to him and it resonates with his experience of Jesus. Therefore the portrait of Jesus as mother warrants closer examination despite its relative lack of attestation in the research.

Rationale for the Image of Jesus as Mother

The image of Christ as mother is rooted in an analogy developed between Jesus' ministry and African concepts of motherhood. Nasimiyu Wasike proclaims God's call for believers to follow Jesus in loving one's neighbor above self and in restoring them to wholeness by nurturing life in all its dimensions. She then establishes the analogy of motherhood:

> In Jesus' life we see him take on the qualities of a mother. He is a nurturer of life, especially that of the weak. Jesus' motherhood is characterized by nourishment, protection, and care for the poor and marginalized. The way Jesus related to people, and especially to the disciples, showed a warm tenderness, affection, receptivity and a readiness to restore life to wholeness.[17]

Having drawn this analogy, Nasimiyu Wasike immediately points out that African women's primary experience in relation to others is as mother. While this reality provides rationale for the christological portrait being advocated, Nasimiyu Wasike objects to the role of mother being overemphasized in African cultures to the extent that it determines women's social status. She emphasizes that "women are not merely child-bearers" and that the concept of mothering goes beyond physically birthing children.[18] Hence, she invites "the African man to follow Jesus and take on the character of motherhood, so that all women and men Christians in Africa mother one another and mother their continent."[19]

Insights from four main sources merge to provide rationale for the image of Jesus as mother: the Bible, the African heritage, the Western Christian heritage, and personal experience. These sources inevitably blend together, yet they are dealt with in turn for the present purpose of analysis. First, the Bible is again set forth as the fundamental wellspring for Christology. The leading proponent for this image, Nasimiyu Wasike, insisted in the interviews that "we have to go to scripture to discover our own Christology, or Christologies, rather than the Christologies of other people, of other continents." She further claimed, "I was depending mainly on the scriptures to see how Jesus is mother, and he's really mother there—nurturing life, protecting life, and playing the role of a mother in our traditional African setting." Citing Jesus' miracle of feeding the five thousand, she questions, "Was not Jesus a mother to the crowd?"[20] The query is based on her observation that in Africa, it is the mother's role to make sure that the children eat. She also refers to John 13, where Jesus' hospitality is symbolized in the Last Supper and his washing the disciples' feet, tasks that also are said to be characteristic of African mothers.

As for the obvious fact that in the biblical record Jesus is not literally a mother, Nasimiyu Wasike explained, "Some people say, 'What? Jesus was not a woman!' Yes, but we are talking about Christ. Physically, Jesus was a man. But Christ is no longer just man. He's a reality that goes beyond the human limitations of sexes." This statement provided one instance, in the present research, of Jesus the historical figure being distinguished from Christ, the risen Lord, who transcends the particularities of human ethnicity and gender. Certainly the image of

Jesus as mother remains problematic for those who interpret it literally, as though the historical Jesus is actually considered to be a mother. Yet for those who interpret it figuratively, as Sam Kibicho explained in the focus group of Kenyan Protestant clergy, "it's a role. In particular, we are talking of Jesus as a servant, this Suffering Servant in Isaiah and also in Matthew. Look at the extent of this serving—our mothers will do that. They will lack in order to sustain life." In view of these theological and hermeneutical considerations, then, some African Christians find biblical warrant for portraying Jesus as mother.

Already it has become apparent that traditional concepts of motherhood in the African heritage shape perceptions of Jesus today. In addition to those aspects noted above, Ghanaian Protestant clergyman Aboagye-Mensah explained, "I think the motherhood Christology has come up because most of us, due to our own traditional backgrounds, are more close to our mothers than we are to our fathers." He suggested that this is partly due to the polygamy system, in which mothers are generally perceived as loving caregivers while fathers remain relatively distant figures representing authority and discipline. Aboagye-Mensah concluded, "So maybe that's why the feminine image is useful when you're talking about Jesus as caring, for then we think more of him in that sense." In the focus group of Kenyan Protestant clergy, Oscar Muriu outlined further concepts of motherhood as applied to Jesus:

> Interestingly, the very roles that you see Jesus depicted in, in the scriptures—
> we perceive him as the shepherd and such—when I look at my upbringing
> and my community interaction, that role was actually fulfilled by women.
> Jesus is a good mother, if I may put it that way, because it's the women in my
> life who have been the peacemakers and the reconcilers, etc. The men in my
> life haven't always been very good at that. In fact if anything, they bring
> disorder and chaos, but it's the women who always, consistently come through
> in these roles. Who love, whatever the cost, who are willing to go to any
> extent to be available, to bring peace, etc. So that, in a sense, the imagery of
> God as a father in the New Testament, particularly in Jesus' own words, for
> me, is better fulfilled in the role of a mother.

Other facets of motherhood derived from the African heritage and contemporary experience await elaboration in the next section. However, these few examples suffice to illustrate the influence that traditional concepts of motherhood exert upon present understandings of Jesus.

The image of Jesus as mother stems, third, from the heritage of Western Christianity. More specifically, in highlighting Jesus as a nurturer of life, Nasimiyu Wasike and her fellow religious sisters look to St. Francis of Assisi as one who both embodies and prescribes the mothering role of Jesus. Mary Savio explained:

> In our tradition as Franciscans, Francis asked his brothers to take turns being
> mother to each other. He told them that in their life, they should have inter-
> vals of prayer, where they would withdraw from the apostolate, looking after

the lepers or the poor. They were to go away in threes or fours, where the three would spend most of the time in prayer, and the fourth brother was to be mother to those three. He was to look for food and feed them and care for them as a mother would care for her child. So, that also is behind the image of Jesus as mother. I mean, for us, that value from Francis, from Italy, fits in very much with our culture.

Savio's statement illustrates how biblical sources, Western Christian traditions, and African cultures converge to sustain the image of Jesus as mother.

The christological portrait from these three sources is reinforced through personal experience, whether of being mothered or of mothering others. John Pobee is among those who spoke candidly of the impact a mother can have in shaping one's perceptions of Jesus. In Pobee's case his serious illness as a child prompted his mother to relinquish her teaching career to ensure that he survived:

> I know what my mother has meant for me. She sacrificed that I may live. I know what my mother has done, and therefore my theology is in a sense a part of my biography. When I talk about compassion and love, the models I use are the love and compassion that I experienced from my mother, and my father also. We're a very close family, so the images come out of my own experiences.

Concomitantly, one's own experience of mothering fosters the appropriation of Jesus as mother. Once again, the role of mother goes beyond physically bearing children, as Nasimiyu Wasike ably demonstrates in her position as mother superior of the Little Sisters of St. Francis. Reflecting on how her experience of "mothering" 520 sisters in Kenya, Uganda, and Tanzania has affected her own understanding of Jesus as mother, she commented:

> It has enhanced it and it has made me experience what I'm talking about, in reality. I could just conceptualize it, but now I have to put it in practice, so that I am really washing my sisters' feet. I am their mother. And as a mother, I have to be able to give, and give, and give. And sometimes you are really exhausted, but you have to continue giving.

While the meaning of Jesus as mother requires further explication in the next section, it is evident that the image arises from a combination of sources including the Bible, the African heritage, Western Christian traditions, and personal experience.

The Meaning of Jesus as Mother

Key aspects of the christological content infusing this image are apparent in the preceding discussion. Most fundamentally, Nasimiyu Wasike presents the concept of mother as "one who nurtures all life without discrimination, favouritism or nepotism."[21] Juxtaposing this definition with biblical accounts of Jesus' ministry, Nasimiyu Wasike insists that "all the followers of Christ, particularly those in Africa, are called today to be mothers that nurture life in all its different dimensions."[22] She sets the christological image against the backdrop of certain forces in contemporary Africa that are said to deny Africans' control over their own destiny and freedom to attain their God-given potential. Examples include the structural adjustment programs and crippling economic debts, the HIV/AIDS pandemic, civil wars, drought, famine, and political killings. In the face of these life-diminishing forces, Nasimiyu Wasike develops the analogy between Jesus' ministry and the role of mothers in traditional African societies. On this basis she portrays Jesus Christ, who is said to be reliving his passion in the people of Africa, as a mother giving birth to a new Africa. The vision is for this Mother Jesus, by working in and through Africans, to "give birth to new and better relationships that will respect life at all levels," and will honor Christ's presence in others despite their ethnic affiliation, their social, economic or political ideology, or their gender.[23] Nasimiyu Wasike sums up the essence of the christological image as follows:

> Africa today needs a Mother's love. African women as mothers have sustained and continued to nurture the life in Africa despite the ethnic wars, the military dictatorships, oppressive governments and economic hardships which deprive many people of the basic necessities. . . . African Christian people—men and women—have to look at Jesus the mother who said, "No one can have greater love than to lay down one's life for his/her friends" (John 15:13). Jesus as mother freely accepted suffering and death on the cross to show his extreme love and liberation for the whole humanity and creation. This is the Jesus that African Christians should emulate. . . . The woman of Africa has given her life for the love of her children but the man of Africa must join hands with women of Africa and follow the example of Jesus the mother.[24]

When challenged as to whether the image of Jesus as mother is not restrictive and more alienating to men than the neutral term *parent,* Nasimiyu Wasike strongly denied any intention of antagonizing men in promoting the motherhood image. On the contrary, she reiterated that "nurturing aspects are not limited to women," and that "if we are all to be mothers, we are all supposed to be nurturers: giving life, saving life." She admitted that she considered employing the term *parent* for Jesus but decided against it for two reasons: first, the need to recover the traditional African concept of mother, which in her estimation has been "downtrodden" or "not respected enough"; and second, *parent* does not convey the same connotations as *mother* in Africa. She explained that "mother, traditionally, was that warmth in the family," and that "traditionally a mother was never killed, because a woman was life! If you kill her, you're killing life!" Lamenting that this convention is no longer honored, Nasimiyu Wasike underlined that it is the traditional respect and intimacy associated with motherhood that she seeks to convey in the christological portrait. In so doing, she illustrates the overlap between the images of Jesus as life-giver and Jesus as loved one.

Certainly, the proposal of Jesus as mother was balanced by additional voices advocating Jesus as parent or as father. For example, Kenyan Catholic clergyman David Kamau outlined the respect that Africans generally have for their parents, based on two beliefs: first, that a parent not only gives birth to a child but also sustains the life of that child even throughout adulthood; and second, that a parent's power to either bless or curse the child is considered very important. On this basis Kamau offered the following perceptions of Jesus:

Now, Christ is our father. Being God-man, he is the father of all fathers. And therefore, when he blesses, you are blessed by the father of all fathers, and therefore you get a lot of benefits. So I can say that Christ is an African parent who bears the Africans, just because he is the giver of life—not only now, physical life, but even eternal life. So I think of Christ as a parent.

While these more inclusive images did emerge in the research, the weight of evidence, and hence the focus of this section, remains on Jesus as mother. Here, various voices corroborate Nasimiyu Wasike's assertion regarding the connotations of motherhood in Africa. For example, Ghanaian Protestant clergyman Abraham Akrong stated:

Mothering is also beyond the quality of women. It's a symbol of nurture and care, that aspect of human life that will not allow the prodigal son to go. That is portrayed more by motherhood than by fatherhood. So, I mean in a real dispassionate way, you could talk of Jesus as mother in terms of the nurture and the loving kindness and the grace and mercy that Jesus shows. These are qualities attached to ideal motherhood, I don't think it's too much tied to gender.

Likewise, Ghanaian Catholic clergyman Charles Palmer-Buckle observed that vernacular songs sometimes address Christ as "Mother Jesus," because "for us, motherhood is a symbol of love, of mercy, of compassion." His further comments warrant citation for the clear explication of rationale and significance provided:

Actually God has always been presented in our culture as both father and mother, and so transferring it to Jesus is nothing very strange. The only thing is that those who use the metaphor do not necessarily think of Jesus as a female, but they think of Jesus as one who expresses these aspects of maternal concern, love, compassion. So it's something that I use myself in my sermons, in my prayers, in my church without any difficulty. He remains a male, but he has these beautiful attributes of the African woman who is motherly, caring, compassionate, merciful, sharing of herself to the point of giving up everything for her children.

Finally, respondents expressed additional concepts associated with motherhood such as provision, protection, and guidance. In sum, Kenyan Circle member Mary

Getui voiced the general consensus of those affirming Jesus as mother, stating, "I look at Jesus not as male or as female, but as those qualities of mother."

Conclusion: Jesus as Mother

While the image of Jesus as mother is by no means the most prevalent christological portrait to arise in the research, a number of respondents certainly affirmed its meaning and significance to them both personally and corporately. Like the image of Jesus as brother, this christological portrait captures the intimacy of relationship that Africans traditionally associate with motherhood. Put simply, Kenyan clergyman David Kamau spoke of his mother as "very close to me, and I think Jesus is someone like that, he is very close to us." The notion of mother potentially deepens African Christians' understanding of Jesus, as Kenyan Catholic Archbishop Ndingi Mwana a'Nzeki indicated. In response to the question of christological images that are especially meaningful to Africans, Nzeki stated that the greatest thing for him is the fact that Jesus died and rose for us. To explain his point about the difficulty of dying for another, he drew upon his own ethnic society, the Akamba, and related the common notion that only a mother will die for her child, in contrast to a father. If a wild animal comes, a father will run for a weapon, leaving the child to die, while the mother will attack the animal at her own peril to save the child. So although Nzeki admits he cannot relate personally to the image of Jesus as mother, since historically Jesus was a man, he nonetheless draws the above parallel and affirms that "Jesus' love for us can be compared with that love of the mother and beyond that."

If appropriating Jesus as mother increases understanding and intimacy with Christ, according to those who affirm this christological image, it also illustrates the process of indigenous formulations of Christology. Ghanaian Protestant clergyman Abraham Akrong highlighted the "wonderful contextualizations" found in vernacular prayers, particularly those of women who address Jesus as "the good mother whose stomach *pains* when something has happened to her children." Akrong explained that this vivid impression of Jesus stems from Akan Christians drawing upon the rich repertoire of traditional titles for God and ascribing them to Christ. He then pointed out the significance of this process:

> I think it is very legitimate, because it helps *explore* the function of Jesus from our *traditional* perspectives, to know him more and more. So I think that the *mother* symbol is fundamental to an African conception of God. And what has happened is that *as* we go along, and Christ becomes significant, some of these parental, motherly symbols which associate Jesus to God, have been transferred to Christ.

Ghanaian Protestant clergyman Aboagye-Mensah concurred, and pointed out further significance in claiming that this indigenous image of Jesus has given him "a much broader view of who Christ is." Citing examples from the gospels of how Jesus cared for individuals, such as the woman with the issue of blood whom he healed and restored to society, Aboagye-Mensah concluded:

So the caring Jesus will come out more for me if I begin to see it in terms of the motherhood of Jesus, which will sound outrageous in Western theology! I think we need to tease out that aspect from the African background. The African understanding of Christ in this way may be able to bring a richer perspective of who Christ is, for me, than perhaps the Western one of the masculine, powerful Christ.

While acknowledging that Christ is victor, as depicted in the masculine imagery, Aboagye-Mensah underlined that at the same time Jesus is very caring, and that the two sides belong together:

My African background, and the Western kind of theology, if I am able to hold the two together, give me a richer perspective of who Christ is, than a small, narrow one. So that again you have a holistic view of Christ—Christ who is powerful, yet Christ who is very caring, who is motherly, and so on.

The image of Jesus as mother not only illustrates indigenous perceptions of Christ in Africa but also serves to recover certain feminine aspects of the Triune God that may not be as adequately acknowledged in Western Christologies. Thus certain African Christians advocate this portrait of Jesus.

Jesus as Lover

Within the sphere of Jesus as loved one, christological portraits of family and friendship overlap in the image of Jesus as lover. Once again, no set question was asked regarding this image, yet respondents attested to its presence and meaningfulness within their contexts. Since this representation of Jesus corresponds closely to the family images discussed above and the friendship images discussed below, the present section is confined to a brief consideration of the prevalence, rationale, meaning, and significance of Jesus as lover.

Ever since Ghanaians encountered Christ, according to Anthony Kornu in the focus group of Catholic clergy, appropriating the love of Jesus has been fundamental to their Christology:

I am talking about Jesus Christ as a lover. In the beginning, maybe those who are mystics are allowed to think of themselves in their relationship with Jesus Christ in terminologies of a love relationship. But now, even in popular music, people sing of Jesus as "my darling Jesus." And even some of the love songs which the youth sing will be transposed gradually into gospel music.

Kornu added that this phenomenon is not simply a popular fad but a reality that touches people deeply regardless of their age. He cited further evidence in the widespread devotion to the Sacred Heart of Christ, which he interprets as follows:

The Sacred Heart devotion is so strong, from the very moment that the church came to some of our areas. People would like to have special communications toward Jesus Christ because he loves us so much and his heart is glowing with love. And yet this heart is pierced, and he offers it and says, "This is my love for you. Give me your heart."

While admitting genuine struggle and failure in his relationship with Christ, Kornu concluded that "the one thing which keeps me going is the deep knowledge and assurance that Jesus loves me."

Contextual evidence corroborates Kornu's testimony regarding widespread perceptions of Jesus as lover. Portraits of the Sacred Heart of Jesus are frequently found in the homes of Catholic respondents in Kenya and Ghana, typifying the "visual Christologies" that reflect a love relationship with Jesus. And Sacred Heart posters are sold on the streets, often among posters of movie stars and sports celebrities. A large statue outside St. Peter's Cathedral in Kumasi, Ghana, portrays Jesus as the Sacred Heart, a scepter in his right hand, and the world, with Ghana highlighted, in his left hand. Taxi drivers in the Akuapem region, Ghana, sometimes advertise "Jesus loves" on the dashboard of their taxis. Altogether, then, the oral interviews and the contextual evidence reveal the importance of a love relationship between Jesus and his followers.

At times the concept of Jesus as lover takes on the particular expression of Jesus as husband. On par with other christological portraits, rationale is found in the merging of biblical and African notions with personal experience. Ghanaian PACWA representative Felicia Opare-Saforo voiced biblical grounds, citing Isaiah 54:5, for women appropriating Jesus in this way:

There are so many women who now know that Christ is their strength and Christ is their everything. They love him, and they adore him, and—even widows, as they read the word of God and get to know that "Your creator is your husband," and all that, they rely on him. So we are relying on Christ and people really actually love him.

Aspects of African tradition and contemporary experience also prompt perceptions of Jesus as husband. In Kenya, Protestant clergyman Peter Bisem acknowledged that among the Kalenjin, traditionally "women have no identity in my community themselves"; their identity is derived from their husbands and sons. Likewise, in Ghana, Protestant clergyman Abraham Akrong stated that in Akan tradition womanhood is defined by "husbands first, children second. If you don't have a husband and a child, your identity as a woman is in crisis." In this cultural context women evidently seek their personal identity in Christ rather than in the dictates of their traditional culture. Furthermore, even those women with a husband and children purportedly turn to Jesus as the one who is ultimately trustworthy and faithful. For example, Ghanaian Protestant clergyman Thomas Oduro described his own Akan society as "masculine, so women right from the beginning are trained to trust or to lean on men." Then, through experiencing disappointment in their relations with various male figures, Christian women come to discover that "the next man that you can trust, who will not disappoint you, is obviously Jesus Christ." Oduro concluded:

> So women see Jesus Christ as somebody who is worthy of trust, a man who is faithful, and a man who you can depend on and get results, both physical and spiritual. Your husband may disappoint you, your father, your brother, but Jesus Christ will never do that. And he can do more than your husband, father, or brother can do.

From the coalescence of rationale grounded in biblical teaching, African traditions and personal experience, the conviction of Jesus as lover is found particularly, but not exclusively, among Christian women. Like other christological images, it functions analogously in that Jesus is understood to fulfill the role of a lover. For example, Ghanaian Circle member Elizabeth Amoah described a common vernacular song, said to be favored by women: "Jesus is my everything, he's my friend, my brother, my husband—everything." "In other words," she continued, "for me, Jesus is someone who has the capacity, the power, to help me go through the struggles of life, in any aspect." Other women respondents echoed this conviction, including Ghanaian queenmother Nana Dokua. She stated that from the Bible and from their experiences in life, Ghanaian Christian women affirm Jesus' protection and provision, saying, "Oye me boafo" (he is my helper). Combining various images of Jesus as loved one, she continued, "He's my daddy, my mom, my husband, my son. Oh, a lot more. The African women, they take him to be everything." She also mentioned that among the women coming to her for advice, a certain widow wept about her problems. Nana Dokua recalled advising her, "Hey! Take Jesus as your personal savior, and he will help you. He will act as your husband, all right?" Thus the concept of a lover, particularly a husband as defined in many African societies, serves as a meaningful construct for appropriating Jesus Christ.

Moreover, several single Christian women, both Protestant and Catholic, voiced the reality and the significance of Jesus as lover to them personally. Kenyan Protestant clergywoman Anne Wambugu recounted having recently received a birthday card from a friend whose written greetings encouraged her to "walk with your 'lover,' Jesus Christ." Wambugu affirmed that this depiction of Jesus resonates deeply with her, saying, "This is a very good statement." Strikingly, Ugandan religious sister Mary Cleophas responded immediately to the question of who Jesus is to her personally:

> Often I look at Jesus as a lover to me. That's the title I give him. When I look at Jesus really coming down, leaving all his Godhead there, reducing himself to my level and then even lower by allowing himself to go through whatever he went through and eventually dying the way he died, I feel it cost a lot of love for somebody to get to that level. And then when I consider what I have personally experienced in life, I find that he's really a lover! He's the savior, but all those things he did because he loves.

The prominence of this christological image for Cleophas and her fellow Little Sisters of St. Francis finds tangible expression in the architectural design of their new Generalate House in Jinja, Uganda. The compound has the chapel in the center and separate blocks of living quarters and offices erected in a circle around it. Built to reflect the traditional homestead, this design is interpreted by religious sister Mary Pius as follows:

> The master of the home, the husband, his hut was in the middle. Then, around that hut there were other huts which belonged to the wives—they used to marry many wives, our ancestors. So, we said, if that is the case, we could have the home of Jesus in the center and we the followers, we take the circle around.

Thus respondents attested to the importance of Jesus as lover in shaping their personal lives and even in designing their physical environment.

Several aspects of the significance of this christological portrait have already emerged, such as the personal identity and sense of belonging found in Jesus. Ghanaian PACWA representative Florence Y. B. Yeboah summed up, "I know he is my lover, and he has made me his own." The intimacy of relationship associated with Jesus as lover was described vividly by a recent convert to Christ, Kenyan Protestant lay woman Sheny Kassam. Having become a believer in the midst of her marital breakdown, she stated enthusiastically that Jesus is

> obviously so real and he is the Son of God and he is Immanuel, the savior, the Christ—everything. But for me, Jesus came just like a prince on a white horse! I know one thing, that for him to choose me and to come and save me, he must be my knight in shining armor! That's the image of Jesus: my knight in shining armor.

She voiced the experiential reality of salvation in terms indicative of a love relationship. Furthermore, respondents clearly look to Christ to fulfill the roles of companion and provider associated with a human lover. However, whether or not the christological reflections convey the particular connotations of lover, certainly the love of Jesus is paramount in the expressed perceptions of these African Christians. Ghanaian Catholic clergyman Matthew Edusei summarized the significance of Christ's love, theologically and experientially, as follows:

> In other words, Jesus brings home to me who God is. And he is *love*. And that love you can see in his ministry and also on the cross. And love is so important to me, as a way of life, as a calling that is precious. Jesus, indeed, exemplifies that to the fullest: "As I have loved, so also you must love." So the grounding of my being, what makes me a human being, the source of it all, is discovered in who Jesus has been, and continues to be in my life, calling me each day to love—that sacrificial love that he came on earth to show us. And grants me the grace to rise up when I fail, to go to him when I need him, so that my life will be re-filled, strengthened, for this love. That makes him so attractive to me!

Without doubt, then, Jesus as loved one features largely in contemporary African Christologies.

JESUS AS FRIEND

Participation in communal life in Africa extends beyond kinship structures to include other relational ties. The present section focuses on Jesus as friend, since this category arose most conspicuously among the wider relational images. This christological image is examined with respect to the data, rationale, meaning, and significance of the image.

THE DATA

Theologians, church leaders, and laity alike identify Jesus as a personal friend. The prevalence of this perception emerged clearly in the oral interviews. Although no question was asked in this regard, thirteen of the thirty individual respondents in Kenya and Uganda initiated comments about Jesus as friend, as did at least seventeen of the thirty-five individuals in Ghana. One additional Ghanaian did not explicitly propose the image, yet she emphasized that "Jesus calls me his friend!" She also spoke of the impact upon women "when one discovers that there is a savior who stays closer than the closest friend or brother, and he becomes real to them." In addition, the image was volunteered in seven of the twelve focus groups. In the majority of cases from individual and group interviews, respondents articulated Jesus as friend in reply, often immediate, to the question of who Jesus is to them personally. For example, Ghanaian Catholic clergyman Charles Palmer-Buckle pondered: "Who is Jesus Christ for me today? First and foremost he is a friend with whom I talk and relate ordinarily." So the extent to which the selected African Christians offered this christological image suggests its importance to them.

In addition, Jesus as friend features clearly in the specified contexts of African Christianity. For example in Kenya, Catholic clergyman Peter Kiarie identified the Kikuyu translation of "What a Friend We Have in Jesus" as a very popular song in his area. Likewise, in Ghana, respondents voiced the impact of hymns expressing the theme of Jesus' friendship upon them personally. Protestant clergyman Dan Antwi explained:

> In the Presbyterian Church we have hymns—they are mostly translated into Twi from some of the old German hymns. But, I have come to a deeper understanding of Jesus through some of the Presbyterian hymns about Jesus. For example, there is one which says, "Yesu mikra adamfo pa" (Jesus, friend of my soul). It's very, very moving, you know, very intimate and it makes you feel that you are with Jesus!

Aside from translated hymns, vernacular compositions, like the following Twi chorus, often reflect Jesus as friend:

Anwanwa Do Ben Ni	*What Wondrous Love Is This?*
Anwanwa do ben ni?	What wondrous love is this?
Odo ben ni?	What love is this?
Anwanwa do ben ni?	What wondrous love is this?
Odo ben ni.	A wondrous love.
Mene Yesu atena, mene n'anante	To live with Jesus
Mafa Yesu se m'adamfo pa	And to walk with Him
Anwanwa do ben ni?	To have Jesus, as my own dear friend
Odo ben ni?	What wondrous love is this?
	What love is this?[25]

Further evidence emerged through participant observation in various meetings with African Christians, when Jesus' friendship was articulated in worship, preaching, testimonies, and prayers. One clear example is the lyrics of a solo sung by Diana Akuwumi at the PACWA Prayer Day in Accra on September 5, 1998:

> *Oh, What a Friend*
> He holds my life
> Jesus the man of Calvary
> Whether day or night,
> Rain or shine, He leads the way
> He holds the troubles and the storms of my life
>   [2d time:] He holds the problems and the pain of
>   my life.
> And he gives me peace, perfect peace
> No man can love me
> As he has done—
> Shedding his blood for me
>
> *Chorus:*
> Oh, what a Friend (x2)
> That Jesus is.[26]

Finally, according to some respondents, certain pictures like the Sacred Heart portray the friendship of Jesus. Discussing that particular picture, Ghanaian Catholic clergyman Joseph Aggrey commented, "See this, the heart, represents *love*. So any time that I see it, I see Jesus to be a loving friend." Hence, the oral interviews and the contextual evidence leave little doubt that the image of Jesus as friend features prominently in the understanding and experience of these African Christians.

RATIONALE FOR THE IMAGE OF JESUS AS FRIEND

The Bible certainly informs perceptions of Jesus' friendship. For instance, Kenyan Protestant lay woman Marcy Muhia alluded to gospel materials in speaking of "Christ who is the friend of sinners, this friend who would lay down his life for me." Similarly, Ghanaian Protestant clergyman Dan Antwi reflected on the overlap between Christology and pneumatology when stating that a "very powerful" image of Jesus is "the idea of the ever-living companion of Jesus— the ascriptions which Jesus gives to the Holy Spirit, who in turn is none other than Jesus in another form." The Western missionary inheritance further shapes this christological image through, for example, the transmission of hymns and catechetical materials.

Although biblical teaching and Western Christianity lend substance to the concept of Jesus as friend for African Christians, it is evidently the common experience of friendship that significantly shapes their expressed Christologies. Many respondents recalled having learned of Jesus' friendship from a very early age, and they voiced the impact that this understanding has had upon them throughout life. One vivid illustration came from Kenyan Circle member Hannah Kinoti, who described her mother's words to her when she was very young:

> Every time she escorted me to the road to catch my bus to go to school, in faraway places from my home district, she would tell me, "Take the hand of the Lord, and don't let it go." So to me, because of that ingrained belief that here, the Lord is with me, Jesus is with me, I see Jesus as my companion, my protector, and my refuge. He's my friend. I know I have turned to him in prayer, many times, and I know my prayers have been answered. So he is, to me, a living companion, one who takes my hand and he doesn't let it go.

Likewise, Ghanaian Catholic clergyman Charles Palmer-Buckle affirmed simply that "Jesus was right from the word go a living, personal friend with whom I grew up." That the experience of friendship significantly influences people's perceptions of Jesus in this regard is manifested further in the next section on the meaning of the christological image.

The Meaning of Jesus as Friend

The many dimensions of friendship expressed in relation to Jesus reveal the richness of this christological portrait. First, respondents delineated impressions of Jesus as a close and faithful companion throughout life's journey. Kenyan Protestant lay woman Marcy Muhia commented that "the image of Christ as one who is a friend, a heart friend, but a really wise heart friend who is able to walk with you through life, in every situation of life, is a strong one for me." In a similar vein, Ghanaian Protestant layman George Hagan observed, "In my day-to-day life, I've come to perceive Jesus Christ as a living reality, a companion in life, somebody who directs or helps to illuminate me in my choices in life."

Inherent in this aspect of friendship claimed with Jesus is the intimacy of self-disclosure, the experience of personal acceptance, and the ensuing emotional bonds. Kenyan PACWA member Judy Mbugua expressed this clearly: "I also see him as my friend, because there are many things I can't tell anybody, not even my husband. But I just find myself on my knees and saying, 'Jesus you understand.' And that makes me feel that we have a special bond, he understands me." Ghanaian Catholic clergyman Charles Palmer-Buckle admitted candidly to further dynamics at play in sustaining such an honest and intimate personal relationship with Christ:

> I feel Jesus as some sort of a friend, somebody with whom I am walking, and I talk to him anytime, anywhere. And I don't only talk to him when I need something or other, I mention him quite often. I quarrel with him from time to time. And I always like to use Jeremiah as my symbol—I like Jeremiah very much because he says, "Lord, you seduced me and I let myself be seduced." And it is a true fact that I'm in love with Jesus, but it is a suffered love. We are fighting, we quarrel! He makes certain demands sometimes, and I fight before I give in. And anytime I have given in, I have felt that he's won but I've also felt happy about it. So, my relationship with Jesus Christ is a very personal sort of relationship.

Furthermore, Kenyan Catholic religious sister Marie Gacambi stressed that Jesus is "the most important friend, who cannot leave you." Recounting her serious car accident and lengthy hospitalization, outlined in Chapter 3, she noted that human friends come and go. She then concluded, "So people get tired, but this is when I recognized that God, and particularly in the person of Jesus Christ, was very close to me." Thus notions of close and faithful companionship are central to the image of Jesus as friend.

A second, related dimension of friendship is Jesus' perceived presence and provision of various needs. Respondents voiced deep awareness of Christ's presence, particularly through the East African Revival Movement. Kenyan Catholic clergyman Peter Kiarie commented generally that "people have a very real feeling of the presence of Christ." To substantiate his observation, he pointed to the prevalence of images or pictures of Jesus in their homes and stated that "with the Revival, Africans really feel very much saved or redeemed by Christ, and he's really part and parcel of their whole life."

From his own personal participation in the movement, Kenyan Protestant clergyman John Gatu related:

> I found in the Revival movement, we talk about walking with the Lord, walking with Jesus Christ. It's a daily experience, in the sense that he's a personal companion, you're not speaking to him far away. It's like the story of the people who went to Emmaus, that idea of a living Lord who you talk to, you relate to, becomes very encouraging and very strengthening—even at times when you feel downhearted, discouraged, at the point of desperation and so on, you have someone to turn to. And the whole experience changes you, and you have something, almost new to talk about. For me, that is probably the most important thing.

Kenyan Protestant lay man Morompi Ole Ronkei stated simply: "I see Jesus as a friend, someone who is there that I can turn to. I see him providing answers when I need them, through reading the Bible. And when the world comes crushing down, he's there." Likewise, Ghanaian Protestant clergyman Emmanuel Martey combined the notions of Jesus as friend and provider, concluding, "So I see him as a companion, a good friend. He provides for my needs, and I know that Jesus is providing for the needs of a lot of Ghanaians."

Not only is Jesus present and provider, but his friendship is also distinguished in effecting liberation/salvation. Ugandan Catholic clergyman J. M. Waliggo interprets the image of Jesus as friend in terms of "an empowerer of anyone who is afflicted and oppressed. So that he is not simply friend of the poor—you can be a friend and the poverty remains." Instead, Jesus is one who identifies with his followers in their situations of need and empowers them to redress those situations through his provision. Similarly, Ghanaian Protestant clergyman Peter Kodjo interprets salvation not in terms of Jesus waving some magical wand, but rather by being a comrade in the struggle. He explained that "Jesus is a friend who has done it before, he knows the road. So when you are in a crisis, you know that Jesus will accompany you, will make it better because he has gone through it. This is what Jesus becomes for us."

Finally, respondents highlighted their conviction that Jesus, as a friend, prays for his followers. Thus the christological image carries rich connotations of Jesus as an intimate and caring companion in life, one who is ever present, one who provides, and one whose friendship makes salvation operative in the concrete realities of life.

Conclusion: Jesus as Friend

The conviction of Jesus' friendship is definitely a strong component in the cluster of close, relational images of Christ. Perceptions of Jesus as friend are notable for their prevalence, indicated by the data, and for the depth of relationship expressed. Universal significance stems from the merging of biblical foundations for the christological portrait and the common human experience of friendship now fulfilled in Christ. Yet the universality of Jesus' friendship takes on local color in particular contexts and in specific lives. For instance, Joshua Aryee's comment in the focus group of Ghanaian Protestant clergy reflects expressions of male friendship in Ghana extended to Jesus:

> Let me say that Jesus is my friend, and time and again, be it in my room or elsewhere, I say, "Lord Jesus, why not put your hand around my neck, and chat with me on this issue?" Anywhere I go, something I picture is Jesus being a friend, walking with him hand in hand, asking him to put his hand around my neck. As a friend, you know, and without Jesus I am nothing.

From the witness of Aryee and many other African Christians, Jesus' friendship is of utmost importance to them.

The oral Christologies revealed two dimensions of this significance. First, Jesus as friend is conceptually relevant in increasing respondents' comprehension and appropriation of the incarnation. For example, Ghanaian Protestant lay man Lawrence Darmani emphasized that Jesus is God, yet he equally underlined the significance of Jesus as friend. Presenting these two facets of Jesus' identity in juxtaposition, Darmani highlighted the consequent closeness of Jesus, particularly in contrast to angels:

> I think about him, as it were, walking with me every time. I see him as a friend I can kneel down and cry unto, somebody I can relate with, not so far away. I see the wisdom in God letting Jesus come like the way he did, instead of maybe coming down like an angel. I know angels visited people, but my conception of an angel is so different than my conception of Jesus Christ. So I know him as Lord, I know him as God, but I want to *establish* that point that he's a friend.

Similarly, in the focus group of Kenyan Circle women, Jane Mwangangi described how the traditional God of the Kikuyu was always present to his people. She then voiced her conviction that this traditional God is linked to Jesus, and the two figures are drawn together when she marveled: "So, that God is a friend to you. So for me, Jesus is a friend and I love him!" Additionally, the image of Jesus as friend is said to convey that "Christ is really a person," and not simply an abstract doctrine. Mwangangi added, "I always experience that love of Jesus. So for me he's a friend, he's not an ideal out there." Thus the reality of the incarnation is evidently grasped more effectively through conceiving of Jesus as friend.

If this christological portrait is significant conceptually, it is even more relevant experientially, according to these African Christians. The overriding impression given by respondents is the awareness of Jesus as a close companion in every aspect of life. A typical statement emerged in the focus group of Ghanaian Protestant laity. Hetty Amissah, who works in catering, professed Jesus as savior and explained his significance to her as follows:

> I take him as a personal friend. He's the center of my life. I do everything in him, I don't leave him out of anything that I do. Even when I'm cooking, I invite him to cook with me, so then I see him as somebody in the kitchen with me.

Moreover, the significance of Jesus as companion was especially highlighted in the reflections of single adults, both women and men. Ugandan Catholic lay woman Mary Kizito responded to the question of who Jesus is to her personally by immediately acknowledging him as friend:

> Maybe because I am single and I always find consolation in having that kind of relationship of a friend I can run to when I'm in trouble, I can talk to him

and I don't have to pick up a phone. He is always there with me. He is part of me, he is my companion.

Likewise, Ghanaian Catholic clergyman Anthony Kornu candidly admitted Jesus' significance to him:

> He's a friend, a friend by my side in all situations. He's the one whom you feel is so close to you. He takes away your loneliness. And especially—you might know that we are celibates, and despite the fact that we have gone in willingly, there are moments when, whether you like it or not, loneliness might like to engulf you. But Jesus Christ as a close companion really does a lot to shield us.

Thus the experiential reality of Jesus' friendship is widely proclaimed and highly significant to these African Christians. As Kenyan Catholic Marie Gacambi summed up, "So, for me, the whole question of Jesus being a friend to me, it is not only intellectually; I have experienced it."

Finally, Kenyan Protestant lay woman Marcy Muhia provided a fitting conclusion in her expressed desire to balance Jesus' friendship with his lordship. From her experience of different denominations in Kenya, she makes a broad distinction between mainline churches, which tend to present Jesus as friend in a more distant way, like "somebody in high places" who will act on your behalf, and Pentecostal churches, which tend to approach Jesus as "buddy, buddy." Cautioning against irreverence toward Christ, Muhia commented, "He has become so human, so like us, that in some ways, the fact that he is God gets buried somewhere in there." So the image of Jesus as friend certainly conveys Jesus' immanence in a meaningful way, yet Muhia rightfully pointed out the need for balancing his closeness as a companion with his transcendence as exalted lord. Once again, the christological images operate ideally not in isolation but in creative tension with one another.

CONCLUSION: JESUS AS LOVED ONE

Core concepts of communal life in Africa are foundational to all of the christological models, yet they are especially evident in the cluster of relational images represented in the third circle, Jesus as loved one. Since the christological portraits in this category are derived from cultural universals of family and friendship, they are generally less controversial than certain other images currently advocated by African Christians. However, the fact that these relational images are relatively more universal in scope does not detract from their particular expression in the specified African contexts. As previously indicated, christological images grounded in concepts of kinship and community are not peculiar to Africa, but they are certainly prominent in Africa. Ghanaian Catholic clergyman Matthew Edusei's comment is indicative in this regard: "The image of Jesus, for me, is of him sitting with others at table, around a meal. And everybody's invited!

Nobody's excluded. That for me is very African. Then the Greek comes in, *koinonia,* the community, family." Edusei went on to state that Jesus exemplifies family in a powerful way, and he concluded emphatically, "God could have come in any form, but he came as a member of a family." Consequently, understanding and appropriating Jesus as a close member of the family and community is especially vital.

As Jesus is interpreted and embraced in terms of these relational images, particular strengths as well as pertinent questions emerge with respect to the expressed Christologies. The criteria set forth in Chapter 2, including the appropriateness of sources and methods and the seven factors of contextual relevance, provide guidelines for assessing the significance of these Christologies for contemporary African Christianity.

In accordance with other christological models, the selected African Christians drew upon all four of the recommended sources in formulating the images of Jesus as loved one, yet to varying degrees. They underlined the Bible as the primary source for African Christologies, and both Old and New Testaments were employed in developing various aspects of Jesus as family member and friend. Theologians, church leaders, and laity delved especially into the gospel accounts of Jesus' earthly ministry to discern his identity and significance both within and beyond his own particular family and community. For example, Kenyan Catholic clergyman Peter Kiarie considered how Jesus lived with his own family and then with the disciples "like an extended family group." On this basis he concluded, "Jesus is a community person! He's not just a loner, he's not just isolated living there, but he actually shared in the life of the people." As African Christians explore the ways in which Jesus lived out his communal life on earth, hermeneutical principles necessarily enter the discussion. Like the rather controversial image of Jesus as ancestor discussed in the previous chapter, affirmation of the disputable image of Jesus as mother evidently hinges on whether it is interpreted literally or figuratively. Thus further developments in the field of contextual hermeneutics will certainly influence the staying power of these more debatable christological images.

The extent to which these relational images of Jesus resonate with the selected African Christians is less likely a function of conscious hermeneutical considerations, however. More likely, the African heritage and the living experience of the church affect the degree of receptivity toward images of Jesus as loved one. That is to say, traditional African concepts of, for example, brother and mother naturally contribute to the substance of the christological images conceived in these categories. Analysis of the rationale and meaning of these various depictions of Jesus has indicated that the biblical revelation of Christ is inevitably interpreted through the lens of African notions of family and friendship. Likewise, personal experience of family and community members is clearly central to the expressed perceptions of Jesus in these relational terms. So, although the Bible is highlighted as the primary source for African Christologies, the relative weight of reasoning from the data in this christological model falls more on the concepts of Christ as interpreted through African tradition and personal experience. However, if these christological portraits are grounded in common human experience of family and friendship, they certainly convey Jesus as one who transcends the human category of brother, mother, lover, or friend. Once again, the christological images function analogously in employing metaphors of interhuman relationships to open avenues for deeper understanding of the divine-human relationship experienced with Christ.

The fourth source for christological construction, contemporary realities, is apparent but comparatively less so. For example, Bujo sets forth the many divisions across Africa, including ethnicity and class, as a basis for his promoting Jesus as universal brother. Similarly, Nasimiyu Wasike urges the image of Jesus as mother against the backdrop of widespread suffering across Africa, said to represent the need for a mother's love and nurture. So although current situations in Africa inspire these relational images according to certain voices, on the whole, contemporary African contexts feature less in the formulation of these particular Christologies.

A twofold movement in articulating images of Jesus as loved one contributes to the effectiveness of the methodologies employed. First, there is clear demonstration of christological construction "from above" in African theologians advocating certain images arrived at through their theological reflections. Pobee develops communal images of Jesus on the basis of biblical exegesis interpreted from an African perspective. Bujo and Nasimiyu Wasike integrate biblical teaching with traditional concepts of family and friendship in response to critical issues in the contemporary contexts of Africa. Mugambi suggests family paradigms for appropriating Jesus in view of the tendencies toward individualistic faith and denominationalism inherited from Western Christianity. Mercy Oduyoye highlights the importance of Jesus as friend to the everyday experience of African Christian women, as discussed in the next chapter where women's Christologies are considered more closely. So African theologians are certainly engaged in formulating Christologies relevant to the relational issues in their respective contexts.

Conversely, images of Jesus as loved one also arise "from below," or in the specified contexts of African Christianity. Evidence from songs, prayers, testimonies, preaching, and "visual Christologies" indicates that these impressions of Jesus in intensely relational terms are deeply significant to the African believers. Moreover, the discussion of Jesus as mother pointed out that sometimes these christological images operate at an unconscious level within Christians, who then affirm the images once someone else articulates them. Hence Ghanaian Catholic clergyman Abraham Akrong rejoices in the "wonderful contextualizations" currently emerging among Akan Christians. He explained that the Akan "have quite a rich repertoire of titles of God," and that as Jesus becomes increasingly significant in Ghana, "some of these titles, like 'mother,' are being transferred to Christ!" He therefore concluded that "a time of Christology of the pew is coming up." Thus the twofold movement of christological formulation, "down" from the theologians and "up" from the people in the pews, reflects the vibrancy and the relevance of African Christologies portraying Jesus as loved one.

Further strengths, as well as certain weaknesses, of this christological model come to light through a consideration of the seven factors of contextual relevance. Present expressions of Jesus as family member and friend contribute less to the issues of historical relevance. So the potential remains for African Christians to articulate these perceptions of Jesus more effectively in relation to, for example, the history of suffering in Africa. To what extent did African Christians perceive Jesus to be a member of their family and community during the centuries of the Atlantic slave trade or the decades of European colonialism? Further reflection on the paradox of claiming Jesus as loved one in the midst of these historical realities will fortify present convictions of Jesus in this capacity.

These relational Christologies definitely have contemporary relevance, according to theologians, church leaders, and laity. Bujo contemplates Christmas in a brutalized Africa and lends powerful expression to the significance of Jesus as the new ancestor who "alone, reunites all the ancestors of different clans; he makes of them a single clan and a single ethnic group." Applying Romans 5:12–21 to the African context, he explains that just as "by a single ethnic and clan ancestor, division has entered the Negro-African world, and thus hatred and massacres, so by a single new ancestor, Jesus Christ, unity and life have been guaranteed us."[27] Therefore Bujo urges his fellow African Christians toward the unity, forgiveness, love, and fraternity obtained in Christ, insisting that allegiance to the clan of Christ must supersede all other clan loyalties.[28] In a similar vein Nasimiyu Wasike advocates Jesus as mother for the potential significance this image holds for nurturing life in Africa amid widespread suffering and death. Furthermore, church leaders and laity have attested to the significance of Jesus as loved one to single adult Christians today. So the cluster of relational images for Jesus clearly speaks to current issues in the contexts of Africa.

In addition, these christological portraits address certain issues with respect to gender appropriateness. Theologically, the image of Jesus as mother is considered to help balance the overemphasis on masculine imagery for God by highlighting the "feminine" qualities associated with Jesus. Experientially, respondents claim that this image of Jesus underlines the importance of mothering as a role that goes beyond biological parenting, thereby addressing a concern of many women in Africa. Similarly, the image of Jesus as husband is said to confront African cultures that define women according to their marital status. These few examples suffice to illustrate how contemporary images of Jesus as loved one contribute toward redressing certain gender concerns in African Christianity.

While the images in this christological model clearly hold potential for contemporary relevance and gender appropriateness, the extent to which this potential is realized determines the credibility of witness. In other words, where these images are actualized, for example in believers surmounting ethnic, class, and denominational divisions by appropriating Jesus as universal brother or nurturing life within the community on the inspiration of Jesus as mother, then the Christologies lend credible witness to Christ. But as long as African Christians display the divisions and the life-denying forces so prevalent across Africa today, then the person of Christ and the expressed Christologies are discredited. Therefore significant challenges remain, not only in articulating images of Jesus as loved one, but in authentically appropriating them.

Greater strengths lie in the combined realms of linguistic, theological, and cultural relevance. Emergent indigenous Christologies indicate that the person of Christ is being conveyed in conceptual categories from Africans' experience of family and community. For example, attention has been drawn to vernacular terms for *mother*, with all the associated meanings, now applied to Jesus Christ. Even in English translation, Nasimiyu Wasike argues that *mother* carries certain connotations in Africa that are not communicated as effectively by *father* or *parent*. Furthermore, Bujo emphasized that "it is not the same to say 'brother' in the West as it is to say 'brother' in Africa. It's not the same to say 'mama.'" Hence he insists that African theology must be written in African languages. So, careful attentiveness to linguistic and conceptual authenticity and clarity is already evidenced in the images of Jesus as communal member. Further progress along these lines promises even greater relevance for these particular African Christologies.

Building upon the linguistic and conceptual relevance, the images of Jesus as loved one bear strong theological relevance for the selected African Christians. Jesus is understood in relation to Africa's pre-Christian heritage when traditional titles for God become transferred to Jesus, as noted above, or when attributes of God, like the traditional Kikuyu concept of his ever-presence, become linked to the notion of Jesus as friend. Moreover, traditional concepts of God, for example as father *and* mother, evidently create greater openness to considering Jesus as mother, something acknowledged to be possibly "outrageous" in Western theology. Yet Aboagye-Mensah asserted that the motherhood of Jesus in the African understanding gives him a richer perspective on Jesus' identity and significance than the more masculine portraits alone. Furthermore, the research data confirm that the images of Jesus as friend and family member serve as a hermeneutical bridge joining biblical and African concepts. Indeed, African Christians claim that appropriating Jesus as brother helps them to grasp his humanity, in terms of his identification and solidarity with humans, his availability and protection, and his relational closeness. Likewise, Ghanaian Catholic clergyman Matthew Edusei affirmed that Jesus as lover "brings home to me who God is, and he is love." So the respondents emphasized that the images of Jesus as family member and friend serve to deepen their understanding and appreciation of the incarnation. These images are also said to convey the relational dimensions of salvation/liberation and to communicate Jesus less as an abstract ideal and more as a "real person." Thus the portraits of Jesus as loved one contribute significantly to the theological relevance of African Christologies.

Finally, the cultural relevance is intrinsically related to the theological relevance outlined above. Since communal life is cardinal to traditional African cultures, believers naturally understand and appropriate Jesus as one who establishes them in communion with God and with one another. Ghanaian Protestant clergyman Abraham Akrong summarized it well in stating:

I think for me—again this is my African background—for me, what Christ came to do for all of us is to help to bring us back into the family of God. And for me as an African, to be in the family of God means a lot, because your family is your security, is your protection, is your past, is your future. So, this is how I would sum up my whole Christology.

The christological and ecclesiological implications of this conviction are far-reaching, as Kenyan religious sister Marie Gacambi pointed out. Drawing upon "African values that can really be used within the church," she emphasized the "communitarian" nature of traditional life and religion in Africa in contrast to mission Christianity which concentrated "more on individualistic saving, taking the individual from the community to be saved by themselves." Against the latter approach, she asserted that "all the miracles of Jesus were to take the individual who was isolated, to bring the individual back to the community." Hence she insisted that the "community aspect" is highly relevant to the church, and she reiterated that the community encompasses the living, the dead, and the unborn. Equally important is the family, "with all the values of the family: values of care, of hospitality, of solidarity, acceptance, respect." She then concluded that Jesus brought these same values upheld by African tradition, and that "these values could enrich very much within the church."

Bujo takes this one step further in stating that Jesus not only endorses the African communitarian values, including hospitality, care of the elderly, the orphaned, and the unfortunate, but also brings them to new fulfillment. Thus Bujo makes the all-important point that "Jesus corrects and completes the traditional morality of Africa. The moral perspective is no longer limited to my clan, my elders, my friends, but extends to the whole human race, in loving service to the Father."[29] Thus, insofar as Jesus is appropriated as loved one, these African Christologies help to recover the communal dimensions of the gospel that are often neglected in the more individualistic expressions of Western Christianity.

The communitarian emphasis in the African Christologies is integral to their comprehensive character, which is an additional aspect of cultural relevance. This chapter has noted that when African Christians portray Jesus as community member, they often reflect an all-encompassing view of his identity and significance. Ghanaian Protestant clergyman Dan Antwi summed up the impact of his African worldview upon his conception of Jesus saying, "*Yesu ye made nyinaa*, Jesus is my all in all, in the sense that life is meaningless without him." Antwi stipulated that *life* signifies "personal life, community life, because as an African, I believe that I am not only here as a person. The fulfillment of my personhood can only be realized in the context of the community; without the community, I am not." Given this communal orientation, he explained that "Jesus then becomes, for me, my all in all—the one who cleanses me, who builds me up and nurtures me into becoming part of the royal family of God." So as Jesus enters the spiritual universe of African Christians, fundamental cultural assumptions regarding the communal nature of existence and the comprehensive character of faith clearly influence the ways in which he is interpreted.

A great strength of this third christological model, Jesus as loved one, thus lies in the realm of cultural relevance. One of the most striking impressions repeatedly voiced by respondents is the deep intimacy with Jesus that the relational images represent. By all accounts, Jesus has indeed found "a place to feel at home" in Africa, for the selected African Christians attested that they have embraced him as family member and close friend. The reality of this evidence from the contemporary African contexts holds tremendous significance, for it demonstrates the universality and the particularity of the Christian faith. Nasimiyu Wasike underlines that "the Son of God comes into the history of every family when in the Incarnation he becomes a member of their own family."[30] Andrew Walls explains further that Jesus must find a home in every cultural context, without becoming so identified with that particular context that others cannot live there.[31] Without doubt the present research indicates that Jesus has entered the homes of these African Christians as an intimate member of the local community. Now as they proclaim their understanding of how Jesus has "tabernacled" among them or "moved into the neighborhood,"[32] they magnify the profile of Jesus as loved one within the global community.

6

Jesus as Leader

Jesus Christ is indeed a great personality whose life conforms to what the Asante expect a great leader to be. . . . He became our rescuer, liberator . . . leader par excellence.

— PETER SARPONG, CATHOLIC BISHOP OF KUMASI, GHANA

Mere chiefs and kings are not his equals
though filled with glory and power,
wealth and blessings, and royalty
in the greatest abundance.
But of them all, he is the leader,
and the chiefs with all their glory follow after him.

— AFUA KUMA, NON-LITERATE LAY WOMAN IN RURAL GHANA

The scandal of the gospel is that Jesus Christ speaks God in suffering. He speaks to us of God who loves, who identifies himself with the person who suffers, who wants people to live, because Jesus Christ died in order for people to live. On the cross Jesus Christ implicates himself, he participates closely in people's struggles for life. From an instrument that is intended to humiliate, he makes an instrument for life, for liberty.

— JEAN-MARC ELA, CAMEROONIAN THEOLOGIAN

INTRODUCTION

When Christians articulate the identity and significance of Jesus Christ, they inevitably draw upon categories from their own social experience. Within this realm of human experience, concepts of leadership are pivotal. John Pobee notes that while various African communities have different ideas and practices of authority, "whatever the leadership concept and practice, they can be a very powerful avenue for articulating the answer to the question 'Who do you Africans say that I am?'"[1]

177

Certainly a wide range of images related to leadership emerges in both textual and oral sources. Though not exhaustive, the following list is illustrative of leadership titles attributed to Jesus: model, guide, teacher, shepherd, chief, king, warrior, liberator, head, judge, master of initiation, rainmaker, sea captain. There are also assorted vernacular titles. Like the christological portraits delineated in previous chapters, these images are derived from the gospel's encounter with the African heritage and contemporary realities. Since certain leadership roles have already been discussed, including the roles of religious specialists like traditional healers and family or clan heads who become ancestors, this chapter concentrates on other leaders in the sociopolitical and religious realms. The first half of the chapter explores the conviction of African Christians that Jesus fulfills the leadership expectations in traditional thought, particularly with respect to concepts of kingship/chieftaincy in some societies. The second half of the chapter focuses on selected expressions of Jesus as liberator elicited by contemporary realities in Africa. The overall purpose of the chapter is to present the rationale for interpreting Jesus as leader in light of African thought and biblical teaching, to investigate the substance of key leadership images in contemporary Christian reflection and practice, and to offer critical assessment regarding the significance of these images for African Christianity.

JESUS AS KING/CHIEF

CONCEPTS OF LEADERSHIP IN TRADITIONAL AFRICA

Because leadership patterns vary among traditional African societies, the initial discussion is contextually grounded in one ethnic group: the Akan of Ghana. However, given the commonalities in concepts of leaders among many African peoples, the relevance of the African heritage to contemporary Christologies in this respect extends beyond this particular people group. Hence evidence from other African witnesses enters into the later discussion regarding Jesus as leader.

Spokespersons regarding traditional Akan leadership include Anglican theologian John Pobee, Methodist leader Robert Aboagye-Mensah, and Catholic Bishop Peter Sarpong. Pobee explains that "the institution of chieftaincy is the focal point of culture and a model for leadership patterns in society."[2] Aboagye-Mensah adds that the "lineage system is vital to the understanding of kingship/chiefship,"[3] with descent and privileges being traced through the mother since Akan society is matrilineal. Each lineage comprises a political unit with its own headman acting as representative on higher councils, from the household head through successive levels of chiefs administering larger political units. At each level the leader is responsible for maintaining defense, law and order, harmonious relationships within the group, and communication among God or the gods, the living, and the departed. In descending order of importance the main leaders include the chief/king *(Ohene)*, the queenmother, and other subchiefs.

Pobee, Aboagye-Mensah, and Sarpong all underline the pervasive influence of religion in the sociopolitical structures of the Akan. Pobee cites sociologist

K. A. Busia regarding the institution of chieftaincy among the Asante, one of the linguistic and cultural groups within the Akan:

> The most important aspect of Ashanti chieftaincy was undoubtedly the religious one. An Ashanti chief filled a sacral role. His stool, the symbol of his office, was a sacred emblem. It represented the community, their solidarity, their permanence, their continuity. The chief was the link between the living and the dead, and his highest role was when he officiated in the public religious rites which gave expression to the community values. He then acted as the representative of the community whose members are believed to include those who are alive, and those who are either dead or are still unborn. The sacral aspect of the chief's role was a powerful sanction of his authority.[4]

Aboagye-Mensah explains further that since the Akan king combines religious, social, and political leadership in occupying the stool, "he is described as the Priest-chief/king."[5] This office is delineated in terms of four main functions and titles of the king. First, he is the priest-chief; he alone has power and authority to gather all the lineages and to sacrifice to the ancestors and God on their behalf. Citing the quotation above from Busia, Aboagye-Mensah concludes, "As Priest-King, he demonstrates that for the Akans there is no deep split between politics and religion; and that both affect the living and the dead."[6] Second, he is the commander of the army responsible for delivering his people from their enemies in battle. Third, he is to remove antisocial acts within the community in order to maintain social cohesion; thus he acts as the legislator and the executive and administrative head. Fourth, he is the custodian of the land or "owner of all the lands," in that he supervises and defends the ancestral lands without having the right to own land privately. Thus the office of kingship is clearly composite.

JESUS AS KING/CHIEF

Following his introduction to Akan leadership, Aboagye-Mensah observes, with lack of surprise, that many African theologians have called for serious consideration to be given to traditional concepts of kingship/chiefship in formulating African Christologies. For example, Pobee is said to speak for many Africans, particularly Akan Christians, when he asserts that "the court of the royal house in Akan society can serve the cause of Christology in Akan African theology."[7] Hence, Aboagye-Mensah's important assertion that

> Akan Christians have no hesitation in transferring to Jesus Christ descriptions and titles which were used for our traditional kings. More strikingly, in this form of transposition they also portray Jesus Christ as one greater and superior to them. They are mere chiefs/kings in comparison to Jesus Christ. Jesus is their leader and is sovereign among them.[8]

Closer examination of Jesus as king/chief entails analysis of the data and the substance of the image before conclusions are reached.[9] For the purpose of this section, the textual and oral Christologies are combined in presentation, together with further evidence gleaned through informal methods of field research.

The Data

Contextual evidence from Kenya, Uganda, and Ghana points to the kingship of Jesus being a prevalent theme in local expressions of Christianity. Participant observation in a wide variety of churches exposed numerous references to Jesus as king in songs, prayers, liturgy, and preaching. Without doubt, the biblical and the Western missionary inheritance at least partially spawn such imagery, as many hymnbooks, for example, attest.[10] Yet, clearly, traditional leadership symbolism further informs christological images of kingship/chieftaincy. For example, in addition to biblical affirmations about Jesus, a traditional greeting reserved for Zulu kings animates the following song that is often sung in Nairobi Chapel:

> *Bayete Inkosi*
> Bayete, Bayete Inkosi
> Bayete, King of Kings
> Bayete, Bayete Inkosi
> Bayete Inkosi means King of Kings
>
> Who can match Your greatness
> Who can know Your power
> Who can search Your riches
> Who can deny You are crowned Lord of Lords
>
> You are crowned King of Africa
> You are crowned Lord of Lords
> You are crowned King of Africa
> Who can deny You are crowned Lord of Lords.[11]

This song also illustrates that the impact of traditional leadership symbolism extends beyond the particular people group represented, for in this case South African Zulu appellations inspire worship within a multi-ethnic congregation in Nairobi, Kenya.

Within the particular context of the Akan, however, christological portraits of kingship/chieftaincy take on added proportion. Catholic Bishop Charles Palmer-Buckle confirmed that "a lot of the Akan songs present Jesus Christ as king, as king of kings, you hear it very, very often, '*Ahenfo mu hene.*'" Protestant clergyman Dan Antwi added, on a more personal note:

The vernacular compositions, the local choruses, have been very, very powerful. Anytime I hear such a piece like "Momanoso Yesu na Oye Ohene," you know, "Lift him up. Jesus is the king!" "Ahenfo mu hene," "he's the king of kings." "Eye-se obiara kotow no," "everybody must bow unto him," it's such a powerful piece that I love very much.

Furthermore, Aboagye-Mensah noted that "Jesus as chief or Jesus as king is also another common terminology people use in prayer." While the meanings of the vernacular terms await further explication below, Sarpong concurs that "in the spontaneous prayers of ordinary people, one hears their kings and chief. They would address Jesus as *Osagyefo, Kantamanto, Kurotwiamansa, Oduyefoo, Paapa, Ahummobro.*"[12]

Besides songs and prayers, several Catholic respondents spoke of liturgical celebrations employing local terminology and customs related to kingship, especially in Easter dramatizations and the annual feast of Christ the King. Describing the latter, Catholic priest Joseph Aggrey related how the Corpus Christi is carried in a palanquin: "We carry Jesus Christ amidst dancing and drumming, and praises, some of which I will say are very traditional. Yes, very traditional." In the focus group of Catholic clergy, Anthony Kornu added:

> [Christians including] traditional chiefs even go and kneel down on their bare knees and go through the whole village. You see it in Cape Coast—all the regalia of chieftaincy! He's [that is, Jesus, symbolized in the Eucharist] even sometimes brought from the king's palace to the church adorned with all the paraphernalia for the procession with the blessed sacrament. Those who are Christian chiefs are there, and they are kneeling down doing obeisance. We associate with him all that goes with kingship and more. So he is chief, king of kings.

One last clue to the importance of Jesus' depiction as king lies in the visual indicators apparent in the Ghanaian context. Figure 6–1 represents many occurrences of this christological image. Also, among the ubiquitous slogans on vehicles are indicators of Jesus' perceived kingship/chiefship, such as one *trotro* (local transport vehicle) publicizing "Osahene Yesu," a Twi military metaphor used of conquering war heroes applied here to Jesus. So simply being in the context of African Christianity, particularly in Ghana, allows ample opportunity to witness the widespread conviction that Jesus is king/chief as expressed in churches and in wider society.

Further corroboration came to light in the oral interviews. In Kenya and Uganda no set question was asked regarding the image of Jesus as king or chief. Nevertheless, Jesus as king emerged as a meaningful category for these selected Christians, as nine of the thirty individual respondents volunteered comments to this effect. In contrast to the fairly common use of "king" in reference to Jesus, only one respondent spoke of Jesus as "chief," and this occurrence was in response to a specific question, not initiated by the respondent. This suggests that the English term *chief* is not applied as readily to Jesus by these particular Christians as it might be in other African contexts. Nor is this observation surprising, since leadership concepts in many ethnic societies in Kenya, including

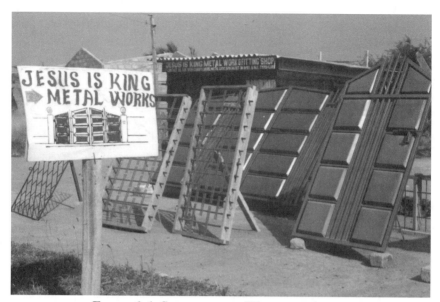

FIGURE 6–1. SIGNBOARD FOR WORKSHOP, ACCRA

the largest people groups of the Gikuyu, Maasai, and Kamba, are based upon rule by elders.[13]

Conversely, in Ghana, where chieftaincy has been more predominant, the christological evidence shifts accordingly. Here, in addition to eight of the thirty-five individual respondents who suggested the image of Jesus as king, four respondents initiated perceptions of Jesus as chief. Therefore, combining the two terms, eleven of the thirty-five respondents volunteered the king/chief image of Jesus as a meaningful christological category.[14] In view of the prevailing patterns of traditional leadership in Ghana, questions were posed to the interviewees in this context concerning Jesus as chief and as *Nana* (a Twi term associated with king/chief and ancestor). Consequently, the Ghanaian material features in the following discussion. Due to the overlapping of terminology including *king, chief,* and other vernacular titles like *Nana*, precise statistical charts isolating any single term, like those in previous chapters, are inadvisable.[15] However, the overall pattern of evidence from the individual interviews in Ghana is decidedly favorable toward the cluster of king/chief/*Nana* images by an approximate ratio of two positive to one negative response. Thus the data from participant observation in the context of Ghanaian Christianity and from the oral interviews leave little doubt as to the widespread conviction of Jesus' kingship/chieftaincy.

Rationale for the Image of Jesus as King/Chief

On par with previous christological images, it is enlightening but insufficient to determine the prevalence of a particular theme in local expressions of Christianity. Further investigation into the meaning and significance of the proposed portrait is required. A consideration of the rationale expressed for the composite king/chief image, plus problems raised with it, will contribute toward this end.

Among the early proponents of Jesus as chief, Pobee provides clear rationale for depicting Jesus in this way. He explains that the Supreme Being in Akan religion is conceived of as a paramount chief so great that he must be approached through subchiefs and his official spokesperson, the *Okyeame*. The *Okyeame* is as the chief in public affairs and exercises royal authority, although such authority is subordinated to the paramount chief. Every chief is said to have an *Okyeame* who serves him in various capacities and who must be competent in public speaking. Moving from the Akan heritage to the Bible, Pobee notes similarities between the two sources regarding the kingship of God. He cites biblical teaching regarding God as king and Jesus as king, yet notes that "Jesus shares in the kingship of God and holds his kingship under God." In order to convey this teaching to local Christians, he suggests:

> In our Akan Christology we propose to think of Jesus as the *Okyeame*, or linguist, who in all public matters was as the Chief, God, and is the first officer of the state, in this case, the world. This captures something of the Johannine portrait of Jesus as the Logos, being at one and the same time divine and yet subordinate to God.[16]

Pobee proposes a further parallel in the sacral role exercised by the Akan chief and by Jesus. However, he distinguishes Jesus' priestly function in that it extends beyond earthly to heavenly rule, as the epistle to the Hebrews argues, and it brings salvation and forgiveness of sin to humanity by virtue of Jesus being both priest and sacrificial victim. Finally, akin to the African chief, Jesus as chief is head of a community, namely, the church. Not only does he represent the community, he also symbolizes its identity, unity, and continuity. He further exercises authority over his people as their judge and the one to whom they owe their allegiance. A new element with Jesus as chief, Pobee stresses, is that his community cuts across political and ethnic boundaries to embrace all humanity.[17]

On the basis of this functional analogy, various honorifics used of chiefs in traditional society are said to capture aspects of New Testament Christology. Pobee proposes the christological title *Nana*, a term traditionally attributed to God and to the ancestors.[18] He cites more examples, in each case setting forth the Akan definition and biblical grounds for its association with Jesus. The first, *Osuodumgyma*, literally means "water that extinguishes fire," fire symbolizing all pain and disaster, and it is attributed to the chief as one who removes all that is inimical to the community, thereby enhancing life. Water, symbolizing life, is likewise important in Jesus' teaching (Jn 4:10). Hence Pobee states, "Jesus is *Osuodumgyma* because he gives life and delivers from the flames of passion, the flames of sin, and gives hope."[19] The next two terms are said to be synonymous: *Kasapreko*, literally meaning "he who speaks once and for all and does not foreswear himself," and *Kantamanto*, "one who does not break his oath." The determination of the Akan chief, whose word stands firm, is likened to that of Jesus in his unswerving devotion to God to the bitter end and, above all, to the absolute assurance of his promises (2 Cor 1:19–20).

A fourth recommended title is *Osagyefo*, meaning "one who saves in battle; therefore, a deliverer." Pobee explains the basic idea of this term as comparable to the Old Testament judges, who saved their people from the tyranny of oppressors. While this appellation is applicable to Jesus as deliverer, according to Pobee, one key difference is that Jesus' deliverance is not through a "literal battle" but rather figurative rescue from "the inimical forces of legalism, self-sufficiency, and the cosmic forces."[20] After delineating the traditional concept of chieftaincy and these praise names attributed to the chief, Pobee concludes with their relevance to contemporary Christianity, namely, that "among the African tribe of the Akan of Ghana a royal priestly Christology aptly speaks to their situation."[21]

Within this brief summary of Pobee's rationale for portraying Jesus as chief, three elements come to light: theological grounds for the analogy in the kingship of God being extended to Jesus, similarities in chiefly functions, and titles of respect associated with the chief that carry christological meaning and significance. These three elements find corroboration among other selected Christians from Ghana.[22]

With respect to the theological grounds for conferring God's kingship/chieftaincy upon Jesus, Aboagye-Mensah provides strong confirmation in his discussion of *Nana* as a christological title. He defines *Nana* as an expression of honor or respect used for the head of a family, such as a grandfather, or the head of a nation, such as kings/chiefs or queenmothers, or for royal ancestors who once ruled the people. The term emphasizes family relations and reflects the bond of love uniting the head of a family or a nation with his or her people. Yet the title is also applied to God, *Nana Nyame*, emphasizing God as "One of great age" and one who creates and unites all the families of the world. Aboagye-Mensah then stresses the significance of this title being extended to Jesus, in that

> the same title is used of human beings and God. The implication is that it can be used of Jesus Christ, the God-man, without much difficulty. Christologically, the title acquires new significance. It is the first time that it is used of one "Person" who unites in Himself the Sovereign God and creaturely man. It means Jesus Christ is also the true head of all individual families, and nations, as well as being the head of the One family of all clans and nations of the universe. In Him the title finds fulfillment as the head of all sovereignty, authority, power or domination in the Church and outside the Church.[23]

Lawrence Darmani voiced similar theological reasoning. From his perspective as a Protestant lay man, he explained that *Nana* is a title for "Supreme" and confirmed that he conceptualizes God as *Nana Nyankopon*. Since he associates the title *Nana* with God, he needs a "bridge" to associate Jesus with *Nana*. That bridge he finds in the Bible, and he explained the significance for him personally as follows:

Because of what I understand from the scriptures, I'm very much privileged to be able to connect Jesus to God, and *therefore* able to use *Nana* for Jesus. Because immediately, I see him not just like the man walking by the shore of Galilee, or being led to the cross to be crucified. But as the God now, who came in the form of man. *Then* I can see Jesus as *Nana*.

Thus the ascription of *Nana* to Jesus clearly carries potential for conveying to Akan Christians the universal rule of Christ and his incarnation. It is worth noting, however, that when probed as to whether the image of Jesus as *Nana* is operative in his own life and specifically in his ministry as editor of *Step Magazine—Ghana,* Darmani replied:

We have not used that word, or that title, *Nana* Jesus, but we have presented him as king. He came in a humble way but in my mind, I see him as a great one who is actually sitting as a chief, as a king! And therefore in my own devotion, prayer, thought, I'm able to see him as the king with powers! Powers to liberate me, powers to guide me and to lead me. In that sense, we have presented him in our publication. So I'm able to say "King Jesus"—that's almost like saying "*Nana* Jesus," just that I've not used the word *Nana*. But otherwise, in my mind, yes, he is *Nana*.

Therefore, even when the vernacular title *Nana* Jesus is not expressed publicly, it evidently functions conceptually within many Ghanaian believers as part of the cluster of king/chief images.

The functional analogy Pobee develops between the traditional Akan chief and Jesus as chief is also witnessed among other Ghanaian Christians. The most obvious parallel, remarked upon by many respondents, is the rule and power exercised by the chief over the subjects. For instance, when asked about the image of Jesus as chief, Protestant lay woman Grace Nartey replied, "Chief, as ruler, as judge, as someone who has authority, yes, one can think of Jesus as chief." She explained further in response to the question of Jesus as *Nana*:

Yes, Jesus is king, Jesus is Lord. Jesus is—you know, the family head or the chief is somebody that one should be able to look up to, somebody that you respect and somebody who provides support and protection. And Jesus does all this and more, so . . .

Protestant clergyman Thomas Oduro brought out another aspect of the subject's allegiance to the chief in the sense of personal identity gained through association, for the chief is "somebody you can be proud of, to relate yourself to." In addition, Protestant lay man Kingsfold Amoah affirmed the fundamental concept of lordship inherent in the image of Jesus as chief. He explains that "when you talk of a lord, a king, then the word *chief* has the same connotations. If I was trying to explain his supremacy and what is meant by *Lord of all lords,* then I could say that he's the greatest chief." Once again, however, a respondent admitted that the image of Jesus as chief is not verbalized in his own experience or ministry. Yet Amoah stated unequivocally that it is meaningful conceptually and that it holds potential for ministry:

> A lot of Ghanaians know a chief as the depository of authority and control and power and that sort of thing. So one could use that same thing that they know and transfer it to describe the lordship of Christ upon their lives. So, just like a chief makes laws and a chief is supposed to be obeyed, and a chief is to be honored, one could use that to present the lordship of Christ.

So whether or not such terms as *chief* and *Nana* were actually voiced in relation to Jesus, they were acknowledged by many respondents as mentally operative and potentially constructive for ministry purposes in Ghana.

The most common reason expressed for affirming Jesus as king/chief/*Nana*, on par with Pobee's third rationale, is the respect or reverence accorded through ascribing these titles. Protestant clergyman Dan Antwi's explanation is telling, for when asked specifically if the term *Nana* comes naturally to him in relation to Jesus, he replied:

> You have the imagery of a chief, a king, lord of lords and king of kings, then in that respect you wouldn't address him in any other way but as you would address a chief—*Nana* would be quite a convenient way. Because, in any case, if Jesus is the heir to the throne of God, then he deserves the title *Nana!*

Striking evidence also came from Nana Addo Birikorang, himself the chief linguist to the regional king. When asked about Jesus as *Nana*, Birikorang responded enthusiastically, with slight laughter, "Jesus is super-*Nana*! Yes! He is super-*Nana*! Because if I go before God, I feel that Jesus is the only means by which I can go unto God." He likewise affirmed Jesus as "super-chief," thus validating Aboagye-Mensah's assertion that Akan Christians transpose titles for traditional kings to Jesus while maintaining his clear superiority over them.

Finally, other Ghanaians echoed Pobee's exposition of traditional Akan accolades capable of expressing facets of New Testament Christology. Although respondents voiced all of the vernacular titles Pobee proposes in this regard, the one most commonly raised was *Osagyefo*, the king/chief who delivers his people in battle.[24] Described as a "brave warrior, conquering king," *Osagyefo* is said to "very aptly describe who Christ is to a believer." Especially instructive here is the conflict that arose between church and state when the title *Osagyefo* was applied to Kwame Nkrumah, Ghana's first president, who led the people of Ghana from colonialism to independence. Certain church leaders vehemently opposed it as "a blasphemous equation of Nkrumah with Jesus the saviour."[25] Pobee explores the use of the term in Asante tradition and in the lyrics of the Fanti Methodist Church, where *Osagyefo* was commonly applied to God. He notes that African and church traditions overlapped, so that the same term was used with different connotations. The conflict that ensued illustrates the extent to which Ghanaian Christians have adopted vernacular appellations for traditional leaders and ascribed them to Jesus. Aboagye-Mensah follows Pobee in criticizing the church's attitude of monopolizing the title for Christ without adequate awareness of the term's usage in its traditional context. He then draws an important conclusion, which explicates the meaning and significance of *Osagyefo* as a christological title:

> In the traditional usage, the title referred to socio-political liberation. The Church in Ghana gave it a religious or divine interpretation. Arguably, the Church understood the term in the spiritual sense. In applying the title to Jesus, we must include both interpretations, traditional and church. Thus Jesus Christ will be understood as the One who delivered and continues to deliver us from socio-political domination and oppression. At the same time He is the One who sets us free from spiritual bondage. In this sense when the title is applied to Him we are stressing the fact that He is concerned about the liberation of our entire life, from the social, political and religious realities that ensnare us. Jesus Christ has come and continues to come to liberate us from all structural and private sins which hold us captive. He is indeed the *Osaagyefoo* and all the other leaders and kings are His subordinate *asaagyefoo*.[26]

The importance of this particular portrait of Jesus warrants further consideration in relation to the next section on liberation theologies.

In addition to *Osagyefo* and the vernacular praise names outlined by Pobee, other chiefly titles are put forward by the selected Ghanaian Christians. For example, Sarpong advocates *Kurotwiamansa*, meaning "leopard," which was traditionally considered the king of the forest and thus applied to the king of Asante. After describing the image of the leopard in terms of its power, fierceness, beauty, and majesty, Sarpong concludes,

> In calling Jesus the leopard, *Kurotwiamansa*, therefore, the Asante is saying that Jesus is feared by the devil; Jesus is the Master of us all; Jesus is beautiful; Jesus is majestic, noble. But these qualities of Jesus are seen in association with the leadership of the Asante people. Jesus is graceful; Jesus is solemn; Jesus is dignified—in the last analysis, Jesus is *the* King. Before him, the King of Asante is no King.[27]

Aboagye-Mensah adds *Oyeadeeyie*, defined as "one who mends, remedies, transforms or restores a person and a thing into its original state," so that the old is transformed into the new. When used of kings, it implies prompt action taken to restore peace to a nation and its people. Therefore, when applied to Jesus, it implies that he is the one through whom God has restored humanity to its original state. Aboagye-Mensah explains, "Through His incarnation, death and resurrection all men have been restored into the image of their Creator and Lord. Thus Jesus Christ is the *Oyeadeeyie par excellence*."[28]

More vernacular titles for Jesus surfaced in the research, yet these examples suffice to illustrate how traditional Akan praise names are applied to Jesus in order to convey his kingship/chieftaincy. Besides this rationale for the image of

Jesus as king/chief, grounds for casting Jesus so have been identified in respondents reasoning theologically from the kingship/chieftaincy of God to that of Jesus and developing analogies between the functions of Akan chiefs and Jesus as chief. Despite the amassing of such evidence, however, not all Ghanaian believers support the christological image of chief. The reasons for their reluctance must therefore be considered.

Problems with the Image of Jesus as King/Chief

From the outset of his proposal regarding Jesus as chief, Pobee acknowledges that the image is necessarily limited. He pinpoints the key danger as the chief analogy being "a *theologia gloriae*, lacking a *theologia crucis*."[29] That is to say, it denotes chiefly power and authority attained through means other than suffering. In contrast, biblical tradition discloses Jesus entering his kingly glory only through humility, suffering, and martyrdom, as symbolized in the cross. Despite the slight modification Pobee makes to his proposal, drawing upon certain chiefs who gain their position through some act of devotion to society, a fundamental tension remains between concepts of power and authority as demonstrated by Jesus and as associated with African chiefs.

Negative connotations surrounding African chieftaincy account for the greatest number of objections raised by the selected Christians in Ghana to the image of Jesus as chief.[30] One example is Catholic priest Matthew Edusei's response to the question of Jesus as *Nana:*

> The image of Jesus as the king of the kings is powerful, and very biblical. He rules over all. Unfortunately, *Nana* has all kinds of connotations—imposing on people, taking the first place. And then the area of service—death on the cross for salvation. Most *Nanas* wouldn't do that, they wouldn't dirty their hands. So we need to be careful how we see Jesus as *Nana.*

Contrary to traditional kings who shared their resources with the people, reservation was expressed about portraying Jesus as chief because of contemporary chiefs "who rather grab and don't share." Catholic lay man George Hagan summarized problematic associations regarding the chiefly lifestyle:

> But the Jesus that people see cannot easily be projected as *Nana*, you see, because we associate in our minds a certain gorgeous way of life with *Nana*. A certain opulence with *Nana*. Jesus as *Nana* will mean Jesus who married so many wives, Jesus who has so much wealth. So the image doesn't quite fit.

Further problems with the christological image stem from traditional chiefs having lost some degree of status, authority, and credibility through the changes brought by colonialism and independence. Protestant clergyman S. S. Quarcoopome explained that the word *chief* has gained derogatory connotations in Ghana due to the British custom of calling African rulers chiefs instead of kings so as to avoid equating them with the king of England. Protestant clergyman Kwesi Dickson added that the British tended to use the chiefs to implement their own colonial policies, thereby influencing people's perceptions of the traditional leaders. He also voiced the present problem of "absentee chiefs," who live and work in distant cities, returning home for festival occasions, in contrast to traditional chiefs, who lived among their people, were known by them, and served them regularly. Hence Dickson concluded that "the *chief* concept has gone through various vicissitudes, and I don't think it's such a vital concept now, christologically."

In light of these and other reservations regarding African chieftaincy, several respondents stressed the distinction between the biblical imagery of Jesus as "king of kings" and "lord of lords" and the traditional chief, as did Edusei above. The pivotal point in these arguments is the conviction of Jesus' divinity. For instance, African chiefs are said to be subject to human weakness and failure and are consequently dethroned, while Jesus' reign is eternal. Earthly kingdoms are necessarily limited to particular territories and peoples, while Jesus' rule is deemed universal. Aboagye-Mensah grants that the Akan king is described as "sacred" as long as he sits on the stool, yet stresses that "he is never considered divine. Even when he dies and becomes an ancestor, he still remains man, for the ancestors are not thought of as deities." Hence he sums up the contrast as follows: "An Akan king is no more than a mere man, but for Jesus Christ we are talking of one who indeed was man like all men and yet more than man. He is the Word-become-man."[31] This fundamental affirmation regarding the supremacy of Jesus over earthly rulers received forceful expression by PACWA representative Florence Y. B. Yeboah. In response to the question of Jesus as *Nana*, she exclaimed, "He is higher than *Nana*. He's the creator of all *Nanas!* He made all presidents and prime ministers, and all *Nanas*." She continued, when asked about Jesus as chief:

> He is greater than every chief! Chief, *Nana*, they are human beings! And like the radiance that fills the heavens, a little atom of his dignity he gives to the *Nana*. And we have no words, we have no mentality to picture his greatness, the awesomeness of his power, and the radiance of his glory. So if we compare him to *Nana*, we are belittling him. We dare not!

Related to these theological objections are those that stem from perceived discontinuities between the African heritage and the Christian faith. Protestant clergyman Samuel Aboa argued that "the chief in our thought is the epitome of our traditional culture, including our religion," and therefore insisted that he cannot "connect Christ with our religion" in this way. Similarly, PACWA leader Felicia Opare-Saforo countered any suggestion of Jesus as chief or *Nana*, declaring that "he's the king of kings, and lord of lords. And I want to take it that way, rather than bringing it to our cultural way of calling our leaders." These two typify respondents who favor biblical terminology over indigenous expressions for Jesus.

A few additional problems are noteworthy. First, feminist theologians have criticized ruler images for Jesus on the basis that human experience of hierarchies, which are usually patriarchal, does not commend itself to the alienated and oppressed. For example, Amoah and Oduyoye stress that "patriarchal/hierarchical structures have little room for the participation and inclusiveness that those whose humanity is being trampled upon yearn for."[32] Second, a few Protestant clergymen remarked that their usual use of English inhibits their use of vernacular titles for Jesus. For instance, while Theophilus Dankwa agrees that *Nana* is fitting for Jesus, he admitted, "For me, personally, I don't think I often refer to Jesus as *Nana*. But maybe that's my problem, that I pray more in English than in Twi!" One final limitation is that the image is naturally context specific. Those Ghanaian respondents not from traditional chieftaincies were less inclined to identify with the image of Jesus as chief; Peter Kodjo, chairman of the Ga Presbytery, for example, said that he is highly critical of chieftaincy.

A variety of factors thus hinder more widespread acceptance of the christological portrait derived from Akan kingship/chieftaincy and its associated titles. Historical and contemporary realities have given rise to certain negative connotations of African chiefs, which in turn fuel attempts to emphasize the theological distinctions between these human rulers and Jesus as divine ruler. Convictions regarding discontinuities between the traditional African heritage and the Christian faith made some respondents reluctant to consider Jesus in indigenous categories of thought. Further obstacles to employing the image were voiced by women concerned about perpetuating authoritarian male images, by those communicating primarily in English, and by those from non-chieftaincy traditions. These factors must therefore be borne in mind when considering the overall effectiveness of the christological image.

Conclusion

Analysis of the research data suggests that the majority of selected Ghanaian Christians favor the images clustering around Jesus as king/chief/*Nana* and other vernacular titles for sociopolitical leaders. Reasons that promote the composite image have been set forth, as well as those that constrain its usage. While the core concept of Jesus' kingship is virtually undisputed,[33] controversy surrounds the depiction of Jesus according to categories derived from traditional Akan/African leadership. Cognitive associations are crucial; Protestant clergyman Abraham Akrong underlined, "because once you use a model, you have to look at the ready meaning that it evokes, whether it's going to hamper or enhance what you intend to do." If the intention is to communicate the identity and significance of Jesus Christ to contemporary Ghanaians, then certainly some respondents believe the African kingship/chieftaincy image hampers that goal. In contrast, the majority are evidently convinced that it enhances their understanding of Jesus; they would presumably identify personally with Catholic bishop Peter Sarpong's verdict:

Asante Catholics consider these [leadership] roles as applicable to, and indeed perfectly fulfilled by the Lord Jesus. They see Jesus as a chief, a king, over them. With the qualities Jesus exhibits—qualities of humility, goodness—the Asante see in him a person who is their leader in a superhuman way.[34]

Indications of the image's relevance for Christian individuals and communities emerged throughout the discussion, confirming Pobee's assertion that a royal priestly Christology speaks aptly to the Akan context. Parish priest Joseph Aggrey affirmed simply, "We can refer to God, or Jesus Christ, as *Nana*. It makes sense to me, and to my people. They will understand that." Protestant clergyman Thomas Oduro assigned even weightier significance to the image of Jesus as chief in suggesting that it communicates more effectively the meaning of the original Greek word translated "lord." In his words:

> The word *lord* in the Greek and its interpretation, to me, does not have a connotation in the Twi version. For instance, in Twi, when you say somebody is "my lord," it means nothing. But if you take the image of somebody as my chief, you don't even need an interpretation. The person already knows what you mean.

Theological relevance is also attributed to the chiefly portrait as an integral part of the ancestral paradigm for Christ. Protestant clergyman Abraham Akrong raised the image and stated that it "is very significant because then Jesus as a chief will stand in the shoes of God the Ancestor. You see, because the chief takes over the personality of the ancestor. So the chief is the ancestor to us." He explained further that ancestorhood functions as a "semantic domain" with related titles that can be employed for various purposes. In particular, he spelled out the concept of chief as potentially valuable in explicating the incarnation according to Akan thought:

> When it comes to an attempt to explain the relationship between God and Christ, the chieftaincy pattern is very, very important. We understand that technically, the chief is the incarnation of the ancestors. And that is why we give them reverence. I'm not saying that the chieftaincy model will exhaust the mystery of the incarnation, but at least it helps people. So if you tell them that "if you see Jesus, you've seen God"; "if you have seen the chief, you've known the ancestors!" it resonates. It's a similar logic.

The portrait of Jesus as African king/chief not only enhances respondents' understanding of Christ, but it may also influence their manner of worship. In the context of discussing Jesus as chief, Protestant lay man Lawrence Darmani related:

> Because I see him as king, I've seen him also as chief, a great chief with a lot of subjects, meaning people who are worshiping him daily. The reason I can

lie down prostrate, really lie down prostrate, before Jesus, is because I'm able to see him as chief.

By way of background, Darmani narrated childhood memories of people removing their sandals, crawling, and then lying prostrate before a certain chief. He also pointed out further postures, such as crossed legs or wearing a hat, on which he commented, "Definitely, I wouldn't be able to do that in prayer. Because in my mind, I've just gone before the chief or the king." Nana Dokua bore similar witness, which is all the more striking in light of her own position as a traditional leader. In response to the question of Jesus as chief, she stated:

> He is king of kings. Chief is *Ohene*, and king is *Ohene*. In our language we say "Ahene mu hene," "king of all kings." So whenever I mention his name, I bow, because I am a chief, a queenmother. So he is my superior. Yes, when worshipping him I can't stand straight like that. I bow!

These personal accounts from a lay man and queenmother alike amplify previous evidence of the christological image in context, such as the liturgical celebrations honoring Christ the King. Contemporary Ghanaian Christianity, as one particular test case, therefore provides strong indication of the prevalence, meaning, and significance of Jesus as king/chief. The next area of investigation concerns sociopolitical leadership images for Jesus advocated in African liberation theologies.

JESUS AS LIBERATOR

INTRODUCTION

Having established that the image of Jesus as king/chief is effective in certain African contexts, such as among Akan Christians, it remains to consider additional christological images of leadership that arose in the research. As Jean-Marc Ela queries, "In this context, what does a Christ dressed up in a leopard's skin like a Bantu chief signify?"[35] The context referred to is that of Africa at large, described as "a grouping of societies that are historical because they are societies that have suffered," and which remains "a land of poverty, oppression, and violence."[36] For all Ela's emphasis on the need for Africans to express the gospel according to their own cultural symbolism, as pointed out earlier with respect to Jesus as healer, he nonetheless maintains that questions of faith posed on the level of culture alone are insufficient. Instead, the "urgent problems of contemporary Africa become the obligatory *locus* of theological research."[37] Ela therefore advocates a critical approach with points of departure in African culture, economics and politics in order to discern and address the mechanisms and structures of oppression at work, for example, in the marginal role given to women in the church. To strengthen his case, he appeals to the "Final Communiqué" from the 1977 Pan-African Conference of Third World Theologians in Accra.

What makes this conference a landmark, according to Ela, is its acknowledgment that the new challenge for African theology lies not only in seeking liberation from cultural captivity but also from political, economic, and social structures. Hence the document's declaration that "African theology must also be *liberation* theology," and the firm resolve expressed by the Accra theologians: "We stand against oppression in any form because the Gospel of Jesus Christ demands our participation in the struggle to free people from all forms of dehumanisation."[38]

While the aim of rediscovering the liberating dimension of the gospel has been fundamental to emergent African theologies, the realization of this goal is inevitably an ongoing process. Critical questions continue to arise, such as those of Mugambi and Magesa with respect to Christology:

Can the title *Liberator* be applied to Christ today? Is it justifiable in terms of the contemporary situation of the African continent? In other words, is Jesus seen as the "One Who makes people free"? Is He preached as such? Indeed, what is the "image" of Christ? What "image" of God are the suffering people of Africa presented with? Particularly, from the perspective of African women's painful existential experience, what is liberation as applied to the power and authority of Christ in the African world?[39]

Although the issues are vast and complex, the present discussion focuses on selected textual and oral Christologies, with particular attention paid to women's Christologies.

TEXTUAL CHRISTOLOGIES

Jean-Marc Ela

Jean-Marc Ela is eminent among Africa's contemporary theologians, particularly in the area of liberation theologies outside of South Africa.[40] Since he does not follow the approach of developing christological titles directly, his contributions concerning Jesus as liberator require more extended explanation. Autobiographical reminiscences about Ela's theological formation bring to light certain convictions that mark his christological reflections; namely, the fundamental role of history, memory, and identity in forging contemporary expressions of the gospel. He recalls critical events that shaped his thinking, including his uncle leading in the political party that struggled during the 1950s for Cameroon's independence. As a child Ela participated in protest through singing at school a national anthem, in vernacular translation, which was composed in French by young Protestant Cameroonians and forbidden by the French authorities.[41] What struck Ela with particular force was that his uncle and parents, active in the independence movement, were devout Christians, while the official churches rejected this movement. Hence his allegiance clearly sided with his Christian parents rather than with the missionaries who considered the nationalist movement to be the work of communists. In an interview he summed up, "And that explains a little the political dimension of my theology, this historical context in which I grew up, since I did not want to renounce my identity. I have that in my memory. My relatives struggled for the independence of Cameroon." He further noted that this background prompted his fundamental view, that "if this God is not *for* the people, is not with the people who seek their liberty, this God, as for me, I don't want a part of him."

Aspects from Ela's early formation resound in his present theological agenda. Although he has not yet written a treatise on African Christology, he has expressed his desire to do so: "I would like to write a theology of Jesus Christ in Africa. To try to meet with Jesus Christ in Africa, in our history, through our memory." His basic reflections along this line are outlined in an article entitled "The Memory of the African People and the Cross of Christ," with additional insights spread throughout various publications. Central aspects of his thought are presented through a brief summary of the critical issues inducing its expression and Ela's contribution to present formulations of Jesus as liberator.

Ela finds rationale for African Christology in the necessity of gaining access to Jesus through the New Testament as it is interpreted in light of the historical perspective of the church. The central question—Who is Jesus Christ to the African?[42]—is said to hold particular significance in light of the future of Christianity lying predominantly in the countries of the South. Hence the need to go beyond "the Byzantine quarrels" to consider what is truly at stake in the current christological debate.

In order to do so, Ela spells out three main critical issues which are interrelated. Without rehearsing the details of these issues, some of which feature in Chapter 2, the key problems are identified briefly in order to pave the way for Ela's proposed Christology. The first major concern is the ethnocentrism of European theology that has dominated Christianity for centuries, resulting in the "Babylonian captivity"[43] of African Christianity to Roman structures, doctrine, and piety. Attendant Christologies include an "abstract" Christ, who, instead of a personal and tangible reality, is portrayed as disincarnate and restricted to the conceptual framework of Greco-Latin philosophies.[44] Other faulty Christologies, arising from the collusion of Western Christianity with colonial conquest and the slave trade, include "an imperial image of Christ,"[45] used to justify oppressive powers, and a "slave-trader"[46] Christ, used to promote faith as escapism from present suffering through promise of heavenly bliss. Against any presentation of Jesus via a theology of the "salvation of souls," Ela repeatedly insists that "salvation in Jesus Christ is liberation from every form of slavery."[47]

A second major area of concern Ela terms "the traps of inculturation" or "the dead-ends of ethnotheology," meaning the tendency to lock African theology in the challenge of inculturation without rendering adequate attention to the concrete subjects of history.[48] Here Ela criticizes attempts to reinterpret Jesus in Africa that limit themselves to a "theology of digging the sources," that is, developed only in relation to traditional African culture.[49] In his estimation, inculturation Christologies alone are insufficient for enabling the Christian faith to face the challenge of current crises such as that of globalization. Therefore his third related concern is the "irruption of the Third World," with its

epistemological rupture from North Atlantic theology in now doing theology
from the "periphery."[50] With characteristic incisiveness, Ela delineates the contemporary context in sub-Saharan Africa in terms of the disillusionment with
flag independences across the continent; the international domination perpetuating injustice in political, economic, social, and cultural spheres; and the internal factors stemming from widespread neocolonialism.[51] It is against this backdrop that Ela questions the meaning of Jesus' portrait as a Bantu chief clad in
leopard skin. Instead, he makes the fundamental assertion that "it is impossible
to attempt an overall interpretation of the Good News from our African situation without making liberation the fundamental axis of a theology which comes
from our people."[52]

From this perspective, what are the key christological questions that Ela identifies? He certainly highlights Jesus' own question to the disciples, "And you,
who do you say that I am?"[53] The discussion above notes his concerns regarding
who Jesus is to the African today and what kind of images have dominated in
the history of African Christianity. Ela's distinctive contribution, however, lies
in the profound christological questions he raises in view of the critical issues
outlined above. For example, after pointing out Jesus' remark, in a pre-capital-
ist society like first-century Palestine, that it is more difficult for a rich person to
enter the kingdom of God than for a camel to pass through the eye of a needle,
Ela queries what Jesus would say today in the face of the oppressive structures
of capitalist-driven globalization.[54] Elsewhere, Ela insists that the African reality requires "a kind of *pedagogy of the discovery of situations of sin and oppression*," situations that contradict God's salvation and liberation in Christ.[55] From
the misery and despair enveloping Africans in the villages and slums, he calls
for an awareness of their kinship with Jesus in humiliation. He then voices an
acute challenge to the church: "After all, it is Jesus himself who walks
unrecognised today in the African people. Mission today calls for an encounter
with a soul-piercing question: 'Why do you persecute me?' (Acts 22:7)."[56]

The contours of Ela's Christology thus take shape around two focal points:
the suffering of Jesus and the suffering of Africans. Neither the scandal of the
cross nor the scandal of Africa "crucified" today can be bypassed, unless the
church falls prey to the temptation of the priest and the Levite who pass by the
suffering victim in the parable of the Good Samaritan.[57] The two nuclei are
brought together in Ela's fundamental question, "How can we articulate the
crucifixion of Jesus and the historical suffering of our people? In other words,
how can we reread in our own way the narratives of the Passion of our Lord
Jesus Christ taking into account the stations of our memory?"[58] Hence, Ela's
lifelong concerns regarding history, memory, and identity underlie his current
challenge for fellow African Christians to "see the crucified [Christ] with our
own African eyes" while "joining him in the tragedy of his Passion."[59]

In order to address his christological query, Ela explores the historical experience of the African in relation to Jesus. He takes up the double challenge he
puts to African theologians: to rediscover the identity of Jesus Christ through
investigating his life, words, and acts; and to rediscover "our own proper identity in such a way that Jesus Christ becomes part and parcel of our memory."[60]

African memory is probed for its impact in shaping historical consciousness plus African imagination and identity. After briefly surveying "the brutal and massive reality of a continent whose life and history are tied to a long, drawn-out agony,"[61] traced through Africa's experience of slavery, colonialism, and post-colonialism, Ela stresses the "imperative not only to see an exclusively suffering Africa, but also an Africa of struggle and resistance."[62] With these dual strands of agony and resistance woven together in Africa's memory, Ela places the continent's history alongside the historical experience of Jesus. Mutuality is made clear when Ela states that "the historical experience of the black person is a theological *locus* that we should pick up in order to read the passion story on the paths of suffering where the crucified Jesus appears as the prototype of the African."[63] He further asserts that *"Africa today is crucified"* and that *"the struggles of our people bring the memory of the Crucified One right into our life and times."*[64]

On the basis of this association in suffering, Ela contends that instead of Africa's condition in history evoking shame, it must be acknowledged as "the very place where the 'great black cry' springs, the cry that joins the anguished appeal of the crucified of Golgotha."[65] The metaphoric merging of these cries is vital to Ela's Christology:

> In uttering "a loud cry" (Mark 15:37; Luke 23:46), Jesus on the cross actual-ized the cry of the poor and the wretched (Pss. 34:7, 69, 70, 72, 77). In his passion he took upon himself the oppression and the injustice borne by the Black Continent. In modern societies where the fact of being an African is a great challenge, tied as it is to a tragic and shameful history, we find here "a memory of the suffering" of the African. The slaughtered Lamb "recapitu-lates" the history of suffering in Africa, where the powers of death have been active for many centuries. . . . In a sense, Jesus the Crucified is the African humiliated and oppressed for centuries.[66]

Ela elucidates how the depth of Jesus' humiliation on the cross reveals both the suffering humanity of Jesus and God's sympathy and passion for humanity. Since Jesus manifests God's presence in the world, the agony Jesus endured on the cross demonstrates the love of God in a definitive way. Therefore, it is through Jesus' revelation of God to humanity in the mystery of the cross that meaning is found for the suffering of Africans in history. Since it is in weakness that God reveals his power, Ela concludes that "it is necessary to learn to contemplate God from 'below,' in the humiliation in which God is engaged in the drama of the crucified throughout history."[67]

Furthermore, Ela points out that Jesus' death on the cross is inseparable from his life and his resurrection. The cross is said to complete the incarnation, through which Jesus reveals the God of the Exodus (Jn 17:6; 8:28; 13:19; Ex 3:14). A central tenet in Ela's theology is that *"God is not neutral."* Rather, he is preoc-cupied with the poor and committed to bringing justice to the oppressed.[68] Jesus' ministry is viewed accordingly, for the incarnation discloses "the ultimate scan-dal of our faith: Jesus Christ made a radical choice in favor of those considered to be the dregs of the world."[69] Ela maintains that this reality has long been concealed by the dominant theology of the rich, which spiritualizes Jesus to such an extent that his humanity, with all its tensions and conflicts, is over-looked. To recover the New Testament perspective, he asserts:

> The incarnation is the supreme event of our faith—God's final word to us (John 1:14; Heb. 1:1–2). It is difficult to realize its full significance unless we grasp it through the world of poverty and oppression. The real world of the gospel is one of hunger, wealth and injustice, sickness, rejection, slavery, and death. It is precisely through the structures of such a world that God is revealed. God is present through Jesus of Nazareth, who, in the incarnation, reveals God's omnipotence in weakness and establishes a form of conspiracy between God and the downtrodden.[70]

Jesus' ministry is then expounded in terms of his announcing the good news, indicating God's option for the poor, and his central act of proclaiming the king-dom of God as the liberation of the oppressed. His actions are interpreted as being rooted in the prophetic tradition of protest against every form of domina-tion and injustice, whether religious, political, economic, or social. Hence, Ela concludes:

> By his life and his action, he constantly takes the side of the poor, the humili-ated, and the defenceless, against the rich, the pious, and the powerful. He does not hate the rich, but he will not tolerate the exploitation or slavery of men and women. He came, as he says himself, to free the oppressed (Luke 4:17–21).[71]

Together with the incarnation, the resurrection of Jesus is acknowledged to be the summit of revelation and the means by which he has conquered death and inaugurated a new world. Ela immediately raises a question however:

> But how can we celebrate the resurrection where millions of men and women live in suffering and oppression? How can the resurrection of Jesus become an historical experience in the struggle for life itself by those who are weak and without power. How does the resurrection of the humiliated begin to-day?[72]

For Ela, these questions lead to the heart of the biblical message and the Chris-tian faith today, as Africans are presently living out the passion of Jesus in his-tory. Aligning the cross of Jesus Christ with the cross of the Third World, he contends that "the very existence of the Third World shows us what sin is and how it is structured in history. The Third World carries within itself the hidden Christ. It is the historic body of Christ today."[73] Consequently, Ela urges Chris-tians to rediscover Jesus in the slums and other places of misery where the poor and oppressed reside, for it is there that salvation in Christ is made visible. The church is thus called to demonstrate this salvation concretely by creating conditions that liberate people and allow them to grow. In Ela's words:

> The church must adopt the practice of Jesus himself. Jesus did not limit his mission to preaching an inner conversion. His concern was precisely for the liberation of the poor and oppressed (Luke 4:16–21). In Jesus, God is glimpsed in the gesture of shared bread and in the act of the person who rises up and walks.[74]

Hence Ela calls for Christianity with "dirty hands" or a willingness to live out the implications of the "dangerous, subversive memory" of Jesus Christ.[75] In other words Christians must recognize the injustices in their current situations, examine them in light of the mystery of the gospel, and thus discover the prophetic character of the poor and marginalized whose very presence manifests the nature of sin. Once exposed, this "sin of the world" is confronted by the gospel when Christ's resurrection takes on reality through transformed lives and structures. Ela therefore concludes, "Only through an active but humble involvement in the dynamics of African society will they [Christians] be able to live and proclaim Jesus Christ as the ultimate Liberator."[76]

African Women's Liberation Christologies

The image of Jesus as liberator is likewise central to, though does not exhaust, African women's Christologies. Previous chapters have highlighted significant contributions of women to other christological portraits, such as those of healer and ancestor. Yet, as Chapter 2 on critical issues emphasizes, women's concerns and experience have become another *locus* for liberation theology in particular. As they reflect upon various forms of oppression suffered under Western Christianity, African religio-cultural traditions, and contemporary socioeconomic and political realities, women offer fresh insights into the identity and significance of Jesus in Africa today. Like women theologians throughout the Third World, African women theologians identify Christology as a fundamental quest in which they seek primarily to articulate the images of Jesus they encounter in the popular religiosity of their own communities. Their departure point is generally located in "the people's struggle for justice, fullness of life, and loving, caring relationship," and their approach is summarized as follows: "The women take into account what the men say, what traditional Christology teaches and what the Bible says, but what they make of all this and of the Christ arises out of their own and other women's experience of the Christ."[77] As a result, their christological reflections often concur with those of their male counterparts, yet add new dimensions to the subject from their perspective.

Common ground is found in the sources and methods considered most relevant to contemporary christological reflection. For example, Elizabeth Amoah and Mercy Oduyoye work not only from Christian scripture but also from the "unwritten scriptures" of the Fante of Ghana. They speak graphically of "the need to rewrap Christology in African leaves,"[78] illustrated through narrating a

Fante legend of a woman who served as a "Christ-figure" by enhancing life and wholesome relations in her community. The biblical and African traditions are also combined with contemporary realities, for instance, in Oduyoye's christological reflections on salvation and liberation, which she situates in a context of racism, sexism, and religious pluralism.[79] Interestingly, like Ela, she contemplates a fundamental "cry" that she identifies as a universal cry for salvation. Note the multiple sources brought to bear on her investigation, outlined with its significance as follows:

> If one studies the Old Testament with the knowledge of the primal worldview of Africa and an awareness of the political and sociological realities that are shaping Africa as part of one's critical equipment, many similarities surface. The primal cry for salvation *(yeshuah)* is taken up in the New Testament and salvation is declared by Christianity to be in Christ. This I believe is the reason for the continued attraction of Christianity to Africans, in spite of the negative burdens associated with its carriers. The Christ of Christianity touches human needs at all levels, and Africans are but ordinary members of the human race feeling the need for salvation.[80]

Especially noteworthy is that in examining the widespread notion that "Jesus saves" in terms of "What does it mean, what does it imply?,"[81] Oduyoye expounds biblical affirmations by drawing upon two vernacular terms introduced earlier in relation to Jesus. Yahweh, the "warrior-savior" of the Hebrew scriptures whose salvation was experienced concretely in military and political terms, is portrayed in the Akan language as *Osagyefo*, or "the one who saves in the battle."[82] Oduyoye points out the extension of the warrior image, previously highlighted regarding Jesus as leader, to cover "the inner battle against evil inclinations" as well (Eph 6:10–20).[83] She defines the second term, *Agyenkwa*, as follows:

> The *Agyenkwa*, the one who rescues, who holds your life in safety, takes you out of a life-denying situation and places you in a life-affirming one. The Rescuer plucks you from a dehumanising ambiance and places you in a position where you can grow toward authentic humanity. The *Agyenkwa* gives you back your life in all its wholeness and fullness.[84]

Through the juxtaposition of biblical and African traditions, Oduyoye explicates Jesus as the Christ, God's chosen instrument of salvation. Salvation is then interpreted in its multifaceted dimensions, summed up as follows:

> Just as in the Hebrew Scriptures, Yahweh rescued people from childlessness and disease, famine and fire, from flood and from the deep sea, from disgrace and humiliation, so we find Jesus in the New Testament snatching women and men away from all domination, even from the jaws of death. He redeems by a strong hand all who are in the bondage of sin and who manifest their being in the service of sin by exploiting their neighbors.[85]

Thus the biblical and African images amalgamate into one multidimensional portrait of Jesus as savior/liberator/redeemer. Its significance to the African context is presented according to the ideal of feminist theology in becoming fully human. Oduyoye concludes:

> The images of the Warrior and of the Liberator are companion images; they give us hope for space in which to be truly human. The Liberator will set us free through the process of redemption. The imagery of God in Christ as Redeemer is one that speaks clearly to Africa.[86]

If African women theologians generally concur with their male counterparts, they also claim to go beyond the christological position of African men or, at times, even to contradict it altogether. The claim is said to be "gleaned not so much from the writings of African women as from the way they live and from their Christianity—their very spirituality, their witness to what Christ means for their lives."[87] Certainly textual evidence of outright contradiction is scant, as they suggest. Many of the objections women authors raise are against Christologies in which "the figure of the Messiah remains powerful and victorious and male,"[88] that is, overlooking the Messiah as suffering servant. Or they criticize certain classical Christologies presented to Africa, like the royal Christ ruling as a magnanimous potentate, for being akin to paternal colonial and missionary rulers without adequately addressing Africa's need for a conqueror to overcome evil forces.[89] They voice further censure regarding images of Christ that focus on a supramundane realm and "the end of the age" with its paradise to come, rather than a Christ who empowers Christians for life in Africa today with all its spiritual and material demands. Yet as Chapter 2 indicates, these faulty images are derived primarily from Western missionary Christianity, and the major contention of African women theologians is that these alienating images of Jesus were created by an elite group of white male theologians and then universalized, leaving the marginalized peoples' images of Jesus unarticulated.[90]

With respect to African men's Christologies, Amoah and Oduyoye briefly survey key christological contributions from John Mbiti, Emmanuel Milingo, Kwesi Dickson, Burgess Carr, Gabriel Setiloane, and John Pobee. Little disagreement is voiced, aside from the reservations regarding Pobee's proposal of Akan "royal Christology." Where African women theologians part company with their male colleagues most vociferously is in their analysis of sexism and, consequently, their formulation of liberation Christologies. Oduyoye relates how the gender question, one of humanity's oldest power struggles, has gained dramatic visibility around the globe since the 1960s, especially through three United Nations–sponsored meetings. Concerning the 1985 meeting held in Nairobi, she contrasts the "snickering" of African men who "pride themselves on having women who have no need to seek liberation as women," with the African women who "announced their position on the liberation struggle and their solidarity with other women."[91] Oduyoye speaks for many African women in their conviction, summed up as follows:

As a Christian African woman, . . . I seek the quality of life that frees African women to respond to the fullness for which God created them. It is my experience that Christianity as manifested in the Western churches in Africa does little to challenge sexism, whether in church or society. I believe that the experience of women in the church in Africa contradicts the Christian claim to promote the worth (equal value) of every person. Rather, it shows how Christianity reinforces the cultural conditioning of compliance and submission and leads to the depersonalisation of women.[92]

In response to this situation, liberation becomes paramount in the praxis and christological reflection of African women theologians. Oduyoye is again representative in defining the term *liberation* as one that "presupposes the existence of an unjustifiable situation that has to be eliminated. All limitations to the fullness of life envisaged in the Christ Event ought to be completely uprooted. Jesus came that we might have life and have it more abundantly."[93] Nasimiyu Wasike points out further presuppositions and the agenda of women's liberation Christologies:

Jesus is calling all the peoples of Africa, women and men and children, not to accept their hardships and pain fatalistically but to work at eliminating the sufferings and creating a better Africa for all. They have to focus on Jesus, the one who enables and empowers and who wants to liberate them from all that denies them life: political oppression, economic oppression, social, cultural and religious oppression.[94]

Women certainly collaborate with the African male theologians in their confrontation of injustice in the socioeconomic and political spheres, bringing women's experiences and perspectives to these issues. Yet it is often in their particular focus on matters of religion and culture that women bring their distinctive voice. For example, Amoah and Oduyoye articulate their view of Jesus as liberator in this way:

This Christ is the liberator from the burden of disease and the ostracism of a society riddled with blood-taboos and theories of inauspiciousness arising out of women's blood. Christ liberated women by being born of Mary, demanding that the woman bent double with gynecological disorders should stand up straight. The practice of making women become silent "beasts" of societies' burdens, bent double under racism, poverty, and lack of appreciation of what fullness of womanhood should be, has been annulled and countered by Christ. Christ transcends and transforms culture and has liberated us to do the same.[95]

In their pursuit of liberation in Christ, what features characterize African women's Christologies? One key emphasis is "the interplay of faith and life,"[96] as demonstrated in the prayers and praises to Jesus of Afua Kuma, the non-literate Ghanaian woman introduced from the outset of this work and acknowledged in various textual and oral sources. Nasimiyu Wasike explains further, pointing out that most African women work sixteen to eighteen hours daily to provide the basic necessities for their families. Consequently,

> they have very little time to seriously reflect on their relationship with other people and with God. Nevertheless, these women believe that their lives are lived in union with God; their theology is not one which is written and articulated but one which is lived and practised in everyday activities and experiences.[97]

Recognizing the shortage of written materials, Nasimiyu Wasike conducted interviews with six African Christian women (two rural women, two women religious, and two university lecturers) concerning the central question, "Who is Jesus Christ in your life?"[98] From her findings she discerns the actual role that Jesus plays in their lives, such as protector from evil powers and provider of strength, comfort, courage, and hope amid the hardships within home, church, and society.

The afflictions that African women face lead to a second characteristic of their Christologies: the deep conviction of Jesus' solidarity with them in adversity. Amoah and Oduyoye put it with stark clarity: "God wears a human face in Christ. God in Christ suffers with women of Africa."[99] Nasimiyu Wasike specifies that Christ "is the one who takes on the conditions of the African woman— the conditions of weakness, misery, injustice, and oppression."[100] Due to this profound sense of camaraderie between Jesus of Nazareth and African women, relational, nurturing images tend to predominate in their christological formulation. One representative expression follows:

> Jesus of Nazareth, by counter cultural relations he established with women, has become for us the Christ, the anointed one who liberates, the companion, friend, teacher, and true "Child of Women"—"Child of Women" truly because in Christ the fullness of all that we know of perfect womanhood is revealed. He is the caring, compassionate nurturer of all. Jesus nurtures not just by parables but by miracles of feeding. With his own hands he cooked that others might eat; he was known in the breaking of the bread. Jesus is Christ—truly woman (human) yet truly divine, for only God is the truly Compassionate One.[101]

Moreover, it is in this context that Nasimiyu Wasike develops the image of Jesus as mother, a theme corresponding to the image of Jesus as life-giver as interpreted by Mary Getui and others in Chapter 3. Once again, the maternal, life-promoting qualities found in Jesus evidently mark African women's written and "lived" Christologies.

Not only do women's liberation Christologies appeal to the life of Jesus in relation to their contexts of suffering, but also to his death and resurrection. Oduyoye condenses widespread views in observing that "for many third world women theologians the resurrection changes all and the living praxis of Jesus empowers them."[102] Nasimiyu Wasike points to the same source for her hope in the transformation of oppressive structures that dehumanize people. Calling Christians to follow Jesus in this task, she offers the following reassurance: "The identification or solidarity with the poor, the oppressed and the downtrodden can seem impractical without the hope and assurance of Jesus Christ's cross and resurrection to affirm that it is God's own undertaking and we are called to participate in it."[103] Perceptions of solidarity between Jesus and African women thus play a significant role in contemporary women's christological reflection and praxis.

A third characteristic of African women's Christologies is the emphasis on the need for holistic Christologies. Nasimiyu Wasike explains:

> The African woman's experience calls for a Christology that is based on a holistic view of life. She needs the Christ who affects the whole of her life, whose presence is felt in every corner of the village and who participates in everything and everybody's daily life.[104]

Amoah and Oduyoye corroborate this view and delineate various facets of contemporary life for which the recommended holistic Christologies bear significance. Their statement clearly summarizes leading aspects of African women's Christologies:

> Having accepted Christ as refugee and guest of Africa, the woman seeks to make Christ at home and to order life in such a way as to enable the whole household to feel at home with Christ. The woman sees the whole space of Africa as a realm to be ordered, as a place where Christ has truly "tabernacled." Fears are not swept under the beds and mats but are brought out to be dealt with by the presence of Christ. Christ becomes truly friend and companion, liberating women from assumptions of patriarchal societies, and honoring, accepting, and sanctifying the single life as well as the married life, parenthood as well as the absence of progeny. The Christ of the women of Africa upholds not only motherhood, but all who, like Jesus of Nazareth, perform "mothering" roles of bringing out the best in all around them. This is the Christ, high priest, advocate, and just judge in whose kingdom we pray to be.[105]

Finally, African women theologians conclude that however Christ has "*been explained*" throughout the centuries in the historical realities of each age and place, "the most articulate Christology is that silently performed in the drama of everyday living."[106] Hence, they are committed to discovering and disseminating the actual working Christologies of African women across the continent. In the process they are fostering creative methodologies to glean insights from these untapped sources, such as Nasimiyu Wasike conducting interviews with various women and Oduyoye exploring the "folktalk" and narratives of African women.[107] These African women theologians are also contributing to new expressions of oral theology, for example, in the "theo-poetics" included in their

FIGURE 6–2. MERCY ODUYOYE AND THE CIRCLE, LEGON, ACCRA

works and the Circle publications.[108] Furthermore, they join with their sisters in EATWOT "to demonstrate that theology is not only written and spoken, but danced, prayed, mimed and cried."[109] This claim is attested through participant observation in meetings with the Circle chapters in Ghana and Kenya, illustrated in Figures 6–2 and 6–3. I would further add the aspect of dress, as observed and photographed among Circle and PACWA women. Figure 6–3 displays the printed fabric of a skirt worn by the coordinator for PACWA—Kenya,

FIGURE 6–3. PRINTED FABRIC WORN BY PACWA MEMBER, KENYA

Naomi Gathirwa. All these expressions, the formal and the informal, create a mosaic of women's Christologies depicting the overall image of Jesus as liberator.

Conclusion

A fusion of men's and women's perspectives therefore emerges from the crucible of African experience eliciting liberation Christologies today. Overlap occurs in the critical issues outlined, although women give prominent attention to sexism, which they claim men often deny or ignore. Shared sources for christological formulation include biblical and African traditions, as well as historical and contemporary socioeconomic and political realities. Men and women theologians generally favor theological methodologies "from below," with conscientious efforts demonstrated in the writings of Ela, Oduyoye, and Nasimiyu Wasike to discern the issues and the images of Jesus in the popular religiosity of their communities. Central to this undertaking is the experience of Africans as a *locus* for theological reflection, with attempts to highlight the agony and the resistance inherent within African history, memory, and identity. A further priority entails identifying the structures of oppression so as to overcome poverty, injustice, and indignity with the liberating power of the gospel. In that ongoing process, women and men theologians share key convictions about Jesus as liberator: his solidarity with them in their historical and contemporary suffering; the immediacy of his presence in the ongoing struggles of life; the relevance of his life, death, and resurrection to all aspects of life; and the integration of salvation and liberation in his call for believers to discover the fullness of life for which he created them. Thus there is widespread consensus that "*liberation* as a socio-political concern and *salvation* as a theological concern are two sides of one coin—two aspects of the aspiration of all people, as individuals and as groups, towards self-realization and self-fulfilment."[110] These aspirations, according to the theologians, are met in Jesus the liberator. The next section examines this image as evidenced in the oral Christologies.

ORAL CHRISTOLOGIES

In keeping with previous chapters, the image of Jesus as liberator is explored in the oral Christologies in an attempt to discern the extent to which it is operative among selected contemporary African Christians, and what meanings and significance are ascribed to it. Since the results of field research in Kenya, Uganda, and Ghana are very similar, they are presented together, with convergences and divergences pointed out as appropriate.

The Data

The image of Jesus as liberator received strong support from respondents across the selected geographical contexts, with virtually every individual agreeing with it in concept if not in its contemporary expression. In Kenya and Uganda, twenty-six of the twenty-nine individuals with whom it was discussed affirmed some notion of Jesus as liberator, and twenty-four of twenty-nine did so without questioning the term (see Table 6–1).[111]

In Ghana, twenty-nine of the thirty-one individuals with whom it was discussed agreed with this depiction of Jesus, while two disagreed with its contemporary expression (see Table 6–2).

Further corroboration is found in the focus groups. The combined results indicate that a positive consensus regarding Jesus as liberator was reached in ten of the twelve groups, while no consensus was achieved in the remaining two groups, whose members expressed dissenting views (see Table 6–3).

Concerning the prevalence of the image in the selected contexts of field research, a few observations are offered, first regarding the extent to which it was suggested by interviewees. In Kenya and Uganda the term *liberator* or Jesus'

Individual Responses	Statistic	Percentage
Positive responses only	24/29	83%
Negative responses only	1/29	3%
Positive and negative responses	4/29	14%
Overall verdict positive: 2/4		
Overall verdict negative: 2/4		
Total responses overall positive	26/29	90%
Total responses overall negative	3/29	10%

TABLE 6–1. INDIVIDUAL RESPONSES IN KENYA AND UGANDA
TO THE IMAGE OF JESUS AS LIBERATOR

Individual Responses	Statistic	Percentage
Positive responses only	22/31	71%
Negative responses only	2/31	6%
Positive and negative responses	7/31	23%
Overall verdict positive: 7/7		
Overall verdict negative: 0/7		
Total responses overall positive	29/31	94%
Total responses overall negative	2/31	6%

TABLE 6–2. INDIVIDUAL RESPONSES IN GHANA
TO THE IMAGE OF JESUS AS LIBERATOR

Focus Group Responses	Statistic	Percentage
Positive responses only	8/12	67%
Negative responses only	0/12	0%
Positive and negative responses	4/12	33%
Overall verdict positive: 2/4		
Overall verdict negative: 0/4		
Overall verdict neutral: 2/4		
Total responses overall positive	10/12	83%
Total responses overall negative	0/12	0%
Total responses overall neutral	2/12	17%

TABLE 6–3. FOCUS GROUP RESPONSES IN KENYA AND GHANA
TO THE IMAGE OF JESUS AS LIBERATOR

work of *liberation* was volunteered by eight out of the twenty-nine individual respondents, with seven of those voicing it positively; one raised it in the context of discussing faulty images of Christ. Similarly, in Ghana, six of the thirty-one individual respondents volunteered the English terms *liberator* or *liberation,* though the equivalent vernacular terms discussed above must also be borne in mind. The image was likewise initiated in two of the twelve focus groups, notably both times by the Circle women in Kenya and in Ghana.

Second, one experience of informal field research is related briefly by way of illustration. On September 10, 1998, I entered Grace Land Enterprises, a gift and flower shop in Koforidua, Ghana. On the wall behind the cashier was a picture of chains falling away from a pair of wrists, and the caption "Jesus can set you free." Striking up a conversation with the young man working, I asked what Jesus had set him free from. He replied, "Certain pains and immorality." Probed further, he explained, "It means, if I couldn't have found Jesus, my life could have been in danger. I was drinking and smoking heavily, and Jesus has changed me. So I have found him very great and precious in my life."

In view of these contextual clues, plus the respondents volunteering the image of Jesus as liberator, some concept along these lines is apparently operative. Further analysis of the interviews is requisite, however, to ascertain the meaning of the christological image, including the rationale for it and problems with it. Only after such investigation can conclusions be reached regarding its significance today.

Rationale for the Image of Jesus as Liberator

Grounds for assent to the image of Jesus as liberator are located primarily in the Bible. Certainly the main passage pinpointed is the programmatic summary of Jesus' mission recorded in Luke 4:18–20, making it one of the biblical texts most commonly referred to throughout the interviews, with seven individual and two focus group respondents either citing or alluding to it. For example, Kenyan Catholic priest Vincent Kamiri immediately responded to the question of Jesus as liberator: "Indeed yes. This is the gospel." He then quoted Luke 4:18–20, summarized Jesus' "manifesto in Nazareth" as proclaiming liberation to the poor, and applied the significance of the image to his parish ministry in Buru Buru, Nairobi. The same Lukan passage was cited as pivotal by Ugandan Catholic priest J. M. Waliggo, for reasons to be further developed in the next chapter. Two respondents referred to the Lukan text as the fulfillment of Isaiah 61, and two related Jesus' ministry to God's liberation of Israel from Egypt in the Old Testament. After introducing God's salvation or redemption of his people, Kenyan Catholic clergyman Peter Kiarie explained: "Christ then comes almost like the new Moses. In the Old Testament it was Moses liberating the people of Israel, so now we have the savior in Jesus Christ."

Appeal to additional biblical texts draws out various facets of how African Christians understand Jesus as liberator. Personal experience manifestly shapes such interpretation, as the following examples illustrate. Interestingly, Kikuyu philosopher Gerald Wanjohi replied to the question of Jesus as liberator as follows:

> I would also accept that completely. Especially for me as a philosopher, he says in the gospel of John, "Know the truth, and the truth will make you free, will liberate you." So, Jesus came to teach us the truth. And it is truth which liberates us. So, I accept Jesus as liberator, because one of the enslaving elements in man is fear, and fear can harm for lack of knowledge. So, if we know, and since Jesus brings us knowledge, in other words, truth, then we are liberated from so many enslaving elements, circumstances.

Other incidents in Jesus' earthly ministry inform perceptions of his role as liberator today. For example, Kenyan Circle member Hannah Kinoti referred to the gospel account of the woman who touched the hem of Jesus' robe, emphasizing how "she had to announce who she was" before being healed. Kinoti then related how Jesus also drew her out so that she could no longer remain quiet about her experience as a woman. She summed up, "I believe this is liberation."

Aside from specific biblical texts believed to shed light on Jesus as liberator, theological rationale for this image is identified in the close association between *savior* and *liberator* outlined above in the textual Christologies. That the two terms are understood as approximate equivalents is evident in Kenyan Catholic lay woman Mary Kizito's comment regarding certain African traditions: "So I look at Jesus as the liberator, or to use another term, the savior, to free us from that kind of bondage with the traditions." The perception that the terms are virtually interchangeable, together with the third term *redeemer,* formed a refrain throughout the interviews. Kenyan Catholic religious sister Marie Gacambi summarized its significance as follows:

> I see Jesus as a liberator—I take it more or less as the savior. Because I don't see saving just in spiritual terms; the African sees the totality of the person. So it is helping me to acquire the fullness of life in all aspects, sociological, psychological, economic, political, spiritual. Because liberation that only looks at the political elements, that's not liberation. But for me, Jesus is enhancing the whole aspect.

Gacambi's observation strikes at the heart of the issue concerning Jesus as liberator. Analysis of the data, indicated above, reveals almost unanimous agreement with the image. However, the crux lies in how the term is interpreted. Undoubtedly the meanings most commonly ascribed to it related to the spiritual dimensions of liberation. For example, Kenyan Catholic Archbishop Mwana a'Nzeki strongly supports the notion of Jesus as liberator; he explained its meaning in this way:

> Of course he is, there is no question about it. He liberated us from death. He is still concerned with people, he is the liberator number one. Meaning he snatched us, he set us free from the slavery of sin, and he continues to set us

free. As a matter of fact anybody who does what is wrong and repents, Jesus forgives. Always!

Other representative expressions included liberation from "original sin" and "punishment of sins," "that sense of guilt" and "former lifestyles," "from ourselves," "internal liberation" from the power of evil, Satan, and psychological hang-ups, "from the clutches of self-condemnation," "whatever problems you have, even the abuse of alcohol," and from the "fear of death," "the unknown," and "the underworld." Further examples cited were liberation from traditional religions and the dual life often experienced by African Christians still adhering to them; cultural captivity, especially for women; and freedom from temptation, evil influences, disease, worries, fears, demons, witchcraft, poverty, materialism, hatred, and the desire for retaliation.

The findings so far confirm the impression of Ghanaian Protestant clergyman Abraham Akrong, who, when asked about Jesus as liberator, replied:

> Only in the spiritual sense, not liberator in terms of liberation theology. If we are moving from where the people really are, I think he's liberator only in the sense of the one who liberates us from demons and witches but not in terms of social, political liberation.

Akrong accounts for the common perception of Jesus as liberator being "solely spiritual" as stemming partly from the impact of charismatic churches with their emphasis on Jesus as liberator from or conqueror over spiritual forces like witches and the devil. More significant, however, he explained,

> it is because African traditional religion itself, which also controls our evaluation of Christianity, still is more for personal well-being and welfare. That is it. And I don't think it's changed. So people see religion as a spiritual source for protection from spirits at work. The other dimension, that you are called to certain change, to transform society, is not developed.

Compounding the situation, according to Akrong, is the fact that Christianity was presented with an emphasis on individual salvation before God, so that people don't connect individual salvation with the redemption of society.

Before addressing these concerns further, it must be noted that some respondents in Kenya and Ghana articulated awareness of the socioeconomic and political dimensions of Jesus' liberation. Regarding Kenyan Christianity, Catholic clergyman Peter Kiarie explained that this reflects a new development, since historically "Jesus was not seen as a political liberator." On the contrary, nationalist thinkers were against Jesus due to the strongly perceived collusion between Christianity and colonialism. Furthermore, recent revival of African traditional religion is said to be "specifically against Jesus," urging that he be removed, "because as long as Jesus is with us, we are not yet free, because he is part of the *mzungu*." Despite these obstacles in the Kenyan context, Kiarie asserted that "the new understanding of the theology of liberation is another development, because now we are seeing Jesus as guaranteeing God-given, inalienable human rights." Similarly, in Ghana, Catholic lay man George Hagan contrasted the Jesus preached by the early missionaries with the Jesus of liberation theology: "This is the Jesus who has been constructed by Africans who are now feeling themselves competent to preach Jesus. This is the Jesus that has been defined and reconstructed by Africans."

Hagan is among those who acknowledge the impact of liberation theologies in South Africa and Latin America and black theology in America. Specifically, he suggested that "the idea of Christ as a companion in the struggle for freedom, that is something that came from America."[112] Whatever precise sources are at play, certainly the theme of Christ's companionship in the struggle came through strongly in the christological reflections of Ghanaian Protestant clergyman Peter Kodjo. Asked who Jesus is to him personally, he responded immediately in terms of Jesus as liberator. Once again, overlap with the christological image of Jesus as life-giver became clear, as Kodjo interprets Jesus' liberation on the premise that "it is almost impossible to understand the face of Jesus outside the context of struggle for life." He described the everyday difficulties faced by most Ghanaians and then explained:

> This is where Jesus' significance comes in vividly, as the one who redeems us from the crisis we have to live with. We are in a context in which we have to struggle for life, and Jesus is the person who has gone through it. And because of Jesus, we also have life. So Jesus as a *savior,* I think is very important for me. Jesus saves, not because he comes like a magical wand, but he's a comrade in the struggle. The experience of Jesus is usually in the struggle, the cutting edges of life. So it's not an intellectual exercise, it is usually an encounter.

Having already integrated the concepts of Jesus' redemption and salvation in life's struggle, Kodjo further incorporated the notion of liberation as he reflected theologically upon his own experience of meeting with leaders and the youth wing of liberation movements throughout Africa. Like the textual theologians discussed above, he stressed the importance of Jesus' life, death, and resurrection:

> My most religious moment is Easter. And for many congregations in which I have worked, forty days' fast is pronounced. Yes! They try to get closer and accompany Jesus on the journey, because they internalize the journey with their own journeys, because some of them are living in very, very frightening situations. And therefore Easter becomes *our* resurrection. The liberation of the community comes out very big in their thinking. So Jesus is savior. Jesus is liberator. Jesus redeems, not as an outsider who comes, but as one of us, because he's gone through everything we've gone through and he's accompanying us through the struggle.

The growing awareness of the socioeconomic and political dimensions of Jesus' liberation extends beyond those who are theologically educated. Protestant and

Catholic lay people in Kenya, Uganda, and Ghana expressed various aspects of this understanding. For example, they voiced expectation that Jesus can liberate from "dictatorship" and "bad governments," "the bondage of leaders who oppress," as well as from "tribal barriers" and "economic handicaps." They further articulated that Jesus is concerned and involved in issues of justice, that his deliverance is to be experienced here and now, that the church has a significant role to play in national politics,[113] and that their personal experience of national liberation from oppressive regimes has enhanced their understanding of Jesus as liberator. Thus, while the aggregate image of Jesus as liberator from the selected oral sources definitely favors the spiritual dimensions of salvation/redemption/liberation, there are indications of reflection upon the socioeconomic and political dimensions as well.

Problems with the Image of Jesus as Liberator

As the data analysis reveals, not all respondents concur with certain presentations of Jesus as liberator. Perceptions hinge on the meaning and methods associated with the liberator image, and further reservations stem from the concept in relation to contemporary experience. The main objection concerns the correlation of Jesus' earthly ministry with some contemporary depictions considered "purely political." Several respondents contend that any portrait of Jesus as a revolutionary freedom-fighter is contrary to the gospel account, since "Christ never fought" but rather "Christ is peaceful. So if you want to liberate yourself by arms, I don't see how you can say that it is Christ who is helping to liberate you." Ghanaian Protestant clergyman Samuel Aboa's summation was typical of the appeal to Jesus' ministry and the problem of his Jewish contemporaries:

> They were expecting somebody like a soldier or a politician using force to liberate them from their colonial powers, from the Romans and the Greeks. But he was quite different. He came to liberate people from what separated them from the source of their life—God.

On this basis, some respondents expressed vehement objection to the portrayal of Christ as liberator on par with Jomo Kenyatta or Kwame Nkrumah. For example, Protestant clergyman J. B. Masinde deeply opposed such proposals as "an intellectual reaction to the colonial Christ that was presented to us," and "a faulty Christology" that leads to a "faulty Christianity." Instead, he maintained that "Christ liberates us from something much more than political bondage," namely, the "bigger slavery to sin." Likewise, Kenyan Catholic priest Peter Gichure criticized Latin American liberation theologians for a certain reductionism:

> Liberated from what, you know? Again, I would be very reserved. If we mean liberator, the one who liberates me from all evil, all evil, even the evil in myself, probably I would understand. But the way it has been used, it's as if liberation is only from certain known evil structures or oppression. And as

long as it remains that way, for example with the Latin American theologians, you're already limiting Jesus. But I think Jesus should be seen as one who stands against all evil: "Deliver us from the evil one."

So strong is this concern about reductionism that some church leaders expressed caution about employing the term *liberator* for Jesus.[114] For example, Mutava Musyimi, general secretary of the NCCK and widely known for his commitment to the political process, clarified:

> I prefer to think of him as a redeemer, not as a liberator. Redeemer is safer for me. Liberator is loaded because there are those who see Jesus in purely political terms. And although we are involved in political issues, we don't see Jesus coming to redeem us in the political sense in which it is understood by liberation theologians. We see Jesus redeeming us, in a holistic way.

Thus common perceptions of Latin American and other expressions being unduly political in orientation hinder more widespread acceptance of Jesus as liberator among these selected African Christians.

Even where respondents agreed with the concept of Jesus as liberator, they expressed further reservations about the christological image in relation to its outworking in contemporary experience. Although Ghanaian Protestant clergywoman Margaret Asabea raised the image herself regarding images of Jesus especially meaningful to Africans, she admitted that she is "battling" with it. She questioned: "What is wrong with the concept of Christ as a liberator, in Africa? Why is it elusive? Why is Christ in the center, in the issues, and yet, to my concept of liberation, we're not getting there. We're not getting the kind of liberation that Christ epitomizes." She then specified that continued suppression "is more painful and more serious when it's happening in the church, against women." Likewise in the focus group of Kenyan Protestant clergymen, Oscar Muriu candidly acknowledged the problem he has personally in accommodating the image:

> Of course theologically I could argue that he is liberator, but if I put it rather crudely, it's not very clear what he has liberated me from. I am still in my political realm, and there hasn't been much liberation there, because so many times we don't relate Jesus to the real world of politics. He hasn't liberated me from my poverty—I am not speaking for myself but for so many who are needy, and accepting Jesus doesn't change the reality of their need, in that sense. And then because so many times we don't relate to the spirit world, we don't sense liberation there. As a born-again Christian, I could argue that he is my liberator, but in my day-to-day life, I don't conceive of him as that.

Thus the oral Christologies indicate almost universal consent that Jesus is liberator, yet dissenting views arise regarding the precise nature of the image, particularly in its sociopolitical interpretation, and the degree to which it is actualized in the selected contexts of contemporary African Christianity.

Conclusion: Jesus as Liberator

Analysis of the oral Christologies reveals almost unanimous assent to the image of Jesus as liberator, with interpretations generally favoring personal and spiritual dimensions such as deliverance from sin, fear, and evil powers. Growing awareness of socioeconomic and political dimensions of liberation is also manifest, together with cautions against portrayals of Jesus in narrowly conceived political terms. In light of the various perspectives voiced from across the continent, the crucial role of context must be underlined in determining the meaning and significance of Jesus as liberator. Ghanaian Protestant clergyman B. Y. Quarshie stressed the importance of working from the particular situation to considerations of the christological image, for in his view it would be meaningful in many contexts in Africa, like South Africa. He makes the important observation that

> at the level of Christ as liberator, in political terms that may be meaningful in a situation where political action is needed. But then on the other hand, Christ as a liberator *need* not be understood in purely political terms. And that is why I say the context is critical, because you could use the category of liberator in nonpolitical terms. And Christ could be liberator in terms of maybe the social ills of the day, or even economic liberation and so on. So it's a category that can be used.

As this christological category gains ground across Africa, several main points from the oral Christologies evidently echo those noted in the textual Christologies. First, the image of Jesus as liberator conveys his solidarity in suffering, as discovered by encountering Christ in the concrete, everyday realities of the struggle for life. For instance, despite his own publications on African theology, Protestant clergyman Emmanuel Martey reflected on his pastoral ministry and emphasized that "Christology for me became not just a theorem, a theological theorem, but a reality in my church, because I saw Jesus liberating people, Jesus delivering people and healing people." Second, respondents voice the deep relevance of Jesus' life, death, and resurrection to the contemporary context, especially to women seeking freedom from bondage to certain church and sociocultural traditions. Ghanaian PACWA representative Florence Y. B. Yeboah stated simply, "On the day of resurrection, Jesus liberated women." Other women rendered testimony to the reality of bondage in their lives, whether female circumcision, traditional customs considered degrading, or stigmas attached to singleness or childlessness. Third, the oral Christologies confirm the intrinsic relation among salvation, redemption, and liberation. Language issues emerged here, with some respondents preferring the English terms *salvation* and *redemption* over *liberation*, due to the sociopolitical connotations of the latter term. Other respondents preferred vernacular terms deemed more appropriate for the composite christological image. For example, Ghanaian Protestant clergyman Peter Kodjo asserted:

> Liberator comes out also in the vernacular—*Ogyefo*. He's a savior—he saves us *from*. Conqueror. It's real for many people. And here the language is very rich because it captures the image a little more vividly. And I would wish that we use Ghanaian languages because the imagery is more real when we use a Ghanaian word. English limits our expression of the concepts.

Finally, the oral Christologies attest to the central affirmation of the need for a holistic image of Jesus as liberator. Kodjo insists that the concept of liberation is not restricted to political emancipation but extends to "all that dehumanizes us in community." Kenyan Circle member Mary Getui specified further: "I would like to look at Jesus as a liberator all round—a liberator from our narrow perspectives, a liberator from our political differences, from our ethnic differences, a liberator from our economic handicaps." Archbishop David Gitari of the Anglican Church of Kenya summed up the personal and communal, plus the spiritual and sociopolitical dimensions of the image in his delineation of Jesus

> liberating people from their sin. And obviously sin can be a very big burden. There are people who have given their testimonies of how they were drug addicts, or alcoholics, but when they went to Jesus, he liberated them, thus restoring them to the fullness of life. But even Jesus as a liberator of a nation like this one, from evil rulers and from corruption and from all that. We know he is still working, and we will continue prophesying so that the liberation can come in all its fullness.

Gitari's closing comment leads to one last observation from the oral Christologies. While respondents voiced the expectation for Jesus to liberate his people here and now, they also recognize the eschatological dimensions of Jesus' salvation/liberation. This important aspect, expressed by Kenyan Protestant lay woman Marcy Muhia, strikes an appropriate note on which to close the present discussion of liberation Christologies:

> There's a part of me that says it's possible to see Kenya liberated now, today. And it's possible to see God's kingdom come, and his will being done here on earth as it is in heaven, now. But at the same time, there's a part of me that accepts that that will not come to fruition until Christ returns. And yet, there's the part of me that says, you know, keep praying. Keep praying.

CONCLUSION: JESUS AS LEADER

Concepts of leadership in Africa provide fertile ground for christological images, as amply demonstrated in the textual and oral sources under consideration.

Attention has focused on two main figures within the realm of sociopolitical leadership: Jesus as king/chief, and Jesus as liberator. While various interpretations surface in relation to these images, a certain congruence emerges between African Christologies derived from traditional categories of leadership and those proposed in contemporary liberation Christologies. Returning to the test case of the Akan in Ghana, Catholic Bishop Peter Sarpong's conclusion encapsulates key themes that have come to light in the examination of both types of Christologies:

> The Asante Christology, therefore, is a Christology that is based upon their conception of leadership in the traditional political set-up—chieftaincy. . . . Jesus came not to destroy the tradition given us but to uphold it for us. He is our leader in the war against the forces of evil, against the oppression of sin, against the domination of anything that is inhuman or dehumanising. Jesus is our military leader. But as he himself said, the war he fights is not for earthly hegemony but to liberate us from the shackles of all that makes it impossible for us to be true sons and daughters of God.[115]

Here the merging of African and biblical traditions becomes explicit as Jesus is interpreted in light of the dual inheritance of African Christians. Yet the significance of the proposed Christology clearly relates to the contemporary realities so central to liberation Christologies. Thus, according to the selected African Christians, Jesus represents both the fulfillment of leadership expectations in traditional African thought and of current yearnings for liberation in all dimensions of life.

Observing the coherence between the traditional king/chief and the liberation Christologies does not dismiss Ela's legitimate question of what the image of Jesus as chief clad in leopard skin signifies in the face of Africa's past and present suffering. Rather, it simply invites the recognition of Jesus as archetypal leader, in all the manifold aspects of that sovereignty, as applied to the needs of particular contexts. Put differently, the approach taken here of christological patterns allows for leadership images to be considered in thematic clusters rather than in isolation or in opposition. In place of the dichotomous approach of inculturation versus liberation Christologies, the integration of leadership images allows for particular images to operate in those contexts where relevant, such as the image of chief among Akan Christians, while also providing a system of cross-checks to guard against irrelevance. Thus, for instance, if the portrait of Jesus as chief does not adequately address gender issues, then the challenges voiced by women's liberation Christologies provide an appropriate corrective. The two approaches are not mutually exclusive, as demonstrated by the Ghanaian women theologians and queenmother clarifying that Akan women hold certain chiefly offices, when this aspect was not brought out in the men's Christologies. Likewise, if images of Jesus' lordship have prevailed in terms of distant, domineering rule, then liberation Christologies rightfully recover the suffering Messiah, whose solidarity with humanity in his life, death, and resurrection continues in the ongoing "crucifixion" of the Third World today.

Taking this approach to the cluster of leadership Christologies, where do the relative strengths lie at present? What enduring questions remain in need of further address? An examination of these questions according to the criteria set forth in Chapter 2 sheds further light on the significance of the selected contemporary African Christologies for African Christianity.

Analysis of the sources and methods employed in the various leadership images reveals appropriate strategies according to the criteria recommended. The textual and oral Christologies attest to all four of the sources advocated, in different degrees. First, the Bible evidently elicits both kingship and liberation Christologies, the latter highlighting Luke 4:18–20 in particular. Second, the African heritage inspires specific images such as Jesus as king/chief/*Nana* and associated vernacular terms. It also provides traditional praise names employed in worship and exposition of New Testament Christologies; oral sources, such as the "folktalk" examined in women's Christologies; and the collective memory of suffering so fundamental to the Christologies of Ela and others. Third, the living experience of the church features to a somewhat lesser extent, for example in the image of Jesus as king/chief operating in worship and being articulated in christological reflection, and the attempts to discover and disseminate the "lived" Christologies of African women. Fourth, contemporary realities are prominent in liberation Christologies that identify African experience, whether of sexism, racism, poverty, or any kind of oppression, as the *locus* for reflection. Hermeneutical strategies demonstrate that any one of the four sources may serve as a departure point for christological formulation, with movement either from the Bible to the African context or vice versa.

As to the question of whether the methods are effective in the pursuit of contextual Christologies, positive indications are found in the extent to which the African heritage and contemporary realities function, as identified above. Moreover, certain theologians demonstrate a conscious and conscientious effort to articulate their Christologies in line with the priorities advocated by EATWOT. For example, Ela quotes from the "Final Communiqué" regarding the need to bring out the liberative dimensions of the gospel, thereby reflecting not only his efforts to do so but also self-critical reflection upon the theological process. Furthermore, Oduyoye represents further refinement of EATWOT priorities as an active participant in the "irruption within the irruption" and a pioneer of new, creative methods in women's Christologies. Critical reflection upon previous methodologies consists in deliberate attempts to uncover sources of oppression, whether perceived to originate in biblical, church, or African traditions or in contemporary realities. While noting the gains made in christological methodologies thus far, the fact that representatives like Ela and Oduyoye are pioneers in this regard also indicates the scope for continued development. To the extent that their fellow African Christians follow in these directions, African Christianity will become more deeply contextual in its identity and expression.

Brief estimation of the seven factors of contextual relevance builds upon the analysis of sources and methods. Areas of strength have already been signaled, primarily those of cultural and linguistic relevance. Widespread evidence contributes to the impression that Jesus has significantly entered cultural perceptions of leadership. Indications have been identified in the textual and oral witness, in the contextual clues found in private and corporate worship as well as in the "lived" and "visual" Christologies, and in the particular instance of conflict between church and state in Ghana, when many Christians considered it blasphemous to use traditional honorifics adopted for Jesus in reference to Nkrumah. Limitations have been noted, such as the cultural specificity of the chief as a christological image and the impact of historical change in concepts of chieftaincy. Nonetheless, striking evidence confirms the opening observation that Africans perceive Jesus as a leader according to traditional categories yet to a superlative degree, such as the African chief Nana Addo Birikorang enthusiastically affirming Jesus as "super-chief" and "super-*Nana*." Furthermore, some respondents claimed that certain vernacular terms like *Osagyefo* and *Agyenkwa* convey the holistic mission of Jesus more accurately than the English terms *savior, redeemer,* and *liberator,* and that employing such vernacular terms enhances their understanding of Jesus and their worship of him.

Areas of moderate strength include contemporary relevance and gender appropriateness, gained foremost through recent expressions of liberation Christologies. Ela and Oduyoye lead in highlighting the "cry" of Africans in relation to current conditions of poverty and oppression across the continent. Nasimiyu Wasike and others add to new articulations of women's Christologies in the face of sexism deemed rampant in church and society. While acknowledging the strides made in liberation Christologies, the impact nonetheless remains moderate due to the enduring tendency to favor interpretations of Jesus as liberator in the spiritual domain more than the socioeconomic and political domains. Despite the emphasis the selected African Christians place on the need for a holistic understanding of Jesus as liberator, comparatively less attention is evidently devoted to christological reflection and praxis in the socioeconomic and political realms.

Before further consideration of this observation, the aspects of historical and theological relevance are certainly manifest, but the force of their presentation is countered by the degree of representation. For instance, Ela is powerful and poignant in his portrayal of the joint sufferings of Jesus and Africa throughout history. As a result, he redresses the critical issue outlined by J. M. Waliggo in Chapter 2 regarding the need to understand the historical suffering of Africans as fundamental to contemporary African Christologies. African Christianity awaits further contributions along these lines in the full-fledged christological treatise that Ela anticipates writing. In the meantime, however, the Christologies represented here would be strengthened by more in-depth reflection upon Jesus in relation to Africa's historical suffering. For the more African Christians are able to recover a sense of Jesus' presence in their history, the less of a newcomer he will seem to their continent.

Finally, the area of perhaps greatest potential and greatest need relates to the criterion of credible witness. The suggestion of greatest potential is confirmed by Ela's remark:

If we actualize the prophetic and subversive project of Jesus Christ in our African societies today, that will not leave anyone indifferent. And consequently, we must develop Christology which emphasizes all the liberating potential of the gospel of Jesus Christ. In this way, at this time, the people will be obliged to pay attention.

The greatest need is summed up in Ela's "brutal" question: "How can we liberate the gospel so that it can become the leaven of liberation," given the current realities in the African church and society?[116] Likewise, Mugambi reflects on the contemporary witness of African Christianity and raises trenchant issues. First, he notes that "Africa is also portrayed as the most religious continent in the world. We are told that Christianity is growing numerically in Africa at such a rate that this will be the most 'christian' continent by the end of the twentieth century." He then queries, "Is this religiosity authentic and genuine, or is it superstition arising from despair?" Even more pointedly, he continues:

It appears as if Africa is overburdened with religion and as if God does not listen to the prayers of Africa. This is very paradoxical. How can the most religious continent in the world be abandoned by God to perish in poverty, in debt and under the yoke of the great powers of the world? What can Africa's religiosity mean at a time when the news about Africa proclaims that nothing good can come out of this continent or from its people?[117]

These are penetrating questions, bearing in mind the honest lament of the Ghanaian and Kenyan clergy quoted above regarding Jesus' liberation being somewhat elusive in their current experience. Even granting the eschatological dimension to Jesus' salvation/liberation, the questions voiced require careful consideration. Do such impressions nullify the foregoing discussion of Jesus as leader? Or are there indications of Jesus' significance to African individuals and communities that, upon cross-examination, provide countering evidence?

Part III explores these major questions concerning the significance of contemporary African Christologies to the African context and to the global church, for in these issues, it must be underlined, African Christianity does not stand alone. On the contrary, the christological questions posed in Africa ultimately bear upon the understanding and witness of Christians worldwide. As Kenyan Catholic clergyman Peter Kiarie noted with respect to Jesus as liberator:

I think we are going to discover him together, internationally. This is my reflection, that there is Jesus the liberator from personal sin, he's my personal liberator from the slavery of the devil, and then Jesus as the liberator of structures, and also of nations. And he'll have an impact even at the international level.

Part III

The Significance of Contemporary African Christologies

7

The Relevance of Christologies
in Africa Today

*It is quite clear that Jesus, in His public ministry, was actively and simulta-
neously involved in both personal and social reconstruction. He mobilized
His followers to become involved in social change, having convinced them of
the necessity and urgency to change their attitudes towards themselves and
the world.*
        —J. N. K. MUGAMBI, KENYAN THEOLOGIAN

*The way in which we present Jesus Christ has a direct impact upon our soci-
eties. The proof, if you like: if I am in exile, it is because I spoke of Jesus
Christ!*
        —JEAN-MARC ELA, CAMEROONIAN THEOLOGIAN CURRENTLY EXILED IN CANADA

*Through these [Christian Scripture in mother tongues], Jesus Christ the Lord
has shouldered his way into the African religious world, and was to be discovered there by faith, not invented by theology.*
        —KWAME BEDIAKO, GHANAIAN THEOLOGIAN

INTRODUCTION

Part II analyzed central themes in contemporary African Christologies in
terms of their rationale, sources, methods, and meaning. Areas of strength have
been noted with respect to the christological images, as well as unresolved controversies and enduring questions. Critical assessment has proceeded on the
basis of priorities voiced by the African Christians, including the use of sources
and methods in christological formulation, plus several aspects of contextual
relevance in christological expression. Important issues have arisen throughout

221

the discussion, yet the overriding concern is that of significance: Is Jesus Christ significant to life in Africa today?

Part III examines this crucial question in light of evidence from the selected textual and oral Christologies. Unlike Part II, in which the data was treated comprehensively, the present chapter is confined to certain indicators of significance according to the selected African Christians. While the christological materials are employed illustratively, their combined witness establishes that Jesus is perceived to be highly relevant to various spheres of life. The discussion opens with a brief consideration of Jesus in recent theologies of reconstruction, followed by an examination of the significance of christological praxis and reflection in Africa today.

JESUS IN RECONSTRUCTIVE THEOLOGIES

Chapter 6 closed with an assessment of the current christological images regarding Jesus as leader. Among the areas of concern, piercing questions were raised about the relevance of Jesus to contemporary life. In particular, J. N. K. Mugambi poignantly expressed the paradox of Africa being the most "religious" and specifically "Christian" continent at the end of the twentieth century, while "its peoples remain the most abused of all in history."[1] Concerned whether Africa's religiosity might be sheer superstition arising from despair, perhaps even a hindrance to progress, Mugambi further questions, "What, precisely is the role of Christianity in particular, and religion generally, in social transformation?"[2]

In order to address this problem, Mugambi advocates "reconstruction" as a new theological paradigm for African Christians in the "New World Order." Without elaborating Mugambi's theological project, the present focus is on the historical and theological context, the rationale, and main proposals in relation to contemporary African Christologies. In turn, these considerations provide a springboard for further analysis of the selected textual and oral Christologies for the perspectives they offer on Jesus' relevance to social transformation.

Mugambi situates his theology of social reconstruction in the context of the dramatic changes in Africa's political landscape in recent history: from decolonization in the 1960s, through disillusionment with independence in the 1970s and 1980s, to the "New World Order" of the 1990s with the demise of the Cold War and the colonial era, including apartheid. Throughout these decades, liberation featured prominently in Latin American, African American, and other third-world theologies. According to Mugambi, "The theme of *liberation* had become commonplace in Africa" by the time the WCC held its Fifth Assembly in Nairobi in 1975, entitled "Jesus Christ Frees and Unites." Moreover, liberation had become "a dominant paradigm on the continent."[3] Mugambi explains the analogy drawn between the history of the Israelites liberated from bondage to Egypt, and modern Africans aspiring for national liberation from colonial rule. He therefore interprets the Old Testament Exodus in a primarily political way. Addressing the Executive Committee of the AACC in Nairobi in 1990, Mugambi voiced the following critique:

> Until now, the majority of renowned African Christian theologians have high-lighted the *Exodus* metaphor and emphasised the theme of *Liberation*. . . . After South Africa (Azania) and Western Sahara resolve their para-colonial crises, the metaphor of the Exodus will become totally inapplicable and ir-relevant. For most African countries that metaphor has been applied for too long, and perhaps should have been replaced at the time of the declaration of African republics.[4]

Mugambi therefore called for a review of the liberation paradigm, question-ing, "If most of Africa had been 'liberated' in the 1950s and 1960s, what hap-pened to that 'liberation'?"[5] He further queried what theological imagery would be more appropriate for Africa in the "New World Order," and along with Charles Villa-Vicencio,[6] proposed reconstruction theology. Thus Mugambi stated to the AACC Executive Committee in 1990 that "we need to shift paradigms from the Post-Exodus to Post-Exile imagery, with *reconstruction* as the resultant theo-logical axiom."[7] Since the 1990s were viewed as a decade of reconstruction in many areas, such as constitutional reforms and economic revitalization, African theology was called to play a culturally reconstructive role like that of Protes-tant theology during the European Renaissance and Reformation.

In developing his reconstructive theology Mugambi identifies further ratio-nale in the dichotomy commonly found between the liberation and salvation paradigms. He explains that the polarization arises from different views regard-ing the role of the gospel in social transformation. While some theologians iden-tify salvation primarily with spiritual conversion and view liberation theology as a "social gospel" that deviates from the biblical message, other theologians insist that the gospel requires involvement in the process of liberation and social transformation. Mugambi argues that the two approaches are not mutually ex-clusive. On the basis of Jesus' ministry of personal and social reconstruction, Mugambi insists that salvation and liberation are theologically complementary. Hence, the following conviction recurs throughout his writings:

> In the African context and in the Bible *salvation*, as a socio-political concept, cannot be complete without *liberation* as a theological concept. Thus Jesus, proclaiming his mission, quoted from the book of Isaiah to indicate the cor-rectness and relevance of his concern (Isaiah 61:1–4).[8]

Mugambi concludes that African theology must seek an integrated approach to the gospel, which overcomes the polarization between liberation and salvation paradigms. Likewise, he contends that African Christologies must overcome the sharp dichotomy between inculturation and liberation. In his view the theol-ogy of reconstruction meets both needs.

The terms *construction* and *reconstruction* are said to originate in engineer-ing, and the notion of *social reconstruction* to belong to the social sciences.

Mugambi turns to African history and biblical traditions to locate processes of social construction, highlighting various motifs in the Old Testament such as the exilic motif in Jeremiah, the Deuteronomic motif associated with Josiah, the restorative motif expressed in Isaiah 61:4, and the reconstructive motif exemplified in Haggai and Nehemiah. For the present purpose of christological investigation, attention is drawn to Mugambi's brief reference to the mission of Jesus being essentially reconstructive of Judaism rather than deconstructive. Without elaborating, Mugambi identifies the Sermon on the Mount (Mt 5—7) as "the most basic of all reconstructive theological texts in the synoptic gospels."[9] Then, in his call for three levels of reconstruction—personal, cultural, and ecclesial— Mugambi introduces the first level by emphasizing that social reconstruction must begin with the individual. He offers evidence in Jesus' teaching regarding the need for transforming personal motives and intentions in order to produce constructive change. Following examples from Matthew and Luke, Mugambi concludes that "the key to social transformation is appropriate disposition of the individual members of the community concerned, especially its leaders."[10]

While christological formulation is not prominent in Mugambi's theology of reconstruction, it does underlie the entire approach of social transformation and reconstruction that he anticipates will characterize African theology in the twenty-first century.[11] For example, in response to his own question of whether Africa's religiosity marks authentic faith or superstitious despair, Mugambi stresses the need for hope among individuals and communities in Africa today. That hope is to be spread through Christian witness, as indicated in the following charge:

> The Churches of Africa are challenged by the scriptures to continually act as God's witnesses on earth in the name of Jesus of Nazareth, whom we affirm to be Christ. Each Christian is challenged to act upon this challenge and endeavour to make it a reality. Do we witness with despair, or with hope?[12]

This challenge presumably forms the basis for the three levels of reconstruction indicated above, and further broken down elsewhere as political, economic, aesthetic, moral, and theological reconstruction.[13]

The question remains, however, as to the extent of innovativeness represented by the proposal for reconstructive theology. Certainly the new terminology, derived from the process of *perestroika* in the former Soviet Union during the late 1980s and the political discourse associated with F. W. De Klerk's 1990 reform initiatives in South Africa, enhances the contextual relevance of African theology in the 1990s.[14] Nonetheless, some question recent theologies of reconstruction regarding their newness and their constructiveness in the lack of clear, concrete proposals.[15] One problem stems from the zeal to find new theological paradigms without adequate appreciation of the gains made in previous theologies.[16] Neither liberation nor inculturation theologies receive due recognition in Mugambi's treatment, nor those who have already succeeded in surmounting previous polarizations between the two trends. For example, Mugambi acknowledges briefly that Jean-Marc Ela's theology "brings about a synthesis of inculturation and liberation."[17] Yet he overlooks other theologians like John Pobee,

Bénézet Bujo, Mercy Oduyoye, and Anne Nasimiyu Wasike, who move in the same direction.

A second problem consists in overlooking the continuity in major theological concerns from past decades to the present time. Mugambi evidently overstated the case in predicting that the Exodus metaphor would become "totally inapplicable and irrelevant" once South Africa and Western Sahara resolved their para-colonial crises. His statement reflects the danger of reducing the theme of liberation to the Exodus metaphor narrowly construed in relation to colonialism, a tendency in Mugambi's reconstructive theology. However, evidence from the present research indicates that the theological concern for liberation is far from passé.[18] Finally, many of the fundamental questions eliciting Mugambi's proposal for theological reconstruction are clearly aligned with those of other inculturation theologies. For example, he introduces his new paradigm with the question, "In a world where national borders are becoming increasingly irrelevant, how can African Christians be faithful to both their own cultures and to the Gospel?"[19] In sum, Mugambi's reconstructive theology is certainly valuable in its contribution to overcoming the polarization between "the so-called 'political theology' of South Africa and the so-called 'cultural theology' of the rest of the continent."[20] It also offers timely recommendations for reforming Christian witness across Africa. Yet the findings from this research corroborate Tinyiko Maluleke's assertion that

> the proposal for some theology of reconstruction is not new in the Third World. Most Third World theologies, insofar as they have been local initiatives aimed at local renewal, have been kinds of theologies of reconstruction. Africans and churches north of the Limpopo have for a long time been engaged in theologies of reconstruction of one sort or another (AACC 1991).[21]

The christological data considered here indicate, first, that theologies of reconstruction are undeniably necessary, and second, that they are currently under way in Africa, whether or not the language of reconstruction is employed. First, the expressed need is clear in Oduyoye's reflections on the reconstruction of Africa: "The future of the Church in Africa is dependent on its ability to embark afresh on its mission to be Christ in Africa."[22] This mission requires responding to "all the poverties of human life." It also means ensuring that the gospel is "set in the context of the real lives of the people to whom it is delivered" and that it makes a difference to those lives. Oduyoye further stresses that "a revisit of both ecclesiology and spirituality is urgent for the theological enterprise of the African Church. The viability of this reconsideration will depend upon the development of a dynamic Christology."[23]

Second, evidence from the present research confirms that the dynamic Christology sought is indeed developing in African Christianity. Part II has investigated christological themes, indicating progress made thus far. The recurring emphasis is that christological formulation is insufficient without considering its significance to the reconstruction or renewal of human lives in the specified contexts. Mugambi expresses common consensus as follows:

The Good News which Jesus proclaims to the world is not theoretical. It is news which in real life rehabilitates individuals and groups that are marginalized by various natural and social circumstances. In contemporary Africa, the Good News understood in this way, ought to . . . help Africans regain their confidence and hope at a time when the print and electronic media portray Africa as a hopeless and helpless continent.[24]

The remainder of this chapter addresses these concerns, reiterated as follows: How is Jesus Christ considered to be significant to life in Africa today? Do the selected African Christians find confidence and hope in him? Do they manifest engagement in theologies of reconstruction or local initiatives in renewal? Once again, the discussion that follows is not to be interpreted as a comprehensive treatment of the issues. Instead, the christological data function as "cairns" along the way of Christian witness in Africa, testifying to believers' experience of Jesus and its perceived impact in their lives.

JESUS IN AFRICA TODAY: CHRISTOLOGICAL PRAXIS

INTRODUCTION

An axiom of third-world theology is that theology entails critical reflection and praxis, or committed action. A hermeneutical connection is upheld between faith and obedience, meaning that people gain a deeper understanding of the gospel by living in accordance with its demands. Theology thus arises in the interaction between action and reflection as Christians live out the faith they articulate.[25] While the two aspects of theology are interwoven, each is considered separately at present for its respective place within emergent African Christologies.

The selected African theologians unanimously maintain that praxis is essential to Christology. Oduyoye underlines that a theology divorced from ethical demands is irrelevant to Africa and that the reason African theologians must review Christology is to highlight the necessity of ethics derived from faith in Christ.[26] Bujo concurs, and castigates African theologians who "are foremost concerned with earning academic degrees as passports to higher careers," and "have no interest in carrying their theologizing into the huts and shanties." He states forcefully:

If our theology . . . restricts itself to an academic exercise taking place exclusively in the lecture halls of universities and highly specialized institutes and seminaries, or mainly at overseas conferences, we must necessarily conclude that it can be *of no relevance or significance whatsoever for our African society.*[27]

To avoid complicity in forming such an elitist Christianity in Africa, social commitment is indispensable to theology. Bujo thus urges professional theologians to maintain close contact with all classes in society yet to exercise a preferential option for the poor on the basis of Matthew 25:35ff. He concludes, "We, African theologians, can no longer afford to merely think socially concerned, or preach socially concerned, or teach socially concerned, but we must also take social action and move from mere orthodoxy to orthopraxis."[28]

If this is the widespread conviction, what is the situation with respect to christological praxis in the selected African contexts? Before coming to the research findings, it is instructive to note C. G. Baëta's observation regarding Christianity's impact in Africa in the twentieth century:

> In numberless institutions of many different kinds as well as in the equally numerous and diverse voluntary organisations and free associations of men, women and children; in the pervasive influence and challenge of its message to men and demand upon their individual lives and their relationships with one another; in countless personal and group decisions made, and lives actually lived very differently from what they would otherwise have been; in the new high hopes and aspirations for individual and social destiny which it has awakened; in the sheer excellence of human performance in devotion and courageous, self-sacrificing service to others, and yet in other ways, Christianity . . . plays a role and exerts a force in tropical Africa which is none the less real or significant because it eludes full and conclusive analysis.[29]

Kenyan Catholic Archbishop Ndingi Mwana a'Nzeki echoes Baëta. Asked if Jesus is relevant to life in Kenya today, he replies, "Very much. Very, very much. People may not be able to express it, but the way they live it, I think he is very relevant." Nzeki then cites examples, such as the fervor of Pentecostals preaching and caring for street children in the slums, and the Catholic cathedral (Holy Family Basilica, Nairobi) being packed out for communion services every morning at 7:20 A.M.

The overall consensus of the interview respondents is that Jesus is definitely relevant to life in their respective contexts, and to all aspects of life. Kenyan Protestant lay man Ole Ronkei's response typifies the widespread response to the question of Jesus' relevance: "Absolutely, definitely. I see him coming into play in *every* part of our lives, in *every* part of *my* life." It is somewhat difficult to isolate particular dimensions of life, given the holistic worldviews generally characteristic of African Christians. However, for the purpose of the present discussion, Mugambi's three levels of theological reconstruction (personal, cultural, and ecclesial) provide a framework with slight modification as follows: personal formation, social transformation, and ecclesial reformation.

PERSONAL FORMATION

The centrality of Jesus to personal formation lies at the heart of the gospel, according to African Christian witnesses. J. B. Masinde, a Kenyan Protestant pastor, expressed it this way:

When all is said is done, all of us need to find out, where do we begin to tackle problems of humanity? It's not in the lab, it's not on the streets, it's not in the parliament, it's in our hearts. And the only thing that seems to adequately address the issues of human hearts, whether it's an African heart or a European heart, is the person of Jesus Christ and his teachings. And that's why I'm saying he is still very relevant to an African. He's relevant to a European. He's relevant to an Indian, because he's the only person who talks about issues of the heart, and addresses them in a way nobody else does.

Whatever the precise issue faced, respondents give account of Jesus' significance to their personal renewal physically, emotionally, morally, and spiritually. Examples of these accounts feature throughout Part II and often reflect universal human needs in accordance with Masinde's observation above. Other evidence conveys more contextual coloring, such as the following statement from Ghanaian Protestant clergyman Thomas Oduro:

We are surrounded by spirits, and we interpret whatever happens to us in the spiritual realm. And, therefore, we always want somebody who is more powerful than the spirits, to protect us, and to lead us through darkness, and to be our guide, and to link us with *Onyankopong*, the Supreme Being. That makes Jesus Christ very, very, very, very relevant. Without him we would have been trying other, lesser deities to test their power and they may disappoint us. So you go to this shrine, disappointed you run to another shrine, disappointment and all that. But, to know Jesus Christ as someone who created all these lesser deities, and therefore is more powerful and is next to God, makes one rest assured that he does not have to run after gods and shrines and fetish priests.

If the issues vary, the common response was one of expressed hope in Christ despite all the odds of the situation. The conviction formed a refrain throughout the oral interviews in Kenya, Uganda, and Ghana. Notably, both the general secretary of the NCCK, Mutava Musyimi, and his deputy, Peter Bisem, highlighted hope as paramount in the significance of Jesus today. Bisem focused more on personal formation, while Musyimi attended to social transformation. Speaking of his own experience and of the struggles of Christians across the continent, Bisem acknowledged that they have known much pain and suffering. Yet he stated, "Jesus comes in as a new picture of hope, irrespective of all that happens, as one who can fill our own person and help us to see God even in the pain that is going on." He explained further, regarding the Kenyan context:

The hopelessness that some people seem to face—in the message of Christ, they are able to see their hope realized, even if not completely in their life. The majority of people would find a lot of solace, a lot of comfort, a lot of hope in Christ. That even though they're in the slums of Mathare Valley or Kibera, the only meaningful hope that seems to address their every context is the message of the gospel. And so people are able to see this man Jesus is so real and so relevant, and they respond to the gospel, in spite of all this, with a lot of zeal, with a lot of dedication.

That hope is firmly grounded in the life, death, and resurrection of Jesus, as poignantly attested in one last illustration of personal renewal. Kenyan lay woman Marcy Muhia related candidly the death of her first child at full term in the pregnancy. Despite intense grief, she affirmed:

> We live in the hope of the resurrection. God knew what it was like for his son to die—same way that I knew what it was like for my son to die. Then God knew the joy of the resurrection, and I too will know the joy of the resurrection. And I think as we wait for that, that is what gives us hope. I think that perspective has made me willing to be an active member of life again.

SOCIAL TRANSFORMATION

A key point in Mugambi's christological reflections outlined above is that social reconstruction must begin with the personal reformation of individuals. Other African Christians confirmed this conviction. For example, with respect to Jesus as liberator, Marcy Muhia stated, "I've seen more and more how the liberation of the individual is the beginning of liberation for the nation. That as each person is set free from their own sins, that person becomes a link in the liberation of the whole nation. That I see as Christ." In Ghana, Catholic Bishop Palmer-Buckle's statement graphically portrayed individuals contributing to social transformation, thereby demonstrating Jesus' significance:

> From my vocation as a bishop, I definitely believe that Jesus owns the answer to the contemporary problems and difficulties and joys and happiness. I see Jesus in the healing of the doctor in the hospital. I see Jesus in the teaching of the teacher who is helping to enlighten the kids. I see Jesus in the mother who, because of her love for her children, would sacrifice herself for her children. I see Jesus in my receptionists who would welcome people into my office and make them feel wanted. I see Jesus in myself, when I stop by an old lady who just wants to see who her bishop is, and I pick her up in my arms, and she strengthens my faith and I strengthen hers. I see Jesus in the orphan who comes to me because he or she has no way of paying his or her school fees, and asks me at a time when I'm tight myself for money, and I have to help. I see him in the priests with whom I work, who are killing themselves in the villages for the good of the people. I see Jesus in the policeman who would fight for justice, honesty and sincerity. I see Jesus in the soldier who would go all out to protect the people, and put order in place. And so for me, Jesus is very, very much alive.

Christological praxis is thus considered fundamental to social transformation. Once again, hope in Jesus forms a motif throughout the textual and oral data. In response to the basic question of who Jesus is, Mutava Musyimi of the NCCK immediately spoke of Jesus as the savior who remains "the major sign of hope and redemption" for the world. He emphasized hope "because of the level and the scale of needs that surround us. And I use the word *need* in its comprehensive sense." Addressing the Kenyan situation, he continued:

> We have major problems in terms of governance, security, economy. The thought-forms that take Jesus and his values seriously provide, in my view, the only kind of hope that I can see, because Jesus comes into situations with a disarming selflessness and teaches us to serve in a way that nobody else does—gives us the capacity to do so in a way that nobody else does. And so whether we are talking about evangelism, discipleship, development projects, advocacy issues, gender issues, the environment, the disabled people, constitution, economies—frameworks of thought that derive their inspiration from him are the only sign of hope that I see.

The natural question is whether such hope is "merely a utopian dream or a realistic hope?"[30] Virtually all the selected African Christians—theologians, clergy, and laity—address contemporary issues in their respective contexts and voice ways in which they believe that obedience to Jesus effects positive change in society. Bujo names "modern African sins" like corruption in the public services that hinders the development and the humanization of Africa, and the modern exercise of power often characterized by personal enrichment and exploitation of the weak. He asserts that corruption and the abuse of power can only be overcome if priority is given to Christ, the proto-ancestor.[31] Ela applies thoroughgoing sociological analysis of political, economic, and social ills that can only be addressed by "the subversive project of Jesus Christ." For his outspoken proclamation of the gospel against political injustices in Cameroon, Ela is currently exiled in Canada. Furthermore, Pobee's prolific writings indicate a wide range of social issues that call for christological reflection and praxis.[32] For instance, he stimulates further consideration of Jesus in relation to poverty in this way:

> Africa is characterized by poverty. They are the poor who are not only materially deprived but also the marginalized, the bruised, the voiceless. Christology in Africa is about how the Word has become flesh in this context of poverty. He is Christ of the Poor. He is the Poor Christ of Africa. He is the Christ of Poor Africans. He is the Christ, the hope of the embattled Africans.[33]

Pobee also concludes that Christians must live out this hope in society:

> The importance of tying in social action and Christology cannot be overstated. It is crucially important for the Christian to let his/her engagement in social action be rooted in a clear understanding of the person of Jesus Christ in whom his/her faith is grounded.[34]

Without minimizing the scale of needs in the African contexts, African Christians maintain that conformity to Christ contributes positively to social transformation. Full-blown analysis of the social impact of Christianity lies beyond the present scope.[35] The following discussion is limited to brief illustrations of the perceived significance of christological praxis according to the selected African Christians in Kenya, Uganda, and Ghana.

Kenya

The vitality of Christian experience in contemporary Kenya is unmistakable. Aside from ample manifestation in the oral interviews, evidence abounds in context: in proliferating churches, mass crusades and open-air preaching, overnight prayer meetings, and in press accounts and popular publications. Vincent Kamiri, a Catholic parish priest in Buru Buru, Nairobi, remarked:

Any time somebody is opening the gospels or the scripture, people are attentive. We [Kenyans] flock into churches. We have problems: problems at home, perhaps as individuals, indeed, as a society. But we have recourse to Jesus. So he is very present in our lives.

Kamiri continued by referring to the Emmaus disciples, who did not immediately perceive Jesus in their midst but came to recognize his presence among them in the breaking of the bread (Lk 24). From this gospel account Kamiri concludes, "Jesus is with us in our difficulties, in our mess, wherever we are. So, he is very present to us, and that is why we shall go to him in our prayers."

Concerning the outworking of this Christian vitality, senior church leaders in Kenya voiced the potentiality and the actuality of social transformation accomplished through obedience to Jesus. John Gatu, former moderator of the Presbyterian Church of East Africa, identified the "selfishness of man" as the root of the suffering in Kenya. He alluded to the gospel accounts of the rich young ruler whom Jesus asked to give away his possessions, and the witness of Zacchaeus upon his conversion in giving back what he had taken from people. Gatu concluded, "I would say from our economic point of view, those are very direct illustrations of what Jesus would have us do with our economy. And it must start with me, and so on." Gatu's comment is not simply a pious platitude; it reflects the real expectation and the historical experience of many believers in the East African Revival. Gatu narrated how, through the influence of the Revival, he renewed his faith in Christ as an adult in 1950, after having "abandoned" it for many years. One of the distinguishing marks of the Revival was a deep conviction that sin required confession and restitution or "putting things right" wherever possible. Hannah Kinoti explains, "Restitution could mean returning to the owner things one had stolen, or a run-away wife returning to her husband, or asking forgiveness from the person one has wronged and thus seeking reconciliation."[36]

The Christian commitment to "putting things right" extends into the political sphere in Kenya. Due to the sensitivity of the subject, specific details are limited here. However, Gatu related one example of how he and other senior church leaders confronted senior government members during political tensions that preceded the 1997 general election. Tensions surrounded the Kenya Constitutional Review in particular, for Parliament had established in 1992 that the Kenyan Constitution was to be rewritten by an independent commission, yet the process had been repeatedly postponed. By 1997 the Kenyan people increasingly insisted that this commission had to be established immediately in order to provide time to rewrite the Constitution before the elections to come in December 1997. Because of the discussions that ensued between senior church and government leaders, Gatu concluded, "*That's* how we had such a smooth general election last year. For me, it was a direct intervention of Jesus Christ in the midst of this land."

Similarly David Gitari, Archbishop of the Anglican Church of Kenya, voiced his perspective on the significance of Jesus during the same period of political tensions in Kenya. One particular incident received international media coverage, and Gitari's account warrants full citation:

He [Jesus] is very, very relevant. In July last year, there was a rally at Uhuru Park of the Opposition. The police went and chased people away, and they came to the Cathedral. They wanted to pray, and the police came and threw tear gas in that Cathedral and injured people. I was telephoned at home by the Provost, so I got the whole story. And that story was reported all over the world. What I did a week later was to preach from Daniel chapter 5: "*Mene, Mene Tekel*, and *Parsin*." And we reminded the President and the police that "your days are numbered and you have been weighed in the balance and found wanting." And that sermon had such a great impact on the President and the politicians, that within two days he called me to State House with other church leaders. And he agreed to the change of the Constitution [in order to make the Kenya Constitution Review Commission independent] before the elections [in December 1997]. Before that he had said, "*Never!*" We had gone to see him and he told us he cannot change. After that sermon he agreed to change. So, I think the gospel preached *prophetically* and *powerfully* has a lot of *impact*.[37]

While the process of political change and constitutional review is undoubtedly complex, there is clear witness to the leading role played by a united front of church leaders in recent Kenyan politics.[38]

Finally, the call for Christian engagement in "putting things right" is extended not only to Kenyan leaders but also to ordinary believers. Participant observation in a church service at Nairobi Chapel allowed exposure to a sermon entitled "Facing Our Giants." Preaching from his written sermon on 1 Samuel 17, Pastor Oscar Muriu addressed "the giants, the Goliaths, the major problems Kenya is facing." He identified nine points:

1. Unemployment—especially with 60% of Kenya's population being youth under the age of 25

2. Poverty, with 50% of our population now living under the poverty line
3. Insecurity due in part to people's increasing desperation, and in part to the fear of guns coming in from the war-torn northern neighbours
4. Future of the street children
5. Debt—both internal and external, and the drag that this has on our economy
6. Land clashes
7. The decaying infrastructure
8. The lack of visionary national and political leadership
9. And the breakdown of the rule of law in this country.[39]

Following exposition of the biblical text, which records David slaying the giant Goliath, Muriu sets forth "five smooth stones" for fighting the Kenyan "giants." The first is prayer, and he comments: "It may be that indeed the only thing that has so far restrained the giants from overwhelming the land sooner, is that Kenyans have been faithful to pray." The second smooth stone is evangelism, "for the gospel can transform society." The third is "speaking out," since God calls Christians "to expose lies and speak out on behalf of the poor and voiceless." The fourth is "non-violent public lobby for responsible stewardship." Muriu explains, "The idea here is to hold our elected officers, public institutions or private businesses to act in accordance with righteousness. To mobilize mass protest so that our collective numbers and voice are heard." He also calls for Christian involvement in the constitutional review process, in order to establish accountability structures to help the public remain honest. The fifth smooth stone is "strategic non-cooperation," or "the selective non-participation in those institutions of government or private enterprise that are unjust, and that oppress people."[40] Thus Muriu seeks to mobilize ordinary Kenyan Christians to live out the gospel of Christ, thereby making an impact politically, economically, and socially.

Obviously, proclamation of the gospel of Christ does not guarantee a righteous society, even in countries like Kenya, where the majority of the population are allegedly Christian. This research does not overlook the severity of social ills, acknowledged above by leading clergy. However, the present discussion remains limited to those indicators of the social impact of christological reflection and praxis in contemporary Kenyan Christianity. From the few illustrations provided, evidence points to at least some degree of vital Christian engagement in social transformation.

Uganda

The discussion of Jesus as liberator in Chapter 6 indicated that Jesus' manifesto in Luke 4:18–20 is pivotal to Catholic priest J. M. Waliggo. In response to the question of who Jesus is to him personally, Waliggo replied:

Really, deep down, I think he *has* to be an African to me, to make sense. And therefore he has to be somebody who knows the suffering the Africans have passed through, and who experiences our marginalization and all the problems that we are going through, even this problem of Christian duality. And who then works with us, in order to achieve total liberation. So, somebody who is an activist for the African liberation, and for removal of every enslavement that would be found in this community of Africans.

John Pobee's observation that "all theology is biography" apparently applies to Waliggo, for the dual themes of suffering and liberation articulated above certainly encapsulate Waliggo's life and thought. In the interview and in later informal conversation, he recounted various experiences of persecution under the Amin and Obote regimes. He also spoke of the humiliation and the alienation of being exiled from 1982 to 1986 in Kenya, Tanzania, Rwanda, and the former Zaire.

After reference to his exile Waliggo continued, "And so, when we managed to remove the oppressive regime, my whole work was to plan how Uganda should be reorganized after the victory." He explained the new role to which he was appointed as general secretary of the Constitutional Commission, with the key task of establishing how to "empower all the people to make a people-centered constitution." For four years he provided oversight to the commission that conducted oral interviews at the grassroots level throughout the country. From the thirty-five thousand memoranda amassed (some up to five hundred pages in length), he and the commission were responsible for writing a draft Constitution of one thousand pages. Afterward, Waliggo worked for the largest newspaper, publishing weekly articles to foster further debate on the issues, before the Constitution was approved in 1995. The Uganda Human Rights Commission was then established to deal with human rights violations and to teach people civic education and the Constitution. Waliggo was appointed to this commission by Parliament, and he continues in that capacity to the present.

In view of Waliggo's experience, it is understandable that Jesus as liberator is the cardinal christological image for him. He declared: "The idea of liberation for me can never go away. If Jesus is revelation, then he becomes relevant in so many realities." He added that "Jesus from the point of view of justice" is critical for him. Commenting upon his own longstanding involvement in justice issues, he assessed his experience of christological reflection and praxis in relation to the Uganda Human Rights Commission as follows:

I've never discovered Christ more clearly than I am now. Never in my whole life, especially when I move into the prison and meet the prisoners and talk to them. At the end I can say, "Ten of you are really unlawfully held. You can come out now." I can come back the next week and see the children in the remand home, the women, and I release them. I felt that before, I could only preach and didn't have that power of Jesus. You left everybody in their own suffering. But now I feel that I am working exactly like Jesus in Luke 4:16–18: "I have come so these may see." When you go into the civic education, you see that the blind are beginning to see, the deaf are beginning to hear. And I've felt if more people within Christianity really had that chance of moving from mere preaching to seeing that the power to liberate is with them, and they are doing it with Jesus, then a lot of things would be solved.

He thus asserted that Christians must extend Jesus' liberative praxis

in the secular world, if one is working in the economic system, in the political system, in the school system, in the health system and so on. Rather than restricting ourselves to something called spiritual, religious. That is only one small aspect where you can liberate people. We need to be integral in our approach.

Waliggo's publications provide notable confirmation of the deep significance of Jesus to his thought and work.[41] His christological reflections revolve around the nucleus of "who is Christ to the suffering people of Africa?"[42] Waliggo stresses the importance first of analyzing christological images, and second, of addressing what difference Jesus makes in the lives of the suffering people of Africa. He articulates a liberation theology founded upon two integral images: "the rejected stone" of the historical Jesus, and "the cornerstone" of the risen Christ. He then underlines the practical tasks entailed in making this Christology a reality by breaking the fetters of hardship and joining the victorious Christ in realizing concrete liberation.[43]

The outworking of Waliggo's christological vision also is clearly manifest in the publication of a seminar to which Waliggo contributed several chapters, integrating his expertise in theology and his experience in justice issues. Especially significant to the present discussion is his chapter entitled "Jesus as the Model of Justice and Peace, Defender of Children and Women, Challenger of Corruption and Oppressive Cultural Practices."[44] Here, in condensed form, Waliggo's Christology derived from Jesus' manifesto in Luke 4:18–20 is applied to contemporary social issues in Uganda. Thus christological reflection and praxis are at the heart of Waliggo's dual roles as theologian and as leader in the Uganda Human Rights Commission. Clearer indication of Jesus' significance to the social renewal of a nation could hardly be found.

Ghana

The vitality of Christian experience noted above with respect to Kenya is likewise attested in Ghana. Lawrence Darmani speaks for many Ghanaians, including theologians, church leaders and laity, who are convinced that Jesus Christ is relevant to life in Ghana today. In an interview Darmani stated:

We've had our share of deep problems and situations that have affected our lives—economically, politically, and even socially. Now Jesus has been with us here in very difficult times. All kinds of evil still goes on in this country. But we've seen situations where Ghanaians have prayed over national problems, like economic hardships and political problems, and the Lord answering them.

As in Kenya, theologians and church leaders assert the need for christological praxis to effect tangible social transformation. Pobee's writings, mentioned above, provide many illustrations of christological reflection in relation to contemporary realities. One noteworthy example is found in *Who Are the Poor?: The Beatitudes as a Call to Community*. In terms similar to John Gatu's, Pobee highlights Zacchaeus's conversion and consequent promise to repay fourfold those whom he had cheated. From this gospel story, Pobee insists that "salvation begins with repentance of one's misdeeds against humanity."[45] Yet it also requires reparation and an amended life with firm resolve not to repeat the offense. Pobee applies this concept of salvation to both individuals and nations. For instance he points out that there has been much discussion of the need to create a just economic international order, yet little progress has been made. He underlines two reasons this situation must be seriously addressed:

> It is not just a question of giving back some of one's gains, whether ill-gotten or otherwise. It is a two-fold issue. First, to realize one's humanity. As long as there are pockets of abject poverty on the face of the earth at this time when we have technological and other material resources to correct the situation, our humanity is at stake. Second, it is an issue of what the example of Christ means for those of us who claim to be Christian: "You know how generous our Lord Jesus Christ has been: he was rich, yet for your sake he became poor, so that through his poverty you might become rich" (2 Cor. 8:9).[46]

Thus Pobee's rationale for redressing international economic injustice is grounded in his conviction that "the real purpose of being Christian . . . is to be human in the image of Christ."[47] It also reinforces Peter Kiarie's assertion that Jesus as liberator must be discovered corporately at the international level, where issues of humanity and credible Christian conversion are at stake.

At the national level in Ghana, church leaders actively address social ills according to the gospel of Christ. The "Communiqué" from the Ghana Catholic Bishop's Conference, July 2–10, 1998, prepared for the "Great Jubilee" of the year 2000, for which "our Holy Father the Pope has requested all Christians to reflect on Christ."[48] On this basis the bishops declared "*a crusade against bribery and corruption*," depicted as "a dangerous social cancer that is eating its lethal way into the fabric" of Ghanaian society. Specific instructions are outlined in the document for prayer and for dealing with bribery in everyday life. The bishops take an ecumenical and interreligious approach in appealing to all Christian churches, Muslims, and followers of traditional religion to join in the campaign "to deliver our nation from the clutches of the bane of corruption." They further address current issues related to the energy crisis and the Cocoa Research Institute, with recommendations for national leaders and citizens in order to enhance economic prosperity. Bishop Peter Sarpong is widely known for his outspokenness on social issues at the national level.[49] In conversation, Sarpong refers to Jesus' teaching about divine judgment based on treatment of the poor and sick, the hungry and thirsty, the stranger and the imprisoned (Mt

25). He applies this passage to the contemporary context in Ghana, for example, "the abject poverty in this society," prisons, street children, blind people, and current ills in the health services. Appealing to Jesus' teaching in the Beatitudes, Sarpong concludes, "Oh! The relevance of Jesus and his doctrine could not be more felt in Ghana than now."

Once again, Christian leaders clearly call for christological praxis to affect society, but what indications are there that the call takes on reality in the lives of ordinary Christians? On par with Kenyan Christianity, Ghanaian Christians evidently find hope in Jesus as expressed tangibly in everyday life. According to Oduyoye:

> Christians live by hope in Africa, that this miracleworking Jesus will work miracles in their daily encounters, and especially in the socioeconomic realm because that's where the suffering is. Everybody's hoping that with Jesus, this *trotro* will bring a lot of money, it will not have an accident, the owner will not have to spend so much money. And that's how people carry on.

Figure 7-1 illustrates Oduyoye's point.

Figure 7–1. *Trotro*, Ghana

Further confirmation occurred in informal conversation with taxi-driver Charles Obeng. Obeng's taxi displays a picture of Jesus and two inscriptions: "Annoiting [*sic*] Power" and "Invite Jesus into Your Life." Questioned about why he placed them there, he replied, "Because I am a Christian" and "because I want the anointing to work with my car." Probed further, he explained that the anointing denotes God's power to protect the car and himself, and to provide business.[50] Obeng also voiced his perspective that, in general, the inscriptions commonly found on vehicles in Ghana do reflect genuine Christian belief. Certainly they do for him personally. Even granting that some vehicle drivers may well display these slogans merely as a fad or a ploy to drum up business, many interview respondents interpreted them as visual indicators of the vibrancy of Ghanaian Christianity.[51] For example, Dan Antwi noted with slight laughter:

> It's amazing how even if you travel around, some of the inscriptions on vehicles, you think that people are Jesus-crazed! But that's exactly what you find—they're not just putting them, but they are increasingly becoming aware of who this Jesus is.

Many marketplace workers adorn their shops with vivid expressions of Jesus' identity and significance to them as well. Figure 7–2 displays how some plumbers in Kumasi publicize their roadside workshop.

Informal conversations with shop owners reveal their hope in Jesus for economic prosperity. Rebeccah Owusu advertises "Wonderful Jesus" across her

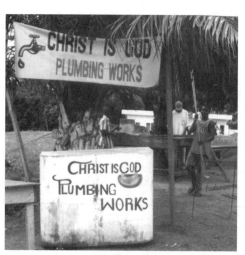

FIGURE 7–2. ROADSIDE WORKSHOP, KUMASI

brightly colored shop in a Kumasi *trotro* station. Asked why Jesus is wonderful, she explained that some people starting businesses look to "fetishes" and "other gods" for success, but she believes that Jesus will help her.[52] Similarly, a dressmaking shop in Kumasi bears the signboard, "Grace High Class Fashion (Don't Despair)." Across the front awning is painted *Hwe dee Awurade aye*," which translates, "See what the Lord has done." Along the side awning is *Yesu Mo*, a common expression of praise that conveys the sense of "congratulations / well done / thank you, Jesus." When asked about the signs, the women workers said that they had had a stall in the Asafo Market, but it had burned down. They had no hope, but this is what God had done for them, and therefore they proclaim, "*Yesu, Mo*."[53]

The Ghanaian evidence thus corroborates that from Kenya and Uganda concerning the significance of Jesus Christ to contemporary life. Across the three African contexts, the witness of selected Christians affirmed the potentiality and the actuality of christological praxis contributing positively to social transformation. Hope in Jesus, against all odds amid contemporary political, economic, and social ills, emerged as a central motif. Evidently this hope is not merely a utopian dream, for concrete manifestations of change were clearly attested: from a priest acting on government authority to bring about tangible liberation in the lives of marginalized peoples to market women celebrating Jesus as the one who enables them to forge a living under difficult economic circumstances. The examples do not dismiss the gravity of suffering in these contemporary situations. But they do illustrate widespread conviction that social transformation at the national and international levels can begin only with individuals. The individuals featured in this section on social transformation signal ways in which Jesus is deemed to be significant today politically, economically, and socially.

ECCLESIAL REFORMATION

Christology is closely related to ecclesiology. The fundamental concern prompting African Christology naturally extends to the central question eliciting African ecclesiology: "How can the Church be truly African and truly Christian?"[54] While the subject commands in-depth attention, the present discussion is restricted to a brief sketch of Jesus' significance to contemporary African ecclesiology according to the selected African Christians.

A dominant model developed in recent African ecclesiology is that of the church as extended family or clan.[55] Important consequences stem from this conception and foster reformation in church polity and practice. Bujo's proposal of Jesus as proto-ancestor forms the basis for his christological-eucharistic ecclesiology. Just as every individual in African tradition shares basic responsibility for strengthening the life-force of the community, so all Christians are to enhance communal life within the church. The challenge is addressed especially to church leaders, who are called "to deepen and to transmit to others the life of Jesus Christ, the Proto-Ancestor." Hindrances to this process, such as "clericalism," "episcopalism," and "sacerdotalism," are decried as "a kind of cancerous growth which slowly but surely chokes the proto-ancestral life."[56] Among the many ecclesial reforms advocated, Bujo underlined in conversation that "our Christology *should* criticize the concept of hierarchy in the Catholic church." He developed the notion of Jesus as the "new Abraham" and the "father of the faithful" on the basis of the gospel account of Jesus choosing the twelve disciples representing the twelve tribes of Israel. He therefore asserted:

> The pope is not a "holy father"; he is a brother, the *eldest* brother, because the father is Christ, according to this text. And then, at the level of the parish, the priest is not a father for the parish; he is a brother among other brothers and sisters.

He directed further recommendations toward priests, religious orders, missionaries, and laity. Again, he wove various proposals for reform within the overall christological pattern of Jesus as proto-ancestor. Thus Bujo concluded that orthopraxis derived from the model of Jesus as life-giver and ancestor could provide "a veritable ferment" for transforming African society today.

Similarly, Pobee related his christological reflections to specific issues within the Anglican Church of Ghana. For instance, he questioned what it means to affirm Christ as "the prince of peace" in confronting one situation of indiscipline and struggle for power at the diocesan level. He concluded, "I want our common affirmation of God, Christ, and the Holy Spirit to be at the center of how we organize our life as a diocese. It's not just a power game! It's not just administration. For me it's a question of our credibility."

Issues of hierarchical structure and power are further questioned in relation to women's participation in the church as the family of God. According to Oduyoye, Christian baptism signifies entry into "a new humanity modeled after Christ," and therefore requires dismantling barriers of classism, racism, and sexism (Gal. 3:28).[57] And, Nasimiyu Wasike asserts:

> For men to be what they have to be, women must be allowed to actualize their potential and to freely participate in all ministerial roles. This is a way in which humanity could be restored to wholeness. Women and men in the Church must be educated to equality, and women's expectations of themselves have to be raised to a model for human justice.[58]

This call does not arise from women alone. For example, Bishop Palmer-Buckle admitted that it remains problematic at present for women to enter the priesthood in the Catholic church. Yet he stressed the need for women in leadership roles such as presidents of parochial councils, and heads of diocesan financial committees, pastoral programs, and lay justice and peace commissions. He concluded:

> I'm looking forward to the day when I have many more women participating in these, because they have a different perspective that has been lacking for quite a while. We can talk about it as men, but we can never feel the way women feel, absolutely not. And so they must be the ones to tell us how they feel about Jesus, their church, issues of justice, compassion, love, and sin. It would be a wonderful contribution, especially to the Catholic Church.

Archbishop David Gitari of the Anglican Church of Kenya voiced further witness:

> St. Paul makes it clear that in Christ there is neither female nor male. Now that we have started ordaining women—I ordained more in Kirinyaga than any other bishop—there are more ordained women in my former diocese and many are doing a better job than men. There are certain things women are able to do which men cannot do. They can penetrate in some places, especially ministering to fellow women, which men could not have done. So I think the church cannot be the church without women playing their role.

The need to redress women's participation in church leadership is far from being met completely. Nonetheless, some gains have apparently been made in this regard. Though the church must be ever reforming, evidence from the textual and oral sources suggests that the African Christologies are exerting influence upon church polity regarding issues of structure, power, and gender.

Church practice is likewise affected by Africans' perceptions of Jesus. Only brief summary statements are offered here by way of example. Jesus' prayer for unity among his followers (Jn 17) is fundamental to the recurring emphasis on ecumenism in African Christianity.[59] While problems of denominationalism continue to breed divisions among local churches, national and international organizations seek to overcome such divisions by portraying believers from other church traditions as "true relatives" within the wider clan of Christ.[60] Moreover, as we've seen above, Jesus as healer features prominently in the preaching, prayers, testimonies, and healing ministries of many African churches. Jesus as ancestor is much less evident in church practices to date, yet indications of the christological image appear for example in vernacular prayers addressed to Jesus as *Nana*, and in certain liturgical innovations. Whichever terms are favored, the image of Jesus as liberator/savior/redeemer is foundational to Christian worship and to Christian witness in church and society.

Furthermore, the extent to which Jesus has found "a place to feel at home" in Africa is widely reflected in church practices. As African Christians have increasingly appropriated Jesus in accordance with African culture, visible changes have occurred for example in preaching and worship. Kwesi Dickson related his experience of being the first Methodist minister to preach in traditional Ghanaian cloth in the early 1970s, and the stir that this created at the time. Now African attire among ministers, or African influence on church vestments, is commonplace. African music, lyrics and dance animate worship in a great number of churches.

Traditional art work and symbols reflect Jesus' entry into the spiritual universe of Africans, thereby inspiring more authentic worship in local churches. For instance, at Holy Trinity Church in Buru Buru, Nairobi, a large mural on the wall behind the altar depicts the life of Jesus in African images. At St. Francis Spiritual Centre in Nairobi the tabernacle is shaped like a traditional African home (see Figure 7–3). In front of the home are maize and local festive drink in African gourds. The significance here lies not only in the African home, where Jesus dwells in the form of the Eucharist, but also in the elements of the Eucharist depicted in local staple foods. Although the indigenous foods are not used in worship at this site, the symbols portray what many Africans Christians call for in celebrating the Eucharist with local foodstuffs.[61]

FIGURE 7–3. TABERNACLE FOR THE CONSECRATED HOST, NAIROBI

Thus there is ample evidence of Jesus' significance to church polity and practice in the selected African contexts. Whatever church traditions have been inherited, the emergence of contemporary African Christologies clearly shapes new ecclesial models and manifestations of African Christianity. Naturally, many issues remain in need of address, yet there is no doubt that Jesus is highly significant to ongoing ecclesial reformation.

JESUS IN AFRICA TODAY: CHRISTOLOGICAL REFLECTION

Reflection and praxis are integral to Christology. Attention focuses upon each in turn for the purpose of highlighting the significance of Jesus to life in Africa today. The present section concentrates on christological reflection, summarizing key aspects of the topic to suggest its significance first to African Christianity and subsequently to world Christianity.

THE FORMULATION OF CONTEXTUAL CHRISTOLOGIES: PERSONAL ENCOUNTER AND COMMUNAL AFFIRMATION

One of the chief distinguishing features of contemporary African Christologies is that they are contextual. Far from abstract, academic pursuits, these Christologies arise from people seeking to discover Jesus while grappling with concrete issues experienced in real life. Pobee stressed that "Christology is always a confession" or "a question of relevant affirmation. What really does it mean to affirm Jesus as savior in this context?" Kwesi Dickson echoed the concern, explaining, "My whole idea is looking at Christ in the realities of my life. The basic thing is who is Christ in my circumstances?" Two main points flow from this common stance, indicating elements of the significance of contemporary African Christologies.

The first point is that for most African Christians, authentic christological reflection arises out of personal encounter with Jesus Christ. Emmanuel Martey set forth the classical definition of theology as "faith seeking understanding." He then asserted: "So if we take Christology as an aspect of theology, then before you even christologize, you should have faith in Jesus Christ. It's very, very important, so that, without faith, I don't know what you are going to write about." Again he stressed the importance of personal knowledge of Christ, declaring that the crucial issue is not "Christology from above or from below, Pannenberg and Barth and the rest. But, the question should be, 'Who is Jesus Christ for us today?' In the final analysis it is, 'But what do you say?'" Peter Kodjo explained that this personal knowledge of Jesus "is not an intellectual exercise, it is usually an encounter. It is only in the encounter that the fact of Jesus becomes very vivid for me personally, and I guess for many people in my experience as a congregational pastor." He further pointed out that the knowledge becomes "discernible in the things which happen daily." He added, "I have realized that I get close to Jesus only when I can find Jesus in the context of life." These insights are in keeping with Mugambi's proposal for "the theological analogy of Encounter" as essential to African Christologies.[62]

So Jesus is experienced personally, according to the selected African Christians, and he is affirmed publicly. Therefore, the second point is that christological reflection arises in the community of faith and in dialogue with other communities of faith. This observation was widely attested in the present research. Dan Antwi stated that "it's the kind of experience people have with Jesus that determines the nomenclature of worship and so on." Consequently, Robert Aboagye-Mensah emphasized that "African theology should more or less be found within the churches." Instead of theologians artificially coining christological titles and trying to incorporate them into church use, Aboagye-Mensah and others call for theologians to listen to the language about Jesus employed in the faith community, to reflect on it, and to then articulate these Christologies on behalf of the community. This does not preclude creative, christological construction by theologians. By and large, however, the evidence from this research strongly supports christological formulation "from below," as theologians articulate the perceptions of Jesus already operative in the lives of African Christians. Abraham Akrong acknowledged that "a time of Christology of the pew is coming up"; for example, titles and attributes of the traditional God are now extended to Jesus.

Certainly all six of the selected African theologians expressed their understanding of the role of the theologian along these lines. Pobee spoke of the theologian as "an articulate individual in the womb of the community of faith." Ela identified the local community in North Cameroon as the vital context of his theology. He described his transition from Strasbourg to Tokombéré as "an intellectual and spiritual revolution" in which all of his prior theology was called into question. In place of academic theology within the concrete walls of libraries, he discovered "theology under the tree." In place of university professors as his masters, he met with the old, the young, and the women in the community. He stressed that the essential thing for him was this immediate contact with the life of Africans in their everyday situations. Instead of starting from the questions posed by classical Western theology, such as whether God exists, he began by listening to the villagers and reappropriating their questions as the departure point for christological reflection. In the same way, Nasimiyu Wasike specified that she writes for "African *women* first."

Yet all of these theologians also anticipate a wider audience for their publications. Nasimiyu Wasike explained that given the plurality of contemporary theologies, she expects that her writings from the perspective of an African woman offer something to African men and to the universal church. Ela stated that his theology aims to be theology in dialogue with that of other cultures. He draws attention to the epistemological rupture that has occurred, breaking the prior monologue of theological discourse arising in the Western context and spreading from there:

For the first time in the history of Christianity, we speak of God not from North America, and from its problems, from its challenges. We speak of God from Africa. Westerners have never done that. They are unaware that in order to understand God now, it is necessary to be listening to questions which are African questions.

Hence, Ela formulates his theology in hopes that it will challenge theologians in North America, Europe, and Asia. Likewise, Pobee underlined that he writes his christological reflections "as an African, but not as an African in isolation." He claims that the test of his theology is whether what he writes is consonant with his home community. Yet he also has foreigners read his work, for "if *they* can understand what I'm saying, then the theology does not become something esoteric for the initiated."

To conclude, christological articulation is born not from creeds and doctrines, in the first instance, but from personal encounter with Jesus Christ. As believers reflect on scripture and on their experience of Christ in the concrete realities of life, they express their convictions in the community of faith, particularly in the context of worship. The present research has confirmed the emergence of creative African Christologies in liturgical contexts, that is, in the songs, prayers, and testimonial confessions of local believers gathered together for worship. It is significant to note that the process of christological formulation attested here reflects a similar process to that of the original emergence of Christologies in the apostolic churches. New Testament scholar Larry Hurtado demonstrates that behind the christological debates and creeds of later centuries lies the "Christ-devotion" of the earliest Christians who encountered and affirmed the Risen Jesus.[63] On the basis of extensive research in first-century Christianity, Hurtado concludes:

> The christological rhetoric of the New Testament and of the later christological controversies and creeds reflects the attempt to explain and defend intellectually a development that began in human terms in profound religious experiences and in corporate worship. Whoever would seek to understand truly the fervent christological discussion of ancient or modern times must first appreciate the religious life that preceded and underlay the ancient development and that continues to inspire sacrificial commitment and intense intellectual effort to this very day.[64]

Parallels between first-century christological formulation and that of twentieth-century Africa merit further investigation. However, the present discussion merely points out that the ongoing affirmation of the identity and significance of Jesus by African Christians gives rise to christological innovations, with theologians playing a specialized role of discerning and articulating the operative Christologies within the community. They do so for the sake of the local community, but also with the intention of dialoguing with other faith communities across denominations and within other religions.

THE IMPORTANCE OF THE VERNACULAR IN CHRISTOLOGICAL REFLECTION

Throughout the present research the importance of the vernacular in christological expression has repeatedly come to light. What remains here is to underscore Pobee's point, noted in Chapter 2, that the vernacular extends beyond language to assume the worldview or "world-taken-for-granted" of a people. With mother tongue so fundamental to cultural identity, it is also vital to christological reflection at every level. First, in the realm of African Christian experience, the impact of the vernacular in enhancing christological expression has become clear. Respondents explained that certain insights about Jesus simply cannot be conveyed as vividly in English as in their mother tongue. Ela voices the need graphically in calling for a "Passover of language":

> In Africa, the confrontation between the message of the gospel and the African universe must bring forth a meaning with the power to transform the lives of African Christians. Today the faith of the church in Africa is in danger of death because the church tends to forget that its cultural dimensions are marked by its Greco-Latin heritage. If the faith of Africans is not to die, it must become a vision of the world that they can feel is theirs; European cultural orientations must be stripped away. There is an urgent need to reject present foreign models of expression if we are to breathe new life into the spoken Word. Our church must experience a Passover of language, or the meaning of the Christian message will not be understood.[65]

It is in this context that Ela advocates the reformulation of the gospel message through the mediation of African culture and symbolism. Thus, the evidence from this research concurs with Kwame Bediako's observations regarding the primacy of vernacular in African Christian experience. From the account of Pentecost in Acts 2, Bediako contends that the ability to hear and respond to the word of God in one's own language is pivotal to authentic religious encounter.[66] Following the process of christological formulation outlined above, the encounter with Christ in African vernaculars has serious implications for theological construction.

Second, Bujo insists that formal christological articulation "must employ an African theological language."[67] Otherwise, there is risk that the Christologies may not take on "flesh and blood" but merely speak to the literate and thereby foster a bourgeois Christianity. He therefore urges mother tongues as

> the means which finally guarantee an active contribution by the simple faithful to a more genuine African theology, outside the academic ivory towers. In this way a process can be initiated that will lead from a clericalist church *for* the people to a church *by* the people and *of* the people.[68]

While publishing Christologies in African vernacular languages remains a moot point, given the logistical obstacles entailed in printing and dissemination, the priority of the vernacular in christological formulation is clear.

Third, at the level of christological analysis, Bujo goes even further in recommending that interpreters of African Christologies must gain competency in the relevant mother tongues. Bujo's ancestral Christology has been misinterpreted due to mistaken presuppositions concerning the English term *ancestor* and its connotations in European culture. Bujo cites additional examples of mis-communication, when Europeans and Africans employ the same term in English but associate it with different meanings (for example, *brother* or *mama*). He therefore stated:

> Christology should start with our own languages, mother tongues. Then we can do a theology which can be understood by our people. And also if somebody wants to discuss it with us, he or she has to first study our languages, because you have a lot of philosophy in the mother tongues.

So vernacular language is crucial to all aspects of christological reflection, from encountering Christ, to articulating that experience, to analyzing that expression of Christology.

JESUS AT THE WELL: AFRICAN WOMEN'S CHRISTOLOGIES

Jesus' encounter with the woman at the well (Jn 4) may be seen as a portrait, or a paradigm, of what is occurring in African women's Christologies. Just as Jesus cut through deep prejudices of race, religion, gender, and class to make meaningful contact with the Samaritan woman, so the women in this study related how Christ meets them directly in their various contexts. Women's contributions to contemporary African Christologies have been highlighted throughout this work but are recapitulated here for their significance to the field of study.

The present research provides ample evidence of women's insights into all of the topics under consideration, not simply gender issues. However, their voices rise distinctively and poignantly with respect to gender concerns that deeply affect them. Significance thus lies in that their christological reflections are often silhouetted against enduring sexism in African societies and churches. In the section above on ecclesial reform, attention was drawn to the impact of women in church life and the need to enhance their participation in leadership. With respect to social issues, women's contributions certainly contribute to reconstructive theologies by overcoming the previous polarization between inculturation and liberation Christologies. Nasimiyu Wasike observed that they are two sides of the same coin. She made the point in the context of vehemently denouncing polygamy:

> Personally I have spoken very, very strongly and loudly against that. This is not inculturation! This is the continuation of enslavement of some human persons, and Jesus liberated us. He set us free! Therefore we cannot continue some of the practices or institutions in our tradition that are actually oppressive and dehumanizing.[69]

Nasimiyu Wasike's verdict on polygamy is not unanimous among African Christians. Yet she joins the chorus of African women (and men) who criticize it as one aspect of African culture deemed incompatible with the gospel of Christ. In

Musimbi Kanyoro's words, polygamy remains "a 'thorn in the flesh' of the Church of Africa."[70]

Oduyoye argues just as vehemently against certain other cultural practices considered violence against women in Africa, such as wife-beating, bodily modifications for beauty (such as fattening, body-piercing for some ornaments, elongated necks), and female circumcision.[71] She asserts:

> The deafening silence of the Church in the face of indescribable cruelty to the girl-child as she is prepared to please men, must surely be an indicator that the whole Church has yet to wake up to its total calling. The global challenge of the Churches' solidarity with women is particularly acute in Africa.[72]

Again, the basis for her charge is the gospel of Jesus Christ, particularly Jesus' teaching against the use of power in "lording over" others.[73] The concern is to break down the systems and attitudes that exploit, abuse, or do violence in any form to others, especially those most vulnerable, like the girl-child.

Other women voiced the significance of Jesus to them in their experience of cultural stigmas against singleness or childlessness. Mary Kizito recounted how her mother became freed from various cultural traditions, such as women not being able to eat chicken, eggs, pork, and certain kinds of fish, and how she herself was not required to kneel down in greeting her father as tradition had stipulated. She then concluded: "So Jesus sets you free! Free, you are not bogged down with traditions, and he himself was breaking some of the traditions!" Additional issues arise for women in political, economic, legal and other social spheres. While acknowledging the gravity of gender issues still in need of address, the selected African women nonetheless believe that Jesus is significant to women's concerns. Marie Gacambi concluded with an honest admission of the hope and the anguish faced by African Christian women today:

> Obviously Jesus is really the one who is inspiring us, because we need to reflect and to theologize on the issues of women. I think our hope is inspired by the belief that Jesus came to break all barriers—no Jews and Greeks, no female, no male. So, I can say that Jesus has a lot to help us forge ahead, but it is not easy. Sometimes we just wonder, really, how long are we to wait? You know, how long are we to wait?

As the women strive for more justice in gender issues, certain themes characterize the Christologies they articulate. One of the central motifs to emerge in the research is the deep sense of Jesus' solidarity with women in their suffering. Inherent in that solidarity is a profound intimacy with Jesus that many African women express. For example, Margaret Asabea marvels that God himself, in Jesus, passed through the birth canal of a woman. She commented:

> I think Christ is more intimate to women than to men! He feels the woes, the wounds, the very heartbeat of a woman. Christ feels it better than any other

person, because he was in the womb with the placenta. The heartbeat of the mother regulated his heartbeat!

This camaraderie between Jesus and African women is further expressed in the supremacy he is said to hold in their lives, and in the strongly relational images with which they identify him. Women in all categories in the research tended to speak of Jesus primarily as friend, companion, lover, husband, and "all in all." Oduyoye commented:

> In the Circle we haven't picked Christology as an issue, and yet through the religion and culture and ecclesiology that we have been doing, there is a lot of christological things that have come out. When we have prayers and worship services, they're very, very christocentric. The hymns . . . choruses . . . are all about this Jesus the companion, Jesus the helper, Jesus the friend. It's that kind of relationship.

The discussion of African women's liberation Christologies in Chapter 6 highlighted additional characteristics of women's Christologies, such as their holistic emphasis and their manifestation of the interplay between faith and life. Oduyoye explains that in Africa there is "a nascent feminism which grants full personhood to the human-male as to the human-female."[74] That is, African women tend not to promote antagonism between the sexes, but rather "the wholeness of the community as made up of male and female beings."[75] Accordingly, she emphasizes, "there is no sexual distinction in the Trinity, but qualities labelled feminine and masculine are all manifested in Christ Jesus who is the image par excellence of God."[76] Jesus thus becomes the model for all humanity, female and male.

It is precisely for this reason that African Christian women insist upon articulating "the feminine experience as a legitimate part of the data for theological reflection, or we will continue to live in our brokenness."[77] Again, it has been noted that women are not alone in voicing this need. Kenyan Catholic priest Peter Gichure acknowledged that women in his society are still oppressed and that theology "is very male dominated." He asserted: "Women theologians must be allowed to do theology, as women. And the church must be able to accept theology by women." Tinyiko Maluleke expresses even stronger censure. After noting the expansion of African women's theological activities since the 1980s, he states, "It is a serious indictment of African male theologies that women's issues have not received immediate and unreserved acceptance."[78] Echoing the same point, more positively, the last word rightfully goes to Oduyoye for her role across the continent in fostering African women's Christologies as part of the recent explosion in theological reflection: "The future Church is one that ensures that women's liberative theology becomes an integral part of the Churches' contribution, made visible in the Church and in the Academy."[79]

CONCLUSION

Recent theologies of reconstruction underline the need for African Christianity to play a vital role in social transformation across the continent today. Whether or not the language of reconstruction is employed, evidence from the present research has disclosed various ways in which African Christologies contribute toward the renewal of individuals and communities. The necessity of christological praxis has been confirmed, and the reality of its impact upon the contemporary context has been illustrated through the combined witness of selected African Christians to personal formation, social transformation, and ecclesial reformation. Notwithstanding the gravity of issues still in need of address, there are definite indications of the significance of Jesus Christ to the lives of contemporary African believers.

Furthermore, as African Christians encounter Jesus personally and affirm his identity and significance within the community of faith, creative christological reflection is born. From the crucible of contemporary realities in Africa where the interface of biblical and African traditions occurs, emergent Christologies display potent signs of how Jesus is consciously appropriated by these Christians. Certainly women's recent contributions have been highlighted in this regard. Additionally, the importance of the vernacular has been underscored for its role in enhancing the authenticity of christological formulation and expression in Africa. Finally, it has been stressed that the Christologies forged within local communities must then engage with christological expressions from other communities ecumenically, internationally, and in interfaith contexts. Thus the significance of Jesus Christ to African Christians lies beyond question, according to the believers informing this discussion. The final question for brief consideration in the next chapter is what import these contemporary African Christologies have for world Christianity.

8

Conclusion:
African Christology in
Contemporary World Christianity

The test of any cultural construct of the gospel is whether it enables growth, change and transformation in and into the image and likeness of God through Christ.

—JOHN S. POBEE, GHANAIAN THEOLOGIAN

Contemporary African Christologies command attention because of Africa's prominent place in world Christianity at the turn of the third millennium. At this juncture what can we conclude about the current status of christological reflection in Africa? Research findings have shown beyond doubt that the selected African Christians voice confident, contextual responses to the fundamental question of Jesus Christ, "Who do you say I am?" The christological confessions affirm that Jesus is consciously appropriated in accordance with biblical and Christian tradition *and* historical and current realities in Africa. In the interface between biblical and African traditions, set within the crucible of African affairs today, emergent Christologies offer fresh insights into the identity and significance of Jesus Christ. They thereby mark important strides in the advance of African Christianity.

Acknowledging progress achieved thus far does not suggest that recent theological agendas have been attained. On the contrary, areas of ongoing controversy and enduring questions have been noted throughout the discussion. The configuration of current Christologies portrayed in four interlocking circles, Jesus as life-giver, Jesus as mediator, Jesus as loved one, and Jesus as leader, elucidates the present shape of Christology in Africa. Approaching the subject through thematic clusters of christological images serves to overcome artificial dichotomies in prevailing paradigms of inculturation and liberation Christologies.

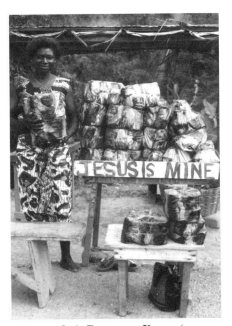

FIGURE 8–1. ROADSIDE *KENKE* (LOCAL STAPLE FOOD) SELLER, GHANA

In-depth analysis reveals that critical issues in the historical, theological, and contemporary contexts prompt particular portraits of Jesus. As these christological images are adopted in contemporary Christian praxis, they serve to redress the very issues that prompted their formulation. The circular motion of Christologies arising *from* and *for* their African contexts has been amply attested in the present research, both in potentiality and in actuality. This observation thereby confirms important developments in relation to the fundamental goal of constructing contextual theology in Africa.

What relevance do these developments in African Christology have for world Christianity? Are they merely exotic expressions of the Christian faith, of passing interest? Or worse yet, as some people might argue, are they simply evidence of syncretism, tainting the gospel with African religions? Brief conclusions from the present research challenge these notions as uninformed and unwarranted. Given the southward shift of world Christianity, Africa marks one of the central zones of theological activity today. To ignore developments in this region, or to treat the African Christologies as exotic manifestations peripheral to the world church, is to betray one's own theological myopia. Indeed, the fact that the African Christologies have not yet gained adequate acknowledgment beyond the continent is more reflective of enduring ethnocentrism within the wider theological community than of the value of the Christologies per se.

The very dynamism of Christianity in Africa today suggests key aspects of the emergent Christologies' significance for world Christianity. Perhaps most fundamental, the present flourishing of Christology in Africa clearly manifests the universality of the gospel. As African Christians understand and convey Jesus in light of biblical revelation and contextual realities, they demonstrate that Christianity can truly find a home in every cultural context. The risk of incorporating cultural elements in ways deemed incompatible with the gospel is countered by the biblical and ecumenical orientation of the African Christologies. Certainly hermeneutical issues of reading the Bible in Africa are becoming increasingly prominent, and rightfully so.[1] Yet the evidence from this research underlines the centrality of the Bible in the christological reflection, including the critical evaluation of christological innovations and the praxis of these African believers. Likewise, the selected Christians manifestly uphold the humanity and the divinity of Jesus as nonnegotiable within their faith, thereby aligning themselves with Christian tradition from apostolic times to the present. While ecumenical perspectives and cooperation need further attention at local levels of African Christianity, the voices highlighted here attest to the importance of christological formulation within the local faith community and in dialogue with other faith communities across denominational, national, and religious borders. So, far from being syncretistic, these African Christologies reflect the whole-hearted acceptance of the gospel in Africa. They thereby demonstrate the universality of the gospel not only in principle but in practice.[2]

Important ramifications flow from the fact that Christianity is developing new local forms shaped by the priorities of those contexts in which it is taking root most firmly, as in Africa. For example, the new diversification of Christianity challenges the tendency in classical Western theology to absolutize certain concepts of Christ or to assume that christological definitions established in the West are necessarily normative for other contexts of faith. In general, the African Christians considered here do not discount creedal and confessional statements from the history of Western Christianity. However, they stress that the christological controversies of other eras and contexts, expressed in foreign languages and thought forms and addressing issues unrelated to their experience, need not govern their christological formulation. Thus African Christians champion the irruption of third-world theologies that break with Western theological agendas and seek to discover the reality of Jesus in relation to current issues in their own respective contexts.

As the word of God "tabernacles" in Africa today, priorities emerging there potentially recover certain aspects of the gospel neglected in the West today. The communitarian aspect of African Christologies, derived from biblical teaching and indigenous worldviews, challenges the rampant individualism in Western Christianity. For example, African concepts of community, encompassing the deceased, the living, and the unborn, invite contemplation by Western Christians steeped in cultural values that often disregard communal life, particularly among generations. Furthermore, the images related to Jesus as life-giver encompass key facets of African worldviews, like the exaltation and celebration of life, and also holistic views of life and healing. These emphases offer correctives for Western worldviews from Enlightenment times, which have tended to elevate the individual and to erect dichotomies between sacred and secular, natural and supernatural. More significant, the African Christologies raise crucial challenges for Western Christianity in the face of geopolitical divisions and economic injustices intensified by contemporary globalization. Attempts to recapture the liberative dimensions of Jesus' mission to the poor and marginalized, and to expose the scandal of Christ's ongoing "crucifixion" in the Third World, compel serious reconsideration of christological reflection and praxis in the West.

At the same time, and through such theological interaction, African Christologies offer means of renewal to churches in the West. Drawing upon an African proverb, Pobee graphically expressed the opportunity for mutual revitalization:

> The Akan have a saying, "The mother feeds the baby daughter before she has teeth, so that the daughter will feed the mother when she loses her teeth." The old

church has lost her teeth. Evidence: empty churches. This new church, the younger church, is now the vibrant part. It owes it to the so-called mother churches to share its insights, so that together they may be renewed and transformed.

The dynamism of African Christianity evidenced in the present research certainly underscores the importance of lived or experiential Christologies. Far from abstract, academic exercises, these Christologies witness to the perceived immediacy of Jesus and his solidarity with believers in the concrete realities of life, particularly for African women. Despite the ongoing challenges acknowledged with respect to christological reflection and praxis in Africa, engagement with the current Christologies provides opportunity for fostering spiritual renewal.

Finally, the fact that African Christians portray local "faces" of Jesus, articulating what they find appealing and relevant in him, forms a significant contribution to world Christianity. The fundamental reality is that no single cultural context can claim a monopoly on understanding Jesus Christ. Rather, the multiplicity of christological images arising in Africa enhances the discovery of the fullness of Christ, which transcends all cultural constructs of the gospel. Emergent African Christologies therefore confirm what Andrew Walls has ably demonstrated through biblical and historical investigation, namely, that the perception and experience of Jesus by different cultures throughout history has expanded our corporate understanding of Christ. Examining what occurred in the apostolic church as Christ was communicated across cultural boundaries, he explains:

> The process was hugely enriching; it proved to be a discovery of the Christ. As Paul and his fellow missionaries explain and translate the significance of the Christ in a world that is Gentile and Hellenistic, that significance is seen to be greater than anyone had realized before. It is as though Christ himself actually grows through the work of mission—and indeed, there is more than a hint of this in one New Testament image (Eph. 4:13). As he enters new areas of thought and life, he fills the picture (the Pleroma dwells in him). It is surely right to see the process as being repeated in subsequent transmission of the faith across cultural lines.[3]

Given the biblical and historical precedents, there is every reason to believe that African Christians are extending this very process in their expressions of Jesus' identity and significance today. Ela is clearly convinced of the ongoing expansion of corporate Christology globally, for he explains, "The Risen One exposes faith to an inexhaustible realm of possibilities. That is why we are searching for a form of speech that will bring the voices of Africa to the life of the world-wide church."[4] Therefore, these voices of contemporary African Christology are of utmost significance to world Christianity. For, as Walls concludes, "It is a delightful paradox that the more Christ is translated into the various thought forms and life systems which form our various national identities, the richer all of us will be in our common Christian identity."[5]

Appendix 1. Qualitative Research Tools

INTERVIEW QUESTIONS
FOR AFRICAN CHRISTIAN THEOLOGIANS

Part One: Reflecting on Theological Formation

1. Reflecting autobiographically, what do you think are the most formative influences in your life that have shaped your theology? Are there any critical experiences that would help me to understand your theology better?

2. a. What is the main context *from* which and *for* which you have written your theology? Please feel free to answer in the plural, "contexts," if need be.
   b. In what way(s) has this context influenced your present understanding of Jesus Christ?

3. Which theologians, African and non-African, have had the greatest impact on your own formulation of Christology—either positively or negatively? Please explain.

Part Two: Setting the Parameters

4. a. In your understanding, what is Christian theology in the African context?
   b. How do you proceed, methodologically, in doing Christian theology in Africa today?

Part Three: Exploring Contemporary African Christologies

5. a. How would you define *African Christology?*
   b. What are the most critical issues regarding African Christologies today?

6. a. What do you think have been your main contributions to the contemporary dialogue concerning African Christologies?
   b. Are there any christological concerns with which you are wrestling at present? If so, please explain.
   c. What do you think needs to be addressed in the future concerning African Christologies?

7. In your view, how does the Christian understanding of God relate to the traditional African worldview(s) in your own context?

8. a. What relevance, if any, do African Christologies have for African society today?
   b. What significance, if any, do they have for world Christianity?

9. a. Are there any final comments you would like to add about contemporary African Christologies?

   b. After observing and responding to these questions I have raised, are there any other aspects of African Christologies to which it is imperative that I attend?

INTERVIEW GUIDE FOR SEMI-STRUCTURED INDIVIDUAL INTERVIEWS AND FOCUS GROUPS

1. When did you first learn about Jesus Christ?
    Further prompts:
    How did you first hear about Jesus?
    Were there any people who were especially significant in telling you about Jesus?
    What did you learn about Jesus at that time?

2. In view of all you've said so far, who is Jesus for you today?

3. Are there any main ideas about Jesus, or images of Jesus, that are especially meaningful to you as an African?
    Possible prompt: There are many metaphors/pictures of God in the Bible that stem from the writer's personal experience, such as David the shepherd testifying to God as "shepherd," or David the warrior addressing God as his "shield" and "fortress." Are there any such images of Christ that resonate specially with your experience as an African? (Note: not just biblical metaphors, but any images deriving from the African worldview.)

4. Do you think Jesus is relevant to contemporary life in Africa? If so, how? If not, why not?
    Further Prompts:
    To political life in Africa/your country?
    To economic life?
    To social life?

5. In your opinion, does Jesus have any particular significance for women in Africa today? If so, please explain.

6. I've heard certain ideas about Jesus discussed by some African Christians. Could you please comment personally on how you might understand these ideas?
    Possible prompts: Have you ever heard of Jesus being understood this way before? Have you thought of him that way yourself? If so, what does each one mean to you? Do they resonate with your own experience of Jesus? (Note: Skip any themes already discussed at the respondent's initiative.)
    a. Jesus as healer/traditional healer
        Kenya: *mganga* in Kiswahili, or other vernacular equivalent
        Ghana: *odunsini* in Twi, or other vernacular equivalent
    b. Jesus as liberator
    c. Jesus as ancestor
        Ghana: *Nana*
    d. Any other image or title for Jesus you would like to discuss?
        Ghana: chief

7. In your understanding, what relationship is there, if any, between Jesus Christ and the God who was worshiped in your home area before Christianity came to Africa?

> Ghana: I've heard that you (the) Akan say, *Yen nkyere abofra Nyame* (Twi: We don't teach any child to know God.) Yet you seem to be very vocal and powerful in preaching Jesus. Why do you insist on preaching Jesus? What *difference* does he make in your religious experience? What is new with him?
>
> Depending upon the respondent, introduce this question as being a more difficult one and repeat it as necessary. Anticipate that some, especially lay Christians, may not have given serious thought to this question before.
>
> In other words, how does Jesus "fit" into the traditional worldview(s) of the African(s).

8. Have you read any books about Jesus besides the Bible? If so, what do you recall about the books?

> *Further prompts:*
> Authors—African, Western, or other?
> Titles?
> In what language(s)?
> Content—ideas about Jesus?

9. Are there any final comments you would like to make about the identity and significance of Jesus to you personally or to African Christians today?

Appendix 2: Interviews with African Christians

INTERVIEWS WITH AFRICAN THEOLOGIANS

Bujo, Bénézet. Professor, University of Fribourg, Chair of Moral Theology and Social Ethics. Fribourg, Switzerland: October 29, 1998.

Ela, Jean-Marc. Professor, l'Université du Montréal à Québec, Department of Sociology. Montreal, Canada: January 8, 1999.

Mugambi, J. N. K. Professor, University of Nairobi, Department of Religious Studies. Nairobi, Kenya: June 10, 1998.

Nasimiyu Wasike, Anne. General Superior of the Little Sisters of St. Francis; Professor, Kenyatta University, Department of Religious Studies. Nairobi, Kenya: April 21, 1998.

Oduyoye, Mercy Amba. Professor, Institute of Women in Religion and Culture, Trinity Theological College, Legon; Founder of the Circle of Concerned African Women Theologians. Legon, Accra: September 3, 1998.

Pobee, John S. Professor Emeritus, University of Ghana, Legon, Department for the Study of Religions; Co-ordinator of the Programme on Theological Education of the World Council of Churches. Geneva, Switzerland: October 28, 1998.

INTERVIEWS WITH CHURCH LEADERS AND LAY PEOPLE

INTERVIEWS IN GHANA

Catholic Clergy

Aggrey, Joseph. Parish priest, Akuapem Region. Mampong, Akuapem: August 31, 1998.

Edusei, Matthew. Priest, National Catholic Secretariat, Accra. Accra: September 1, 1998.

Palmer-Buckle, Charles. Bishop of Koforidua. Koforidua: September 10, 1998.

Sarpong, Peter Kwasi. Bishop of Kumasi. Kumasi: September 7, 1998.

Catholic Laity

Ackah, Samuel. Teacher, Presbyterian Teacher's College, Akropong-Akuapem. Akropong-Akuapem: September 16, 1998.

Asubonteng, Samuel. Executive Secretary, National Catholic Laity Council, Accra. Accra: September 1, 1998.

Hagan, George. Professor, University of Ghana, Legon, Director of the Institute of African Studies. Legon, Accra: July 28, August 6, 1998.

Kulipoe, Constantine. High school teacher, Aburi. Mampong-Akuapem: August 26, 1998.

Sackey, Brigid. Lecturer, University of Ghana, Legon, Institute of African Studies. Legon, Accra: August 3, 1998.

Protestant Clergy

Aboa, Samuel K. Former Principal of Presbyterian Teachers' College, Akropong. Mampong-Akuapem: August 17, 1998.

Aboagye-Mensah, Robert. Superintendent Minister of the Methodist Church—Dansoman Circuit, Accra; Lecturer, Trinity Theological College, Legon. Accra: September 20, 1998.

Akrong, Abraham. Professor, University of Ghana, Legon, Institute of African Studies. Legon, Accra: July 27, 1998.

Antwi, Dan. Principal, Trinity Theological College, Legon. Legon, Accra: July 24, 1998.

Asabea, Margaret Victoria. Presbyterian Minister; Chaplain, Women's Teacher Training College. Akropong-Akuapem: July 2, 1998.

Dankwa, Theophilus B. Pastor, Accra Chapel. Accra: August 16, 1998.

Dickson, Kwesi. President of the AACC; Professor Emeritus, University of Ghana, Legon. Legon, Accra: September 2, 1998.

Kodjo, Peter. Chairman of the Ga Presbytery. Accra: September 3, 1998.

Martey, Emmanuel. Lecturer, Trinity Theological College, Legon. Akropong-Akuapem: August 24, August 28, 1998.

Oduro, Thomas. Principal, Good News Theological College, Accra. Akropong-Akuapem: August 14, 1998.

Quarcoopome, S. S. Senior Research Fellow, University of Ghana, Legon, Institute of African Studies; Resident pastor, Charismatic Evangelistic Ministry, Legon. Legon, Accra: August 4, 1998.

Quarshie, B. Y. Lecturer, University of Ghana, Legon, Department of Religions; Former Chairman of a Presbytery. Accra: July 29, 1998.

Senavoe, Juliana. Principal, Christian Service College, Kumasi. Akropong-Akuapem: July 18, 1998.

Protestant Laity

Amoa, Yeboa. Managing Director of Ghana Stock Exchange, Accra. Accra: July 28, 1998.

Amoah, Kingsfold. Director, Ghana Road Fund, Accra. Accra: August 18, 1998.

Dankwa, Virginia. Ophthalmologist, Accra. Accra: August 16, 1998.

Darmani, Lawrence. Editor, *Step Magazine—Ghana*, Accra. Accra: July 30, 1998.

Glover-Quartey, Alex. Management Consultant, Accra. Accra: September 18, 1998.

Nartey, Grace. Administrator, Ridge Church, Accra. Accra: September 2, 1998.

Odotei, Irene. Lecturer, University of Ghana, Legon, Institute of African Studies. Legon, Accra: August 4, 1998.

The Circle of Concerned African Women Theologians

Amoah, Elizabeth. Senior Lecturer, University of Ghana, Legon, Department of Religions. Edinburgh, Scotland: November 16, 1998.

Harlley, Emily Asaa. Public Services Commission, Accra. Akropong-Akuapem: August 26, August 28, 1998.

Pan-African Christian Women's Alliance

Opare-Saforo, Felicia. Businesswoman, Accra; National Coordinator of PACWA—Ghana. Akropong-Akuapem: August 3, 1998.

Yeboah, Florence Y. B. National Director of GHACOE (Ghana Congress on Evangelisation) Women's Ministry, Accra. Accra: July 30, 1998.

Traditional Leaders

Birikorang, Nana Addo. *Apesamakahene* (Chief Linguist, or official spokesman, of the Traditional Council of Akuapem). Akropong-Akuapem: August 27, 1998.

Dokua I, Nana. *Okuapehemmaa* (Queenmother of Akuapem Traditional Region). Akropong-Akuapem: September 18, 1998.

INTERVIEWS IN KENYA

Catholic Clergy

Gichure, Peter. Lecturer, St. Thomas Aquinas Seminary; Catholic University of East Africa, Nairobi. Nairobi: June 3, 1998.

Kamau, David. Vicar at Holy Family Basilica, Nairobi. Nairobi: May 29, 1998.

Kamiri, Vincent. Parish priest, Nairobi. Nairobi: May 28, 1998.

Nzeki, Ndingi Mwana a'. Archbishop of the Roman Catholic Church in Kenya. Nairobi: May 29, 1998.

Catholic Laity

See Ugandan Christians interviewed in Nairobi.

Gacambi, Marie Therese. Lecturer, Catholic University of East Africa, Nairobi. Nairobi: June 3, 1998.

Kiarie, Peter. Lay theologian and evangelist; former Director of Education at the Catholic Secretariat, Nairobi. Ruiru, Kenya: June 5, 1998.

Wanjohi, Gerald. Retired Professor, University of Nairobi; Former Chairman of the Department of Philosophy. Nairobi: June 26, 1998.

Protestant Clergy

Bisem, Peter. Deputy General Secretary, National Council of the Churches of Kenya, Nairobi. Nairobi: June 7, 1998.

Gatu, John. Former Moderator of the Presbyterian Church of East Africa. Nairobi: June 8, 1998.

Gitari, David. Archbishop of the Anglican Church of Kenya. Nairobi: May 19, 1998.

Kivunzi, Titus. Bishop of the Africa Inland Church. Nairobi: June 8, 1998.

Masinde, J. B. Pastor, Deliverance Church, Umoja, Eastlands. Nairobi: June 11, 1998.

Musyimi, Mutava. General Secretary, National Council of the Churches of Kenya, Nairobi. Nairobi: May 29, 1998.

Wambugu, Anne. Lecturer, Pan African College, Nairobi. Nairobi: May 21, 1998.

Protestant Laity

Correa, Mabel. Beauty therapist, Nairobi. Nairobi: June 8, 1998.

Kassam, Sheny. Pastor, Solid Rock Church; former businesswoman, Nairobi. Nairobi: June 9, 1998.

Muhia, Marcy. Director of Worship, Nairobi Chapel. Nairobi: May 20, 1998.

Muriithi, John Njoroge. Fruit hawker, Nairobi. Nairobi: June 12, 1998.

Ole Ronkei, Morompi. Director of Compassion—Africa, Nairobi. Nairobi: June 2, 1998.

The Circle of Concerned African Women Theologians

Getui, Mary. Chair of Religious Studies Department, Kenyatta University, Nairobi. Nairobi: May 20, 1998.

Kinoti, Hannah W. Professor; former Chair of Religious Studies, University of Nairobi. Nairobi: June 11, 1998.

Pan-African Christian Women's Alliance
Gathirwa, Naomi. National Coordinator of PACWA—Kenya; Consultant in Gender and Development, Nairobi. Nairobi: June 13, 1998.
Mbugua, Judy. Coordinator of PACWA—Africa, Nairobi. Nairobi: May 29, 1998.

INTERVIEWS IN UGANDA

Catholic Clergy
Waliggo, John Mary. Secretary for Justice and Peace Commission, Uganda. Jinja: May 7, 1998.

Catholic Laity and Religious
Kizito, Mary. Lecturer, Daystar University, Nairobi. Nairobi: June 7, 1998.
Ssemakula, Peter Nelson. Political refugee in Nairobi; MA student at the American University, Nairobi. Nairobi: May 31, 1998.
Sr. Mary Cleophas. Little Sisters of St. Francis. Jinja: May 6, 1998.
Sr. Mary John. Little Sisters of St. Francis. Nkokonjeru: April 30, 1998.
Sr. Mary Pius. Little Sisters of St. Francis. Jinja: May 2, 1998.

Protestant Laity
Nabwire, Sarah. Political refugee; Housegirl, Nairobi. Nairobi: June 20, 1998.

ADDITIONAL TAPED INTERVIEWS

Kanyoro, Musimbi. General Secretary of the Y.W.C.A.; Executive Director of the Women's Dept. for the Lutheran World Federation; Coordinator for the Circle of Concerned African Women Theologians. Geneva, Switzerland: October 30, 1998.
Korse, Peter. Catholic Missionary; Chaplain to the Little Sisters of St. Francis, Jinja. Jinja: April 29, 1998.
Sr. Mary Savio, Little Sisters of St. Francis; colleague whom Anne Nasimiyu Wasike included in her interview. Nairobi: April 21, 1998.

FOCUS GROUPS

IN GHANA

Catholic Clergy
National Catholic Secretariat, Accra: September 4, 1998. Participants based on site.
Dasaah, Aidan C. . Priest.
Kornu, Anthony. Priest.

Catholic Laity
National Catholic Secretariat, Accra: September 4, 1998. All participants employees.
Abban, Isabella. Nurse Educator and Health Coordinator.
Akantu, Gilbert K. Accountant.
Amoo-Adare, Afua. Women's Desk.
Asubonteng, Samuel. Executive Secretary.

Avornyo, Raphael. Coordinator for AIDS Programme.
Tetteh, Emmanuel. Personnel Administration.

Protestant Clergy
Akrofi-Christaller Memorial Centre, Akropong-Akuapem: August 13, 1998. All participants attending a workshop on Gospel and Culture.
Antwi, Stephen. Pastor, Bible Church of Africa, Accra.
Aryee, Joshua. Pastor, Presbyterian Church of Ghana, Accra.
Asare, Johnson. Cross-cultural Church Planter, Tamale.
Lamptey, Joseph. Canon, Holy Trinity Cathedral, Accra.
Marbell, Bernard E. Teacher, Maranatha Bible College, Accra.
Mills, Joseph C. Teacher, Assemblies of God Bible Institute, Saltpond.

Protestant Laity
Ridge Church, Accra: September 2, 1998. All participants members of Ridge Church.
Adu-Asante, Joseph. Accounting Officer, Accra.
Amissah, Hetty. Caterer, Accra.
Sackey, Grace. Nurse; Florist, Accra.

The Circle of Concerned African Women Theologians
Trinity Theological College, Legon, Accra: September 18, 1998. Meeting of the Circle.
Dowuona, Rebecca F. A. Teacher; Student, Trinity Theological College.
Nyarko, Laurene R. Minister, Youth Training Centre of Methodist Conference, Aburi.
Obu, Helena. Pastor, Teacher; Student, Trinity Theological College.

Pan-African Christian Women's Alliance
PACWA Prayer Day, Accra: September 5, 1998.
Agyei, Mary. Not working [place unspecified].
Arthur, Agnes. [work unspecified], Accra.
Dadebo, Gladys. Student teacher, Accra.
Forson, Grace. Unemployed, Accra.
Hyde, Mary Anna. Evangelist, Accra.
Nyarko, Christiana O. Politician, Accra.
Nyinaku, Grace. Customs Officer, Accra.

IN KENYA

Catholic Clergy
St. Francis Church, Ruiru, Kenya: June 7, 1998. Priests working in this parish.
Chege, Elijah. Priest.
Jabedo, Francis. Priest.
Mwangi, Njoroge. Priest.

Catholic Laity
Home of Mrs. Ruth Odera, Kileleshwa, Nairobi: June 3, 1998. All participants members of Consolata Shrine, Base Christian Community in Kileleshwa.
Awange, Peres Alice. Secretary, Nairobi.
Kariuki, Gervase. School maintenance worker, Nairobi.
Kulemo, Angelic. Housegirl, Nairobi.

Makoriwa, Frances Therese. Teacher, Secretarial College, Nairobi.
Muketi, Mary. Unemployed, Nairobi.
Mwango, Catherine. Deputy Executive Director, African Centre for Technology Studies, Nairobi.
Odera, Ruth Phoebe. Senior Supplies Officer, Nairobi.
Okeyo, Salome A. Primary school teacher, Nairobi.
Olwana, Salome Rose. Civil servant, Nairobi.
Otieno, Charles. Civil servant; Administrator, Nairobi.
Owuor, Rose. High school teacher, Nairobi.

Protestant Clergy
   Daystar University: May 18, 1998.
Adoyo, Boniface. Pastor, Nairobi Pentecostal.
Gachinga, John. Pastor, Nairobi Baptist.
Kibicho, Sam. Minister, Presbyterian Church of East Africa—St. Andrews, Nairobi.
Muriu, Oscar. Pastor, Nairobi Chapel.
Obwa, Samuel. Director, Institute of Christian Ministries and Training, Daystar University, Nairobi; Church leader in Africa Inland Church, Ngong Road, Nairobi.
Wambugu, Ann. Lecturer, Pan African College, Nairobi.

Protestant Laity
   Member's home in Ngong Town, Kenya: June 12, 1998. All participants members of a Bible Study from the African Inland Church, Ngong Road, Nairobi.
Jamwah, Ruth Atieno. Christian Education Dept., Africa Inland Church, Nairobi.
Kanyi, Anne. Church worker, Nairobi.
Komen, Simon. Engineering consultant, Nairobi.
Nguhiu, James Mwangi. Veterinary Surgeon; University lecturer, Nairobi.
Nguhiu, Purity. Veterinary Surgeon, Nairobi.
Obwa, Leah Osimbo. Teacher, Nairobi.

The Circle of Concerned African Women Theologians
   J. J. McCarthy Home of Assumption Sisters in Kileleshwa, Nairobi: May 15, 1998. Weekend seminar of the Circle. The following members were present but not all participated in the focus group discussion.
Ayanga, Hazel. Lecturer, Moi University, Eldoret, Kenya.
Choge, Emily. Student; Lecturer, Moi University, Eldoret, Kenya.
Gacambi, Marie Therese. Lecturer, Catholic University of East Africa, Nairobi.
Gachiri, E. L. Roman Catholic religious sister; Teacher; Retreat Director [place unspecified].
Gecaga, Margaret. Student; Lecturer, Kenyatta University, Nairobi.
Getui, Mary. Chair of Religious Studies Department, Kenyatta University, Nairobi.
Muchocho, Evelyne. Lecturer, Egerton University, Njoro, Kenya.
Muriithi, Sicily Mbura. Minister, Presbyterian Church of East Africa, Chogoria, Kenya.
Muthei, Ruth. Lecturer, Kenyatta University, Nairobi.
Mwangangi, Jane Nyaguthu. Minister, Anglican Church of Kenya, Kerugoya, Kenya.
Njiri, Edith. Minister, Anglican Church of Kenya, Kutus, Kenya.
Okemwa, Pacificah. Lecturer, Teacher's Training College [place unspecified].
Otieno, Pauline A. Student; Lecturer, University of Nairobi.
Owuor, Margaret A. Student; Lecturer, Egerton University, Njoro, Kenya.
Wamue, Grace. Lecturer, Kenyatta University, Nairobi.

Pan-African Christian Women's Alliance
Presbyterian Church of East Africa—St. Andrews, Nairobi: June 13, 1998. PACWA Meeting.
Gitere, Elizabeth W. Businesswoman, Githunguri, Kenya.
Koinange, Mary M. W. Evangelist; Social Development Officer, Nairobi.
Mathu, Jane Nyaguthii. Social Worker; Probation Officer, Nairobi.
Muia, Rose M. Evangelist; Teacher, Nairobi.
Ndirangu, Rachel. Businesswoman; Teacher, Nairobi.
Sakuda, Rose W. Evangelist, Ngong Hills, Kenya.

Notes

1 EXPLORING AFRICAN CHRISTOLOGIES TODAY

1. John Mbiti, *New Testament Eschatology in an African Background* (Oxford: Oxford University Press, 1971), 190.

2. J. N. K. Mugambi and Laurenti Magesa, "Introduction," in *Jesus in African Christianity: Experimentation and Diversity in African Christology*, ed. J. N. K. Mugambi and Laurenti Magesa (Nairobi: Initiatives, Ltd., 1989), x.

3. A. F. Walls, "Towards Understanding Africa's Place in Christian History," in *Religion in a Pluralistic Society*, ed. J. S. Pobee (Leiden: E. J. Brill, 1976), 180.

4. See, for example, Emmanuel Martey, *African Theology: Inculturation and Liberation* (Maryknoll, N.Y.: Orbis Books, 1993), 78.

5. John V. Taylor, *The Primal Vision: Christian Presence amid African Religion* (London: SCM Press, 1963), 7.

6. Ibid., 16.

7. E. Sambou, quoted in Anselme T. Sanon, "Jesus, Master of Initiation," in *Faces of Jesus in Africa*, ed. Robert J. Schreiter (Maryknoll, N.Y.: Orbis Books, 1991), 85.

8. J. Galilee Shembe, *Izihlabelelo zaManazaretha* (Durban: Elite Printers, 1940), 75.

9. Gerhardus Cornelis Oosthuizen, *The Theology of a South African Messiah: An Analysis of the Hymnal of "The Church of the Nazarites"* (Leiden: E. J. Brill, 1967), 37.

10. Afua Kuma, *Kwaebirentuw Ase Yesu: Afua Kuma Ayeyi ne Mpaebo* (Accra: Asempa Publishers, 1980), 6, 46, 5.

11. Afua Kuma, *Jesus of the Deep Forest: Prayers and Praises of Afua Kuma*, trans. Jon Kirby (Accra: Asempa Publishers, 1981), 6, 46, 5.

12. John S. Mbiti, "Some African Concepts of Christology," in *Christ and the Younger Churches*, ed. Georg F. Vicedom (London: SPCK, 1972), 51.

13. See Martey, *African Theology*, 78; Raymond Moloney, "African Christology," *Theological Studies* 48, no. 3 (September 1987): 505.

14. Aylward Shorter, "Folk Christianity and Functional Christology," *AFER* 24, no. 3 (June 1982): 134.

15. Kofi Appiah-Kubi, "Christology," in *A Reader in African Christian Theology*, ed. John Parratt (London: SPCK, 1987), 69.

16. Charles Nyamiti, "Contemporary African Christologies: Assessment and Practical Suggestions," in *Paths of African Theology*, ed. Rosino Gibellini (Maryknoll, N.Y.: Orbis Books, 1994), 70.

17. John Baur, *2000 Years of Christianity in Africa: An African History 62–1992* (Nairobi: Paulines Publications Africa, 1994), 304.

18. Ukachukwu Chris Manus, "African Christologies: The Centre-Piece of African Christian Theology," *Zeitschrift für Missionswissenschaft und Religionswissenschaft* 82 (1998): 3–23. See "Christology," *Voices from the Third World* 7, no. 1 (March 1985); Joseph Doré, ed., *Chemins de la Christologie Africaine* (Paris: Desclée, 1986);

"Christologies in Encounter," *Voices from the Third World* 11, no. 2 (December 1988); Mugambi and Magesa, *Jesus in African Christianity*; Schreiter, *Faces of Jesus in Africa*; John S. Pobee, ed., *Exploring Afro-Christology* (Frankfurt: Peter Lang, 1992).

19. For the rise of African theology, see, for example, Baur, *2000 Years of Christianity in Africa*, 288–306; Bénézet Bujo, *African Theology in Its Social Context*, trans. John O'Donohue (Nairobi: St. Paul Communications; Maryknoll, N.Y.: Orbis Books, 1992), 37–73; Martey, *African Theology*, 7–35; John Parratt, *Reinventing Christianity: African Theology Today* (Grand Rapids, Mich.: William B. Eerdmans, 1995), 1–13; Josiah U. Young III, *African Theology: A Critical Analysis and Annotated Bibliography* (Westport, Conn.: Greenwood Press, 1993), 13–42. Accounts of the rise of African Christology are less common. For one example, see Ukachukwu Chris Manus, *Christ, the African King: New Testament Christology* (Frankfurt: Peter Lang, 1993), 49–70.

20. Kwame Bediako, "The Significance of Modern African Christianity—A Manifesto," *Studies in World Christianity* 1, Part 1 (1995): 58–59.

21. Quoted in Baur, *2000 Years of Christianity in Africa*, 292–93.

22. John Pobee, conversation with author, Pretoria, South Africa, January 25, 2000; see also John S. Pobee, "I Am First an African and Second a Christian," *Indian Missiological Review* 10, no. 3 (July 1989): 268–77.

23. See Adrian Hastings, "Cultural Revolution," in *African Christianity: An Essay in Interpretation* (London: Geoffrey Chapman, 1976), 37–59.

24. Justin S. Ukpong, "Current Theology: The Emergence of African Theologies," *Theological Studies* 45 (1984): 508.

25. See, for example, Jean-Marc Ela, *My Faith as an African*, trans. John Pairman Brown and Susan Perry (Maryknoll, N.Y.: Orbis Books, 1988), xiii.

26. Desmond Tutu, quoted in Kwame Bediako, "Understanding African Theology in the Twentieth Century," *Bulletin for Contextual Theology* 3, no. 2 (June 1996): 2.

27. Bediako, "Understanding African Theology in the Twentieth Century," 2.

28. Kwesi A. Dickson, *Theology in Africa* (London: Darton, Longman, and Todd, 1984), 145ff.

29. Parratt, *Reinventing Christianity*, 78.

30. Hastings, *African Christianity*, 50–51.

31. Adrian Hastings, *A History of African Christianity 1950–1975* (Cambridge: Cambridge University Press, 1979), 231.

32. Hastings, *African Christianity*, 52.

33. Scholars debate the appropriateness of the term *primal*. John V. Taylor, Harold Turner, and Andrew Walls advocate it as a replacement for more pejorative classifications like animistic, pagan, or primitive religions; however, some religious phenomenologists object to it (see James L. Cox, "The Classification 'Primal Religions' as a Nonempirical Christian Theological Construct," *Studies in World Christianity* 2 (April 1996): 55–76; Rosalind Shaw, "The Invention of African Traditional Religion," *Religion* 20 (1990): 339–53.

34. Bediako, "Understanding African Theology in the Twentieth Century," 2.

35. Ibid., 4.

36. See Kwame Bediako, *Theology and Identity: The Impact of Culture upon Christian Thought in the Second Century and in Modern Africa* (Oxford: Regnum Books, 1992).

37. Bediako, "Understanding African Theology in the Twentieth Century," 2.

38. Enyi Ben Udoh, "Preface," in *Guest Christology: An Interpretative View of the Christological Problem in Africa* (Frankfurt: Peter Lang, 1988).

39. Ibid., 2, 10–11.

40. Ibid., 64.

41. Ibid., 74–75.

42. Ibid., 266.

43. Bediako, *Theology and Identity*. Among his christological reflections are "Biblical Christologies in the Context of African Traditional Religions," in *Sharing Jesus in the Two Thirds World*, ed. Vinay Samuel and Chris Sugden (Bangalore: Partnership in Mission-Asia, 1983), 115–75; *Jesus in African Culture: A Ghanaian Perspective* (Accra: Asempa Publishers, 1990), reprinted in *Emerging Voices in Global Christian Theology*, ed. William A. Dyrness (Grand Rapids, Mich.: Zondervan, 1994), 93–121. Page references below are to the original edition.

44. Bediako, "Biblical Christologies in the Context of African Traditional Religions," 132. For more extensive treatment of his analysis of the western missionary inheritance, see Bediako, *Theology and Identity*, 225–66.

45. Bediako, "Biblical Christologies in the Context of African Traditional Religions," 125.

46. Ibid.

47. Bediako, *Jesus in African Culture*, 5.

48. Bediako, "Biblical Christologies in the Context of African Traditional Religions," 143–44.

49. Bediako, *Jesus in African Culture*, 5; see also 13.

50. Ibid., 9.

51. Ibid., 41–42.

52. Charles Nyamiti, *Christ as Our Ancestor: Christology from an African Perspective* (Gweru, Zimbabwe: Mambo Press, 1984), 16.

53. See Charles Nyamiti, "African Theology: Which Directions? Which Methodologies?" *African Christian Studies*, Occasional Paper nos. 3 and 4 (November/December 1985): 3–7; idem, "My Approach to African Theology," *African Christian Studies* 7, no. 4 (December 1991): 35–53.

54. For example, see Martey, *African Theology*, 124; Bujo, *African Theology in Its Social Context*, 67–68; Aylward Shorter, "Ancestor Veneration Revisited," *AFER* 25, no. 4 (August 1983): 197–203.

55. John Mbiti, "Apartheid, Revolution and Christology," review of Takatso A. Mofokeng, *The Crucified among the Crossbearers: Towards a Black Christology* (Kampen: Uitgeversmaatschappij J. H. Kok, 1983), *International Review of Mission* 75 (July 1986): 332–33.

56. Mofokeng, *The Crucified among the Crossbearers*, x.

57. Ibid., 35.

58. Ibid., 42.

59. Bediako, "Understanding African Theology in the Twentieth Century," 6–7.

60. J. N. K. Mugambi, *African Christian Theology: An Introduction* (Nairobi: East African Educational Publishers, 1989), 5.

61. Rosino Gibellini, "Introduction," in *Paths of African Theology*, ed. Rosino Gibellini (Maryknoll, N.Y.: Orbis Books, 1994), 6.

62. J. N. K. Mugambi, *From Liberation to Reconstruction: African Christian Theology after the Cold War* (Nairobi: East African Educational Publishers, 1995), 19.

63. Nyamiti, "Contemporary African Christologies," 63.

64. Bénézet Bujo, oral interview, Fribourg, Switzerland, October 29, 1998.

65. John S. Pobee, "In Search of Christology in Africa: Some Considerations for Today," in Pobee, *Exploring Afro-Christology*, 9–10.

66. David Bosch, *Transforming Mission: Paradigm Shifts in Theology of Mission* (Maryknoll, N.Y.: Orbis Books, 1991), 427.

67. Anne Nasimiyu Wasike, "Witnesses to Jesus Christ in the African Context," *Propositum* 3, no. 1 (June 1998): 18.

68. Pobee, "In Search of Christology in Africa," 11.

69. Ibid., 19–20.

70. Pan-African Conference of Third World Theologians, "Final Communiqué," in *African Theology en Route*, ed. Kofi Appiah-Kubi and Sergio Torres (Maryknoll, N.Y.: Orbis Books, 1979), 192.

71. Ibid., 193.

72. Bujo, *African Theology in Its Social Context*, 70.

73. Akintunde E. Akinade, "'Who Do You Say That I Am?'—An Assessment of Some Christological Constructs in Africa," *Asia Journal of Theology* 9, no. 1 (April 1995): 184.

74. Samuel Amirtham and John S. Pobee, eds., *Theology by the People: Reflections on Doing Theology in Community* (Geneva: World Council of Churches, 1986), ix.

75. Ibid., 5–7.

76. Mercy Amba Oduyoye and Musimbi R. A. Kanyoro, "Introduction," in *The Will to Arise: Women, Tradition, and the Church in Africa*, ed. Mercy Amba Oduyoye and Musimbi R. A. Kanyoro (Maryknoll, N.Y.: Orbis Books, 1992), 1.

77. Anne Nasimiyu Wasike, "Christology and an African Woman's Experience," in Mugambi and Magesa, *Jesus in African Christianity*, 123.

78. Dickson, *Theology in Africa*, 109.

79. Pobee, "In Search of Christology in Africa," 11.

80. Ibid.

81. Henry Okullu, *Church and Politics in East Africa* (Nairobi: Uzima Press, 1974), 54.

82. See also Mercy Amba Oduyoye, *Hearing and Knowing: Theological Reflections on Christianity in Africa* (Maryknoll, N.Y.: Orbis Books, 1986), 45–50; Ela, *My Faith as an African*, 5.

83. John S. Mbiti, quoted in Bediako, "The Significance of Modern African Christianity—A Manifesto," 52.

84. Bediako, "The Significance of Modern African Christianity—A Manifesto," 53.

85. Ibid., 58–59.

86. Ibid.

87. Robert C. Bogdan and Sari Knopp Biklen, *Qualitative Research for Education: An Introduction to Theory and Methods* (Boston: Allyn and Bacon, 1982), 30, quoting G. Psathas, *Phenomenological Sociology* (New York: Wiley, 1973).

88. I have slightly edited oral sources to enhance readability. For the original citations, see Diane Barbara Stinton, "Jesus of Africa: Voices of Contemporary African Christology from Selected Textual and Oral Sources" (Ph.D. diss., University of Edinburgh, 2001).

89. For further information, see the bibliography of oral sources herein.

90. See "Interview Guide for Selected African Christian Theologians" in Appendix 1. I tape recorded, transcribed, and verified transcripts with each theologian, except J. N. K. Mugambi, who preferred to write responses to the interview questions and to discuss them with me. All interviews were in English except that with Jean-Marc Ela, which was in French and for which I had some translation assistance.

91. At the invitation of Nasimiyu Wasike, general superior of the Little Sisters of St. Francis, I traveled to Uganda for the seventy-fifth anniversary celebrations of their

religious order. This increased the degree of participant observation and the opportunities for individual interviews, both within that religious community and beyond it.

92. For the sake of theological analysis, the oral voices are introduced throughout the text according to these categories. However it must be acknowledged that, in reality, the speakers, whether theologians, church leaders, or laity, do not necessarily identify themselves by these labels—particularly those of Protestant or Catholic.

93. See "Interview Guide for Individual Interviews and Focus Groups" in Appendix 1. I tape recorded and transcribed all interviews and analyzed them using QSR N4 software for qualitative data analysis. Interview transcripts are recorded on CD-Rom at the Centre for the Study of Christianity in the Non-Western World, University of Edinburgh.

94. The dotted lines indicate a possible, though not presumed, direct relationship between the selected African Christians and the six theologians. In other words, I did not assume that the respondents were familiar with the textual Christologies. Nor did I mention the theologians or their works unless respondents volunteered such awareness on their part. Some respondents knew the theologians personally, others knew their works, while still others did not voice any such awareness. However, the primary purpose of the interview was not to discern the respondents' knowledge of these particular theologians but to probe *their* perceptions of Jesus Christ.

95. Mugambi and Magesa, "Introduction," 10.

2 Understanding Origins of African Christologies

1. John S. Mbiti, "Some African Concepts of Christology," in *Christ and the Younger Churches*, ed. Georg F. Vicedom (London: SPCK, 1972), 51.

2. Ibid., 52.

3. Pan-African Conference of Third World Theologians, "Final Communiqué," in *African Theology en Route*, ed. Kofi Appiah-Kubi and Sergio Torres (Maryknoll, N.Y.: Orbis Books, 1979), 192.

4. Ibid., 193.

5. Charles Nyamiti, "African Christologies Today," in *Jesus in African Christianity: Experimentation and Diversity in African Christology*, ed. J. N. K. Mugambi and Laurenti Magesa (Nairobi: Initiatives, 1989), 18.

6. Ibid., 28.

7. Laurenti Magesa, "Christ the Liberator and Africa Today," in Mugambi and Magesa, *Jesus in African Christianity*, 82–83.

8. Nyamiti, "African Christologies Today," 28.

9. John Parratt, *Reinventing Christianity: African Theology Today* (Grand Rapids, Mich.: William B. Eerdmans, 1995), 51.

10. Cf. Justin S. Ukpong, "Christology and Inculturation: A New Testament Perspective," in *Paths of African Theology*, ed. Rosino Gibellini (Maryknoll, N.Y.: Orbis Books, 1994), 40–61.

11. Mercy Amba Oduyoye, *Hearing and Knowing: Theological Reflections on Christianity in Africa* (Maryknoll, N.Y.: Orbis Books, 1986), 3.

12. Jean-Marc Ela, "Le motif de la libération dans la théologie africaine," *Les nouvelles rationalités africaines* 2, no. 5 (October 1986): 46, my translation.

13. John S. Pobee, "Jesus Christ—The Life of the World: An African Perspective," *Ministerial Formation* 21 (January 1983): 5; see also idem, *Toward an African Theology* (Nashville, Tenn.: Abingdon, 1979).

14. Pobee, "Jesus Christ—The Life of the World," 5.

15. J. N. K. Mugambi, *From Liberation to Reconstruction: African Christian Theology after the Cold War* (Nairobi: East African Educational Publishers, 1995), 77.

16. See, for example, Mongo Beti, *The Poor Christ of Bomba*, trans. Gerald Moore (Oxford: Heinemann, 1971); Okot p'Bitek, *African Religions in Western Scholarship* (Kampala: East African Literature Bureau, 1970); Ali M. Mazrui, *The African Condition—A Political Diagnosis* (London: Faber and Faber, 1980).

17. See Kwame Bediako, *Christianity in Africa: The Renewal of a Non-Western Religion* (Edinburgh: Edinburgh University Press; Maryknoll, N.Y.: Orbis Books, 1995).

18. This view must be balanced by a comment Gatu made later in the interview. After denouncing missionary shortcomings in the spread of the gospel in Kenya, particularly with respect to the crisis regarding female circumcision among the Gikuyu, Gatu ended more charitably by acknowledging the human limitations of missionaries.

19. Anne Nasimiyu Wasike, "Witnesses to Jesus Christ in the African Context," *Propositum* 3, no. 1 (June 1998): 18.

20. J. N. K. Mugambi, *African Christian Theology: An Introduction* (Nairobi: East African Educational Publishers, 1989), 56.

21. See Kwame Bediako, *Theology and Identity: The Impact of Culture upon Christian Thought in the Second Century and in Modern Africa* (Oxford: Regnum Books, 1992), 239.

22. Bénézet Bujo, *African Theology in Its Social Context*, trans. John O'Donohue (Nairobi: St. Paul Communications; Maryknoll, N.Y.: Orbis Books, 1992), 9.

23. Ibid., 69.

24. "SPG" refers to the Society for the Propagation of the Gospel, an Anglican missionary society established in Britain in 1701.

25. John S. Pobee, *Toward an African Theology* (Nashville, Tenn.: Abingdon, 1979), 81.

26. For example, see John S. Mbiti, *African Religions and Philosophy* (Nairobi: Heinemann, 1969), 92; idem, *Introduction to African Religion* (London: Heinemann, 1974), 201–2.

27. Elizabeth Amoah and Mercy Amba Oduyoye, "The Christ for African Women," in *With Passion and Compassion: Third World Women Doing Theology*, ed. Virginia Fabella and Mercy Amba Oduyoye (Maryknoll, N.Y.: Orbis Books, 1988), 37.

28. Ibid.

29. Bujo, *African Theology in Its Social Context*, 9.

30. Jean-Marc Ela, "De l'assistance à la libération: Les tâches actuelles de l'église en milieu africain," *Foi et développement* 83 (January-February 1981): 5, my translation.

31. Mugambi, *From Liberation to Reconstruction*, viii.

32. Oduyoye, *Hearing and Knowing*, 9.

33. Jean-Marc Ela, "The Memory of the African People and the Cross of Christ," in *The Scandal of a Crucified World: Perspectives on the Cross and Suffering*, trans. and ed. Yacob Tesfai (Maryknoll, N.Y.: Orbis Books, 1994), 18.

34. Ibid., 18–19.

35. See Bediako, *Theology and Identity*; idem, "Understanding African Theology in the Twentieth Century," *Bulletin for Contextual Theology* 3, no. 2 (June 1996): 1–11; Andrew Walls, "Africa and Christian Identity," *Mission Focus* 6, no. 7 (November 1978): 11–13.

36. Bujo, *African Theology in Its Social Context*, 94.

37. John S. Pobee, *Christ Would Be an African Too* (Geneva: WCC Publications, 1996), 22.

38. Jean-Marc Ela, "Globalisation et paupérisation: Un défi à la théologie africaine," in *Liberation Theologies on Shifting Grounds: A Clash of Socio-Economic and Cultural Paradigms*, ed. G. de Schrijver (Leuven: Leuven University Press, 1998), 159, my translation.

39. Mercy Amba Oduyoye, "Reflections from a Third World Woman's Perspective: Women's Experience and Liberation Theologies," in *Irruption of the Third World: Challenge to Theology*, ed. Virginia Fabella and Sergio Torres (Maryknoll, N.Y.: Orbis Books, 1983), 247–48.

40. Ibid., 249.

41. Ibid., 250.

42. Ibid., 254. See also Oduyoye, *Hearing and Knowing*, 120–37; idem, "The Roots of African Christian Feminism," in *Variations in Christian Theology in Africa*, ed. John S. Pobee and Carl F. Hallencreutz (Nairobi: Uzima Press, 1986), 32–47.

43. Anne Nasimiyu Wasike, "Christology and an African Woman's Experience," in Mugambi and Magesa, *Jesus in African Christianity*, 129.

44. Ibid., 129–30.

45. Ibid., 123.

46. Amoah and Oduyoye, "The Christ for African Women," 35.

47. Mercy Amba Oduyoye, "The Passion Out of Compassion: Women of the EATWOT Third General Assembly," *International Review of Mission* 81, no. 322 (1992): 315.

48. Ibid., 316.

49. Mugambi and Magesa, "Introduction," in Mugambi and Magesa, *Jesus in African Christianity*, xiv.

50. Oduyoye, *Hearing and Knowing*, 9.

51. John S. Pobee, "African Symbolism and the Interpretation of Christianity," in *Variations in Christian Theology in Africa*, ed. John S. Pobee and Carl F. Hallencreutz (Nairobi: Uzima Press, 1986), 53.

52. Ibid., 54.

53. Pan-African Conference of Third World Theologians, "Final Communiqué," 193.

54. J. N. K. Mugambi, "Theological Method in African Christianity," in *Theological Method and Aspects of Worship in African Christianity*, ed. Mary N. Getui (Nairobi: Acton Publishers, 1998), 5.

55. Ibid., 26–27.

56. F. Welbourn and B. M. Ogot, *A Place to Feel at Home* (London: Oxford University Press, 1962).

57. Pan-African Conference of Third World Theologians, "Final Communiqué," 194.

INTRODUCTION TO PART II

1. Kwame Bediako, "Understanding African Theology in the Twentieth Century," *Bulletin for Contextual Theology* 3, no. 2 (June 1996): 1.

2. Charles Nyamiti, "Contemporary African Christologies: Assessment and Practical Suggestions," in *Paths of African Theology*, ed. Rosino Gibellini (Maryknoll, N.Y.: Orbis Books, 1994), 66.

3. Charles Nyamiti, "African Christologies Today," in *Jesus in African Christianity: Experimentation and Diversity in African Christology*, ed. J. N. K. Mugambi and Laurenti Magesa (Nairobi: Initiatives, 1989), 17, 29.

4. J. N. K. Mugambi, *From Liberation to Reconstruction: African Christian Theology after the Cold War* (Nairobi: East African Educational Publishers, 1995), 9–10.

5. Desmond M. Tutu, "Black Theology and African Theology—Soulmates or Antagonists?" in *A Reader in African Christian Theology*, ed. John Parratt (London: SPCK, 1987), 54.

6. Jean-Marc Ela, "De l'assistance à la libération: Les tâches actuelles de l'église en milieu africain," *Foi et développement* 83 (January-February 1981): 4, my translation; idem, "The Memory of the African People and the Cross of Christ," in *The Scandal of a Crucified World: Perspectives on the Cross and Suffering*, trans. and ed. Yacob Tesfai (Maryknoll, N.Y.: Orbis Books, 1994), 19–20.

7. Jean-Marc Ela, *My Faith as an African*, trans. John Pairman Brown and Susan Perry (Maryknoll, N.Y.: Orbis Books, 1988), vi.

8. Bénézet Bujo, *African Theology in Its Social Context*, trans. John O'Donohue (Nairobi: St. Paul Communications; Maryknoll, N.Y.: Orbis Books, 1992), 7.

9. This phrase originated with Cameroonian theologian Engelbert Mveng referring to the violence of colonialism, but it has been adopted by many other African theologians. According to Mveng, "It consists in despoiling human beings not only of what they have, but of everything that constitutes their being and essence—their identity, history, ethnic roots, language, culture, faith, creativity, dignity, pride, ambitions, right to speak . . . we could go on indefinitely" (Engelbert Mveng, "Third World Theology—What Theology? What Third World?: Evaluation by an African Delegate," in *Irruption of the Third World: Challenge to Theology*, ed. Virginia Fabella and Sergio Torres [Maryknoll, N.Y.: Orbis Books, 1983], 220).

10. Bujo, *African Theology in Its Social Context*, 71.

11. Bénézet Bujo, *African Christian Morality at the Age of Inculturation* (Nairobi: St. Paul Publications—Africa, 1990), 125.

12. Ibid., 126.

13. Nyamiti, "African Christologies Today," 32.

14. Emmanuel Martey, *African Theology: Inculturation and Liberation* (Maryknoll, N.Y.: Orbis Books, 1993), 130.

15. Ibid., 125–26.

16. Ibid., 126.

17. Ibid., 128.

18. Ibid., 131.

19. For example, see Robert J. Schreiter, *Constructing Local Theologies* (London: SCM Press, 1985), 6; and Stephen B. Bevans, *Models of Contextual Theology*, ed. Robert J. Schreiter (Maryknoll, N.Y.: Orbis Books, 1992).

20. Avery Dulles, *Models of the Church* (Garden City, N.Y.: Doubleday, 1974), 21–22.

21. Ibid., 18; see also 23–25.

3 JESUS AS LIFE-GIVER

1. Bénézet Bujo, *African Christian Morality at the Age of Inculturation* (Nairobi: St. Paul Publications—Africa, 1990), 103.

2. The use of the term *traditional* in relation to aspects of African culture is not intended to be derogatory in any way, as it might be considered in other contexts. The aim is to discern those beliefs, customs and values derived from African realities prior to the coming of Europeans and Christianity that exert enduring influence upon African worldviews. Furthermore, in reality, the traditional and the modern intermingle in contemporary Africa and cannot be separated. However, they are distinguished here for purposes of analysis.

3. Bénézet Bujo, *African Theology in Its Social Context*, trans. John O'Donohue (Nairobi: St. Paul Communications; Maryknoll, N.Y.: Orbis Books, 1992), 17.

4. Ibid., 17–19; Bujo, *African Christian Morality at the Age of Inculturation*, 74–75.

5. Bujo, *African Theology in Its Social Context*, 20.

6. Vincent Mulago, "Vital Participation: The Cohesive Principle of the Bantu Community," in *Biblical Revelation and African Beliefs*, ed. Kwesi A. Dickson and Paul Ellingworth (London: Lutterworth Press, 1969), 138.

7. Bujo, *African Theology in Its Social Context*, 21.

8. Bujo, *African Christian Morality at the Age of Inculturation*, 78.

9. John S. Pobee, "Life and Peace: An African Perspective," in *Variations in Christian Theology in Africa*, ed. John S. Pobee and Carl F. Hallencreutz (Nairobi: Uzima Press, 1986), 17.

10. Mulago, "Vital Participation," 139–40.

11. Placide Tempels, *Bantu Philosophy*, trans. Colin King (Paris: Présence Africaine, 1959).

12. Bujo, *African Theology in Its Social Context*, 56.

13. Ibid., 57.

14. Bénézet Bujo, *Christmas: God Becomes Man in Black Africa* (Nairobi: Paulines Publications Africa, 1995), 32.

15. Ibid., 33.

16. Bujo, *African Christian Morality at the Age of Inculturation*, 83.

17. Bujo, *Christmas*, 33.

18. Pobee, "Life and Peace," 19.

19. Ibid., 21.

20. John S. Pobee, "Jesus Christ—The Life of the World: An African Perspective," *Ministerial Formation* 21 (January 1983): 6.

21. Ibid., 7.

22. Ibid., 7–8.

23. Twi lyrics and English translation provided by Yeboah following the interview.

24. Mercy Amba Oduyoye, "Wholeness of Life in Africa," in *An African Call for Life: A Contribution to the World Council of Churches' Sixth Assembly Theme: "Jesus Christ—the Life of the World,"* ed. Masamba ma Mpolo, Reginald Stober, and Evelyn V. Appiah (Nairobi: Uzima Press for the World Council of Churches, 1983), 113.

25. Ibid., 114.

26. Ibid., 117.

27. Ibid., 115.

28. Bujo, *Christmas*, 8.

29. Ibid., 32–33.

30. Ibid., 77.

31. Kofi Appiah-Kubi, "Christology," in *A Reader in African Christian Theology*, ed. John Parratt (London: SPCK, 1987), 76.

32. Cécé Kolié, "Jesus as Healer?" in *Faces of Jesus in Africa*, ed. Robert J. Schreiter (Maryknoll, N.Y.: Orbis Books, 1991), 128.

33. Jean-Marc Ela, *My Faith as an African*, trans. John Pairman Brown and Susan Perry (Maryknoll, N.Y.: Orbis Books, 1988), 44, 50.

34. Philomena Njeri Mwaura, "Healing as a Pastoral Concern," in *Pastoral Care in African Christianity: Challenging Essays in Pastoral Theology*, ed. D. W. Waruta and H. W. Kinoti (Nairobi: Acton Publishers, 1994), 67–68.

35. Ela, *My Faith as an African*, 50–51.

36. John S. Pobee and Gabriel Ositelu II, *African Initiatives in Christianity* (Geneva: WCC Publications, 1998), 29; see also John S. Pobee, "Healing—An African Christian Theologian's Perspective," *International Review of Mission* 83 (April 1994): 247–55; John S. Pobee, "Health, Healing and Religion: An African View," *International Review of Mission* 90, nos. 356/357 (January/April 2001): 55–64.

37. Mwaura, "Healing as a Pastoral Concern," 70.

38. For a criticism of mission Christianity for not having penetrated deeply into African traditional religiosity, see John S. Mbiti, *African Religions and Philosophy* (Nairobi: Heinemann, 1969), 236–39. See also Bujo, *African Christian Morality at the Age of Inculturation,* 107; and Pobee, "Health, Healing and Religion, 60–61.

39. Jean-Marc Ela, "De l'assistance à la libération: Les tâches actuelles de l'église en milieu africain," *Foi et développement* 83 (January-February 1981): 2, my translation.

40. Kolié, "Jesus as Healer?" 141.

41. Ibid.

42. Ibid., 141–42.

43. I designed the interview questions in an attempt to elicit the respondents' own views about Jesus as far as possible. Then, if a respondent had not initiated comments on a particular image of interest to me, I raised it for discussion in the later stages of the interview. This was the approach taken with the image of Jesus as healer and also the related one of Jesus as traditional healer (see the Interview Guide in Appendix 1).

44. In a semi-structured interview, the questions planned serve only as a general guide to conversation. The result is that not every question is necessarily addressed to every respondent. In the present case, the image of Jesus as healer was not volunteered by five respondents, nor was the question asked due to time constraints in the interview.

45. *Legon Praise*, 2d ed. (Legon, Accra, Ghana: Legon Interdenominational Church, n.d.), 8.

46. This does not suggest that all African Christians assume that the traditional concept of God among their ethnic societies is identical with the God of the Bible, for the research clearly indicates that this is not the case. However, Ole Ronkei represents those African Christians who do find such continuity in their understanding of God and reveals the impact this has upon their view of Jesus as healer.

47. The significance of Jesus to childless women is noted here, for women's acceptance of this condition goes against traditional African views of human wholeness requiring fecundity. Jesus' significance in this regard is reiterated in Chapter 7.

48. Bénézet Bujo, "Pour une éthique africano-christocentrique," in *Combats pour un christianisme africain: Mélanges en l'honneur du Professeur V. Mulago,* ed. A. Ngindu Mushete (Kinshasa: Faculté de Théologie Catholique, 1981), 27, my translation.

49. Pobee, "Healing—An African Christian Theologian's Perspective," 251; see also Pobee, "Health, Healing and Religion: An African View."

50. Anne Nasimiyu Wasike, "Christology and an African Woman's Experience," in *Jesus in African Christianity: Experimentation and Diversity in African Christology,* ed. J. N. K. Mugambi and Laurenti Magesa (Nairobi: Initiatives Ltd., 1989), 133.

51. *Daily Nation*, December 3, 1996; Anne Nasimiyu Wasike, "Witnesses to Jesus Christ in the African Context," *Propositum* 3, no. 1 (June 1998): 28–29.

52. Ela, "De l'assistance à la libération," 3, my translation.

53. Ibid.

54. Mercy Amba Oduyoye, *Hearing and Knowing: Theological Reflections on Christianity in Africa* (Maryknoll, N.Y.: Orbis Books, 1986), 44.

55. Elizabeth Amoah and Mercy Amba Oduyoye, "The Christ for African Women," in *With Passion and Compassion: Third World Women Doing Theology*, ed. Virginia Fabella and Mercy Amba Oduyoye (Maryknoll, N.Y.: Orbis Books, 1988), 39.

56. Pobee, "Healing—An African Christian Theologian's Perspective," 250.

57. Oduyoye, *Hearing and Knowing*, 44.

58. Nasimiyu Wasike, "Witnesses to Jesus Christ in the African Context," 13.

59. Ela, *My Faith as an African*, 67.

60. Ibid., quoting *Jeune Afrique* (March 12, 1980).

61. Ibid., 76.

62. Ibid.

63. Ibid., 78.

64. Ibid., 79.

65. Ibid., 78.

66. Ibid., 79–80.

67. Kolié, "Jesus as Healer?" 132.

68. R. Buana Kibongi, "Priesthood," in Dickson and Ellingworth, *Biblical Revelation and African Beliefs*, 50.

69. Ibid., 54.

70. Ibid., 55.

71. Gabriel M. Setiloane, "Where Are We in African Theology?" in *African Theology en Route*, ed. Kofi Appiah-Kubi and Sergio Torres (Maryknoll, N.Y.: Orbis Books, 1979), 64.

72. Matthew Schoffeleers, "Christ in African Folk Theology: The *Nganga* Paradigm," in *Religion in Africa: Experience and Expression*, ed. Thomas D. Blakely, Walter E. A. van Beek, and Dennis L. Thomson (London: James Currey, 1994), 74.

73. Ibid. While Schoffeleers provides no formal definition of "folk theology," he identifies it as being derived from "the population at large" as distinct from the "intellectual elite" or "professional theologians." This interpretation is adopted for the present purpose.

74. *Mganga* is the Swahili noun form equivalent to *nganga* in other Bantu languages. I posed the question using the term *mganga*, because most educated Kenyans speak Swahili as the national language. However, I added the phrase "or traditional healer" to allow respondents to discuss the equivalent figure in their own ethnic society and vernacular.

75. The "Total Responses Overall Positive" figure of fourteen is derived from adding the eight "Positive Responses Only" with the six "Overall Positive Responses." The same method applies for totaling the negative responses, and this forms the pattern for subsequent tables.

76. No focus groups were conducted in Uganda since the research undertaken in this country was an unexpected extension of the original research design focusing on Kenya.

77. *Mganga* and its vernacular equivalents may be used in reference to more than one religious specialist, as the data reveal. The singular *traditional healer* is used as a generic term encompassing the variety of roles and individual specialists delineated in the ensuing discussion.

78. *Daktari* is a modern Swahili adaptation of "doctor."

79. *Odunsini* is the Twi word for "traditional healer." I chose to use it in the interviews because Twi is a major language in Ghana and therefore widely understood. Again, however, I placed it in apposition to "traditional healer," allowing respondents to discuss this figure in their own vernacular and ethnic society.

80. Peter K. Sarpong, "Asante Christology," *Studia Missionalia* 45 (1996): 203.

81. Schoffeleers, "Christ in African Folk Theology," 85.

82. In keeping with the qualitative research approach taken, no claim is made that the statistics presented based on this sample are proportionately representative of the population at large.

83. Schoffeleers, "Christ in African Folk Theology," 73.

84. See "Presuppositions" in Chapter 1 above; cf. J. N. K. Mugambi, *From Liberation to Reconstruction: African Christian Theology after the Cold War* (Nairobi: East African Educational Publishers, 1995), 67–68; Nasimiyu Wasike, "Witnesses to Jesus Christ in the African Context," 1, 3; Charles Nyamiti, "Contemporary African Christologies: Assessment and Practical Suggestions," in *Paths of African Theology*, ed. Rosino Gibellini (Maryknoll, N.Y.: Orbis Books, 1994), 64.

85. Schoffeleers, "Christ in African Folk Theology," 85.

86. Ibid. For Schoffeleers's reference to Kolié's view, see 86 n. 3.

87. For example, John Gatu, Mary Getui, David Gitari, and Hannah Kinoti in Kenya; Kwesi Dickson and Emmanuel Martey in Ghana.

88. Kwame Bediako, "The Significance of Modern African Christianity—A Manifesto," *Studies in World Christianity* 1, Part 1 (1995): 53.

89. John S. Mbiti, quoted in Bediako, "The Significance of Modern African Christianity," 52.

90. Bediako, "The Significance of Modern African Christianity," 53.

91. Schoffeleers, "Christ in African Folk Theology," 79.

92. Ibid., 86.

93. Ibid.

94. Aylward Shorter, *Jesus and the Witchdoctor: An Approach to Healing and Wholeness* (London: Geoffrey Chapman, 1985), 12–13. For further discussion of the tensions between Western and traditional African approaches to healing and their theological significance, see Gerard Jansen, "Western Medicine—Secularised and Secularising: A Medical Missiological Problem," *Missionalia* 25, no. 3 (November 1997): 344–59.

95. Aylward Shorter, "Folk Christianity and Functional Christology," *AFER* 24, no. 3 (June 1982): 136–37.

96. Kibongi, "Priesthood," 55.

97. Ibid., 56.

98. Pan-African Conference of Third World Theologians, "Final Communiqué," 195.

99. Ibid.

100. Of the individual respondents, only two out of the sixty-five mentioned AIDS as an example of current suffering, without elaborating on the crisis. Of the focus groups, AIDS was mentioned in four out of the total of twelve groups, with members from two groups discussing the significance of Jesus in relation to the pandemic.

101. John S. Mbiti, "Some African Concepts of Christology," in *Christ and the Younger Churches*, ed. Georg F. Vicedom (London: SPCK, 1972), 55.

102. John S. Mbiti, "'Ho Soter Hemon' [Our Savior] as an African Experience," in *Christ and Spirit in the New Testament*, ed. Barnabus Lindars and Stephen S. Smalley (Cambridge: Cambridge University Press, 1973), 403.

103. Oduyoye, "Wholeness of Life in Africa," 121.

104. See, for example, Kolié, who acknowledges Ela's influence in "Jesus as Healer?" 149 n. 19; and Mwaura, "Healing as a Pastoral Concern."

105. Kolié, "Jesus as Healer?" 132.

106. See Pobee, "Healing—An African Christian Theologian's Perspective," 251; idem, "Health, Healing and Religion," 61–64.

107. Kolié, "Jesus as Healer?" 128.

108. Ibid., 142.
109. Ibid., 148.

4 JESUS AS MEDIATOR

1. Laurenti Magesa, *African Religion: The Moral Traditions of Abundant Life* (Maryknoll, N.Y.: Orbis Books, 1997), 77, 193.

2. John S. Mbiti, *African Religions and Philosophy* (Nairobi: Heinemann, 1969), 68.

3. John S. Mbiti, *Introduction to African Religion* (London: Heinemann, 1975), 62.

4. Mbiti, *African Religions and Philosophy*, 78, see also 75–91; Mbiti, *Introduction to African Religion*, 65–76.

5. Mbiti, *Introduction to African Religion*, 63–64.

6. Kofi Appiah-Kubi, "Christology," in *A Reader in African Christian Theology*, ed. John Parratt (London: SPCK, 1987), 71.

7. François Kabasélé, "Christ as Ancestor and Elder Brother," in *Faces of Jesus in Africa*, ed. Robert J. Schreiter (Maryknoll, N.Y.: Orbis Books, 1991), 117.

8. In addition to Bujo and Ela, cited below, see J. N. K. Mugambi, *The African Heritage and Contemporary Christianity* (Nairobi: Longman Kenya Ltd., 1989), 66–67; Anne J. Nasimiyu, "Vatican II: The Problem of Inculturation" (Ph.D. diss., Duquesne University, 1986), 249; Vincent Mulago, "Vital Participation: The Cohesive Principle of the Bantu Community," in *Biblical Revelation and African Beliefs*, ed. Kwesi A. Dickson and Paul Ellingworth (London: Lutterworth Press, 1969), 137–58; Peter K. Sarpong, *Ghana in Retrospect: Some Aspects of Ghanaian Culture* (Tema, Ghana: Ghana Publishing Corporation, 1974), 33; and Aylward Shorter, "Ancestor Veneration Revisited," *AFER* 25, no. 4 (August 1983): 199. See also Jomo Kenyatta, *Facing Mount Kenya: The Tribal Life of the Gikuyu* (London: Secker and Warburg, 1956); Kofi Asare Opoku, *West African Traditional Religion* (Accra: FEP International Private Ltd., 1978); Daniel Wambutda, "Ancestors: The Living Dead," in *Traditional Religion in West Africa*, ed. E. A. Ade. Adegbola (Ibadan: Daystar Press, 1983), 128–37.

9. Bénézet Bujo, *African Theology in Its Social Context*, trans. John O'Donohue (Nairobi: St. Paul Communications; Maryknoll, N.Y.: Orbis Books, 1992), 25–26.

10. Jean-Marc Ela, *My Faith as an African*, trans. John Pairman Brown and Susan Perry (Maryknoll, N.Y.: Orbis Books, 1988), 14.

11. Ibid., 24–26.

12. Bénézet Bujo, *African Christian Morality at the Age of Inculturation* (Nairobi: St. Paul Publications—Africa, 1990), 73.

13. Charles Nyamiti, *Christ as Our Ancestor: Christology from an African Perspective* (Gweru, Zimbabwe: Mambo Press, 1984), 15.

14. Ibid., 15–16.

15. Sarpong, *Ghana in Retrospect*, 35.

16. Shorter, "Ancestor Veneration Revisited," 199.

17. Mbiti, *African Religions and Philosophy*, 83.

18. Magesa, *African Religion*, 78.

19. Ibid.

20. Mbiti, *African Religions and Philosophy*, 85. Mbiti's terminology breeds confusion, however, for he does not specify the relationship between ancestors and the living dead.

21. Shorter, "Ancestor Veneration Revisited," 198–99.

22. Ibid., 202.

23. Richard J. Gehman, *African Traditional Religion in Biblical Perspective* (Kijabe, Kenya: Kesho Publications, 1989), 184.

24. Ibid., 185–86.

25. John Parratt, ed., *The Practice of Presence: Shorter Writings of Harry Sawyerr* (Grand Rapids, Mich.: William B. Eerdmans, 1994), 43.

26. Ela, *My Faith as an African*, 18. See also idem, "Ancestors and Christian Faith: An African Problem," in *Liturgy and Cultural Religious Traditions*, ed. Herman Schmidt and David Power (New York: Seabury Press, 1977), 38.

27. For only one recent example in an extensive field of literature, see T. Merrigan and J. Haers, eds., *The Myriad Christ: Plurality and the Quest for Unity in Contemporary Christology* (Leuven: Leuven University Press and Uitgeverij Peeters, 2000).

28. John S. Pobee, *Toward an African Theology* (Nashville, Tenn.: Abingdon, 1979), 46.

29. Ibid., 81.

30. Ibid., 82.

31. Ibid., 83.

32. Ibid., 94.

33. Ibid.

34. The image of Jesus as chief is explored in Chapter 6.

35. Pobee, *Toward an African Theology*, 98.

36. Bujo, *African Theology in Its Social Context*, 9.

37. Ibid., 76–77.

38. Ibid., 27; see also idem, "Nos ancêtres, ces saints inconnus," *Bulletin de théologie africaine* 1, no. 2 (July-December 1979): 165–66; idem, "Pour une éthique africano-christocentrique," in *Combats pour un christianisme africain: Mélanges en l'honneur du Professeur V. Mulago*, ed. A. Ngindu Mushete (Kinshasa: Faculté de Théologie Catholique, 1981), 23–24; Bujo, *African Christian Morality at the Age of Inculturation*, 76–78.

39. Bujo, *African Theology in Its Social Context*, 78.

40. Ibid., 29–30.

41. Ibid., 79.

42. Ibid., 81.

43. Bénézet Bujo, *Christmas: God Becomes Man in Black Africa* (Nairobi: Paulines Publications Africa, 1995), 66.

44. Bujo, *African Christian Morality at the Age of Inculturation*, 82.

45. Ibid., 83.

46. Ibid., 82.

47. Ibid., 103.

48. Bujo, *African Theology in Its Social Context*, 82.

49. Ibid., 83; see also Bujo, *Christmas*, 66.

50. Bujo, *African Theology in Its Social Context*, 84.

51. Bujo, *African Christian Morality at the Age of Inculturation*, 83.

52. Bujo, "Pour une éthique africano-christocentrique," 23.

53. Bujo, *African Theology in Its Social Context*, 91.

54. Bujo, *African Christian Morality at the Age of Inculturation*, 89.

55. Ibid., 84.

56. Bujo, *African Theology in Its Social Context*, 91.

57. Matrix tables prepared in the research analysis reflect that Catholics were divided almost equally in their views, while the Protestants were clearly more negative than positive, reflecting a ratio of approximately two negative to one positive.

58. Although Aboa used the term *equate* in the passage cited, the context of conversation makes clear that he does not equate Jesus with the African ancestors literally but only analogously.

59. Birikorang related how he and others believe the Akan are descendants of Manasseh, who remained in Egypt. He remarked that this perceived physical kinship brings Jesus "very, very, very close."

60. It must be underlined, however, that this is not the case for all African societies. Women feature among the ancestors for many people groups, particularly among matrilineal societies like the Akan, according to Mercy Amba Oduyoye and John Pobee. However, Bisem's point warrants attention because women are often overshadowed by men in the expressed concepts of ancestors.

61. Kabasélé, "Christ as Ancestor and Elder Brother," 123–24.

62. Nyamiti, *Christ as Our Ancestor*, 9.

63. Ernst Wendland, "'Who Do People Say I Am?': Contextualizing Christology in Africa," *AJET* 10, no. 2 (1991): 15.

64. Ibid., 16–20.

65. Tite Tiénou, quoted in Wendland, "'Who Do People Say I Am?'" 16.

66. For example, see Elizabeth Amoah and Mercy Amba Oduyoye, "The Christ for African Women," in *With Passion and Compassion: Third World Women Doing Theology*, ed. Virginia Fabella and Mercy Amba Oduyoye (Maryknoll, N.Y.: Orbis Books, 1988), 38–39.

67. For example, see Bujo, "Nos ancêtres, ces saints inconnus," 173–78; also oral interviews with Marie Gacambi and Mary Kizito. For opposing views, see Ela, *My Faith as an African,* 28–29; Ela, "Ancestors and Christian Faith," 47; Kabasélé, "Christ as Ancestor and Elder Brother," 125–26.

68. Cf. Kwame Bediako, who contends that Jesus fulfills the role of the African ancestors and thereby displaces their mediatorial function (*Jesus in African Culture: A Ghanaian Perspective* [Accra: Asempa Publishers, 1990], 41–42), and François Kabasélé, who argues that Jesus does not abolish ancestral mediation but makes it subordinate to his own ("Christ as Ancestor and Elder Brother," 126).

69. In an informal tape-recorded interview, Korse explained, "Sometimes I say, 'You who are gone before us, our parents, grandparents, uncles, aunties, our colleagues, our friends'" (Jinja: April 29, 1998).

70. Kabasélé, "Christ as Ancestor and Elder Brother," 126.

71. Kwame Bediako, "The Doctrine of Christ and the Significance of Vernacular Terminology," *International Bulletin of Missionary Research* 22, 3 (July 1998): 110.

72. Ibid.

73. C. F. D. Moule, quoted in Fergus J. King, "Angels and Ancestors: A Basis for Christology?" *Mission Studies* 11, no. 1 (1994): 23.

74. King, "Angels and Ancestors," 24.

75. Bediako, "The Doctrine of Christ and the Significance of Vernacular Terminology," 110–11.

5 JESUS AS LOVED ONE

1. Vincent Mulago, "Vital Participation: The Cohesive Principle of the Bantu Community," in *Biblical Revelation and African Beliefs*, ed. Kwesi A. Dickson and Paul Ellingworth (London: Lutterworth Press, 1969), 143.

2. Ibid., 139.

3. François Kabasélé, "Christ as Ancestor and Elder Brother," in *Faces of Jesus in Africa*, ed. Robert J. Schreiter (Maryknoll, N.Y.: Orbis Books, 1991), 123.

4. John S. Pobee, *Toward an African Theology* (Nashville, Tenn.: Abingdon, 1979), 88.

5. John S. Pobee, *Skenosis: Christian Faith in an African Context* (Gweru, Zimbabwe: Mambo Press, 1992), 66.

6. J. N. K. Mugambi, "Conclusion: Christological Paradigms in African Christianity," in *Jesus in African Christianity: Experimentation and Diversity in African Christology*, ed. J. N. K. Mugambi and Laurenti Magesa (Nairobi: Initiatives Ltd., 1989), 139.

7. Bénézet Bujo, *Christmas: God Becomes Man in Black Africa* (Nairobi: Paulines Publications Africa, 1995), 52.

8. John S. Mbiti, quoted in Anne J. Nasimiyu, "Vatican II: The Problem of Inculturation" (Ph.D. diss., Duquesne University, 1986), 258.

9. Nasimiyu, "Vatican II," 257.

10. Pobee, *Toward an African Theology*, 89.

11. Ibid.

12. Mugambi, "Conclusion," 139.

13. *Legon Praise*, 2d ed. (Legon: Legon Interdenominational Church, n.d.), 49.

14. Quoted in John S. Pobee, "Confessing Christ à la African Instituted Churches," in *Exploring Afro-Christology*, ed. John S. Pobee (Frankfurt: Peter Lang, 1992), 147.

15. Harry Sawyerr, *Creative Evangelism: Towards a New Christian Encounter with Africa* (London: Lutterworth Press, 1968), 73–74; see also Aylward Shorter, "Folk Christianity and Functional Christology," *AFER* 24, no. 3 (June 1982): 134.

16. Bujo, *Christmas*, 36–37.

17. Anne Nasimiyu Wasike, "Witnesses to Jesus Christ in the African Context," *Propositum* 3, no. 1 (June 1998): 21.

18. Anne Nasimiyu Wasike, "Christology and an African Woman's Experience," in Mugambi and Magesa, *Jesus in African Christianity*, 131.

19. Nasimiyu Wasike, "Witnesses to Jesus Christ in the African Context," 21.

20. Ibid.

21. Ibid.

22. Ibid.

23. Ibid., 23.

24. Ibid., 29.

25. *Legon Praise*, 29.

26. Lyrics provided by the soloist, Diana Akuwumi.

27. Bujo, *Christmas*, 33.

28. Bénézet Bujo, *African Theology in Its Social Context*, trans. John O'Donohue (Nairobi: St. Paul Communications; Maryknoll, N.Y.: Orbis Books, 1992), 112.

29. Ibid., 88.

30. "Culture and Identity: Report of Section I of the Bangkok Conference," *International Review of Missions* 62 (April 1973): 189, quoted in Nasimiyu, "Vatican II," 108.

31. Andrew F. Walls, *The Missionary Movement in Christian History: Studies in the Transmission of Faith* (Maryknoll, N.Y.: Orbis Books, 1996), 25.

32. John 1:14 (*The Message: The New Testament in Contemporary English,* trans. Eugene H. Peterson [Colorado Springs, Colo.: NavPress, 1994]).

6 JESUS AS LEADER

1. John S. Pobee, "In Search of Christology in Africa," in *Exploring Afro-Christology*, ed. John S. Pobee (Frankfurt: Peter Lang, 1992), 17.

2. John S. Pobee, *Christ Would Be an African Too* (Geneva: WCC Publications, 1996), 24.

3. Robert Kwasi Aboagye-Mensah, "Socio-Political Thinking of Karl Barth: Trinitarian and Incarnational Christology as the Ground for His Social Action and Its Implications for Us Today" (Ph.D. diss., University of Aberdeen, 1984), 425.

4. K. A. Busia, quoted in John S. Pobee, *Toward an African Theology* (Nashville, Tenn.: Abingdon, 1979), 94–95. *Asante* is the indigenous term that was used in the nineteenth century and has recently regained currency over the anglicized form *Ashanti.* Therefore, *Asante* is employed in the discussion, while quotations, of course, retain their original usage.

5. Aboagye-Mensah, "Socio-Political Thinking of Karl Barth," 431.

6. Ibid., 433.

7. Pobee, *Toward an African Theology*, 94.

8. Aboagye-Mensah, "Socio-Political Thinking of Karl Barth," 437–38.

9. The combined expressions *king/chief* and *kingship/chieftaincy* appear in the literature, indicating dual terms for the single office of traditional leadership. Respondents, however, expressed some degree of nuance concerning the English terms in relation to Jesus. That is to say, presumably no African Christian would disavow Jesus as king, yet not all agree with the ascription of chief to Jesus.

10. For example, *Asempa Hymns* contains English choruses adapted from various vernaculars plus classic hymns from British Christianity expressing the theme of Jesus as king (see *Asempa Hymns* [Accra: Asempa Publishers, 1982], nos. 7, 62, 64).

11. Nairobi Chapel song sheet, April 26, 1998.

12. Peter K. Sarpong, "Asante Christology," *Studia Missionalia* 45 (1996): 202.

13. It is worth noting that the functions and qualities expected of elders in these societies are closely akin to those of the king/chief in other people groups. For an in-depth study of Jesus as elder in the context of the Gikuyu, see P. N. Wachege, *Jesus Christ Our Muthamaki (Ideal Elder): An African Christological Study Based on the Agikuyu Understanding of Elder* (Nairobi: Phoenix Publishers Ltd., 1992).

14. One interviewee suggested both images, king and chief, hence the total of eleven respondents.

15. Respondents repeatedly explained the approximate equivalence between two or sometimes three of the terms *king, chief,* and *Nana.* For example, Protestant clergyman Theophilus Dankwa responded to the specific question of Jesus as chief, explaining, "Well, chief, *Nana*, king all go together, if one is thinking in terms of his kingship, his rule and authority." In addition, respondents sometimes answered the question of Jesus as chief using vernacular terms such as the Twi *Ohene.* Because of the difficulty in isolating particular terms, it is advisable to treat this leadership image in terms of a cluster of descriptions carrying slightly different nuances and to seek to discern the overall pattern of response for the composite image.

16. Pobee, *Toward an African Theology*, 95.

17. Ibid., 95–96.

18. Ibid., 94; see also Chapter 4 above.

19. Pobee, *Toward an African Theology,* 96.

20. Ibid., 96–97.

21. Ibid., 97.

22. While the present discussion focuses on the Ghanaian context, further support is found elsewhere in sub-Saharan Africa. For example, see Douglas W. Waruta, "Who Is Jesus Christ for Africans Today? Prophet, Priest, Potentate," in *Jesus in African Christianity: Experimentation and Diversity in African Christology*, ed. J. N. K. Mugambi and Laurenti Magesa (Nairobi: Initiatives, 1989), 40–53; François Kabasélé, "Christ as

Chief," in *Faces of Jesus in Africa*, ed. Robert J. Schreiter (Maryknoll, N.Y.: Orbis Books, 1991), 103–15.

23. Aboagye-Mensah, "Socio-Political Thinking of Karl Barth," 445. Despite expressing strong theological support for *Nana* as a christological title in this context, he admitted in conversation that the term has not taken root among local Christians as might have been expected since the 1960s and 1970s, when it was advocated by theologians like Pobee. He accounts for the situation by noting that the term *Nana* is much more closely associated with God, *Nyankopon*, than with *Nana Yesu*. Although he affirmed that people are using the term for Jesus, in the end he stated, "Let me stick my neck out and say that it is terminology more within the theological setup than within a church situation."

24. This title was introduced by nine of the thirty-five individual Ghanaian respondents: two in publications, including Aboagye-Mensah and Sarpong, and an additional seven in conversation.

25. John S. Pobee, *Kwame Nkrumah and the Church in Ghana 1949–1966* (Accra: Asempa Publishers, 1988), 143.

26. Aboagye-Mensah, "Socio-Political Thinking of Karl Barth," 449–50.

27. Sarpong, "Asante Christology," 204–5.

28. Aboagye-Mensah, "Socio-Political Thinking of Karl Barth," 451.

29. Pobee, *Toward an African Theology*, 97.

30. The contrast between the prescribed role of traditional chiefs and the actual role of contemporary chiefs and dictatorial politicians also forms a refrain throughout the writings of Bénézet Bujo (e.g., *African Christian Morality at the Age of Inculturation* [Nairobi: St. Paul Publications—Africa, 1990], 106). See also Harry Sawyerr's earlier critique of the christological image in "The Basis for a Theology for Africa," in *The Practice of Presence: Shorter Writings of Harry Sawyerr*, ed. John Parratt (Grand Rapids, Mich.: William B. Eerdmans, 1994), 104–5.

31. Aboagye-Mensah, "Socio-Political Thinking of Karl Barth," 442.

32. Elizabeth Amoah and Mercy Amba Oduyoye, "The Christ for African Women," in *With Passion and Compassion: Third World Women Doing Theology*, ed. Virginia Fabella and Mercy Amba Oduyoye (Maryknoll, N.Y.: Orbis Books, 1988), 41. They also criticize Pobee's portrayal of Jesus as *okyeame* or chief linguist, stating that for Pobee the *okyeame* "can be nothing else but male. Whereas in the Akan system of rule the *okyeame* can be either a man or a woman" (ibid., 43). However helpful their clarification is in this regard, there is no evidence of gender restriction in Pobee's publication (see Pobee, *Toward an African Theology*, 94ff.).

33. One Ghanaian respondent consented that Jesus is king of kings but cautioned that he is a "spiritual king" whose "kingdom is not of this earth." One Kenyan respondent made a similar comment.

34. Sarpong, "Asante Christology," 194.

35. Jean-Marc Ela, "The Memory of the African People and the Cross of Christ," in *The Scandal of a Crucified World: Perspectives on the Cross and Suffering*, trans. and ed. Yacob Tesfai (Maryknoll, N.Y.: Orbis Books, 1994), 28.

36. Ibid., 27.

37. Jean-Marc Ela, "Christianity and Liberation in Africa," in *Paths of African Theology*, ed. Rosino Gibellini (Maryknoll, N.Y.: Orbis Books, 1994), 140.

38. Quoted in Ela, "Christianity and Liberation in Africa," 139–40.

39. J. N. K. Mugambi and Laurenti Magesa, "Introduction," in Mugambi and Magesa, *Jesus in African Christianity*, xiv.

40. Philip Gibbs notes that Ela used the term *liberation* in a 1963 publication ("L'Église, le monde noire"), before Vatican II and before the term became popular in Latin American theology (Philip Gibbs, *The Word in the Third World: Divine Revelation in the Theology of Jean-Marc Ela, Aloysius Pieris, and Gustavo Gutiérrez* [Rome: Editrice Pontificia Università Gregoriana, 1996], 104).

41. Ela explained the significance of the song as follows: "And from a very young age, we sang it at school to show that we have a soul, we have a conscience, we have a history, we have a country, the Cameroon, the cradle of our ancestors. We sang like that to affirm ourselves before the Europeans, before the French, in the historical context in which we began to raise the great question of independence. And therefore, I participated closely in that, in my childhood, in my formation."

42. Ela, "The Memory of the African People and the Cross of Christ," 18.

43. The term is akin to Pobee's concept of the "North Atlantic captivity of the church," yet Ela is even more scathing in criticizing certain aspects of mission and African Christianity (see Jean-Marc Ela, *My Faith as an African*, trans. John Pairman Brown and Susan Perry [Maryknoll, N.Y.: Orbis Books, 1988], 154).

44. Ela, "The Memory of the African People and the Cross of Christ," 20.

45. Ela, *My Faith as an African*, 111.

46. Jean-Marc Ela, "Le motif de la libération dans la théologie africaine," *Les nouvelles rationalités africaines* 2, no. 5 (October 1986): 43, my translation.

47. For example, see Ela, "Christianity and Liberation in Africa," 142.

48. For the first, see Jean-Marc Ela, "Globalisation et paupérisation: Un défi à la théologie africaine," in *Liberation Theologies on Shifting Grounds: A Clash of Socio-Economic and Cultural Paradigms*, ed. G. de Schrijver (Leuven: Leuven University Press, 1998), 161–65; for the second, see Ela, "The Memory of the African People and the Cross of Christ," 19–20.

49. In this context Ela criticizes theologians like John Mbiti, and theological anthologies like that of Robert Schreiter, *Faces of Jesus in Africa*. Concerning the latter, see Ela, "The Memory of the African People and the Cross of Christ," 19–20. Ela also voiced this critique during the oral interview.

50. Ecumenical Association of Third World Theologians, "Final Statement" (Tanzania 1976), in *The Emergent Gospel: Theology from the Developing World*, ed. Sergio Torres and Virginia Fabella (London: Geoffrey Chapman, 1978), 259ff., referred to in Ela, "The Memory of the African People and the Cross of Christ," 18; see also Virginia Fabella and Sergio Torres, eds., *Irruption of the Third World: Challenge to Theology* (Maryknoll, N.Y.: Orbis Books, 1983).

51. For example, see Ela, "Christianity and Liberation in Africa," 137–39; such sociopolitical analysis underlies virtually all of Ela's theological reflections.

52. Ela, "Le motif de la libération dans la théologie africaine," 38, my translation.

53. Ela, "The Memory of the African People and the Cross of Christ," 17.

54. Ela, "Globalisation et paupérisation," 168–69.

55. Ela, "Christianity and Liberation in Africa," 143.

56. Ibid.

57. This striking analogy recurs in Ela's writings. For example, see Ela, "The Memory of the African People and the Cross of Christ," 18–19, quoted in Chapter 2, the section entitled "Theological Issues."

58. Ela, "The Memory of the African People and the Cross of Christ," 19.

59. Ibid., 20.

60. Ibid.

61. Ibid., 21.

62. Ibid., 27.

63. Ibid., 28. Here Ela acknowledges Bénézet Bujo, "Pour une éthique africano-christocentrique," in *Combats pour un christianisme africain: Mélanges en l'honneur du Professeur V. Mulago,* ed. A. Ngindu Mushete (Kinshasa: Faculté de Théologie Catholique, 1981), 21–31.

64. Ela, "Christianity and Liberation in Africa," 146.

65. Ela, "The Memory of the African People and the Cross of Christ," 28; see also Jean-Marc Ela, *African Cry.* trans. Robert R. Barr (Maryknoll, N.Y.: Orbis Books, 1986).

66. Ela, "The Memory of the African People and the Cross of Christ," 31.

67. Ibid., 32.

68. Ela, *My Faith as an African,* 104.

69. Ibid., 105.

70. Ibid.

71. Ibid., 108.

72. Ibid., 110.

73. Ibid., 99.

74. Ela, "Christianity and Liberation in Africa," 142.

75. Ibid., 152, 146. Ela adopts the second phrase from the German theologian Johannes B. Metz and uses it throughout his writings.

76. Ela, *African Cry,* 87.

77. Mercy Amba Oduyoye, "The Passion out of Compassion: Women of the EATWOT Third General Assembly," *International Review of Mission* 81, no. 322 (1992): 316.

78. Amoah and Oduyoye, "The Christ for African Women," 35, 37.

79. Mercy Amba Oduyoye, *Hearing and Knowing: Theological Reflections on Christianity in Africa* (Maryknoll, N.Y.: Orbis Books, 1986), 97–98. Although Oduyoye identifies these contemporary realities as the context for her christological reflection, she does not attend to them as directly here as she does elsewhere. For example, in addition to her monographs and edited works, see "The Roots of African Christian Feminism," in *Variations in Christian Theology in Africa,* ed. John S. Pobee and Carl F. Hallencreutz, 32–47 (Nairobi: Uzima Press, 1986); "'In the Image of God': A Theological Reflection from an African Perspective," *Bulletin de théologie africaine* 4, no. 7 (January-June 1982): 41–53; "Naming the Woman: The Words of the Akan and the Words of the Bible," *Bulletin de théologie africaine* 3, no. 5 (January-June 1981): 81–97; and "Violence against Women: Window on Africa," *Voices from the Third World* 18, no. 1 (June 1995): 168–76.

80. Oduyoye, *Hearing and Knowing,* 98–99.

81. Ibid., 97.

82. Ibid., 99.

83. Ibid., 100.

84. Ibid., 98.

85. Ibid., 101.

86. Ibid., 102.

87. Amoah and Oduyoye, "The Christ for African Women," 43.

88. Ibid., 36.

89. Ibid., 37.

90. Anne Nasimiyu Wasike, "Witnesses to Jesus Christ in the African Context," *Propositum* 3, no. 1 (June 1998): 18.

91. Mercy Amba Oduyoye, *Daughters of Anowa: African Women and Patriarchy* (Maryknoll, N.Y.: Orbis Books, 1995), 2–3.

92. Ibid., 9. See also Musimbi R. A. Kanyoro and Nyambura J. Njoroge, eds., *Groaning in Faith: African Women in the Household of God* (Nairobi: Acton Publishers, 1996). The theme of liberation is fundamental throughout the Circle publications.

93. Oduyoye, *Daughters of Anowa*, 4.

94. Nasimiyu Wasike, "Witnesses to Jesus Christ in the African Context," 25.

95. Amoah and Oduyoye, "The Christ for African Women," 43.

96. Ibid., 41–42.

97. Anne Nasimiyu Wasike, "Christology and an African Woman's Experience," in Mugambi and Magesa, *Jesus in African Christianity,* 130.

98. Ibid., 125.

99. Amoah and Oduyoye, "The Christ for African Women," 44.

100. Nasimiyu Wasike, "Christology and an African Woman's Experience," 130.

101. Amoah and Oduyoye, "The Christ for African Women," 43–44.

102. Oduyoye, "The Passion out of Compassion," 316.

103. Nasimiyu Wasike, "Witnesses to Jesus Christ in the African Context," 27.

104. Nasimiyu Wasike, "Christology and an African Woman's Experience," 130.

105. Amoah and Oduyoye, "The Christ for African Women," 45.

106. Ibid.

107. Oduyoye employs the term *folktalk* in reference to the myths, folktales, and proverbs that shape the popular ideology that governs people's lives (see *Daughters of Anowa*, 14 n. 12).

108. See Oduyoye's poem on wholeness, mentioned in Chapter 3 above; also see "Woman with Beads" in the opening pages of *Daughters of Anowa;* and Mercy Amba Oduyoye, ed., *Transforming Power: Women in the Household of God* (Accra: Same-Woode Limited, 1997), 148–69.

109. Oduyoye, "The Passion out of Compassion," 313.

110. J. N. K. Mugambi, *African Christian Theology: An Introduction* (Nairobi: East African Educational Publishers, 1989), x.

111. One respondent did not explicitly agree or disagree, but rather pointed out that Jesus did not liberate his people in the way the people expected, that is, from Roman subjugation, and this was the root cause of their rejection of him. This response is interpreted as "Negative only" in the summary table. Four additional respondents discussed positive and negative factors related to the image, with two respondents concluding more negatively about its current usage.

112. Hagan explained that Americans had a consciousness of what liberation had brought to them, and that Kwame Nkrumah was influenced, particularly by the black religious leaders, in his political thought and his Christian belief by this struggle for liberation.

113. On the basis of his Ph.D. research on the role of the church in Kenyan politics, Morompi Ole Ronkei concludes that church leaders "did not go to the extent of liberation theology, as you saw in Latin America. But they went to an extent of total engagement with the political system in this country over a very long time period. So, would I call that liberation? Yes, I would certainly use that term, because the church was influential in liberating this country from deteriorating into dictatorship."

114. For example, in addition to Kenyan clergymen Masinde, Gichure, and Musyimi, cited here, there is also Africa Inland Church Bishop Titus Kivunzi. In Ghana, Catholic Bishop Palmer-Buckle and Protestant clergyman Theophilus Dankwa expressed the same reservation.

115. Sarpong, "Asante Christology," 194.

116. Ela, *My Faith as an African*, 112.

117. J. N. K. Mugambi, "The Future of the Church and the Church of the Future in Africa," in *The Church of Africa: Towards a Theology of Reconstruction* (Nairobi: AACC, 1991), 29, 32.

7 THE RELEVANCE OF CHRISTOLOGIES IN AFRICA TODAY

1. J. N. K. Mugambi, *From Liberation to Reconstruction: African Christian Theology after the Cold War* (Nairobi: East African Educational Publishers, 1995), 33; cf. idem, "The Future of the Church and the Church of the Future in Africa," in *The Church of Africa: Towards a Theology of Reconstruction* (Nairobi: AACC, 1991), 29; J. N. K. Mugambi, ed., *The Church and the Future of Africa: Problems and Promises* (Nairobi: AACC, 1997), 41.

2. Mugambi, *From Liberation to Reconstruction*, 35.

3. Ibid., 4, 10.

4. Mugambi, "The Future of the Church and the Church of the Future in Africa," 34; see also Mugambi, *From Liberation to Reconstruction*, 14.

5. Mugambi, *From Liberation to Reconstruction*, 5.

6. For example, see Charles Villa-Vicencio, *A Theology of Reconstruction: Nation-Building and Human Rights* (Cambridge: Cambridge University Press, 1992).

7. Mugambi, *From Liberation to Reconstruction*, 5.

8. J. N. K. Mugambi, *African Christian Theology: An Introduction* (Nairobi: East African Educational Publishers, 1989), 12.

9. Mugambi, *From Liberation to Reconstruction*, 13.

10. Ibid., 16.

11. Ibid., 40. For a more concentrated expression of his christological reflections, see J. N. K. Mugambi, "Conclusion: Christological Paradigms in African Christianity," in *Jesus in African Christianity: Experimentation and Diversity in African Christology*, ed. J. N. K. Mugambi and Laurenti Magesa (Nairobi: Initiatives Ltd., 1989), 136–61.

12. Mugambi, "The Future of the Church and the Church of the Future in Africa," 30.

13. See J. N. K. Mugambi, "Social Reconstruction of Africa: The Role of the Churches," in *The Church and Reconstruction of Africa: Theological Considerations*, ed. J. N. K. Mugambi (Nairobi: AACC, 1997), 1–25.

14. For example, see Villa-Vicencio, *A Theology of Reconstruction*, 3–8.

15. See Tinyiko Sam Maluleke, "The Proposal for a Theology of Reconstruction: A Critical Appraisal," *Missionalia* 22, no. 2 (August 1994): 245-48; idem, "Recent Developments in the Christian Theologies of Africa: Towards the Twenty-First Century," *Journal of Constructive Theology* 2, no. 2 (December 1996): 42–44. Along with the central thrust of Mugambi's theology of reconstruction, important emphases such as the need for ecumenical and multidisciplinary approaches have been attested in other theologians under consideration here.

16. See Tinyiko Sam Maluleke, "Half a Century of African Christian Theologies: Elements of the Emerging Agenda for the Twenty-First Century," *Journal of Theology for Southern Africa* 99 (November 1997): 16–17.

17. Mugambi, *From Liberation to Reconstruction*, 10.

18. See also Maluleke, "The Proposal for a Theology of Reconstruction," 256; Maluleke, "Recent Developments in the Christian Theologies of Africa," 44.

19. Mugambi, *From Liberation to Reconstruction*, xiv; see also Mugambi, "The Future of the Church and the Church of the Future in Africa," 40; Mugambi, "Social Reconstruction of Africa," 3–4.

20. See Kwame Bediako, "Africa and Christianity on the Threshold of the Third Millennium: The Religious Dimension," *African Affairs* 99, no. 395 (April 2000): 312.

21. Maluleke, "The Proposal for a Theology of Reconstruction," 255–56. Examples of African theologians cited in this regard include Jean-Marc Ela, John Mbiti, Kwesi Dickson, John Pobee, and Charles Nyamiti (256 n. 34).

22. Mercy Amba Oduyoye, "The Church of the Future in Africa: Its Mission and Theology," in *The Church and Reconstruction of Africa*, ed. J. N. K. Mugambi (Nairobi: AACC, 1997), 73.

23. Ibid., 76.

24. Mugambi, "The Future of the Church and the Church of the Future in Africa," 46.

25. Sam Amirtham and John S. Pobee, eds., *Theology by the People: Reflections on Doing Theology in Community* (Geneva: WCC Publications, 1986), 6.

26. Mercy Amba Oduyoye, *Hearing and Knowing: Theological Reflections on Christianity in Africa* (Maryknoll, N.Y.: Orbis Books, 1986), 96.

27. Bénézet Bujo, *African Christian Morality at the Age of Inculturation* (Nairobi: St. Paul Publications—Africa, 1990), 124–25.

28. Ibid., 129.

29. C. G. Baëta, quoted in Kwame Bediako, *Theology and Identity: The Impact of Culture upon Christian Thought in the Second Century and in Modern Africa* (Oxford: Regnum Books, 1992), 440.

30. Mugambi, *African Christian Theology*, 99.

31. Bénézet Bujo, "Pour une éthique africano-christocentrique," in *Combats pour un christianisme africain: Mélanges en l'honneur du Professeur V. Mulago*, ed. A. Ngindu Mushete (Kinshasa: Faculté de Théologie Catholique, 1981), 30.

32. For example, see John S. Pobee, *Toward an African Theology* (Nashville, Tenn.: Abingdon, 1979), 99–119, 141–56.

33. John S. Pobee, "In Search of Christology in Africa," in *Exploring Afro-Christology*, ed. John S. Pobee (Frankfurt: Peter Lang, 1992), 16.

34. John S. Pobee, *Who Are the Poor?: The Beatitudes as a Call to Community* (Geneva: WCC Publications, 1987), 3.

35. See Paul Gifford, *African Christianity: Its Public Role* (London: Hurst & Company, 1998); idem, "Christian Fundamentalism, State and Politics in Black Africa," in *Questioning the Secular State: The Worldwide Resurgence of Religion in Politics*, ed. David Westerlund (London: Hurst & Company, 1996), 198–215; idem, "Some Recent Developments in African Christianity," *African Affairs* 93 (1994): 513–34; Paul Gifford, ed., *The Christian Churches and the Democratisation of Africa* (Leiden: E. J. Brill, 1995).

36. Hannah W. Kinoti, "Christology in the East African Revival Movement," in Mugambi and Magesa, *Jesus in African Christianity,* 68.

37. See also Paul Gifford, "Introduction: Democratisation and the Churches," in Gifford, *The Christian Churches and the Democratisation of Africa*, 1–13.

38. Since 1998, when this field research was undertaken, the Kenya constitutional review process has continued to be highly contentious. It is noteworthy that the initiative for establishing an independent review commission has been spearheaded by the NCCK and the Catholic Secretariat, who together formed a strategic group called the *Ufungamano* Initiative. Among the leaders who introduced this initiative are Mutava Musyimi, general secretary of the NCCK; Catholic Archbishop Ndingi Mwana a' Nzeki; and Anglican Archbishop David Gitari, all of whom feature in this research. As a result of the *Ufungamano* Initiative, driven largely by this united front of senior church leaders together with key politicians, lawyers, and other religious leaders, an independent commission was established in 2000. Despite considerable opposition from certain members

of senior government and the judiciary, the commission, chaired by Prof. Yash Pal Ghai, issued *The People's Choice: Draft Report of the Constitution of Kenya Review Commission* on September 18, 2002 (see the *Daily Nation* [Nairobi], September 19, 2002).

39. Oscar Muriu, "Facing Our Giants," text provided by the author (April 19, 1998), 1.

40. Ibid., 10–12.

41. In addition to the works cited below, see John Mary Waliggo, "Making a Church that is Truly African," in *Inculturation: Its Meaning and Urgency*, ed. J. M. Waliggo et al. (Kampala: St. Paul Publications—Africa, 1986), 11–30.

42. John M. Waliggo, "African Christology in a Situation of Suffering," in Mugambi and Magesa, *Jesus in African Christianity*, 93.

43. Ibid., 109.

44. John M. Waliggo, "Jesus as the Model of Justice and Peace, Defender of Children and Women, Challenger of Corruption and Oppressive Cultural Practices," in *The Second National Seminar on the Implementation of African Synod: The Church as Family of God in Uganda Based on Justice and Peace, 28th April to 3rd May 1997*, by the National Commission of Justice and Peace and the Pastoral Department (Kampala: Uganda Catholic Secretariat, August 1997), 55–59.

45. Pobee, *Who Are the Poor?*, 48.

46. Ibid.

47. John S. Pobee, *Christ Would Be an African Too* (Geneva: WCC Publications, 1996), 8.

48. Peter K. A. Turkson, "Communiqué" (Koforidua: Ghana Catholic Bishops' Conference, 1998), 1.

49. For example, Sarpong is featured in the media for his leadership in the war against corruption. See also Peter Sarpong and John Onaiyekan, "Communiqué" (Kumasi: The Bishops of the Association of Episcopal Conferences of Anglophone West Africa Triennial Plenary Assembly, August 22–31, 1998).

50. Charles Obeng, informal conversation, Accra, September 13, 1998.

51. Although the question cannot be fully dealt with here, the majority of interview respondents in Ghana with whom it was discussed contended that the shop signboards and vehicle slogans generally provide evidence of authentic Christian belief.

52. Rebeccah Owusu, informal conversation, Kumasi, July 14, 1998.

53. Informal conversation, Kumasi, July 14, 1998; translation of the conversation and signboards by research assistant Joseph Bansu.

54. J. N. K. Mugambi and Laurenti Magesa, "Introduction," in *The Church in African Christianity: Innovative Essays in Ecclesiology*, ed. J. N. K. Mugambi and Laurenti Magesa (Nairobi: Initiatives Ltd., 1990), 1.

55. For example, see John Mary Waliggo, "The African Clan as the True Model of the African Church," in Mugambi and Magesa, *The Church in African Christianity*, 111–27.

56. Bénézet Bujo, *African Theology in Its Social Context*, trans. John O'Donohue (Nairobi: St. Paul Communications; Maryknoll, N.Y.: Orbis Books, 1992), 97–98.

57. Oduyoye, *Hearing and Knowing*, 137.

58. Anne Nasimiyu Wasike, "African Women's Legitimate Role in Church Ministry," in Mugambi and Magesa, *The Church in African Christianity*, 68.

59. See J. N. K. Mugambi, "The Ecumenical Movement and the Future of the Church in Africa," in Mugambi and Magesa, *The Church in African Christianity*, 5–28; idem, "Towards Ecumenical Consensus on Baptism, Eucharist, and Ministry," in *Christian Mission and Social Transformation: A Kenyan Perspective*, ed. J. N. K. Mugambi (Nairobi: National Council of Churches of Kenya, 1989), 108–17; John G. Gatu,

"Ecumenism," in Mugambi, *Christian Mission and Social Transformation*, 103–7; John Pobee, ed., *Towards Viable Theological Education: Ecumenical Imperative, Catalyst of Renewal* (Geneva: WCC Publications, 1997).

60. Waliggo, "The African Clan as the True Model of the African Church," 125. Examples of Christian organizations committed to ecumenism include the AACC, the NCCK, the Council of Churches in Ghana, the Association of Episcopal Conferences in Eastern Africa, and the Association of Episcopal Conferences of Anglophone West Africa.

61. For example, see Jean-Marc Ela, *African Cry*, trans. Robert Barr (Maryknoll, N.Y.: Orbis Books, 1986), 1–8.

62. J. N. K. Mugambi, *The African Heritage and Contemporary Christianity* (Nairobi: Longman Kenya Ltd., 1989), 162; see also Mugambi, "The Future of the Church and the Church of the Future in Africa," 33.

63. Larry Hurtado employs the term "Christ-devotion" to encompass Christology, or "the beliefs about Jesus held by earliest Christians and the factors that shaped them," and also "the wider matters of the role of Jesus in the beliefs and religious life of ancient Christians" (Larry W. Hurtado, *One God, One Lord: Early Christian Devotion and Ancient Jewish Monotheism*, 2d ed. [Edinburgh: T & T Clark, 1998], viii).

64. Ibid., 128; see also Larry W. Hurtado, *At the Origins of Christian Worship: The Context and Character of Earliest Christian Devotion* (Carlisle, Cumbria: Paternoster Press, 1999); idem, "Religious Experience and Religious Innovation in the New Testament," *Journal of Religion* 80 (2000): 183–205.

65. Jean-Marc Ela, *My Faith as an African*, trans. John Pairman Brown and Susan Perry (Maryknoll, NY: Orbis Books, 1988), 44.

66. Kwame Bediako, *Christianity in Africa: The Renewal of a Non-Western Religion* (Edinburgh: Edinburgh University Press, 1995), 60.

67. Bénézet Bujo, "African Theology: Which Direction to Take and What Methodology to Use?" *African Christian Studies* Occasional Paper nos. 3/4 (November/December 1985): 10.

68. Bujo, *African Christian Morality at the Age of Inculturation*, 128–29.

69. See also Anne Nasimiyu Wasike, "Polygamy: A Feminist Critique," in *The Will to Arise: Women, Tradition, and the Church in Africa*, ed. Mercy Amba Oduyoye and Musimbi R. A. Kanyoro (Maryknoll, N.Y.: Orbis Books, 1992), 115–16.

70. Musimbi Kanyoro, "Polygamy: A Dilemma for the Church in Africa," in *Culture, Women and Theology*, ed. John S. Pobee (Delhi: The Indian Society For Promoting Christian Knowledge, 1994), 171.

71. Mercy Amba Oduyoye, *Daughters of Anowa: African Women and Patriarchy* (Maryknoll, N.Y.: Orbis Books, 1995), 164–66.

72. Oduyoye, "The Church of the Future in Africa," 75. See also T. M. Hinga, "Christianity and Female Puberty Rites in Africa: The Agikuyu Case," in *Rites of Passage in Contemporary Africa: Interaction between Christian and African Traditional Religion*, ed. James L. Cox (Cardiff: Cardiff Academic Press, 1998), 168–79; Pacificah F. Okemwa, "Clitoridectomy Rituals and the Social Well-Being of Women," in *Groaning in Faith: African Women in the Household of God*, ed. Musimbi R. A. Kanyoro and Nyambura J. Njoroge (Nairobi: Acton Publishers, 1996), 177–85.

73. Oduyoye, "The Church of the Future in Africa," 83 n. 5.

74. Mercy Amba Oduyoye, "The Roots of African Christian Feminism," in *Variations in Christian Theology in Africa*, ed. John S. Pobee and Carl F. Hallencreutz (Nairobi: Uzima Press, 1986), 37.

75. Oduyoye, *Hearing and Knowing*, 121.

76. Ibid., 137.

77. Ibid., 136.

78. Maluleke, "Half a Century of African Christian Theologies," 20.

79. Oduyoye, "The Church of the Future in Africa," 78.

8 CONCLUSION: AFRICAN CHRISTOLOGY IN CONTEMPORARY WORLD CHRISTIANITY

1. For example, see Gerald O. West and Musa W. Dube, eds., *The Bible in Africa: Transactions, Trajectories, and Trends* (Leiden: E. J. Brill, 2000).

2. See Andrew Walls, "The Christian Tradition in Today's World," in *Religion in Today's World: The Religious Situation of the World from 1945 to the Present Day*, ed. Frank Whaling (Edinburgh: T & T Clark, 1987), 76; Kwame Bediako, "Africa and Christianity on the Threshold of the Third Millennium: The Religious Dimension," *African Affairs* 99, no. 395 (April 2000): 313.

3. Andrew F. Walls, *The Missionary Movement in Christian History: Studies in the Transmission of Faith* (Maryknoll, N.Y.: Orbis Books, 1996), xvii.

4. Jean-Marc Ela, *My Faith as an African*, trans. John Pairman Brown and Susan Perry (Maryknoll, N.Y.: Orbis Books, 1988), 143.

5. Walls, *The Missionary Movement in Christian History*, 54.

Bibliography

SIGNIFICANT TEXTS
OF THE SELECTED AFRICAN THEOLOGIANS

Amirtham, Sam, and John S. Pobee, eds. *Theology by the People: Reflections on Doing Theology in Community*. Geneva: WCC Publications, 1986.

Amoah, Elizabeth, and Mercy Oduyoye. "The Christ for African Women." In *With Passion and Compassion: Third World Women Doing Theology*, edited by Virginia Fabella and Mercy Oduyoye, 35-46. Maryknoll, N.Y.: Orbis Books, 1988.

Bujo, Bénézet. *African Christian Morality at the Age of Inculturation*. Nairobi: St. Paul Publications—Africa, 1990.

———. *African Theology in Its Social Context*. Translated by John O'Donohue. Nairobi: St. Paul Publications; Maryknoll, N.Y.: Orbis Books, 1992.

———. *Christmas: God Becomes Man in Black Africa*. Nairobi: Paulines Publications Africa, 1995.

———. "Pour une éthique africano-christocentrique." In *Combats pour un christianisme africain: Mélanges en l'honneur du Professeur V. Mulago*. Bibliothèque du Centre d'Etudes des Religions Africaines, no. 6, edited by A. Ngindu Mushete, 21-31. Kinshasa: Faculté de Théologie Catholique, 1981.

Ela, Jean-Marc. *African Cry*. Translated by Robert R. Barr. Maryknoll, N.Y.: Orbis Books, 1986.

———. "Ancestors and Christian Faith: An African Problem." In *Liturgy and Cultural Religious Traditions*, edited by Herman Schmidt and David Power, 34-50. New York: Seabury Press, 1977.

———. "De l'assistance à la libération: Les tâches actuelles de l'église en milieu africain." *Foi et développement* 83 (January-February 1981): 1-9.

———. "Christianity and Liberation in Africa." In *Paths of African Theology*, edited by Rosino Gibellini, 136-53. Maryknoll, N.Y.: Orbis Books, 1994.

———. "Globalisation et paupérisation: Un défi à la théologie africaine." In *Liberation Theologies on Shifting Grounds: A Clash of Socio-Economic and Cultural Paradigms*. Bibliotheca Ephemeridum Theologicarum Lovaniensium, no. 135, edited by G. de Schrijver, 153-75. Leuven: Leuven University Press, 1998.

———. "The Memory of the African People and the Cross of Christ." In *The Scandal of a Crucified World: Perspectives on the Cross and Suffering*, translated and edited by Yacob Tesfai, 17-35. Maryknoll, N.Y.: Orbis Books, 1994.

———. "Le motif de la libération dans la théologie africaine." *Les nouvelles rationalités africaines* 2, no. 5 (October 1986): 37-51.

———. *My Faith as an African*. Translated by John Pairman Brown and Susan Perry. Maryknoll, N.Y.: Orbis Books, 1988.

Mugambi, J. N. K. *African Christian Theology: An Introduction*. Nairobi: East African Educational Publishers, 1989.

————. *The African Heritage and Contemporary Christianity*. Nairobi: Longman Kenya Ltd., 1989.

————. "The Future of the Church and the Church of the Future in Africa." In *The Church of Africa: Towards a Theology of Reconstruction*. African Challenge Book Series no. 2, 29-50. Nairobi: AACC, 1991.

————. *From Liberation to Reconstruction: African Christian Theology after the Cold War*. Nairobi: East African Educational Publishers, 1995.

Mugambi, J. N. K., ed. *The Church and the Future of Africa: Problems and Promises*. Nairobi: AACC, 1997.

————. *The Church and Reconstruction of Africa: Theological Considerations*. Nairobi: AACC, 1997.

Mugambi, J. N. K., and Laurenti Magesa, eds. *The Church in African Christianity: Innovative Essays in Ecclesiology*. African Christianity Series. Nairobi: Initiatives Ltd., 1990.

————. *Jesus in African Christianity: Experimentation and Diversity in African Christology*. African Christianity Series. Nairobi: Initiatives Ltd., 1989.

Nasimiyu, Anne J. "Vatican II: The Problem of Inculturation." Ph.D. diss. Duquesne University, 1986.

Nasimiyu Wasike, Anne. "Christology and an African Woman's Experience." In *Jesus in African Christianity: Experimentation and Diversity in African Christology*, edited by J. N. K. Mugambi and Laurenti Magesa, 123-35. Nairobi: Initiatives Ltd., 1989.

————. "Witnesses to Jesus Christ in the African Context." *Propositum* 3, no. 1 (June 1998): 17-29.

Oduyoye, Mercy. "An African Woman's Christ." *Voices from the Third World* 11, no. 2 (December 1988): 119-24.

————. "The Church of the Future in Africa: Its Mission and Theology." In *The Church and Reconstruction of Africa*, edited by J. N. K. Mugambi, 66-83. Nairobi: AACC, 1997.

————. *Hearing and Knowing: Theological Reflections on Christianity in Africa*. Maryknoll, N.Y.: Orbis Books, 1986.

————. *Introducing African Women's Theology*. Introductions in Feminist Theology, no. 6, edited by Mary Grey and others. Sheffield: Sheffield Academic Press, 2001.

————. "The Passion Out of Compassion: Women of the EATWOT Third General Assembly." *International Review of Mission* 81, no. 322 (1992): 313-18.

————. "The Roots of African Christian Feminism." In *Variations in Christian Theology in Africa*, edited by John S. Pobee and Carl F. Hallencreutz, 32-47. Nairobi: Uzima Press, 1986.

————. "Wholeness of Life in Africa." In *An African Call for Life: A Contribution to the World Council of Churches' Sixth Assembly Theme: "Jesus Christ—the Life of the World,"* edited by Masamba ma Mpolo, Reginald Stober, and Evelyn V. Appiah, 113-22. Nairobi: Uzima Press for the World Council of Churches, 1983.

Oduyoye, Mercy Amba, and Musimbi R. A. Kanyoro, eds. *The Will to Arise: Women, Tradition, and the Church in Africa*. Maryknoll, N.Y.: Orbis Books, 1992.

Pobee, John S. *Christ Would Be an African Too*. Gospel and Culture Studies. Vol. 9. Geneva: WCC Publications, 1996.

————. "Healing—An African Christian Theologian's Perspective." *International Review of Mission* 83 (April 1994): 247-55.

———. "Health, Healing and Religion: An African View." *International Review of Mission* 90, nos. 356/357 (January/April 2001): 55-64.

———. "Jesus Christ—The Life of the World: An African Perspective." *Ministerial Formation* 21 (January 1983): 5-8.

———. *Skenosis: Christian Faith in an African Context*. Gweru, Zimbabwe: Mambo Press, 1992.

———. *Toward an African Theology*. Nashville, Tenn.: Abingdon, 1979.

———. *Who Are the Poor?: The Beatitudes as a Call to Community*. Risk Book Series no. 32. Geneva: WCC Publications, 1987.

Pobee, John S., ed. *Exploring Afro-Christology*. Frankfurt: Peter Lang, 1992.

Pobee, John S., and Carl F. Hallencreutz, eds. *Variations in Christian Theology in Africa*. Nairobi: Uzima Press, 1986.

WORKS RELATED TO AFRICAN CHRISTIANITY

Aboagye-Mensah, Robert Kwasi. "Socio-Political Thinking of Karl Barth: Trinitarian and Incarnational Christology as the Ground for His Social Action and Its Implications for Us Today." Ph.D. thesis, University of Aberdeen, 1984.

Akinade, Akintunde E. "'Who Do You Say That I Am?'—An Assessment of Some Christological Constructs in Africa." *Asia Journal of Theology* 9, no. 1 (April 1995): 181-200.

Appiah-Kubi, Kofi. "Christology." In *A Reader in African Christian Theology*, edited by John Parratt, 69-81. London: SPCK, 1987.

Appiah-Kubi, Kofi, and Sergio Torres, eds. *African Theology en Route*. Maryknoll, N.Y.: Orbis Books, 1979.

Bediako, Kwame. "Africa and Christianity on the Threshold of the Third Millennium: The Religious Dimension." *African Affairs* 99, no. 395 (April 2000): 303-23.

———. "Biblical Christologies in the Context of African Traditional Religions." In *Sharing Jesus in the Two Thirds World*, edited by Vinay Samuel and Chris Sugden, 115-75. Bangalore: Partnership in Mission-Asia, 1983.

———. *Christianity in Africa: The Renewal of a Non-Western Religion*. Edinburgh: Edinburgh University Press; Maryknoll, N.Y.: Orbis Books, 1995.

———. "The Doctrine of Christ and the Significance of Vernacular Terminology." *International Bulletin of Missionary Research* 22, 3 (July 1998): 110-11.

———. *Jesus in African Culture: A Ghanaian Perspective*. Accra: Asempa Publishers, 1990.

———. "The Significance of Modern African Christianity—A Manifesto." *Studies in World Christianity* 1, Part 1 (1995): 51-67.

———. *Theology and Identity: The Impact of Culture upon Christian Thought in the Second Century and in Modern Africa*. Oxford: Regnum Books, 1992.

———. "Understanding African Theology in the Twentieth Century." *Bulletin for Contextual Theology* 3, no. 2 (June 1996): 1-11.

Bevans, Stephen B. *Models of Contextual Theology*. Faith and Cultures Series, edited by Robert J. Schreiter. Maryknoll, N.Y.: Orbis Books, 1992.

Dickson, Kwesi. *Theology in Africa*. London: Darton, Longman and Todd, 1984.

Doré, Joseph, ed. *Chemins de la Christologie Africaine*. Paris: Desclée. 1986.

Dulles, Avery. *Models of the Church*. Garden City, N.Y.: Doubleday, 1974.

Fabella, Virginia, and Mercy Amba Oduyoye, eds. *With Passion and Compassion: Third World Women Doing Theology*. Maryknoll, N.Y.: Orbis Books, 1988.

Fabella, Virginia, and Sergio Torres, eds. *Irruption of the Third World: Challenge to Theology*. Maryknoll, N.Y.: Orbis Books, 1983.

Gibellini, Rosino, ed. *Paths of African Theology*. Maryknoll, N.Y.: Orbis Books, 1994.

Hastings, Adrian. *African Christianity: An Essay in Interpretation*. London: Geoffrey Chapman, 1976.

Healey, Joseph, and Donald Sybertz. *Towards an African Narrative Theology*. Nairobi: Paulines Publications Africa, 1996.

Kanyoro, Musimbi R. A., and Nyambura J. Njoroge, eds. *Groaning in Faith: African Women in the Household of God*. Nairobi: Acton Publishers, 1996.

Kuma, Afua. *Jesus of the Deep Forest: Prayers and Praises of Afua Kuma*. Translated by Jon Kirby. Accra: Asempa Publishers, 1981.

———. *Kwaebirentuw Ase Yesu: Afua Kuma Ayeyi ne Mpaebo*. Accra: Asempa Publishers, 1980.

Magesa, Laurenti. *African Religion: The Moral Traditions of Abundant Life*. Maryknoll, N.Y.: Orbis Books, 1997.

Maluleke, Tinyiko Sam. "Half a Century of African Christian Theologies: Elements of the Emerging Agenda for the Twenty-First Century." *Journal of Theology for Southern Africa* 99 (November 1997): 4-23.

———. "The Proposal for a Theology of Reconstruction: A Critical Appraisal." *Missionalia* 22, no. 2 (August 1994): 245-258.

———. "Recent Developments in the Christian Theologies of Africa: Towards the Twenty-First Century." *Journal of Constructive Theology* 2, no. 2 (December 1996): 33-60.

Manus, Ukachukwu Chris. "African Christologies: The Centre-Piece of African Christian Theology." *Zeitschrift Für Missionswissenschaft Und Religionswissenschaft* 82 (1998): 3-23.

———. *Christ, the African King: New Testament Christology* (Frankfurt: Peter Lang, 1993).

ma Mpolo, Masamba, Reginald Stober, and Evelyn V. Appiah, eds. *An African Call for Life: A Contribution to the World Council of Churches' Sixth Assembly Theme: "Jesus Christ—The Life of the World"*. Nairobi: Uzima Press for the World Council of Churches, 1983.

Martey, Emmanuel. *African Theology: Inculturation and Liberation*. Maryknoll, N.Y.: Orbis Books, 1993.

Mbiti, John S. "Some African Concepts of Christology." In *Christ and the Younger Churches*, edited by Georg F. Vicedom, 51-62. London: SPCK, 1972.

———. "'Ho Soter Hemon' [Our Savior] as an African Experience." In *Christ and Spirit in the New Testament*, editd by Barnabus Lindars and Stephen S. Smalley, 397-414. Cambridge: Cambridge University Press, 1973.

Mofokeng, Takatso Alfred. *The Crucified among the Crossbearers: Towards a Black Christology*. Kampen: Uitgeversmaatschappij J. H. Kok, 1983.

Mulago, Vincent. "Vital Participation: The Cohesive Principle of the Bantu Community." In *Biblical Revelation and African Beliefs*, edited by Kwesi A. Dickson and Paul Ellingworth, 137-58. London: Lutterworth Press, 1969.

Mwaura, Philomena Njeri. "Healing as a Pastoral Concern." In *Pastoral Care in African Christianity: Challenging Essays in Pastoral Theology*, edited by D. W. Waruta and H. W. Kinoti, 62-86. Nairobi: Acton Publishers, 1994.

Nyamiti, Charles. "African Christologies Today." In *Jesus in African Christianity: Experimentation and Diversity in African Christology*, edited by J. N. K. Mugambi and Laurenti Magesa, 17-39. Nairobi: Initiatives Ltd., 1989.

————. *Christ as Our Ancestor: Christology from an African Perspective*. Mambo Occasional Papers—Missio-Pastoral Series no. 11. Gweru, Zimbabwe: Mambo Press, 1984.

————. "Contemporary African Christologies: Assessment and Practical Suggestions." In *Paths of African Theology*, edited by Rosino Gibellini, 62-77. Maryknoll, N.Y.: Orbis Books, 1994.

Parratt, John. *Reinventing Christianity: African Theology Today*. Grand Rapids, Mich.: William B. Eerdmans, 1995.

Ross, Kenneth R. "Current Christological Trends in Northern Malawi." *Journal of Religion in Africa* 27 (May 1997): 160-76.

Sarpong, Peter K. "Asante Christology." *Studia Missionalia* 45 (1996): 189-205.

————. *Ghana in Retrospect: Some Aspects of Ghanaian Culture*. Tema, Ghana: Ghana Publishing Corporation, 1974.

Schoffeleers, Matthew. "Christ in African Folk Theology: The *Nganga* Paradigm." In *Religion in Africa: Experience and Expression*, edited by Thomas D. Blakely, Walter E. A. van Beek, and Dennis L. Thomson, 73-88. London: James Currey, 1994.

Schreiter, Robert J. *Constructing Local Theologies*. London: SCM Press, 1985.

Schreiter, Robert J., ed. *Faces of Jesus in Africa*. Faith and Cultures Series, edited by Robert J. Schreiter. Maryknoll, N.Y.: Orbis Books, 1991.

Shorter, Aylward. "Ancestor Veneration Revisited." *AFER* 25, no. 4 (August 1983): 197–203.

————. "Folk Christianity and Functional Christology." *AFER* 24, no. 3 (June 1982): 133-37.

————. *Jesus and the Witchdoctor: An Approach to Healing and Wholeness*. London: Geoffrey Chapman, 1985.

Taylor, John V. *The Primal Vision: Christian Presence Amid African Religion*. London: SCM Press, 1963.

Tempels, Placide. *Bantu Philosophy*. Translated by Colin King. Paris: Présence Africaine, 1959.

Torres, Sergio, and Virginia Fabella, eds. *The Emergent Gospel: Theology from the Developing World*. London: Geoffrey Chapman, 1978.

Udoh, Enyi Ben. *Guest Christology: An Interpretative View of the Christological Problem in Africa*. Studies in the Intercultural History of Christianity, Band 59. Frankfurt am Main: Peter Lang, 1988.

Ukpong, Justin S. "Christology and Inculturation: A New Testament Perspective." In *Paths of African Theology*, edited by Rosino Gibellini, 40-61. Maryknoll, N.Y.: Orbis Books, 1994.

Waliggo, John M. "African Christology in a Situation of Suffering." In *Jesus in African Christianity: Experimentation and Diversity in African Christology*, edited by J. N. K. Mugambi and Laurenti Magesa, 93-111. Nairobi: Initiatives Ltd., 1989.

Walls, Andrew. "Africa in Christian History: Retrospect and Prospect." *Journal of African Christian Thought* 1, no. 1 (June 1998): 2-15.

————. "Africa and Christian Identity." *Mission Focus* 6, no. 7 (November 1978): 11-13.

————. "The Christian Tradition in Today's World." In *Religion in Today's World: The Religious Situation of the World from 1945 to the Present Day*, edited by Frank Whaling, 76-109. Edinburgh: T & T Clark, 1987.

————. *The Missionary Movement in Christian History: Studies in the Transmission of Faith*. Maryknoll, N.Y.: Orbis Books, 1996.

————. "Towards Understanding Africa's Place in Christian History." In *Religion in a Pluralistic Society*, edited by J. S. Pobee, 180-89. Leiden: E. J. Brill, 1976.

Wendland, Ernst. "'Who Do People Say I Am?': Contextualizing Christology in Africa." *AJET* 10, no. 2 (1991): 13-32.

Young, Josiah U., III. *African Theology: A Critical Analysis and Annotated Bibliography* (Westport, Conn.: Greenwood Press, 1993).

Index

299

Also in the Faith and Cultures Series

Faces of Jesus in Africa, Robert J. Schreiter, C.PP.S., Editor

Hispanic Devotional Piety, C. Gilbert Romero

African Theology in Its Social Context, Bénézet Bujo

Models of Contextual Theology, Stephen B. Bevans, S.V.D.

Asian Faces of Jesus, R. S. Sugirtharajah, Editor

Evangelizing the Culture of Modernity, Hervé Carrier, S.J.

St. Martín de Porres: "The Little Stories" and the Semiotics of Culture, Alex García-Rivera

The Indian Face of God in Latin America, Manuel M. Marzal, S.J., Eugenio Maurer, S.J., Xavierio Albó, S.J., and Bartomeu Melià, S.J.

Towards an African Narrative Theology, Joseph Healey, M.M., and Donald Sybertz, M.M.

The New Catholicity: Theology between the Global and the Local, Robert Schreiter, C.PP.S.

The Earth Is God's: A Theology of American Culture, William A. Dyrness

Mission and Catechesis: Alexandre de Rhodes and Inculturation in Seventeenth-Century Vietnam, Peter C. Phan

Celebrating Jesus Christ in Africa, François Kabasele Lumbala

Popular Catholicism in a World Church: Seven Case Studies in Inculturation, Thomas Bamat and Jean-Paul Wiest, Editors

Inculturation: The New Face of the Church in Latin America, Diego Irrarázaval, C.S.C.

The Bible on Culture: Belonging or Dissenting?, Lucien Legrand, M.E.P.

On Being Human, Miguel H. Díaz

Doing Local Theology, Clemens Sedmak